CW01661596

TRUE STORIES *of*
COURAGE, LOYALTY, AND FRIENDSHIP

THE NEWFOUNDLAND DOG

TRUE STORIES *of*
COURAGE, LOYALTY, AND FRIENDSHIP

THE NEWFOUNDLAND DOG

Robert C. Parsons

ILLUSTRATED BY MEL D'SOUZA

FLANKER PRESS LIMITED
ST. JOHN'S

Library and Archives Canada Cataloguing in Publication

Parsons, Robert Charles, 1944-
The Newfoundland dog : true stories of courage, loyalty and friendship / Robert C. Parsons.

Issued also in electronic formats.
ISBN 978-1-926881-65-2

1. Newfoundland dog. 2. Human-animal relationships--Anecdotes. I. Title.

SF429.N4P37 2012 636.73 C2011-908595-X

PRINTED IN CANADA

MIX
Paper from responsible sources
FSC www.fsc.org FSC® C016245

This paper has been certified to meet the environmental and social standards of the Forest Stewardship Council® (FSC®) and comes from responsibly managed forests, and verified recycled sources.

Illustrated by Mel D'Souza Cover Design: Adam Freake Cover Art: Lee Ann Shepard

FLANKER PRESS
PO BOX 2522, STATION C
ST. JOHN'S, NL, CANADA
TOLL FREE: 1-866-739-4420
WWW.FLANKERPRESS.COM

16 15 14 13 12 2 3 4 5 6 7 8 9

Canada
Canada Council for the Arts Conseil des Arts du Canada
Newfoundland Labrador

We acknowledge the financial support of the Government of Canada through the Book Publishing Industry Development Program (BPIDP) for our publishing activities; the Canada Council for the Arts which last year invested $24.3 million in writing and publishing throughout Canada; the Government of Newfoundland and Labrador, Department of Tourism, Culture and Recreation.

CONTENTS

ILLUSTRATIONS

FOREWORD

THOSE WHO ARE familiar with the tales of Robert Parsons's many well-researched books concerning ships and the sea may wonder, as I did, why all of a sudden the interest in a dog?

Then as the stories reveal themselves, it just as suddenly becomes plain to see.

True, there are several interesting tales that do not involve the famous Newfoundland dog's heroics while on the stormy seas, yet it seems very evident that the author, during the research for his previous books, must have, in many instances, heard the bark of the Newfoundland dog.

This book is not just about one or two instances of a dog saving a child from a watery grave, or a dog being loyal to its owner. It's about the manner in which the Newfoundland dog's character and intelligence are manifested in its actions.

Perfection is a rare quality. Are we to see that the Newfoundland dog is perfect? Well—almost. Yes, it bites, but maybe the reader will find a justification for such action.

As a boy growing up in Grand Bank I was familiar with toilets perched precariously over a tide-flushing landwash. Thus it was with great delight to read how "Champ" exacted his revenge.

War is always terrible, and even though "Gander" became a national hero, he, like many humans, paid the supreme sacrifice.

The intelligence displayed by the Newfoundland dog is evident in the many fascinating tales related by the author. Could the black fur of this great dog turn white? Could the dog be a thief? Could it hoard money? The stories are packed with intrigue and sometimes have uncanny conclusions.

Robert Parsons, in his inimitable style, has uncovered many tales that make us proud of the noble Newfoundland dog.

FRANK TIBBO
GANDER, NL

AUTHOR'S NOTE

IN A WAY this book began around 1987-88 in a library reference room somewhere with film rolling on a microfilm reader. Back then I was looking for information on a ship, a crew, a wreck, or a marine incident. But as I searched and scrounged I found many interesting items in the news, tidbits I had to read. I was distracted in a way from my purpose, of researching and recording Newfoundland's marine history. However, some inner voice said, "Get a copy of this unique story." And I did.

So it happened that in 20 years of research and pack-ratting I had collected many bits of information on diverse topics, ranging from the local to the international. Most of what I tucked away for future use was of Newfoundland the place—its events, history, people—and Newfoundland the dog.

Back then, I had also interviewed many of the

Newfoundland and Labrador old salts, skippers, captains, shipowners, their families, or descendants. Again the main interest was the sea, but odd bits of the unusual crept in—tales of weather phenomena, exotic ports, foods eaten, lumber camps, knitting, tricks played on other sailors, funerals at sea. You get the general idea: tales of the worldly, wonderful, and weird. Yes, and stories of ship mascots, usually the great Newfoundland dog.

More than 20 years later, as my ship stories began to dwindle, I turned to tales of the strange but true. One book emerged of the unusual: *Any Strange News: True Stories Behind the Headlines* (2006). It had a short run and quickly sold out. Then in 2009 I wrote a series of tales of true crime, mischief, and mayhem in *Courting Disaster*, published by Flanker Press. Stories in both books had been garnered from my collection of newsworthy events great and trivial.

Toward the end of 2010, I again combed my massive files—the stuff a rat that likes shiny objects would take down into its burrow—for stories other than "of the sea." In the material there were many Newfoundland dog stories that I believed had never been in print. I also had brief notes in my research book of dates, information, stories, and facts I had seen on diverse topics, including animals. I went looking for the source of these notes.

The accounts thus collated of the heroic Newfoundland dog ranged from tales of ship mascots to stories of American watchdogs and everything else in between with a time frame between the 1860s and the

1960s. It was roughly one hundred years' worth of unique Newfoundland dog stories. I thought, at least, they were unique and interesting enough for a wider audience.

When I combed through the books I had already written I found there were two or three Newfoundland dog stories already published in those. These were reproduced (with some revision or additional information) for this volume. One example is "Dan, the Hero of Bareneed," which had previously appeared in *Any Strange News*. Only with one tale of the Newfoundland dog did I debate whether to include it or not: "Rigel, of the *Titanic*."

Unless the gender of the dog was specifically mentioned in original sources, I refer to the Newfoundland in the masculine. Another final decision I had to make was where to place the stories in this work. A story of loyalty and intelligence shown by our faithful friend might well have taken place during a rescue at sea. Thus I arbitrarily chose the chapter in which the story appears herein.

Not in all stories in *The Newfoundland Dog: True Stories of Courage, Loyalty, and Friendship* does the loyal companion emerge as a hero or unscathed. As a precaution to those who love the Newfoundland dog and feel pain or sorrow at its death, if the dog comes to harm or pays the ultimate sacrifice, that story appears as the last in the chapter.

I quickly discovered I was at one severe disadvantage as I began to compile the stories: I had never owned a dog (well, except for a few short years when I was about ten years old), let alone a Newfoundland. I tried to compensate for this by talking to as many people as possible who owned or had once owned that faithful companion. I consulted as many books of reference as necessary. There are many Newfoundland dog owners to thank. You know who you are.

Frank Tibbo, a fellow Grand Banker and author, kindly agreed when I asked him to write a foreword for me. Likewise, Mel D'Souza, who not only gave me much encouragement when I sent him that preliminary or early batch of stories, but also sketched the illustrations—and then some more. My appreciation goes out to both you guys.

Well, that's it, good reader. I have departed from a well-traversed sea lane and now begin a journey for the Newfoundland dog afficionados.

I am grateful for the opportunity of reworking or rewriting the stories in *The Newfoundland Dog: True Stories of Courage, Loyalty, and Friendship*. I have made every effort to identify rightful owners and obtain proper permission to reproduce them. If errors occur in this regard or with the information please notify the author, and efforts will be made in any subsequent editions to correct the errors or omissions.

ROBERT C. PARSONS
GRAND BANK, NL
JANUARY, 2012

ROBERTPARSONS@PERSONAINTERNET.COM

"Preserving Newfoundland
and Labrador's Marine History,
One Tale at a Time."

ACKNOWLEDGEMENTS

MEL D'SOUZA, ILLUSTRATOR, also my first reader, gave me the incentive to forge on; Frank Tibbo, an author himself and writer of the foreword, was also an early reader, giving positive encouragement; my wife, Sadie, who read the initial batch of stories and gave perceptive advice and encouragement. Others with whom I had early correspondence were Burton Janes, William "Bill" Tibbo (formerly of Harbour Breton), and the current mayor of Grand Bank, Darrell LaFosse, the son of the late Freeman LaFosse.

Several tales originated in the *Daily Examiner* and *Daily Patriot* (both of PEI); *New York Times; New York Herald; Evening Telegram; Royal Gazette; Fishermen's Advocate; Western Star; Otago Times; Boston Herald; San Francisco Sportsman; Harbour Grace Standard*; and *Twillingate Sun*. I studied various "dog" books from which I found the chapter introductions.

Finally, the good folks at Flanker Press, who have produced many fine books by Newfoundland and Labrador authors, were efficient, helpful, and above all patient and friendly with my project. I thank them.

TRUE STORIES *of*
COURAGE, LOYALTY, AND FRIENDSHIP

THE NEWFOUNDLAND DOG

1

INTELLIGENCE

The large and handsome animal which is called from its native country the Newfoundland Dog, belongs to the group of spaniels, all of which appear to be possessed of considerable mental powers, and to be capable of instruction to a degree that is rarely seen in animals . . . In this country [England], the Newfoundland Dog is raised to its proper position, and made the friend and companion of man.

ILLUSTRATED NATURAL HISTORY (MAMMALIA)
REV. J. G. WOOD, 1853

CAROLINA'S DOG

CAPTAIN STEPHEN LEMIST commanded the ship *Carolina* out of Boston, with his second mate, John Codman. Lemist, in the story as told by Codman, had on board a fine, shaggy, black Newfoundland dog named "Neptune." Nep, as he was affectionately known, was the pet of all hands as well as his master.

Nep had full liberty of the quarterdeck and availed of that privilege by walking about there. At times he put his paws upon the taffrail, the wide rail around the stern of a ship. Sometimes he would get up on the rail and look about. To the crew, the balancing act on the taffrail looked dangerous, but no action or coaxing could prevent the dog from standing on the rail, looking at birds, the sea, and other ships.

One summer, *Carolina* was bound from New Orleans

and was being towed up the Mississippi River accompanied by four other vessels—all linked together in a row, like ducks. It was a civil, calm tow and Nep was walking on the rail as was his occasional custom. However, this time he lost his balance and fell overboard.

It was impossible to stop the vessel without affecting the tow and all ships in it. At any rate, even if *Carolina*'s crew wanted to turn around, the captain of the tow tug would not consent to do so. So Captain Lemist and the distraught crew had no choice but to leave the dog to his fate. They watched it swimming as their ship moved farther and farther upriver.

For a while Nep swam after the flotilla but, finding he could not keep up, he struck out for the western shore of the Mississippi, sensing that he was nearer to that side. The only satisfaction the crew had was that the dog's life was in no danger and that he was a good swimmer. They felt sure he would reach land.

Downhearted and mourning the loss of a dear shipmate, *Carolina*'s crew had no choice but to return to their duties. Although Nep might survive, they sadly agreed they had parted company with the Newfoundland forever.

Captain Lemist took the loss the hardest. Mate Codman said after, "I can see the captain now as he laid his head upon the binnacle [the housing for the compass] and sobbed like a child."

Carolina was positioned 50 miles below New Orleans at the time of the accident. In due time it docked at a levee, where the crew remained for three days discharging cargo. The ship was consigned a freight of cotton and tobacco for London, England, and was towed up to Lafayette, some three to four miles above, to load.

Codman says *Carolina* was berthed on the eastern side of the Mississippi, the third outside in a tier of vessels, side by side extending out from the wharf. The cargo was carried on planks over the decks of the other vessels between *Carolina* and the shore.

One morning, after *Carolina* had been there two days, the crew was astonished to see Nep walk on board.

Codman relates his and his shipmates' joy was equal to that of Nep's. Wagging his tail, Nep began to cry and whine in a dog's language of delight. He jumped on every one of his old friends, entirely ignoring the stevedores whom he did not know.

Nep then rushed down the companionway in search of the captain, who was not on board at the time. A few minutes later Nep came back on deck, looking dejected and mournful. Codman says the dog took no further interest in him or any of the crew, except for a few inquiring looks.

"I expect to be believed," says Codman, "for I am telling the truth when I say there were big tears in the dog's eyes."

Codman knew the captain had gone ashore to the consignee's office in Lafayette. "Come on, Nep. Let's go," he said. Nep understood quickly as he jumped on the stages and planks over the other vessels' decks and followed the mate down to the office.

There Nep was grabbed up in his fond master's arms. Codman says, "There is not a particle of fiction in this pathetic yet happy story."

But the mystery! How Nep found his ship was beyond the understanding of all crew. They merely guessed that he had travelled 50 miles up the river on the western side. He then came to the ferry, somehow got a passage across without molestation, crossed over to New Orleans, and then found his way up to Lafayette. How did he know his ship was on the eastern side? But he did.

He then walked over the decks of two ships to reach his old home again.

"How did he find us?" said Codman. The crew could see he yearned to tell them, and Nep could see it was in their minds and on their lips. But, alas, he could not speak.

A KISS FOR THE RIGHT GUY

THE *BOSTON HERALD* verifies this is a true story and there is no reason to doubt it. On Thursday, February 1, 1872, a gentle, handsome Newfoundland dog walked into the school that once stood on Poplar Street, Boston. He entered the dressing room or cloakroom in the back of a classroom and took down the cap and coat of his young master.

The Newfoundland looked inquiringly at all the children in the room and failed to see the owner of the cap and coat. Walking into another classroom on the same floor, he found the person he was looking for. The Newfoundland went up to the desk, dropped the garments near the desk, and affectionately kissed the boy.

THE SHILLING UNDER THE STONE

THE STORY IS told of a gentleman, perhaps wanting to show the intelligence of his Newfoundland dog, who tested his loyal companion with a shilling. He was travelling somewhere in England with a friend on horseback. The man put a marked shilling under a stone near a road, first showing the shilling to his Newfoundland dog. He then, with his friend, rode on for three miles.

When the Newfoundland received a signal from his master, the dog turned back to find and retrieve the shilling. The two gentlemen rode home, but to their disappointment and surprise the faithful animal did not return that day.

As the tale was later told by observers at the scene, the dog had gone to the spot where the shilling had been deposited, but the stone was too heavy for the agility or strength of the dog. He stayed at the spot howling until two horsemen came riding up.

They were attracted by his inordinately distressed howls and stopped to look at the dog. One of them got down from his horse and, seeing the stone near the dog, turned it over with his foot. He saw the shilling and put it into his pocket, not realizing it was the object of the dog's distress.

The dog followed their horses for 20 miles until the horsemen stopped at an inn. He remained quietly in the background, where the two had a meal, then the dog followed the chambermaid to the bedroom. The maid admitted the dog, thinking he was part of the group.

Meanwhile, the dog hid under one of the beds. The man who had the shilling in his pocket hung his trousers on a nail by the bedside. When both travellers were asleep, the dog took the trousers in his mouth and, leaping out of the window that had been left open because of the sultry heat, ran off.

Eventually he reached his master's home with his prize. When the master looked through the pockets, he was able to trace the owner and return the trousers and the sundry objects in it—except the shilling. The master and the travellers were able to piece together what had happened, verifying the intelligence and cunning of the Newfoundland dog.

In time the story entitled "A Sagacious Newfoundland Dog" was published in *Nature* (a prestigious British journal founded in 1869 and still in existence today), and on October 9, 1879, was reprinted in a Newfoundland newspaper.

A RAINY DAY SOLUTION

A HANDSOME NEWFOUNDLAND dog named "Jack" lived in California in the San Francisco area. Every evening at nine o'clock, Jack and his master went for a walk. One evening Jack did something for the first time, and the owner believed it was the dog's intelligence and not instinct that prompted the action. So much so the man sent the story to *Cassell's Saturday Journal* and it also appeared in the *San Francisco Breeder and Sportsman* in July, 1894.

Jack's master always used an orange-wood walking stick and always carried it with him on the walk. Every evening at the stroke of nine by the clock in the home, Jack rushed to the hat rack in the hall and nosed about the walking sticks and umbrellas until he found the orange-wood stick.

He immediately appeared before his master, carrying it in his teeth. Jack wagged his tail, pranced about happily, and demonstrated as plainly as possible he wanted a walk. He showed he would be a broken-hearted dog if his friend and master didn't take that evening stroll.

One evening the family was in the parlour with some guests that were visiting. A shower had come on and by 9:00 p.m. it was raining hard. The strokes had hardly died away when in pranced Jack with the favourite walking stick in his mouth.

"No, Jack," said his master. "We cannot go out tonight. It is raining too hard."

The guests, who had never seen these actions by a dog, were amazed to witness this show of faithfulness and determination, murmuring words of delight and generally praising Jack. The host wanted to stay home to talk to his guests. Jack seemed undaunted and again presented the stick.

"We'll get wet. Just listen to the rain," said the master. And with that he turned once again to talk with his guests. They could hear Jack in the hallway upsetting the rack and umbrella container, pulling things over. They figured Jack was putting the walking stick back in the rack, like the wise dog he was.

A few moments later Jack gave a pleading bark and bounded in with an umbrella in his mouth, the first time he had ever presented this object.

Everyone, guests and all, rushed around looking for a raincoat and hat for the man of the house. And that gentleman, carrying the umbrella so persuasively offered him, took Jack out for his evening walk without further delay.

THE MISER

TALES OF CANINE economy and frugality are not rare, most of which centre around dogs that hoard or bury food, bones, and other objects that take their fancy. Instances of a dog money miser are more unique. However, there is the story of "Dandie," a Newfoundland dog belonged to a gentleman living in Edinburgh, Scotland.

Dandie had a propensity for money and showed great interest in coins whenever he saw them handled by his master or others in the household. Thus he frequently had money given to him because, in addition to obvious wisdom often shown by Dandie, he would occasionally go to the bakers and buy his own bread.

But Dandie received more money than his needs called for, so he took to hoarding it. His master discovered this trait when Dandie appeared one day with a breakfast roll when it was known that no one had given him any money.

Suspicion aroused, the master asked the maidservant to search the room the Newfoundland usually slept in. Her error was that she allowed the dog in the room the same time as it was being investigated.

Dandie appeared quite unconcerned until the girl approached the box where the dog slept. Dandie then seized the servant by her gown and tried to drag her away. He became so incensed and violent that she called the master. He had to hold Dandie while a search was made of the blanket in the box. Seven pence-halfpenny were found hidden in the bed.

Dandie did not give up his miserly habits after this, but showed a great dislike afterward for the servant who had discovered his cache. From that point on, the Newfoundland was careful to search out a different place of concealment for his coins.

FOR THE WANT OF A BROOM

THE MAN, WHO is given the name Mr. Smith for the sake of anonymity, lived on Main Street. He didn't mind saying he was the owner of what he called "a very smart Newfoundland dog" and went on to give an example of his friend's intelligence.

On a snowy winter's day, Smith was busy shovelling snow from his front veranda and stone walkway leading to the street. After he had done all he could do with a shovel, he decided to finish the job with a broom, sweeping away the last few crumbs of snow. His Newfoundland, "Leo," was keeping company, watching and waiting cheerfully to help in any way he could.

However, the broom was behind Smith's house on the rear porch step, usually stuck up in the corner. Smith ordered Leo to go there and get it.

He started off happily and at full speed, apparently delighted to be able to do something for his master. Yet he returned in a moment without the broom.

"What do you mean, sir," said Smith. "Go and get the broom!"

Again Leo bounded through the snow on his way to the back step, but again returned a moment or two later empty-handed or empty-mouthed.

"No broom, sir?" said Smith, in obvious reproof. "Go and get that broom, I tell you!"

For the third time Leo dashed through the snow, but again no broom.

This time his master stooped as if to pick up something with which to punish the dog for his disobedience or non-compliance. Smith told him with threatening gestures and in a stern tone to "Go and get that broom immediately."

Leo lowered his tail and, this time more disconsolately, went off through the snow to find what his master wanted. He was gone just a few moments longer, but this time came back with the broom in his mouth. With every demonstration of joy and delight, he said wordlessly to his master, "I have brought you a broom and here it is!"

Hours later, Smith happened to meet or speak to his next-door neighbour. "When you are finished with my broom," said the neighbour, "can you bring it back? I have some snow to clear myself."

"I have your broom? I don't think so," said Smith.

"Oh yes, you have. I'm quite sure, for this morning I was looking out my window and saw your dog running through the snow to my back step. Then he went to your house with my broom in his mouth. He carried it around to you shovelling in the front."

It was discovered that Mrs. Smith had removed the broom from its usual place. Leo, forced to get a broom or receive a stern chiding, did the next best thing to please his master by taking the neighbour's broom.

THE NEWFOUNDLAND WHO WAS A THIEF

FOR TWO WEEKS in mid-March, 1895, a milk thief had been at work in Boston's Eleventh Precinct, around Morton Street. Several well-filled milk cans disappeared from the doorsteps of houses, never to be recovered. Despite a neighbourhood watch, no one could spot the thief.

Finally, and in desperation, according to the *Boston Traveler*, one of the milkmen went to the nearest police station and asked that an officer be given special detail to help the milkman watch for the culprit. Both, incognito, kept a lookout on Morton Street.

Just before daybreak on a Tuesday morning, after the milk had been delivered to the customers along the street, the policeman and the milkman took up a position in a doorway to watch. They waited until 6:00 a.m. No thief appeared, at least not one with two legs.

As the sun broke over the Boston rooftops, the watchers were making up their minds that there was little use remaining any longer. Then a large Newfoundland dog came around the corner and slowly ambled up the street.

"There's your thief," remarked the policeman as he watched the dog cautiously peering into every doorway as he walked along.

"What! The dog?" said the milkman, incredulously.

"I'm sure. Yes. Keep your eye on him."

The Newfoundland paused before a doorway where a can of milk stood, then walked slowly up the steps and smelled the can. In a moment he took the can in his teeth, walked down to the street, and started off the way he had come.

The milkman, true to his profession of delivering and safekeeping the milk, wanted to shout and frighten the dog away. But the policeman asked him to wait and see what the dog would do.

Both followed him a short distance to see him turn down another street and climb up into the veranda of a house. He set the can down for a moment and studied it. Then he picked it up in his teeth again and shook the can gently.

In a moment the wooden plug dropped out of the milk can and, setting the can down on its side, the dog began to lap the milk contentedly as it poured out. Both men watched him until he finished, then the dog proceeded to destroy the evidence. Picking up the can again in his teeth, the Newfoundland left the veranda.

He went around to the backyard of the house and into

a clump of bushes at the rear. The dog who was a thief was lost to view from a few moments, but then came out again, proceeding to the veranda. He lay down and soon fell asleep.

The policeman and the milkman went out into the bushes to look around. There they discovered 14 empty milk cans. Caught in the act, the Newfoundland was arrested, taken to a police station, tried, and finally freed because no law applicable to four-footed criminals could be found.

2

LOYALTY

The Newfoundland is smart and loyal. The breed is easily trained as they are eager to please their masters. They are neither easily frightened nor excitable. Relative to other breeds, Newfoundland puppies, especially older puppies, tend to be calm, but obedience training is a must for these giant dogs.

http://www.doggiewoggie.com/dog-breeds/newfoundland

AN APPEAL FOR CHARITY

AROUND THE TURN of the twentieth century, the City of New York had in place the institution of Commission of Charities. The commissioner was entrusted with the care and management of charities, poor houses, hospitals, jails, and orphanages in the great city. Other commissioners cared for outlying towns and villages. In 1912 the commissioner for New Rochelle, south of New York City, was Vincent De Paul Crennan.

On Sunday, January 21, 1912, as he was sitting down in his home enjoying dinner, Crennan heard whining and scratching at his door. It was a large Newfoundland dog, carrying in his mouth a note crudely written as if by a child. It read:

> Dear Mr. Crennan:
>
> Please, Mr. Crennan, if Rover brings this to you, won't you please

> come and help us. Mamma and Papa and Willie are all sick, and now I am sick too, and we have no coal, or nothing to eat.

On the back, the note bore the name and address of a family on Union Avenue, West New Rochelle. Crennan recalled he had provided for that family some days ago. The family truly deserved help for the father was out of work, the mother invalided, and two children, Willie and a ten-year-old daughter, depended on the parents and the graces of charity.

Then to further devastate the family, all came down with the grippe, a contagious viral disease akin to severe influenza. The father fell sick on Monday, January 15, and the son two days later. The ten-year-old tried in vain to do housework, cook, and act as a nursemaid. She saw it was work in vain, for without proper nourishment and warmth her family would only get worse. In addition, the extra duty and lack of food was wearing her down. Finally, she hit upon another plan.

She and "Rover" walked to Commissioner Crennan's house on Friday to ask for help. He gave the family groceries and meat. The food was soon gone and by early Sunday morning the little girl had used up the last of the coal. Then in the cold house she caught a chill, which developed into influenza and perhaps would lead to the grippe. This time she was too sick to walk to the commissioner's house. She sent the faithful Newfoundland dog, Rover.

When Commissioner Crennan reached the home that mid-Sunday afternoon, he delivered a bag of coal, some meat, and groceries from his own larder. Once Crennan got the fire going and a pot of vegetables boiling, he spoke to the girl (whose identity and that of her family remained anonymous). She told the commissioner how she managed to get a message to him.

"Rover was lying in front of the cold stove," she said, "and I thought he might find you because he went with me on Friday. So I wrote the note and gave it to him, and told him to take it to you."

"All the News That's Fit to Print"

The New York

L. LXI...NO. 19,721. NEW YORK, MONDAY, JANUARY 22, 1912.—EIGHTEEN

SENDS HER DOG FOR HELP.

Rover Goes Straight to Charities Commissioner and Brings Relief.

Special to The New York Times.

NEW ROCHELLE, N. Y., Jan. 21.—Vincent De Paul Crennan, Commissioner of Charities of New Rochelle, was interrupted at dinner to-day by the whining and scratching of a big Newfoundland dog at his kitchen door. The dog carried in his mouth the following note, scrawled in a child's handwriting:

Dear Mr. Crennan: Please, Mr. Crennan, if Rover brings this to you, won't you please come and help us. Mamma and papa and Willie are all sick, and now I am sick too, and we have no coal, or nothing to eat.

The note bore the name and address of a family in Union Avenue, West New Rochelle, whom the Commissioner had helped a few days ago. The mother is an invalid, the father, who is out of work, was taken ill with grip last Monday, and their son on Wednesday. Their ten-year-old daughter tried to do the housework and cooking besides acting as nurse.

She and Rover called on Commissioner Crennan on Friday, and he gave them groceries and meat. This morning the girl used the last of the coal, and caught a heavy cold. When Commissioner Crennan reached the house this afternoon, carrying a bag of coal, meat, and groceries from his own cellar, the little girl told him how she managed to get a message to him.

The editors of the *New York Times* had literally hundreds of stories for its daily paper and often had difficult decisions which news items made the front page. On January 22, 1912, the paper with "All the News That's Fit to Print" as its slogan put the story of Crennan's Newfoundland dog on its front page.

Crennan glanced down at Rover, now asleep by the warm stove. To him it seemed incredible that the dog knew what the note contained or understood what the girl intended for him to do and where he had to go. As if to read the disbelief on the commissioner's face, the girl concluded her story and she had no doubt of the dog's intelligence and loyalty: "Rover understands everything you say to him. But I did not know he would remember your name or where you lived. But he did, and he is a good dog."

WAITING FOR HIS MASTER

THE *BUFFALO ADVERTISER* ran a brief news story in a February, 1876, edition of what it called "remarkable circumstances" of faithfulness in a dog. Someone residing on one of the main thoroughfares of Hamburg, New York, called the police station on a Thursday to report that a large Newfoundland dog was standing on the side of the road about a mile from town. It had been there since Tuesday.

Despite coaxing and entreaties, the dog refused to move. A small, four-wheeled wagon was next to it. Someone had released the dog from the wagon on Wednesday or Thursday, but the dog stood by it, anxiously waiting for someone to appear. The wagon was partially filled with willow branches. The police surmised these had been cut by the dog's master from a willow grove close by.

It was Friday morning before the police removed the dog and finally determined who owned it—a local man, Mr. Selrick, a basket maker. Selrick had been arrested on Wednesday morning. Apparently the weather turned cold and he left the dog and wagon at the place they were found to "get a drink."

At the local bar or tavern he took a number of "drinks" until he was intoxicated and forgot all about his dog, the wagon, the willow sticks, and the making of baskets. Arrested for being drunk in public, he had no money to pay a fine and was given 30 days in the local Work House.

The Newfoundland, presumably, was cared for by a concerned citizen or relative. However, the *Advertiser* said, it was a good illustration of the fidelity of an animal, who had stayed for three days without food, waiting without question for his master, as opposed to his master's neglect and wastefulness.

THE LOST LUNCH

A MR. JOHN NEWCOMB lived in Dover, New Jersey. He was a shoemaker by trade and walked to his work at Sussex and Clinton streets. His closest friend was "Nero," a large Newfoundland dog. Occasionally he left his lunch (or dinner) home. Maybe he was in a hurry or maybe he liked to give his dog some work and duty, so he would send Nero to fetch the lunch containers from home.

On May 20, 1904, Nero again went on that errand, as Mrs. Newcomb had the meal prepared back home. It was in two pails: one contained the food; and the coffee she put in a glass bottle, which she put in a separate pail.

Nero took both in his great jaws and off he went on a dog trot, happy to be of service to his master. For some reason Nero decided he could shorten the journey by a quarter-mile (as determined after) by going across some vacant lots. Then he would have to walk across a footbridge over a canal.

The bridge was but a narrow plank and, in crossing it, Nero had to watch his step. So careful was he that he slackened his grip on the handle of the coffee bottle and it dropped into the water.

Forgetting also that he had the pail in his mouth, Nero jumped in after the coffee container and thus lost the pail. Frantically he began to swim around in the canal, occasionally ducking his head under in hopes of seeing either or both.

Two boys who knew the dog and Mr. Newcomb saw what had happened and, after watching the dog swim around for over half an hour (the boys thought at any minute the dog would retrieve the containers), they went to the shoe store and told Mr. Newcomb about the drama that had unfolded before them.

Newcomb hurried over to the canal and found the dog still swimming about, plunging here and there, seemingly trying to find and get the lost lunch. He called repeatedly for Nero to come out of the water, but the faithful Newfoundland refused to leave the canal. All efforts to get him to land were futile.

It could be readily seen the dog was becoming exhausted, but still he swam around, yelping and crying piteously. The dog appeared to be heartbroken at having met with an accident and not being able to deliver his master's lunch.

Then Mr. Newcomb saw that the only way to get the

dog out of the water would be to fetch up the pails from the bottom of the canal. Somehow, with a pole or hook, he was able to do so. This took about 15 minutes: the dinner pail first, then after that the coffee bottle.

Only then, with both objects fished up from the bottom and safely in the master's hands, would Nero consent to come out. He reached the shore, but was so weak he could not crawl and had to be hauled onto dry land. Nero, after swimming for more than an hour, quickly recovered.

THE RIGHT HAND FOR THE NEWFOUNDLAND

GENERAL SIR GEORGE Napier, 1784-1855, served in the British army in the Peninsular War (a conflict between France, England, Spain, and Portugal) and lost his right arm in the 1810 storming of Ciudad Rodrigo, a city in Spain. Later in Sir George's life he knew a man who had "a dog," which later sources claim was a Newfoundland.

The tale, which appeared in 1868, some years after Napier had passed away, reinforced and "illustrated the wonderful manner in which instinct in all animals appears to develop from constant and intimate association with humans."

That instinct or training became evident when this particular Newfoundland was in company with Sir George Napier. For whatever whim or caprice the friend of

Sir George Napier had, the man trained the Newfoundland to accept food, morsels, and tidbits from the table with only the right hand. If anyone offered food with the left hand, the dog would refuse to take it.

On one occasion, Napier, with several other guests, dined at this friend's home. The guests heard of the Newfoundland's training and were amusing themselves by tempting the well-bred dog to lower his high standard of etiquette. They offered food with the left hand, but all in vain. Not one of the seven gentlemen with Napier could bribe the dog to accept any dainty, however savoury or aromatic, with the left hand. Yet the Newfoundland eagerly ate the same food presented with the right hand.

When Napier offered food with his left (and only) hand, the wise animal glanced at the general's empty sleeve, perceived Napier had no right hand, and accepted the gift. The men tried the experiment again and again, but the Newfoundland's discrimination and training never faltered.

DUTY CALLS

"CAESAR'S" STORY WAS cosmopolitan: a Newfoundland dog in a story that happened in London, England, and carried in the Prince Edward Island newspaper the *Daily Examiner* of August 5, 1882.

A London merchant felt obliged to tell his tale of loyalty and intelligence as exemplified in Caesar. Both master and dog had gone from home together, and while they were away the master found a key in his pocket which he should have left behind at his home. He gave the key to the dog and told him to take it back—a trot that would take the Newfoundland about a half-hour.

Caesar dutifully started back with the key in his mouth. On the way he was met and attacked by a butcher's dog, a vicious and short-tempered cur. Caesar received a beating, but somehow tore himself away from his enemy and delivered the key in safety.

Caesar then returned by the road he had come, and stopped by the butcher shop, looking for the dog that had accosted him. Once found, there ensued a battle that the *Daily Examiner* says "lasted a long time." It did not end until the cur that had dared to interfere with a Newfoundland in the execution of his responsibility had been dispatched. The antagonist was "put beyond all chance of doing the like again."

A LOAF OF BREAD

EDDIE GERROLD, AGE nine, went into the woods at the rear of his father's house to gather nuts. By October they were plentiful in the groves and forest behind his father's house in Watervliet, New York. Eddie obtained a little bag from his mother and started off to the woods, happy as a lark. As the evening of Thursday, October 22, 1875, drew to a close, he hadn't returned and his anxious parents went out to search for him.

With help from volunteer searchers, they continued looking and calling out to him all day Friday. On the evening of that day, the parents returned home tired and footsore, sad and disappointed. They almost gave the child up as lost.

About 9:00 a.m. Saturday, as most of the residents of the small town were in Mr. Gerrold's house making more plans and generally sympathizing with the family, "Jack," a large Newfoundland, entered the house and seemed uneasy. Jack, while not exactly a house pet, had hung around the Gerrold family since he was a month old. On that morning he whined, barked at intervals, and paced around as if there was something on his mind.

He was put outside the door for disturbing the family and friends as they talked and discussed important issues regarding the missing Eddie. Jack remained by the door for some time, then ran into a Mrs. Scovill's house, next door to the Gerrolds.

He grabbed a loaf of bread that the lady of the house had just taken out of the oven and put near the stove to cool. Jack ran off in the direction of the woods with the loaf in his mouth. When Mr. Scovill returned to his house from the Gerrolds', his wife told him about the incident with the dog. Mr. Scovill was surprised to hear this, for Jack was always quiet, gentle, and honest. It was totally out of character. Thus Scovill returned to the Gerrold house and told the story.

Both Mr. Scovill and Mr. Gerrold felt pretty certain that the dog had some idea of where the child might be located. New hope lifted the family and friends as they waited for the dog to return. Maybe the talk turned to finding a sniffer dog, a bloodhound, for the search.

At any rate, Jack returned in about an hour and showed the same anxiety that people had noticed earlier. After trying several moves and devices to get the family to follow him, Jack finally started in the general direction where little Eddie had gone.

With half the population of Watervliet following him, Jack led them through many winding paths until finally the Newfoundland and his entourage reached a chestnut grove. There they found Eddie lying under a tree with his leg broken.

Eddie finished the account: he was up in a tree, shaking it with all his might to get the nuts to fall, when he fell heavily to the ground. He said he blacked out or fainted in pain.

But the first thing that met his gaze when he regained consciousness was Jack standing over him. This was Friday evening, and the dog never left his side but kept barking with all his might until Saturday morning. By this time, Eddie related, he was hungry and tried to reach some chestnuts that lay on the ground a little distance from him.

When Jack saw this he started off and returned some time later with a loaf of bread in his mouth. He laid the bread by the boy's side and he ate most of it. Then Eddie became lonesome and anxious and began to cry. Jack left again, this time returning with help. Eddie was carried home. A doctor came from a nearby town and set his broken limb.

A MOST DEVOTED FRIEND

IN THE HISTORICAL accounts of the State of Wisconsin, an upper Midwestern state in the United States, there is a brief anecdote of a Newfoundland dog. When the Civil War in the United States (1861-1865) broke out, Wisconsin's immigrants quickly joined up to fight for their new homeland. Company F of the Sixth Infantry, for example, was composed entirely of Germans from Milwaukee. These soldiers were the early settlers or first-generation descendants of settlers.

One of Company F's officers, Captain Werner von Bachelle, had trained as a soldier in the French army before emigrating to America. Colonel Rufus Dawes told a heartfelt and true story about him.

Dawes wrote that when von Bachelle enlisted, he brought with him "a fine Newfoundland dog which had been trained to perform military salutes, to march and other remarkable actions." In military camp, on the march, in the line of battle, this dog was von Bachelle's constant companion.

Both dog and master were on the front line at Antietam, Maryland, on September 17, 1862, reportedly the bloodiest day in American military history. Dawes recalled that bullets flew as thick as hail. Of the 280 men he brought to the field of battle, 150 were killed or wounded.

"At the farthest point of advance," Dawes wrote, "Captain Werner von Bachelle, commanding Company F, was shot dead."

Many left alive, when recounting their losses after the skirmish, inquired about the dog. "The Newfoundland was by his side when he fell. Our line of men left the body when they retreated, but the dog stayed with his dead master and was found on the morning of September 19, lying dead upon his master's body. We buried him with von Bachelle.

Dawes concluded, "As far as we knew, no family or friends mourned for poor von Bachelle, and it is probable that he was joined in death with the most devoted friend he had on earth."

LOYAL, TILL DEATH

IN SALEM, MASSACHUSETTS, in mid-November, 1888, the local police had a prolonged, traumatic, and fatal fight with a Newfoundland. The loyal friend belonged to a man, John Gynan. Apparently Gynan was depressed and wished to leave this life, and did so by committing suicide by hanging himself.

A well-to-do bachelor who lived alone at South Salem Point, Gynan's only companion was a large Newfoundland dog. When Gynan's body was discovered, the dog was lying beneath it. The shoes of the dead man showed that the loyal companion had tried to revive his master. The dog had licked them repeatedly, nudged them, and tugged on them, to no avail.

While two policemen were cutting the dead man down, the dog stood by with his eyes riveted on his master's face. But the moment they tried to move the body, he became ferocious. He bit both until they backed off, and the two police beat a welcomed retreat.

Then the dog caressed the dead man's face, whining mournfully all the while. The police tried to coax the dog away, but he showed his teeth every time they approached. Savage growls warned them to keep their distance.

The standoff continued for over an hour and, although the police saw the dog as intelligent and a true friend to the end, they had to use more force, and one policeman fired two shots at the faithful animal.

The Newfoundland dog, mortally wounded, then ran down the stairs to the only exit to the street and again blocked the way, snapping at all who approached. Even as the end was near, the dog was determined that no one, including his master, would go out through that door.

He became so aroused and fanatical, it became absolutely necessary to kill the dog. Fourteen bullets were fired at close range before the dog lay still. Then the dead body of the master was carried over the inanimate form of the pet dog lying in front of the door.

3

RESCUE, BY WATER

The Newfoundland: Noted for sea rescues, the gentle, patient Newfoundland stands 26-28 inches (66-71 cm) and weighs 110-150 pounds (50-68 kg). Powerful hindquarters, a large lung capacity, large webbed feet, and a heavy, oily coat enable it to swim in cold waters. It has also been used as a watchdog and draft animal. The typical Newfoundland is solid black; the Landseer Newfoundland is usually black and white.

THE BRITANNICA CONCISE ENCYCLOPEDIA

DAN, THE HERO OF BARENEED

IN THE FALL of 1916, when the trauma of conflict on sea and land was at its midpoint, a folk poem by an anonymous writer, simply entitled "To Dan," appeared in the local papers. Dan was not a soldier of war nor a heroic seaman, for as the subheading for the 14-stanza poem says, he was "The Dog Hero of Bareneed."

Not everyone who read the weekly papers in 1916 wanted an overdose of war news, casualties, shipping losses, and the politics of strife-torn Europe. Editors were delighted when light, folksy items appeared that helped people forget for a moment or two the hunger, insecurity, troubles, death, and disaster that global conflict brings to everyone's threshold. Although the story of "Dan" happened in the fall of 1900, the poem was printed 16 years later.

Bareneed, a fishing community located at the base of

the Port de Grave peninsula, about two kilometres southwest of the community of Port de Grave, is an old established fishing town in Conception Bay, Newfoundland. Some of the earliest names recorded there (in the 1864 Hutchinson's *Newfoundland Directory*) are Batten, Hennebury, and Richards. Indeed, it was young Wilfred Richards who plays a principal part in this tale.

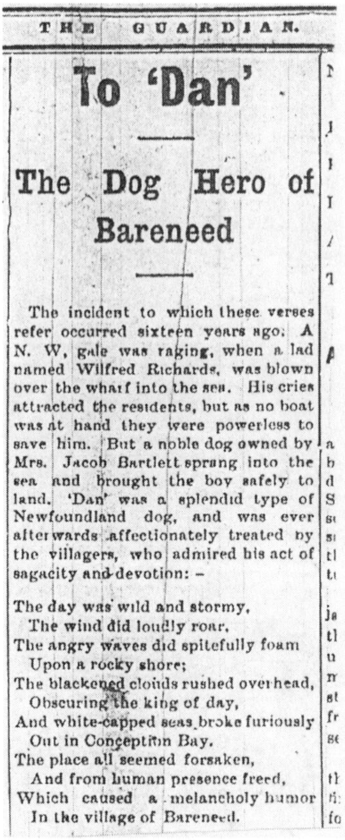

THE GUARDIAN.

To 'Dan'

The Dog Hero of Bareneed

The incident to which these verses refer occurred sixteen years ago. A N. W. gale was raging, when a lad named Wilfred Richards, was blown over the wharf into the sea. His cries attracted the residents, but as no boat was at hand they were powerless to save him. But a noble dog owned by Mrs. Jacob Bartlett sprang into the sea and brought the boy safely to land. 'Dan' was a splendid type of Newfoundland dog, and was ever afterwards affectionately treated by the villagers, who admired his act of sagacity and devotion: –

The day was wild and stormy,
The wind did loudly roar,
The angry waves did spitefully foam
Upon a rocky shore;
The blackened clouds rushed overhead,
Obscuring the king of day,
And white-capped seas broke furiously
Out in Conception Bay.
The place all seemed forsaken,
And from human presence freed,
Which caused a melancholy humor
In the village of Bareneed.

Wilfred had gone down to the wharf during a northwest gale, but a sudden gust of wind blew him into the water. His cries attracted residents, but no boat was at hand to reach him. Quite possibly all small craft had been pulled ashore because of the gale and no one quite knew what to do.

Young Richards may have been in the water for a minute or two, when a great Newfoundland, described in the preamble to the poem as "a noble dog owned by Mrs. Jacob Bartlett," sprang into action. He jumped overboard and brought the boy to safety. Dan either grabbed the clothes of Wilfred and pulled him to safety, or the lad may have clung to Dan's neck.

At any rate, Dan saved the life of Wilfred Richards and the dog was forever after treated affectionately by the people of Bareneed. When he died his grave was marked and, for years after, tended with honour.

"To Dan"

The day was wild and stormy,
The wind did loudly roar,
The angry waves did spitefully foam,
Upon a rocky shore.

The blackened clouds rushed overhead,
Obscuring the king of day,
And white-capped seas broke furiously,
Out in Conception Bay.

The place seemed also forsaken,
And from human presence freed,
Which caused a melancholy humor,
In the village of Bareneed.

When lo, a little wanderer,
Quite carelessly did stray,
A-seaward down the village slope,
To gaze out o'er the bay.

Unconscious of the danger,
He smiles upon the sea,
With boyish pride he watched the waves,
No trace of fear has he.

When suddenly a wilder gust,
Bore down with lightning speed,
Which left him helpless, struggling,
In the waters of Bareneed.

His cries for help are answered soon,
By many an anxious heart,
But still, alas, no means are near,
The let the men depart.

The angry waves then seemed to mock
The helplessness of man,
But God reserved another means,
To the Thwart the billows greed;
For nobly to the rescue springs,
"Dan," the hero of Bareneed.

Bold "Dan" had watched, with pity,
The people on the quay,
He saw young Wilfred Richard,
Still floating out the bay.

With love that was almost human
As if from on High 'twas lent,
He sprang out in the harbour,
To save his little friend.

He swam toward the drowning lad,
While many wished Godspeed;

And brought young Richards safe ashore,
That evening in Bareneed.

Now sixteen years have flown since then,
And "Dan" has passed away,
But he surely was the noblest dog,
Around Conception Bay.

He was always loved by Wilfred,
And his memory still holds green;
In a quiet nook in the village,
His grave may still be seen.

And when those hardy fisher folk,
Discuss some noble deed,
Their thoughts revert to brave old "Dan,"
The hero of Bareneed.

THE GENTLEMAN

ACCORDING TO THE *Ottawa Free Press* there was a Newfoundland dog in Detroit that deserved to be called a gentleman. That is, if he wasn't already addressed by that epithet. In fact, he was generally called "Deko"—a dog that loved to romp with children. Children knew and loved him. Deko was easily recognizable, as he had a crooked tail.

Deko also loved to hang around a certain wharf in Detroit, especially where the passenger ferries docked. In those times, a ferry operated by the Ogdensburg line ran between the major cities and towns in Lake Michigan to Detroit in Lake Erie

Sometime in mid-November, 1877, the steamer docked in Detroit. Hetty, the daughter of a passenger from Albany, saw Deko and ran down the gangplank to play with the dog. While running as fast as she could go with her head turned so she could see the dog, she misjudged the distance to the end of the wharf and fell into the river.

Deko stood at the edge of the wharf and waited a few seconds until Hetty's head appeared above the surface. Then he jumped in after her. Taking one of the little girl's shoulders in his huge mouth, gentleman Deko kept her afloat until two men had put out a small boat and pulled Hetty aboard.

When Deko's heroic exploits were reviewed, the reason for the crooked tail was publicized—it may have already been well-known in Minnesota, but people in Detroit wanted to hear the story again and again.

Deko had been unfortunately present at a thwarted bank robbery, perpetrated by the infamous Younger Brothers. At that time Deko, through the wanderings or work of his master, was in downtown Northfield, Minnesota, during the hour of what became known as "the Northfield Raid." Several movies have been produced of this event, including *The Younger Brothers* and *The Great Northfield Minnesota Raid*.

Cole, Bob, and Jim Younger robbed banks and trains in the northern states. After more than a decade of life as outlaws, the Youngers' exploits were halted by a thwarted attempt on September 7, 1876, when they tried to rob the First National Bank of Northfield (in that time the largest bank west of the Mississippi).

When members of the gang rode into Northfield, they wore flowing garments to conceal their guns. Once inside, they dropped their coats and demanded the money from the vault. The bank clerk on duty was killed when he refused to open the safe. When the townspeople were alerted and the shooting started, the robbers dropped everything and fled. In the melee that followed, a town resident was killed, as were two gang members.

Another victim was wounded: Deko, the Newfoundlander, received a bullet in the tail, leaving him with a lopsided wagging appendage for the rest of his life. The next year Deko's owner moved to Detroit. During the dog's residence on the Detroit River, he learned the sound of various ship whistles and which ones invariably stopped at the wharf near which he lived.

When a Northern Transit boat signalled, Deko recognized it. He then proceeded to the hotel where one of the shipping clerks resided. The clerk was escorted to the wharf by Deko before the boat pulled in.

The gentleman Newfoundland stood guard on the boat at the top of the gangway until all the freight was moved and jumped ashore when he heard the order, "Haul in!" He then waited for the next Northern Transit boat to make its appearance.

But gentleman Deko, innocent bystander at a bank robbery, guardian of the gangway, was best known for saving the life of young Hattie in the Detroit River.

JUMBO JUMPS IN

"IN THE WORLD over," says the newspaper the *Western Star* of February 20, 1901, "the Newfoundland dog is hailed as a life saver and members of this species have been decorated with medals therefore by the Humane Societies in Europe."

The town of Prowseton could attest to that praise issued in the *Western Star*, but in the everyday working world of the Newfoundland fisherman, it is unlikely the town dog was ever decorated as a lifesaver.

A resettled fishing community in the province of Newfoundland and Labrador, Prowseton was located on the west side of Placentia Bay, on a small peninsula between Great Sandy Harbour and Little Sandy Harbour. The village was for many years known as Seevely's or Sibley's Cove, but in 1915 its name was changed to avoid confusion with Sibley's Cove, Trinity Bay, and Sibleys

Cove near Long Harbour, Placentia Bay (now known as Mount Arlington Heights). The name Prowseton was chosen by the Newfoundland Nomenclature Board to honour Judge D. W. Prowse, who had recently died.

The town never had a large population (it went over 50 once, in 1951), but Hickey was the most common name, with others being Foote, Hynes, Miller, and Pine. However, in the 1920s Prowseton was large enough to have a postal operator or master, a man by the name of J. Gibbons.

The Daily News

FOUNDLAND, FRIDAY, JUNE 29, 1928.

NFLD. DOG SAVES BOY FROM DROWNING

When Lad Falls Over Wharf at Prowseton "Jumbo" Jumps in and Rescues Exhausted Lad

Prowseton, June 28—(Special to Daily News)—John Walter Gibbons, son of J. Gibbons postal operator, of Prowseton, had a narrow escape from drowning today. Whilst the boy was fishing for tomcods he tripped and fell head first into deep water. A large Newfoundland dog

Newspaper clipping from the *Daily News* (June 29, 1928) lauding the praises of a Newfoundland dog, Jumbo.

On June 29, 1928, Gibbons's young son, John Walter, was fishing for tomcods, as boys are wont to do, from the head of the small wharf. Somehow he tripped and fell head first into deep water.

"Jumbo," a large Newfoundland owned by Patrick Hickey, saw what happened, jumped overboard, and swam to the boy. Little John Walter grabbed hold of the dog and held fast until Jumbo reached shore. The boy was exhausted, but alive. In a short while he was none the worse for his experience. But his father, the postal operator, wired the story to St. John's that day, saying Jumbo was a hero that saved the life of his son who would have undoubtedly drowned. The Newfoundland deserved a medal. However, there is no record of Jumbo ever receiving one.

THE DEBATE ON THE BRIDGE

LONGMAN'S MAGAZINE FIRST put in an appearance in November 1882 in Britain and ceased publication in 1905, focusing on fiction with debuting works by Thomas Hardy, Henry James, Edith Nesbit, Robert Louis Stevenson, H. Rider Haggard, Rudyard Kipling, and others. Issued monthly, it also carried short non-fiction articles on general human interest.

In one of its 1890 issues, *Longman's* gave an illustration of what a fine specimen of animal the Newfoundland dog was in a short piece called "A Great Dog." "The Newfoundland is a particular favourite of mine. He is the most magnanimous fellow in the world and smaller dogs may insult him with impunity unless a river happens to be near." Then, if a little mutt is too venturesome and insolent, it might find itself taking an involuntary bath.

Some time previously, the author says, a particularly fine Newfoundland was sitting on a narrow wooden bridge studying a bone. A predatory mastiff came along on the same bridge. This dog was unable to distinguish between *meum et tuum,* that is, what's mine and what's yours. Thus a smart argument arose.

The debate became more violent, so much so both fell into the deep stream below. The nearest landing place was about a hundred yards downriver. The Newfoundland, true to his breed, swam without much difficulty to land.

He gave himself a good shake and was preparing to leave when, suddenly, he became aware of the other dog, his enemy of just a few moments previously. The Newfoundland dog realized the other dog was more of a soldier than a sailor. It would rather stand on terra firma than swim in liquidum. In other words, the mastiff was wildly beating the water and drowning.

One look was enough. In went the shaggy-coated Newfoundland and, seizing the other by the collar, brought his opponent safely to land. The two dogs eyed each other with lordliness for some seconds, then silently and solemnly wagged their tails and with dignity departed company. Magnanimous, noble, honourable?

"Some will," says the writer, "say that this was nothing but instinct; they may be right. I prefer to give my four-footed Newfoundland the benefit of the doubt."

WHERE'S THE DOG?

THIS UNCREDITED POEM accompanied an illustration that probably came from an unidentified book or a calendar. The image shows a ship, a dog rescuing an inert child in the water, and a group of several men rowing a small boat in the direction of the dog and child. The poem beneath the illustration goes like this:

THE NEWFOUNDLAND DOG

Hark, Hark! To that cry! 'Tis the child. Hark again!
Lower boats on the starboard, quick, quick, or 'tis in vain!
'Tis the child we have played with, quick, quick, let us save
The fair boy we all love from a deep ocean grave.

He is sinking: he floats again! Look! There he drifts
On the dark rolling billow, see, see, how it lifts.

Now, now he is lost in the trough of the sea.
Where's the dog? The Newfoundland! Quick bring him to me!

Brave Carlo! Go seek him, away! Fetch him out!
And the dog has leap'd off while the ship puts about.
Away! Hie on him, boy! Dash over the spray!
Strong swimmer, bold diver, go deep as you may.

See the child has gone down, seek him, Dog. Look around!
Now the boats! Pull men! 'Tis for life! Ere the billows close over the drown'd.
Oh! God preserve the child! Amen and Amen.
See! He has found him! Good boy! Ah! Good dog! Brave Carlo, again.

A moment, Hurrah! They are safe in the bow.
Good dog; where's the man that is nobler than thou?
Thou shall live in our hearts, for tho' soulless and mute,
Yet God's beautiful image was saved by the brute.

The poem and illustration, believed to have originated in the mid-nineteenth century, of a Newfoundland saving a life.

A DEBT REPAID

"SULTAN," A LARGE Newfoundland dog, lived near the Harlem River, a navigable tidal strait running between Manhattan and the Bronx in New York City. In early September, 1897, Mrs. Abbie Schumacher of One Hundred and Eighty-second Street, Harlem, decided she would like to go for a row on the river.

Rowing the boat were James Harrison and his son, William. Mrs. Schumacher took her 13-year-old daughter, Mina, with her. They were about to pull away from the shore when Sultan bounded up to the side of the boat.

With a series of barks and tail wagging, Sultan indicated he would like to go for a row as well. Mina had to beg her mother and the two men to allow her dog to accompany them. Finally, after a considerate amount of coaxing, the other three relented and Mina invited Sultan aboard, whereupon he lay quietly on the bottom of the rowboat. He was deeply grateful, but said nothing.

But at the newly constructed ship canal at Spuyten Duyvil, the little boat capsized, perhaps through a sharp turn or movement of a passenger. All, including the dog, were thrown into the water. Mrs. Schumacher clung to the overturned boat. William Harrison, who was a strong swimmer, struggled to keep his father afloat. Little Mina went underwater, drifted away, and undoubtedly would have drowned within a few minutes.

Sultan, the other excellent swimmer in the group, studied the situation quickly and swam for Mina. He grabbed her dress with his teeth, held her head above water, and struck out for shore.

When young Harrison had safely cared for the older people, he swam after the dog and the child. But as he drew near, Sultan growled between his teeth as he clung to Mina, helping her to the shoreline. William Harrison wisely kept his distance.

Sultan safely landed his charge on shore and repaid Mina for her influence in allowing him into the boat in the first place. Mrs. Schumacher, interviewed later, said she would rather lose her home than see anything happen to Sultan.

4

RESCUE, BY LAND

The large Newfoundland dog Heck, belonging to the St. Elmo Hotel, in the neighbouring oil town of Eldred, Pennsylvania, was known throughout the northern oil field for its great strength and almost human intelligence . . .

"There is no doubt in my mind that but for the intelligence and activity of Heck the fire in the hotel would not have been discovered in time for a single person to have escaped from the building.

The noble animal understood from the half-crazed movements of the child's mother that there was another child in danger and to rescue whom he gave his own life . . ."

PORTER IN ST. ELMO'S HOTEL
NEW YORK TIMES, SEPTEMBER 23, 1884

JACK GILL'S WARNING

MR. GILL WAS an electrician who worked nights in the historic neighbourhood of Jamaica Plain in Boston, Massachusetts. On October 23, 1899, he left for work, leaving his Newfoundland, "Jack Gill," or just "Jack," as he was called, as custodian of his house, his wife, and infant boy.

Some time during the night an overheated stove set fire to a wooden partition next to the chimney. The blaze was within a foot of a door connecting the down stairway to the front exit when Mrs. Gill was awakened by Jack. Jack had barked for a moment or so but somehow realized the woman was too deep in sleep to be awakened in time. Thus he went to the bedside and pulled on the bedclothes. Mrs. Gill, seeing the thick smoke, grasped the situation in an instant.

Flames were near her, giving her not a second to lose.

Near the open door at the top of the stairwell, which had not yet been touched or scorched by the fire, stood the dog with the infant between his massive paws. While Mrs. Gill was rousing herself from deep sleep, the dog had sensed there was no time to lose and brought the child to where he could be easily seen and picked up by the mother.

Mrs. Gill sprang out of bed, grabbed the child, and groped though the smoke toward the stairs. Leading the way in the dark and blinding smoke was Jack, down the stairs and to the door. With great difficulty Mrs. Gill opened the door, but a moment after Jack's charges reached the street, the house was ablaze from cellar to attic.

It was a feat of valour, substantiated by Mrs. Gill, that prompted everlasting love from the master—Jack had saved the woman of the home and his playmate, the little boy, from death by smoke inhalation or fire on Bourne Street, Jamaica Plain.

THE GOOD DOCTOR'S DOG

ROBERT NELSON, BORN in Truro, Nova Scotia, studied and trained to be a doctor, and came to Carbonear, Newfoundland, around 1871 to begin practice. In time he had patients and emergency calls in the outlying towns around Carbonear and many parts of Conception Bay. To accompany him on his long and lonely journeys, Doctor Nelson acquired a Newfoundland dog, said to "possess all the admirable qualities of its breed."

One cold winter's day, Dr. Nelson set out to journey to Blackhead, about 15 miles (24 kilometres) away. Along with the horse and sleigh, he took his Newfoundland with him, but the weather nearly took the doctor's life. The incident is described in the *Harbor Grace Standard* of January 18, 1879, which said, "We are sorry to learn the Dr. Nelson of Carbonear, on the night of Thursday last (January 16) well nigh fell victim to the inclemency of the weather while engaged in his humane work of administering to the ailments of his patients."

But for the fact that the doctor's loyal friend, the Newfoundland dog with him, saved his life. The report continues:

> Dr. Nelson had just driven to Blackhead to see a sick person. After performing his office of mercy, he took the road to home, but when within several miles of Carbonear, he felt so cold that he decided to jump out (of his winter conveyance) and run a little beside it to restore warmth to his body.
>
> To his horror, however, he sank helpless to the ground. Both his feet were frostbitten. To make matters worse, his horse had started off, leaving him with no help but his favourite Newfoundland dog. This faithful creature remained beside him all that long and intensely frosty night, shielding him from the fearful fate of being frozen to death.
>
> Apparently with the coming of daylight Nelson managed to find some human habitation or some other person found him for the story continues. "We are sorry to learn, as it is, that Dr. Nelson's legs are badly frostbitten, so much so, indeed, that it is feared one of the legs will have to be amputated."

After this report the story is silent, but the fact was that because of his unanticipated overnight sojourn in very cold outdoor temperatures, both Dr. Nelson's legs were amputated. The good doctor, a well-respected and skilful physician, recovered and continued his practice until he died in Western Bay in 1906.

THE ST. ELMO HOTEL FIRE

"HECK" WAS HIS name. Everyone in the oil town of Eldred, Pennsylvania, seemed to know Heck, the large Newfoundland dog. Not only was he recognized affectionately by sight, but many knew of his great strength and almost human intelligence. On September 18, 1884, those noble qualities were put again to a test.

Heck's owner, an employee of the hotel, slept upstairs. However, the porter of Eldred's St. Elmo Hotel, a small man who was kind-hearted and civil, was a special friend of Heck. When the porter slept in a little room back of the office at St. Elmo, the dog lay down at night and slept on the floor of the office. On that Thursday night in September, the porter had had too much to drink and lay in a deep, heavy sleep.

Some time during the night he was awakened by the loud barking of Heck, who was jumping wildly up and down on the porter's bed. At one point Heck grabbed the pillow under the porter's head and pulled it away.

The still inebriated and sleepy porter tried to make the dog go away, but the Newfoundland persisted in his efforts. It finally dawned on the muddled mind of the porter the hotel was on fire. The lower level where he slept was full of smoke and he could hear the crackling of the flames.

The porter jumped from the bed, but with the effects of alcohol he fell to the floor and would have stayed there, unable to get up to help himself. The faithful dog at once seized him by the coat collar (the porter in his haste to sleep had not removed his outer clothes). Heck dragged him out of the room and halfway to the other door when the porter, whose name has not been preserved in history, managed to get to his feet.

He unlocked the door and staggered onto the street. Meanwhile, the fire was gaining headway rapidly. St. Elmo was filled with guests and not one had been warned or roused from sleep.

Heck, as soon as he realized his friend was safe, dashed back into the building and ran upstairs, barking loudly. He first stopped at his master's door, where he howled and scratched at the door until the man was aware of the danger and rushed out of the hotel, as there was no time to lose. There was no need for Heck to guide him to the door, as the dog seemed to realize his owner knew of the great danger and knew the way out.

But the dog gave the alarm at every door and in some instances guided the guests downstairs to the outer door. Each one of these, being strangers in the hotel and not aware of where quick exits were located, said after that the dog seemed to understand this, as he looked after their safety.

Many guests, seeing the flames and smoke, seemed to panic in the rush. The hotel dog alone kept his cool and complete control of himself, taking active steps to save people. He ran in and out of the burning building, guiding some half-dressed man or woman downstairs, only to return at once to search for others.

One of the last he guided out was a woman with a child in her arms. By now the smoke was so thick, the woman tripped on the stairs while in the hurry and fell. The child was thrown to the floor, but before she could find and recover the child in the smoke-filled entranceway, others standing near the door pulled her outside.

Heck saw this and, jumping in through the smoke pouring from the office door, gripped the child's clothes in his teeth and carried her safely outside. Ironically this last rescue of the last person, a small child, ultimately led to the death of heroic Heck.

The mother of the child, as soon as she recovered somewhat from smoke inhalation and was restored by fresh air, became aware her child was not in sight. Not knowing the child was safe and located in another part of the street, she began to call frantically, "Anna is still in there. Anna is in that fire!" The woman made a dash for the building as if to rush into the flames to look for the child.

At this point, as a dozen hands held the woman back from an emotional attempt to get into the building, Heck disappeared with a bound over the burning threshold and into the hotel. The faithful animal never appeared again. His remains were later found in the burnt-out ruins of St. Elmo Hotel.

All present at the fire agreed but that for the intelligence and activity of Heck, the fire in the hotel would not have been discovered in time for most to make it out alive. More lamentable was that the esteemed animal mistook the half-crazed shouts and movements of the child's mother as meaning that there was another of her children still inside.

As well, the public were sure that to rescue this child the dog gave his own life. The remains of Heck were given a fitting burial and his loss was regretted and written up in honour as that of any citizen of the day.

THE BOYLE BUSINESS RESCUE

THE NEWFOUNDLAND NEWSPAPER the *Twillingate Sun* carried a brief sketch of a heroic event and that piece was published two months after the event had actually happened. On March 8, 1890, the *Sun* said, under the bold banner "A Newfoundland Dog," that the animal saved six lives in Allegheny City.

"The dog," said the *Sun* (as quoted from the American journal *Scientific American*), "by loud barking roused his master, the man called for assistance and succeeded in rescuing from the burning building, the members of three families." The *Sun*'s short tale of loyalty, intelligence, and rescue can be fleshed out in more detail through the Pittsburgh, Pennsylvania, media.

A little after midnight on January 17, 1890, a fire broke out in the armoury, or army drill centre, on the first floor of the Boyle Building in Allegheny City, across from downtown Pittsburgh. Several other businesses were located on the first or ground floor while families lived on the second and third floors.

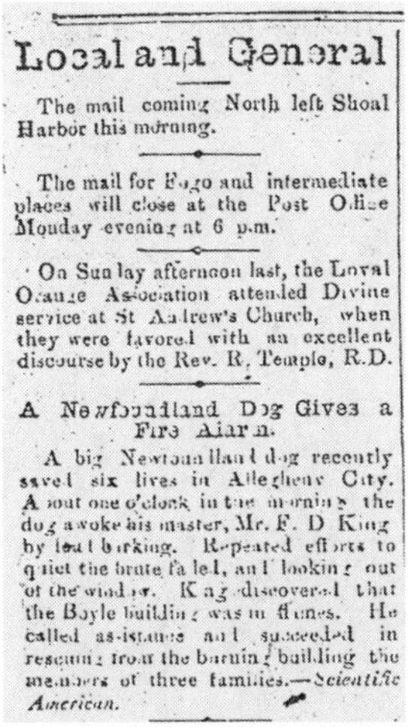
Local and General

The mail coming North left Shoal Harbor this morning.

The mail for Fogo and intermediate places will close at the Post Office Monday evening at 6 p.m.

On Sunday afternoon last, the Loyal Orange Association attended Divine service at St Andrew's Church, when they were favored with an excellent discourse by the Rev. R. Temple, R.D.

A Newfoundland Dog Gives a Fire Alarm.

A big Newfoundland dog recently saved six lives in Allegheny City. About one o'clock in the morning the dog awoke his master, Mr. F. D King by loud barking. Repeated efforts to quiet the brute failed, and looking out of the window. King discovered that the Boyle building was in flames. He called assistance and succeeded in rescuing from the burning building the members of three families.—*Scientific American.*

A faded clipping from the *Twillingate Sun* of March 8, 1890, carries the short story of a heroic Newfoundland dog.

About 1:00 a.m., a Newfoundland, unfortunately unnamed, began to bark at the bed of his master, F. D. King. King, sleeping soundly in one of the first-floor kitchens in the Boyle Building, was awakened by the dog, but tried to get back to sleep. Repeated efforts to quieten down the pet failed, so King got up to look out the window.

He saw the Boyle Building was in flames and gave an alarm. The janitor of the building was the first to respond and both men ran to the floors above to rouse the families. Smoke was beginning to fill the corridors and rooms, but all three families—six people—got out in the nick of time. They gathered in the freezing January temperatures, clad only in nightclothes, on the street opposite the Boyle Building. In time Mr. King and his Newfoundland companion joined them.

Firemen eventually gained control of the fire, but the Boyle Building was extensively damaged. The *New York Times,* commenting on the rescue, said: "The dog had saved six lives and today was hero of Boyle's Block."

A BATTLE WITH THE WOLVES

ON SATURDAY, OCTOBER 9, 1897, Sam Dodge left his home in Montgomery County, Ohio, to go to what was then called "Indian Territory." He left his wife and his five-year-old daughter, Bessie, on the ranch along with the family dog, a Newfoundland, whose name is not known.

While Mrs. Dodge was preoccupied with some household tasks, Bessie, missing her father, wandered away looking for him. As soon as the mother noticed the child was not around the home, immediately notified neighbours and a search for the child began. She also realized the Newfoundland dog was gone as well.

On Sunday evening, October 10, little Bessie was found ten miles from her home. She was asleep with the Newfoundland dog standing beside her on guard and protecting her. The dog was torn and bleeding and near him lay the bodies of two wolves. Seeing these wolves, the searchers thought Bessie might have been bitten or hurt. They looked for wounds or bruises on Bessie, but she was unharmed.

The searchers carried Bessie and the wounded dog back to her home. But on Monday, the dog died from the injuries inflicted by the wolves. Sam Dodge returned from his expedition within a day or two and ordered a marble monument to be placed at the head of the faithful animal's grave.

5

RESCUE, BY SHIP

No animal, perhaps, can show more real courage than this dog, the Newfoundland dog. His perseverance in what he undertakes is so great, that he never relinquishes an attempt which has been enjoined him as long as there is a chance of success.

I allude more particularly to storms at sea and consequent shipwreck, when his services, his courage, and indefatigable exertions, have been truly wonderful. Numerous persons have been saved from a watery grave by these dogs.

ANECDOTES OF DOGS
EDWARD JESSE, 1858

THE BURIN BANKER *NIGHTINGALE*

AROUND EARLY JULY, 1903, the bank fishing vessel *Nightingale* sailed into Burin harbour, Newfoundland, with a black flag flying at half-mast, indicating one or more crew members had been drowned or lost on a voyage.

Nightingale fished the productive grounds off the southern Avalon Peninsula. Captain Thomas Shave was in command of the 52-net-ton banker owned by Charles F. Bishop of Burin, built in LaHave, Nova Scotia, in 1892. *Nightingale,* a six-dory vessel, had 14 men aboard. The crew, all of Burin, had procured 900 quintals.

As well, Captain Shave carried a mascot which the *Evening Telegram* of July 18, 1903, identifies as "a dog"; however, Bruce Hynes's book *The Noble Newfoundland Dog* says it was a Newfoundland. The four-legged friend certainly had the characteristics of a loyal lifesaver, as was brought out when the captain had the sad duty to relate the events when two of his crew fell into the sea.

In the early morning of July 3, the *Nightingale* was nine miles off Cape Pine. Captain Shave asked two of his crew, Thomas Deer and John Isaacs, to take the riding sail off the stern davits. As the two were doing this, the plank or step to the davit gave out just as the vessel gave a lurch in the seas.

Both men fell head first over the stern taffrail and into the sea. Both men sank quickly and, although it was July, the sea was still cold. Some other crew working on deck saw the two go over the rail and they put out a dory as soon as they were able. Others on deck threw an oar, a fish tub, and other wooden objects near the men in hope that something to keep them afloat would drift near them.

The ship's dog also saw what happened to Isaacs and Deer. He jumped over the side and swam to Isaacs, who grabbed the dog's shoulder and fur. The dog seemed to understand the situation and kept Isaacs up until the men in the dory came along and pulled the drowning man in over the side.

Thomas Deer seemed to be paralyzed by the sudden immersion and lower temperature of the ocean. He seemingly made no effort to reach an oar that was within his grasp. Even the faithful dog swam near him, but Deer didn't seem to see or comprehend this. He fell back and sank within sight of his shipmates. Both the

Newfoundland and John Isaacs reached the deck of the *Nightingale* none the worse for the cold dip in the ocean.

Sadly, Captain Shave abandoned his voyage and changed his course for Burin. As he entered the harbour, the flag of distress flew at half-mast. The heroism and courageous action of the mascot Newfoundland dog was underplayed in the trauma and retelling of the event. The captain had the sad duty to inform the family and town that Mr. Deer, aged 28, married and with one child, was lost at sea.

LIFELINE

DESPITE THE GREAT number of wrecks and shipping disasters around Newfoundland and Labrador's shores, coupled with the fact that folks in many island villages kept a Newfoundland dog, there are few tales of the faithful swimmers going out to wrecks to help distressed mariners.

According to some media accounts, a dog swam out to the wreck of the SS *Ethie* aground at Martin's Point, Bonne Bay, on December 11, 1919. Those reports said the heroism of the animal helped save lives. For years it was debated if a four-legged friend carried a rope to the *Ethie.* Time and research determined that there was a mixed-breed on shore, but it was a small dog owned by Rueben Decker, who discovered the wreck. It was not a Newfoundland and it didn't swim out to the wrecked steamer, despite the newspaper headlines around the world.

From the beach, Rueben Decker's dog "Wisher" watched the rescue of the *Ethie* unfold. However, on the coast of Kent, England, some years previous to the above incident, a Newfoundland did carried a rope through stormy seas to shipwrecked sailors. How he did it demonstrated again the intelligence, courage, and strength of the breed.

A heavy gale had blown up and watchers on the shore saw a storm-driven wooden vessel staggering toward the coast. In time it struck the bottom about 100 feet from the shore and began to fall to pieces as the white surf rolled over the vessel (unfortunately not named). Eight men could be seen clinging to the wreck. It was obvious to the watchers the ship's small boat, if still intact, could not be gotten out over the side. And the landsmen knew no ordinary boat could be launched from the shore through the breakers to go to their aid.

At that time no life-saving crews and boats were in place on the stormy coasts of England (as was the case in later years). There was only one way the men could get off the wreck—if a line could be stretched from the shore to the stranded vessel. However, there was no way a line could be floated against the high wind, surf, and current pounding the shoreline.

Why the men on the vessel could not get a line ashore is not clear, but it may have been due to currents foiling any attempt parallel to the shore. Maybe a line became caught in the rocks or debris. Perhaps the exhausted men had all they could do to cling to the wreck, much less find and attach a float.

It was feared that the unfortunate mariners would perish at any moment. Then a man came down to the beach accompanied by a Newfoundland dog. He realized that (as perhaps others did as well) if a line could reach the ship from the shore, the sailors might be saved. The man saw how it could be done.

Putting a short stick in the mouth of the dog, he pointed to the vessel. The courageous Newfoundland seemed to understand at once and, springing into the sea, fought his way through the waves. However, the tide, wind, and surf were too heavy. He could only reach to within a few feet of the vessel's side.

But he was seen by the crew. They tied a piece of wood from the vessel to a line and threw it toward the swimmer. The wise Newfoundland understood the object and seemed to know it was attached to a line on the ship and it must be brought to shore. He seized the wood and dragged it toward the beach and through the surf, delivering it to his master.

A heavier line was attached to the one the dog brought ashore. By this means a "breeches buoy" was set up and every person on board was saved from a watery grave.

LAKE MICHIGAN AND THE *STAMPEDE*

ON SATURDAY, DECEMBER 10, 1887, a sudden and furious gale swept down Lake Michigan. One of the vessels out in the storm was the schooner *Stampede*, belonging to Sheboygan, Wisconsin. While the vessel was off South Point, Milwaukee, the winds tore the sails out of bolt ropes and broke both masts off. Aboard were the captain, six sailors, and a large Newfoundland dog.

The captain rigged a storm sail on the stump of the mast and managed to keep the head of the vessel before the wind. The *Stampede* narrowly escaped striking the shore, sheered clear just in time, and went off down Lake Michigan.

Temperatures had dropped to intense cold, causing the spray from every wave that broke over the schooner to form into layers of ice. Rigging, the pieces of the mast, superstructure, and decks were covered in ice.

It was necessary for the captain to keep his men at the pumps constantly, for the vessel had strained in the storm and was taking in water almost as fast as it could be pumped out. They remained at the pumps all day Sunday and all night, as the schooner was in imminent danger of foundering in the high seas.

At 3:00 a.m. Monday they drifted past Chicago and put up signals or flares of distress. These were seen and a tug came out from the city to help, but by the time it reached the general area, the tug could not find *Stampede* in the snow and darkness and returned to port.

By 8:00 a.m. the captain, in an attempt to save himself and the crew from certain drowning, had managed to run *Stampede* aground at a remote and desolate place a little distance below South Chicago. High waves began to pound the schooner and it was breaking up in the surf.

Of the seven men aboard, only the cook and captain were in relatively good shape. The others, through the stretch of hard work and exposure at the pumps, were almost immobile with the cold. Their hands and feet were badly frozen.

There was no way to reach shore. Presumably the ship's boat had washed away or was damaged by waves. The captain saw no solution except through the Newfoundland dog (unnamed). The dog alone could reach shore with a rope, but what then? The rope would need to be attached to the shore somehow.

The only solution was to send into the sea the two bodies in better condition—two who might reach shore—the dog and the cook. The latter was stronger and suffered less than the remaining men.

The captain tied a rope around the cook, who had volunteered to reach land—either he must attempt or all would perish on the disintegrating schooner. The dog and cook were lashed together.

When the cook entered the water, at once the cold almost paralyzed him. However, the dog, oblivious to the severe conditions, struck out for land, partly towing the cook. The loyal Newfoundland reached the shore. His weakened companion fell on the beach, unable to help himself, and perhaps would have soon perished from hypothermia.

However, the dog began barking loudly and furiously for help. Soon enough, it came through a farmer going by that area in a wagon. On the beach he found the prostrate and nearly unconscious man.

He carried the sailor to a farmhouse and summoned help for those on the stranded vessel. The Newfoundland had, of course, brought ashore a rope. To this a crowd of rescuers attached a heavier line, a hawser, and within hours a bosun's chair was attached to the hawser.

The captain, still attempting to keep warm and to survive, lashed one of the frozen sailors to the bosun's chair and the people on shore began to pull him in. Halfway from the vessel he stuck fast, perhaps on some outcrop of rock, or the rope jammed. He could neither be pulled back to the ship nor to the shore.

Every time *Stampede* rolled in the surf and there was some slack on the line, the suffering sailor would be half submerged in the waves. When the vessel rolled the other way he was jerked in the air. For nearly an hour he hung there in great agony. The people on the shore were utterly powerless to help.

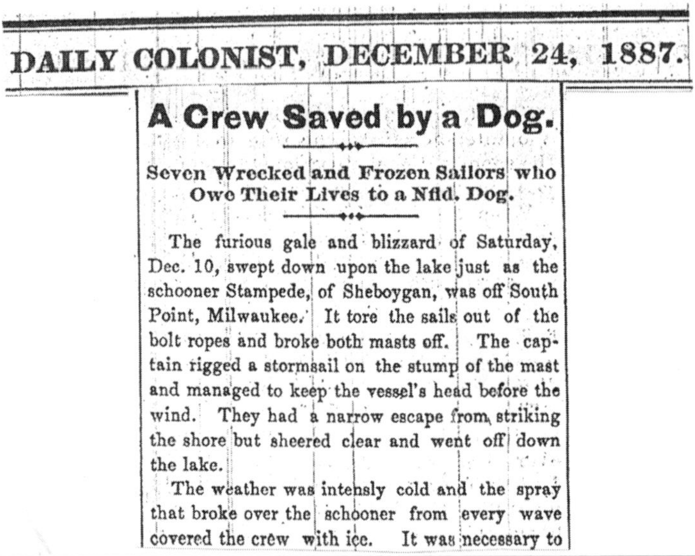

DAILY COLONIST, DECEMBER 24, 1887.

A Crew Saved by a Dog.

Seven Wrecked and Frozen Sailors who Owe Their Lives to a Nfld. Dog.

The furious gale and blizzard of Saturday, Dec. 10, swept down upon the lake just as the schooner Stampede, of Sheboygan, was off South Point, Milwaukee. It tore the sails out of the bolt ropes and broke both masts off. The captain rigged a stormsail on the stump of the mast and managed to keep the vessel's head before the wind. They had a narrow escape from striking the shore but sheered clear and went off down the lake.

The weather was intensly cold and the spray that broke over the schooner from every wave covered the crew with ice. It was necessary to

The *Daily Colonist*, December 24, 1887, says: "Seven Wrecked and Frozen Sailors who Owe Their Lives to a Nfld. Dog."

To add to the life-threatening drama, the remaining five people on the schooner were in danger of being cast into the water at any time as *Stampede* was breaking apart. Seemingly the heroic effort of the Newfoundland dog would be in vain.

In the intervening time, a life-saving crew, people trained in water rescue, arrived on the scene. They rescued the sailor stranded on the hawser and eventually got a rescue boat out to take off the remaining crew.

All were taken to a hospital, where most had frozen hands or feet amputated. As for the gallant dog who not only dragged a rope ashore but also the near-dead cook, there was no mention of reward. Beyond headlines in the *Daily Colonist* (December 24, 1887), his efforts went unheralded.

THE NEWFOUNDLAND AND SABLE ISLAND

ACCORDING TO GOVERNMENT records and sources—official and otherwise—scores of ships and many lives have been lost on Sable Island. The 18-mile-long sandbar lies in the oft-traversed routes between Europe and Nova Scotia. Its low, crescent-shaped land mass and treacherous shoals are often hidden by fog, waves, and storm.

Such were the great number of wrecks and deaths, Nova Scotia established a life-saving station on the sand-spit in 1801 and these men of the station, complete with a doctor, became the first permanent inhabitants of the island. Two lighthouses, one on the eastern tip and one on the western tip, were built in 1872. Up to the time of the lights, the island used "watchmen" to search for wrecks or lights from vessels in danger near the island.

On February 12, 1872, the vessel *Lilly Parker*, out of Swansea, Wales, was wrecked on the island, resulting in the death of all aboard, except one. And the life of that one survivor, a woman, was the direct result of the ship's Newfoundland dog.

On that stormy night, watchmen on duty at the "Left Bar" of Sable Island heard the whining of a dog near their station. Where had the dog come from? A wreck, maybe? At once they went outside, saw the dog, and determined it was real enough and friendly. The men attached a lantern around the neck of the dog and followed it to the beach.

The dog led them to the edge of the water and there lay a woman and a child—presumably her child, as it was clasped in her arms—and both were alive, but barely. Cold salt water and February's freezing temperatures had done its death-dealing duty.

The little girl, about two years old, and the woman were carried to the Sailor's Hospital and the doctor on the island, about a half-mile away. The woman lay insensible for about two days. The child died from exposure the following morning, February 13. The doctor's report at this point only stated that "Her appearance was refined and beautiful."

When the mother regained consciousness she asked where she was. She was told by Dr. Aylward she had been saved from some wreck (the island watchmen and officials had not yet determined the name of the ship) and was in the hands of those who could take care of her.

She earnestly thanked those around her, but immediately after, as her memory returned, asked, "Where is Robert? Where is my Robert, Captain Fletcher?" No one could tell her. The doctor-surgeon could only say that as nothing had yet been learned of a wreck, Captain Fletcher might be safe.

The woman wept bitterly for some moments and again, turning suddenly to the doctor, asked for a child. Dr. Aylward decided not to inform the woman of the death of the child at that time. The following night, the woman had recovered more so that he was able to inform her that her child had died of exposure, how she had been found, and the harrowing news that her husband, Captain Fletcher, had not been heard of.

In time she recovered sufficiently that her story could be pieced together. On January 3, 1872, the bark *Lilly Parker* left England, bound for Halifax, Nova Scotia, with merchandise and salt. It had several crew aboard and the ship's mascot dog, a great Newfoundland. Five days into the journey the foretop mast and foretop gallant mast were carried away in a severe winter gale that lasted over two days.

Captain Fletcher put up jury, or temporary, masts and *Lilly Parker* continued westward. Again it ran into heavy weather during which a large amount of sails were ripped apart. After 30 days at sea, the vessel sailed into a hurricane that destroyed the vessel's foremast and mizzenmast. Seas tore a breach or gap in the bulwarks and forced the bark onto its beam ends, or pushed down until its masts were nearly parallel to the sea.

Thus disabled, the bark continued on until, by the

captain's reckoning on the morning of February 12, *Lilly Parker* had drifted 500 miles off course and into the latitude of Sable Island.

Late that day a strong northeast wind came on. The sea rose to what the woman described as "a fearful height." When the wind increased the ship lost its rudder. Thus the captain and sailors were unable to keep the vessel off any land—that land they determined was the desolate and dangerous shoals of Sable Island.

The ship, tossed like a sodden log, drifted on a lee shore, striking heavily on an underwater ledge that stretched beyond the northernmost point of Sable Island. With bows stove in, or crushed, *Lilly Parker* disintegrated rapidly. With such a storm raging, it was useless to suggest any plan of escape or of self-rescue.

Beyond this description, that is, beyond the point when the ship fell apart on Sable Island, Mrs. Fletcher was unable to give details. Her confused memory was a blank. She could only say definitely that the bark suddenly broke in two parts. Those on board were either thrown into the sea or had some brief time to grab some portion of the wreck. All was confusion and trauma.

Some crew screamed for ropes to be thrown to them, some for boats to be launched. The captain, her husband, called, "Bella, Bella!" But after this, Mrs. Fletcher remembered little, except some semi-conscious feeling of being dragged ashore by someone, or something.

She had held her baby firmly clasped to her during the awful ordeal. There were no other survivors and it had been her faithful Newfoundland dog that had saved the woman and her child, dragging both ashore through the raging surf. Furthermore, there was no doubt both would have died of hypothermia, but the dog found help in time to save one.

The stately animal, worn out by the rescue, had only been able to whine piteously, first by the woman's side; then it had sensed that other humans—the life station men, as it turned out—were near. It was the lamentation of the Newfoundland these men had heard.

Mrs. Fletcher later stated her husband was Captain Robert Fletcher of Liverpool and both had resided at Hope Street, Mount Pleasant, in that city. *Lilly Parker* was owned by Hick, Brook and Harley of Swansea, but she could only name three other crew: mate William Carter, a married man who lived in Liverpool with five children; and the second mate, Charles Carter, brother of the mate, also married. "Jip" Judson was the cook and he was a native of Demerara.

At first the sole survivor was offered a passage on board the ship *Fils d'Orson,* which had stopped briefly at Sable Island for water. Doctor Aylward deemed it safer she wait until the usual monthly boat from Halifax visited Sable Island.

At this point there was no further word of the heroic Newfoundland dog, but no doubt he was feted and fondly remembered by Mrs. Fletcher of the bark *Lilly Parker.* However, when the *New York Times* picked up the story on February 29, 1872, its banner, fifth entry down, read: "She and Her Child Rescued by the Newfoundland Dog."

PRICE FOUR CENTS.

PERILS OF THE SEA.

Story of the Wreck of the Bark "Lilly Parker."

Drifting on a Lee Shore Without Masts or Rudder.

The Captain's Wife and a Dog the Only Survivors.

She and Her Child Rescued by the Newfoundland Dog.

Death of the Little Girl from Cold and Exposure.

The *New York Times*, February 29, 1872, headlines the wreck of *Lilly Parker*.

WISE, FAITHFUL, AND FATAL

IN ITS TIME and around St. John's, Newfoundland, the story became one of the best ever heard of the faithfulness and determination of a dog. Mr. Thomas J. Shortall, an eyewitness, told the story to the *Daily Colonist* and on October 1, 1888, it appeared in print. According to Shortall, during that summer he was on the banks fishing in the schooner *Mary Ellen*.

A small schooner of 24 tons and carrying three dories, *Mary Ellen* was owned by Alan Goodridge and Sons, who ran a business on the Southern Shore with a branch in St. Mary's. In fact, said Shortall, Captain Tremblett left Salmonier in St. Mary's Bay on June 16, 1888, bound for the banks. In addition to the crew of seven men, the vessel had aboard a mascot dog, identified in another source as a Newfoundland. "Hero" was his name and, as events unfolded, he lived up to the definition of his name, one of distinguished courage or ability, admired for brave deeds and noble qualities.

About 7:30 p.m. *Mary Ellen* was bound out for the banks and was about 35 miles southeast of Cape Pine. The wind was west-northwest, blowing a strong breeze with a heavy, choppy sea.

The wind was pretty much on the port quarter, says Shortall, and the schooner was running at about eight knots. Captain Tremblett had James Murphy and another man run the log line to determine the ship's speed. The captain himself stood in a companionway looking at the "glass" or barometer.

Suddenly, *Mary Ellen* gave a lurch and James Murphy, holding the log reel, was thrown into the sea. Shortall and others on deck shouted to him to hold on to the reel and line, but in the high seas it was pulled from his hand.

Murphy was not able to swim a stroke and would have sunk within a moment or two. The captain gave orders to throw the dory over the side, and one was gotten out as soon as possible. But before the bottom of the dory touched the water—before a man could get into it—a dark form rushed up the cabin steps and plunged over the taffrail at the stern.

It was Hero, the schooner's dog. He had been asleep, but was roused by the bustle and shouts. He went over the stern in the direction of the floundering man, but by now *Mary Ellen* had gone some distance ahead.

Yet Hero saw him right from the outset and made

straight for him. Murphy was sinking when the dog reached him, and in 20 seconds would have gone down. Hero grabbed him by the cheek first, but afterward let go of this grip and caught him by the hand.

The faithful dog then endeavoured to swim back to the schooner. By the way in which the dog held Murphy's hand, the man was slowly being drowned, for as he was pulled along his head went under water.

Using the little strength left to him, Murphy tore his hand from the dog's mouth and, in panic, partially put his arm and upper body on the dog's back. This gave Murphy a little reprieve, but the dog was now partly under water. Yet it swam on.

The men in the dory pulled with all their might. The dog struggled and pulled, but his efforts and strength were growing weaker. Hero made no attempt to shake or throw the man off, although he must have known instinctively his own life was in danger.

Just a few seconds before the dory reached both, the dog sank and Murphy was going down too, but he was caught by the men in the dory. Pulled on board, he was unconscious when the men lifted him on the schooner.

Some time after his crewmates rolled and pumped him, James Murphy came to. The vessel, which in the meantime had hove to—went nearly stationary head into the wind—proceeded on to the fishing banks. Murphy recovered in short time and, with the exception of cuts and teeth marks to the hand and face, was fit to work.

Hero, the Newfoundland, was gone. All the crew

agreed but for the dog's strength, intelligence, and determination, *Mary Ellen* would have had to return to port with a black flag at half-mast, indicating death on board.

Shortall finished up his tale, saying that while they were sorry for poor Hero, they were very thankful to God for sparing the life of James Murphy. Murphy was 19 and the sole support of a needy family.

The account of the *Daily Colonist* ends, stating that, "At the finish of the story and at the remembrance of the heroic conduct of the faithful brute, tears filled Shortall's eyes."

6

SURVIVAL

[The Newfoundland dog] can stand any amount of hardship which would speedily kill any other living creature. He can dig a hole for himself in the snow and snooze peacefully in a temperature of twenty-five below zero.

EVENING HERALD
JANUARY 20, 1898

HOW "BERG" GOT HIS NAME

MANY RESIDENTS OF Newfoundland and Labrador communities, more especially those along the northern coasts, kept a dog. The most common breeds were those that could easily be trained to fetch birds shot from rocky points, or those that could pull a small cart or a wood slide or help haul a seal carcass killed on the ice floes.

Unlike the environmental conditions today, two or three generations ago an icefield often extended off Newfoundland's northern coasts from November right up to early May. As well, a seal or two on the floes could be killed by landsmen, helping augment a shortened food supply in early and late spring. One common beast of burden in that era was the Newfoundland dog, which could effortlessly pull a seal carcass several miles over the rough ice to land.

Quite often these dogs had no name, and if the animal did it certainly could not utter it, in case a stranger wanted to know. (The author recalls teaching and boarding in Card's Harbour in 1966, where the man of the house had a working dog which he merely called Phss! "Here, Phss," he'd say. I asked him if that was the dog's name, to which he replied, "No, just a sound, a word to get his attention.")

It may have been one of those of the gentle race from the Fogo district that became separated from seal hunters just a few weeks before the ad, below, appeared in *The Fishermen's Advocate*. At any rate, in early May, 1933, the Western Union Cable Ship *Cyrus Field* (named after the financier who masterminded the first transatlantic telegraph cable in 1854) was off northern Newfoundland. It butted its way through pans of ice as it repaired the sub-Atlantic cable lines under the ocean—those which carried code between Europe and America.

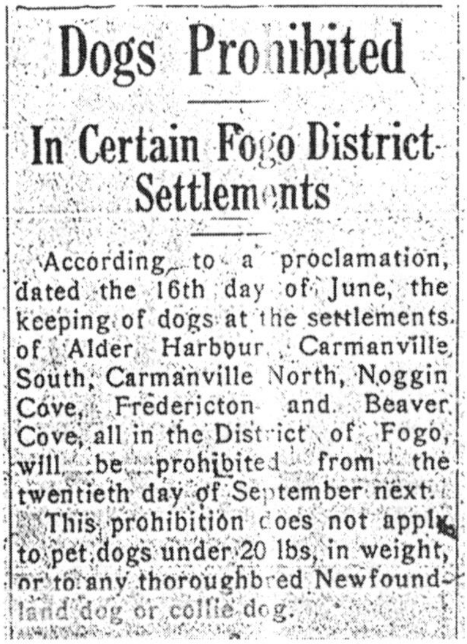

Dogs Prohibited

In Certain Fogo District Settlements

According to a proclamation, dated the 16th day of June, the keeping of dogs at the settlements of Alder Harbour, Carmanville South, Carmanville North, Noggin Cove, Fredericton and Beaver Cove, all in the District of Fogo, will be prohibited from the twentieth day of September next.

This prohibition does not apply to pet dogs under 20 lbs, in weight, or to any thoroughbred Newfoundland dog or collie dog.

A notice in the *Fisherman's Advocate* of June 30, 1933, demonstrates the value of the Newfoundland dog. As of September 20, 1933, all dogs in the Newfoundland towns of Alder Harbour, Carmanville, Noggin Cove, Fredericton, and Beaver Cove (Fogo district) were prohibited—except pet dogs under 20 pounds, collies, and Newfoundland dogs. Other large breeds and mongrels were sheep molesters and killers.

It was the heaviest ice *Cyrus Field* had encountered in 28 years of repairing cable. Captain Richard Beadon posted ship's lookouts in the crow's nest and at other stations. As it steamed along looking for clear water, the crew could see an occasional seal.

"Seal on the ice 200 yards from the edge," called Quartermaster Young.

"Strange seal," replied Flack, Officer of the Watch. "I'll have a look with the telescope." Then he added, "It's not a seal, Captain Beadon. It's a dog."

"Can't be. This far out?"the captain said. "You must be mistaken."

"Sir. I'm sure it is a dog and we have to rescue it. It's moving and alive."

As a true humanitarian, and fond of animals, Captain Beadon didn't hesitate. Upon closer approach the crew and officers lined the rails and the small black speck came closer. Frightened by the sound and appearance of the ship, the dog, now seen to be a black Newfoundland, ran away across the ice.

The dog attempted to jump to another small berg and fell into the water. As the ship turned, the ice packed closer together and the dog was able to crawl upon a small berg. Panting and exhausted, it lay still as the ship edged alongside.

Man's love for the most loyal and intelligent of his four-legged friends prompted each and every member of the crew to volunteer to go over the side in rescue. Bosun McCreadie was on the ice almost immediately with rope in hand. Cable Foreman Weeden climbed down over the side and caught the dog's harness with a boathook.

Gentle hands lifted it on board. The first to hold the Newfoundland was Engineer Dorn, an amateur dog breeder himself. Dr. Hutchinson, the ship's physician, administered first aid treatment. The dog was "lean-flanked" and almost all in, to the point of death, but a few days of warmth, food, and pampering restored the dog to excellent health.

The Western Union Cable Ship *Cyrus Field*.

Every man vied for ownership, especially Young, who saw him first; Flack, who positively said it was a dog; McCreadie, the first over the side; Weedon, who attached the lifting device; and Doran, who was the first to hold him. Finally, to settle it all, the whole ship's company adopted the Newfoundland. Right away he was named "Berg" and the crew agreed there was a special meaning to the name, as he had been found on a small iceberg.

When *Cyrus Field* docked in Halifax on May 28, Berg was at the rail. With his death-defying experience on the ice floes somewhere between Cape Bonavista and the Horse Islands now a drifting memory, Berg was at the rail barking happily.

According to the Halifax media, "the dog is believed to have been one of a number lost by seal hunters off the Newfoundland coast several weeks ago." Other information gathered later, perhaps by *Cyrus Field*'s wireless operators, said that the Newfoundland was one of five dogs cut away by seal hunters from a sledge when the ice rifted open off Horse Island, 140 miles west of where Berg was found.

His companion dogs must have perished. Berg managed to survive. Most likely he killed and ate young seals while on the ice as the ice pack was blown miles out to sea and eastward.

Nevertheless, Berg turned out to be very appreciative and a friendly soul. Needless to say, he was the pet of every member of *Cyrus Field*.

WASHED OVERBOARD

NEWFOUNDLAND DOGS WERE often carried as mascots on ships, especially fishing schooners of the east coast. In heavy weather, with waves breaking across the deck, a wise and caring captain would keep his friend below deck, or perhaps lashed on, as he would demand of his seamen working on deck or at the wheel. But as is so often the sad tale of the sea, scores and scores of seamen lost their lives when washed overboard in high seas.

In an unidentified and undated newspaper clipping (next page), the lead-in says "Nfld. Dog's Great Swim—Vancouver, Feb. 14" and continues: "The steamer *Fred J. Wood* arrived from the Pacific coast and reports picking up a large black Newfoundland dog one hundred miles from land. The animal was almost dead from exhaustion but recovered and now seems none the worse for its experience. It wore no collar, and was apparently lost overboard from some passing ship."

Nfld. Dog's Great Swim.

Vancouver, Feb. 14.—The steamer Fred J. Wood arrived from the Pacific coast, and reports picking up a large black Newfoundland dog one hundred miles from land. The animal was almost dead from exhaustion but recovered, and now seems none the worse for its experience. It wore no collar, and was apparently lost overboard from some passing ship.

Newfoundland Pup Brings Luck

Henry Ford Makes a Record Catch of Halibut.

Portland, Maine—The fishing schr. Henry Ford, out of Gloucester, was here to-day with a record catch of 45,000 lbs. of halibut

A faded and old clipping telling of a Newfoundland washed overboard and later to be found by a passing ship.

The tale from the Pacific coast mirrors a similar event on North America's east coast. In the tale above, the dog certainly had luck on its side. Then again, a Newfoundland picked up at sea may shed its lustre and luck on the fortunate vessel that finds it, as amply illustrated by the schooner *Henry Ford*.

The banker *Henry Ford*, out of Gloucester, put into Portland, Maine, with a record catch of 45,000 pounds of halibut. Captain Clayton Morrissey attributed the catch to a strange story of luck that had as its hero a seven-month-old Newfoundland pup.

In mid-April, 1926, Morrissey sailed *Henry Ford* into the smoother waters near Miquelon, off Newfoundland's south coast. Travelling over high seas, battling strong winds, and beating ice from the ropes and rigging for two cold weeks wearied the crew to the point of exhaustion. Morrissey sailed into calmer waters so his men could clear away the ten tons of frozen spray-ice on all the topsides.

At that point—from Morrissey down to the newest recruit on his 25-man roster—all were down in the mouth, for not only had the elements exhausted them, but fish was scarce.

And then, out from the grey distant sea and sky came a swimming dog—swimming away from the land and toward the ship. The crew paused from its ice chopping to welcome the hardy animal. Like the Newfoundland found off the Pacific coast some years before, this Newfoundland too was exhausted, but soon recovered.

As curious as it was to tell, *Henry Ford*'s luck changed overnight. The seas calmed and normal fishing could resume. For a fortnight the sailors laboured to catch and process the halibut. When Morrissey, his crew, and newly found mascot arrived in Portland, the vessel had a record catch for a single voyage to the halibut banks.

Captain Morrissey had no explanation for how the dog came to be swimming in the sea and that it had no identification. But once the Newfoundland was rescued, he said he took no chances of the dog being washed overboard. He had the dog tied on the rudder post. "I wouldn't take $500 for her right now," he told newspapermen in Portland.

HIS HAIR TURNED WHITE

MANY ARE THE tales of a person's hair suddenly turning grey or white overnight from extreme stress or fright. History records that the hair of some condemned prisoners, for example Sir Thomas More (1535) and Marie Antoinette (1793), turned white overnight before their executions.

Locally I have heard of stress and worry causing hair to turn white in a few days. As told by George Squires of Grand Bank, when the schooner *Mikado* went missing and was later posted as lost with crew in the fall of 1897, William Bond, father of the ship's youngest crewman, 18-year-old Robert Bond, spent so many hours grieving over his son's fate that his hair turned white within a few short weeks.

This is the story of a Newfoundland dog's fur, or

hair, as the print media termed it, turning white from stress as reported by the Rome, New York, *Sentinel* of July 1, 1887.

About four weeks previously, the water levels on the Mohawk River flowing through Rome were relatively high. A Mr. Barber of Lyonsdale put his black Newfoundland dog into the river at that place, perhaps for a swim, or a bath, or whatever.

The powerful current carried the dog downstream and he passed over the dam. Instead of carrying him on downstream, a water eddy carried the dog to some dry rocks just below the dam. The dog knew he could not swim to land as the current would pull him downstream or pull him under, thus taking his life.

The Newfoundland had to remain on the rocks until the water receded and the current slowed. He remained there for 21 days and nights, without food. During that time his hair turned nearly white. That this tale is true was substantiated by a prominent resident of Rome, New York.

ERNST LOST, ERNST SAVED

WHEN THE CAPTAIN AND CREW of the German bark *Ernst* were taken from their sinking craft by the SS *La Bourgoyne* in late July, 1896, they lamented that they could not take their large, handsome Newfoundland dog with them on the rescue boat. *La Bourgoyne*'s boat was so crowded with rescuers and rescued that an extra 100 pounds, the approximate weight of the dog, would sink the small craft.

Their four-legged friend had been a companion to all on *Ernst* for the whole voyage. Sadly, they said their goodbyes as they abandoned ship. However, the dog, as it turned out, was saved by another vessel and brought safely to port.

Captain Ocklemann of the German oil tanker *Mannheim* from Geestmunde bound to New York sighted the *Ernst*. Wallowing in the water at latitude 48.48 north, longitude 29.43 west, *Ernst* was still flying its distress signals. Ocklemann approached the vessel as closely as he could and sailed around it several times, blowing his steam whistle.

No signs of life could be seen until someone caught sight of a dog rushing frantically up and down the deck. Captain Ocklemann sent his mate over in *Mannheim*'s lifeboat. When the mate set foot on *Ernst*, the Newfoundland jumped up on him, licked his hands, and gave him such a welcome that the mate could hardly make his way to the cabin.

The mate found no one aboard but saw evidence the bark had been hastily abandoned. There was no salvage or tow that could save the nearly submerged vessel. It was about to sink, yet it lay directly in the path of transatlantic ships, becoming a potential menace to navigation. He decided the bark must be set afire to ensure a quick sinking.

The mate built a large fire in the after cabin and, picking up what papers and official documents of the ship he could find, called the dog and both got into the boat. The exuberant animal seemed overwhelmed with joy. It whined grateful appreciation nearly constantly.

The last anyone aboard the tanker saw of *Ernst* were the flames pouring out of two hatches. Meanwhile, the grateful Newfoundland soon settled himself in his new quarters and could be seen running around *Mannheim*'s deck, playful and contented.

Captain Ocklemann planned to keep the dog and named him "Ernst," after the ill-fated ship from which he was snatched.

ROVER'S ARCTIC CRUISE

IN 1881 THE United States Congress chartered the Newfoundland sealing steamer *Proteus* to transport the Arctic expedition of Adolphus Greeley as far as Ellesmere Island, with an agreement to return for the explorers in two years. An American army officer, Ernest Garlington, was placed in charge of the 1883 voyage. SS *Proteus* reached Smith Sound in June, 1883, where Garlington overruled Captain Richard Pike's (born in Carbonear) objections that it was too early in the season to continue northward. Shortly after weighing anchor, *Proteus* was crushed by pack ice and sank. The crew escaped in lifeboats and were eventually picked up in northern Greenland by the second American relief ship, *Yantic*.

On its voyage northward, *Proteus* carried three breeds of dog—21 Eskimo sled dogs, which were to be used to pull supplies over the ice; "Rover," owned by Captain Pike, was a crossbreed of a setter and a Newfoundland; and yet another "Rover," a purebred Newfoundland. The latter Rover was bought by Lieutenant Garlington in St. John's, Newfoundland—*Proteus*'s last port of call.

When *Yantic* docked in New York in late September, 1883, only one dog was still alive: Rover, the Newfoundland. He jumped about on *Yantic*'s deck and tugged at his tether, but wagged his tail good-naturedly all the time. He thought more of a pat on the head than a bone. The sailors said he had to be kept tied on or he would jump overboard and swim ashore.

This was Rover, the Newfoundland dog on the Greeley relief ship *Proteus* when the vessel was crushed in the ice on July 23 off Cape Sabine while trying to reach Lady Franklin Bay. *Proteus*'s crew set to work throwing clothing, provisions, and other stores out of the doomed ship upon the ice. Some cargo was lost, but enough was saved to ensure the comfort of the group. The crew launched three open boats after the sides of *Proteus* were broken in. Rover curled up in the bow of one of them, taking his chances of reaching safety with the humans.

The 21 Eskimo dogs were described as a treacherous set. However, Garlington's Rover could whip three or four of them at a time and kept them at bay in the bow of *Proteus*. When *Proteus*'s timbers cracked, the sled dogs were seized with terror, running about, howling dismally, and refusing to leave the ship. They were so wild and unruly they could not be taken into the small boats.

The sailors, knowing the vessel was soon going down, seized the sled dogs by the tail and neck and put them out on the ice. There they ran into nooks of ice and howled louder. Doctor J. S. Harrison, the surgeon of the expedition, said after that when one of these dogs fell or went down, the others pounced on it.

Captain Pike decided his Rover could not be taken into the boat, and it too was put out upon the ice. Dr. Harrison figured the vicious sled dogs would set upon Pike's Rover when the shipwrecked crew sailed away.

On July 25, the group set out to cross Smith Sound and, while traversing the rough ocean, Garlington's Rover became seasick. Harrison said he put his head over the side and paid tribute to the deep in a very human way. In Melville Bay on August 24 the crew found *Yantic*, which brought them—and the Newfoundland Rover—to St. John's.

A NIGHT IN THE WOODS

FREEMAN LAFOSSE WAS proud of his two dogs, a feeling that went hand in hand with respect and concern for their well-being. And the dogs reciprocated with loyalty, hard work, and companionship. If that were not enough, on one cold winter's night they gave back the greatest gift, saving their master's life.

Mr. LaFosse passed away a number of years ago, but he often told the story of survival in the country back of Parsons Harbour. Parsons Harbour, a resettled fishing community on the south coast of Newfoundland, is located at the mouth of Rencontre Bay. For most of its history, Parsons Harbour was known as New Harbour. It was renamed, after a prominent local family in the 1940s, to avoid confusion with numerous other New Harbours in Newfoundland.

Most of its people were fishermen who did some subsistence farming. Firewood was a valued commodity on the bleak coast and most men went into the woods to cut their fuel—Freeman as well. "Bullet" and "Boswain," or Bosun for short, were working dogs. Most of Freeman's children feel sure the dogs were Newfoundlands. They had the shape, the insulated fur or hair, and the characteristics of the breed. Bosun was the offspring of Bullet, and just as strong, intelligent, and loyal as the mother.

Freeman always kept dogs, as did many families, not only in Parsons Harbour, but in many Newfoundland communities. They hauled supplies into the country on fall hunting trips and pulled the meat out after a kill. Newfoundlands pulled firewood out of the countryside in winter and accompanied their masters in the boats in bird hunting season. Never a downed game bird would go astray once the Newfoundland saw it fall.

Freeman always maintained the dogs were not pets. Therefore, they were not allowed in the house. If dogs grew accustomed to heat, they would suffer more out in the cold, while working. Especially the paws. If kept indoors, a dog's paws would often get sore once they were put outside in the cold. However, a dog that remained outside didn't develop this problem.

The dogs were kept tied on during the spring, summer, and fall months. This was not so much to keep them from roaming (roaming dogs were a menace to sheep in some parts of Newfoundland), but to prevent the wearing down of their toenails. In winter a working dog needed traction, and long nails gave them this when pulling wood over snow and across frozen ponds. Dogs were kept under the house out of the weather. They were well-sheltered and warm in winter and were in the shade in summer.

One winter, Freeman recalled, he was cutting firewood in the area called Upper Pond, about two miles in the back country behind Parsons Harbour. Bullet and Bosun went with him and both had their own slide. When the wood was cut and trimmed, they pulled a load each. Freeman always claimed that between the two dogs, they could pull nearly a cord of wood in one trip.

Freeman always kept his weather eye peeled for signs of approaching storm, but on this day the weather turned bad quickly. It was two miles to reach home and, rather than take a chance on the open country in high winds, blinding snow, and low temperatures, Freeman chose to stay in the woods. The heavy spruce or fir would offer some protection. Maybe the wind and snow might slack off when evening came and he would trudge his weary way home.

But the storm grew worse. Losing no time, he made a rough shelter out of sticks and boughs. He then cut many soft pine boughs to lie on. Into the hole he crawled. Bullet and Bosun followed suit and lay down, one on each side of their master. That's where they spent a long night, asleep.

As it turned out, the night became bitterly cold. Freeman said after that if it wasn't for the dogs' body heat and the insulating effect of their fur, he would not have made it through the night. He was sure his life was spared because of his two dogs. In his later years, he often told the tale of Bullet and Bosun, but with a hint of sadness as he remembered two faithful friends, yet finishing with a smile and saying, "it was the most comfortable night I ever spent in the woods."

SOLE SURVIVOR

VARIOUS ARTICLES FROM the English vessel *Floating Light* drifted ashore in mid-February, 1865. Heavily laden with bales of cotton, the ship had been bound from Bombay, India, to a port in the Bristol Channel, either Swansea or Cardiff. Various articles, ship debris, and bales of cotton belonging to *Floating Light* drifted onto beaches in the channel near Milford (Haven). Some flotsam came to shore farther east at Caldey Island, Wales.

From the shipper's marks on the cotton bales, port authorities identified the cargo as being from the vessel *Floating Light*. Judging from the estimated time of arrival in port, weather conditions, and ocean currents, vessel owners determined it went down off Caldey Island. Nothing had been heard from the crew for three weeks. Thus *Floating Light* was unfortunately written in ships' rosters as "Lost with Crew," an all-too-frequent occurrence in the era of sail.

Known to be on board *Floating Light,* according to the *Royal Gazette* of March 7, 1865, was a black Newfoundland dog. Although unnamed, it had various markings, including a white breast, by which the dog was known. The *Gazette* went on to say in commentary on *Floating Light,* "a remarkable instance of canine endurance has come to hand from Milford."

On March 4-5, an account from Milford said a black curly Newfoundland dog with a white breast come on shore a few days before at Hagerstown (Hagestown), near Milford. The dog was standing on a bale of cotton. The markings on the bale indicated it belonged to the cargo of *Floating Light,* known to be lost with crew three weeks previously.

The description of the dog, plus the proof on the bale of cotton, led all concerned to say both were from the ill-fated ship. Those telling the story had no hesitation or doubt of this fact. However, the two questions posed were: Where had the dog been for three weeks? And how had it subsisted and survived?

Like the *Carolina*'s dog in a previous story, those connected with it could see the animal looked longingly in their faces as if it wanted to tell a story. If its tongue could utter words, the sole survivor of *Floating Light* would surely enlighten all. All that could be done was done to give the unrequited tale to the world under the heading "A Strange Dog Story."

7

MASCOT

[The Newfoundland dog's] powerful swimming ability plus his docility and intelligence were great assets to any ship's company, and it became customary to take at least one web-footed Newfoundland on voyages as a "ship dog."

The specific service he rendered was to swim ashore with a line, thus establishing communication with help on land. Untold numbers of lives were saved because of the swimming help of the "ship dog" and his ability to find footing on rough rocks in a heavy sea where the best of watermen might not survive. In less rough water he could also haul a small boat ashore by its painter.

THIS IS THE NEWFOUNDLAND
(MRS.) MAYNARD K. DRURY, 1979

SLEEPING WITH THE DOG

MANY OF THE old sea captains, the fish killers, those veteran skippers who brought in great quantities of salt cod to home ports, often carried a dog on board on trips to the Newfoundland Banks. It was a mascot, and if the vessel brought in good catches, then the dog became more than a mascot. It was a good-luck token. One of those skippers (like Captain Thomas Shave in a previous story) who welcomed a dog on board was Captain John Thornhill, a noted highliner—one who regularly brought in large catches. Born on Brunette Island in Fortune Bay, he resided in Grand Bank and commanded banking schooners in that port.

In 1922, when the bank fishing season ended, Captain John had broken all catch records up to that time when he landed a season's total of 6,500 quintals of fish at LaHave,

Nova Scotia, from April to September. That year he had charge of the schooner *Marion Belle Wolfe*. Thornhill was paid the captain's share of $1 per quintal of cod landed, giving him $6,500 for summer's work while the dorymen, mostly Newfoundlanders, on *Marion Belle Wolfe* cleared $600 a man. These wages, earnings, hard cash were unprecedented in a rural Newfoundland town in that era.

Fishermen who sailed with Captain John said his skill, hard work, fierce determination, and his relentless motivating of his men put him at the top. In his time, he was one of the highest and most consistent procurers of fish. Yet, John attributed some of his success to luck and to the fact he always carried a Newfoundland dog on his schooner. While agreeing a dog mascot on a fishing vessel was fine, his people (his wife, Dinah, was the author's great-aunt, his grandmother's sister) thought a Newfoundland dog would be better off on land, residing in the Thorndyke, John's Queen Anne–style home in Grand Bank.

Marion Belle Wolfe, a ten-dory banker owned in LaHave, had a late start at fishing in the spring of 1922. Usually Newfoundland's south coast schooners were at the banks by early March, but Captain John left Grand Bank on or about April 10. It may have taken extra time for him to get to LaHave with a skeleton crew to pick up *Marion Belle Wolfe* and to return to Grand Bank to get his full complement of bank fishermen.

En route to the fishing grounds, his first stop was at St. Pierre for some supplies. One popular ship broker on the French Islands was the Folquet Brothers firm. When

Thornhill transacted business there, he inquired how other bankers, especially the French fleet, were faring. Folquet told him he had heard of good fishing on the southern edge of the Grand Bank, an area not usually frequented by Newfoundland schooners.

Acting on this sound advice, Thornhill sailed *Marion Belle Wolfe* south-southeast for 240 miles to the area bank fishermen called "muddy grounds." The banking schooner reached there after dark. The crew filled the trawl tubs and prepared the banking dories. While waiting for daylight, Captain Thornhill got out a handline and attached several baited hooks to it. He dropped the line over the side of the schooner. If fish grabbed it, that would indicate whether they were plentiful.

When the baited line was pulled up, there was a large fish on every hook. Yes, there was fish there. Perhaps the Newfoundland dog (its name is now lost in time) was a good omen—that combined with Thornhill's knowledge gained from the French fishing interests.

Fish! And more fish! It is said through family tradition that the dorymen found time to sleep for only eight hours from that Monday to Saturday. They caught up on sleep on Sunday since, as was the Newfoundland custom, no fishing was done on the Sabbath Day.

After the dories came back to the schooner filled to the gunnels with cod taken from the baited trawls, there was no rest for the dory fishermen. The fish had to be dressed, or cleaned, salted, and stored away in the holds by the fishermen. Nova Scotian fishing schooners usually carried four men who were "dressers," those whose only work was to gut, clean, and salt the fish when it came aboard. Those manning the dories got some much-needed rest. But the crew of *Marion Belle Wolfe* still had work to do once the fish was caught.

When Newfoundland schooners like *Marion Belle Wolfe* were into good catches, the weary men grew delirious from the lack of rest. At the fish splitting tables set up on the deck, sleep-deprived workers unwittingly performed some strange and amusing actions.

One man knocked on the table with the end of his knife and called out "Jennie" several times. When his mate asked him about it, he explained he thought he was in Grand Bank rapping on the door of his home and calling to his wife to let him in. Another man bent over in sleep, weaving his knife back and forth in a half-split cod. He later sheepishly said he was cutting out a pattern for his daughter's dress.

Captain Thornhill's mascot Newfoundland was lying on the quarterdeck, causing one doryman to say, "If that man can lie down and have a nap, then so can I." No one could convince him otherwise as he walked over and stretched out beside the dog and fell asleep.

Thornhill's crew had salted away 1,900 quintals when *Marion Belle Wolfe* was forced to return to Newfoundland to replenish food supplies and to get fresh bait. Thornhill landed at Epworth, near Burin, and sent a telegram to Grand Bank to say he had procured 1,900 quintals. The telegraph operator in Grand Bank wired back, asking if there was some mistake in the number, and should it be "900"?

One of the most recognizable and iconic photos of a schooner: the LaHave, Nova Scotia, schooner *Marion Belle Wolfe* anchored at Burin in November, 1929. A house washed out to sea by the November 18 tidal wave, or tsunami, is affixed to the stern.

Thornhill learned that another LaHave schooner was in Grand Bank, and he sailed there to transfer 1,000 quintals to that vessel. *Marion Belle Wolfe* quickly left for the productive grounds again, making several voyages to the southern edge of the Grand Banks and bringing bumper loads each time.

Thornhill's prowess as a banking captain enabled him, with the earnings made in 1922, to buy part shares in another LaHave banking schooner, *Vera P. Thornhill*, named for his daughter. Thus John Thornhill became one of the few fishing captains on Newfoundland's south coast who was also a vessel shareholder. He always claimed his reputation came from a combination of work and chance, perhaps luck rubbed off by his fellow sailor, a Newfoundland dog.

CAPTAIN AUGOT'S MASCOT

CAPTAIN MICHAEL "MIK" Augot of Harbour Breton, Newfoundland, always carried a mascot dog with him on fishing voyages. In the 1930s he owned a large black Newfoundland named "Monge," a name probably derived from blancmange, or simply called "monge," a popular Newfoundland dessert of milk, sugar, and flour. The Newfoundland monge was well-known in Harbour Breton. One of Augot's long-time crewmen, Philip Tibbo, often asked Augot if he could take the dog with him while bird hunting up around Western Head. Monge retrieved every bird, further cementing the friendly bonds between Tibbo and Monge.

At sea, the dog usually hung around the after quarter-deck where the captain had his cabin and bunk, but at times he would go forward to the forecastle and hang around the bunk of his friend, Phil Tibbo. Monge knew and was loyal to Tibbo as well as his master, the captain. No crewman was allowed to sit or lie on that bunk while Tibbo was not around.

In his many years as a bank fishing captain, Augot had several unique experiences at sea, but one of his closest brushes with death came in July, 1937, while Monge was with him. His schooner, *Pauline E. Lohnes*, was rammed by an ocean liner while it was anchored on the fishing banks some miles south of Cape Race.

In the early evening of July 17, light fog surrounded the *Lohnes*. The sea was relatively calm and five of the vessel's ten dories were still out, tending trawl lines. Monge, the mascot Newfoundland dog, lay around the deck, sleeping, or was otherwise mildly interested in the proceedings as fish was being dressed, gutted, cleaned, salted, and stored in the hold.

Suddenly, Captain Augot, Monge, and the crew came fully alert when they heard the ominous shriek of a steam whistle. It was an approaching vessel, but as yet Augot couldn't see anything through the fog. However, he ordered that the schooner's small foghorn be kept going continuously.

A few moment's later he saw a large steamer bearing directly down on his schooner and he began firing the swivel, a small cannon used to signal or warn dorymen. Perhaps, too, the onrushing steamer would hear that sound.

Both signals were useless in alerting the charging ship,

which evidently did not see *Pauline E. Lohnes*. With not a second to lose, the men gutting or processing fish on deck jumped into a dory tied on to the side of the schooner and pushed off.

Captain Augot, his son, and Monge remained aboard, hoping the liner might miss or slightly graze their schooner. But the steamer *Jean Jadot,* whose name they soon determined, struck the forward section of *Pauline E. Lohnes*.

The impact caused the *Lohnes*'s foremast to come tumbling down, bringing with it the maintop which had broken off. The forward deck and forecastle went to splinters. If *Jean Jadot* had struck at night, when most of the schooner's 22 crew would have been asleep in the forecastle, the ramming would have meant death by drowning or being killed upon impact.

When *Jean Jadot* struck, somewhat forward of amidships, the steamer's forward momentum pushed the schooner's bow under water and turned it for a while on its side. This was when Mik Augot and his son, the only two humans left aboard, were attempting to make their escape. Monge, momentarily forgotten in the melee, rushed about on deck. He had intuitively sensed the danger and threat to lives.

In a burst of superhuman strength that comes in times of crisis, the captain and his son freed another dory. This was partly caught under the side of the sinking schooner. Somehow they got aboard, but lost one of the oars in the attempt, although the captain received a slight injury to his arm. Monge was still aboard rushing from one section of the foundering ship to another.

Within five minutes of impact, the *Lohnes* went down, bow first. Two of the dories that had been still tending fishing gear arrived in the area, no doubt attracted by the foghorn and swivel gun. As the men rowed nearer, they saw the whole spectacle, but could not reach the schooner's side in time to attempt rescue.

When the last dories pulled up alongside a few minutes later, the occupants were surprised to see a large Belgian steamer where home base, the *Pauline E. Lohnes,* should be. As officers on *Jean Jadot* saw these dories pull up, the captain shouted to them to rescue one last occupant on the sinking vessel: the dog, Monge.

Monge ran to and fro along the sides of the sinking schooner until its stern went under. Then he leaped into the cold Atlantic. With directions from those on the side of the liner, the dorymen found Monge and pulled him aboard a dory. He too was taken aboard the *Jean Jadot* with the rest of the *Lohnes*'s crew.

There were no casualties and the steamer's doctor treated Captain Augot's arm. All, including Monge, were carried to New York, *Jean Jadot*'s ultimate destination. From New York they were transported by train northward to Canada toward Halifax and eventually home.

However, before the voyage was finally over, once more the focus came upon Monge. Apparently on one of the railway lines, animals were prohibited on the trains. All 22 men had tickets, but Monge—well, he was four-legged with no ticket!

"If Monge, this Newfoundland dog, a mascot who is a perfect gentleman, loyal and intelligent, is not allowed on this train, then none of us will board," said Captain Augot. The crew agreed. Train officials relented and made an exception to the rule once they heard how the dog had just survived a shipwreck.

Monge again took his rightful place as one of the crew with Captain Mik Augot, his son, Phil Tibbo, Harry Day, Garfield Day, Sam Strickland, Ralph Mullins, and the other Harbour Breton seamen.

SAILOR, THE PROHIBITION DOG

PROHIBITION, A LEGAL ban on the manufacture and sale of alcoholic beverages, was enforced by the 18th Amendment to the United States Constitution on January 16, 1920. Sometimes called the Volstead Act after Senator Andrew Volstead, who lobbied vigorously for its enactment. Prohibition lasted until 1933. In its heyday the dry spell generated a wave of organized criminal activity in the United States, including: the bootlegger; the speakeasy, or illegal saloon; and the rum-runner, who transported the contraband liquor.

For handsome prices, the rum-runners often purchased fast, manoeuvrable fishing schooners unlikely to be suspected as rum carriers. Much of the illegal booze came from St. Pierre, an island near Newfoundland's south coast. Nova Scotian or Newfoundland schooners, often owned and manned by south coast sailors, took the products to the three-mile limit off the eastern seaboard of the United States. There at Rum Row they were met by buyers who took the goods to markets on shore.

In 1992, this author talked to Gordon Noseworthy of Fortune, who sailed on a rum-runner or two, delivering the spirits to Rum Row. As we sat in his cozy kitchen in Fortune, he recalled the "good times" on board his father's command, the tern (three-masted) schooner *Cote Nord*. He remembered the amusing incidents, memorable characters, and rum-running schooners like *Thorndyke*. He also recalled some of the principals of the trade, saying:

> Jack McCarty, born in Bay St. George, was skipper of the *Thorndyke* when all this [Prohibition] was going on. My father, George Hezekiah "Ki" Noseworthy, and McCarty were good friends. On one occasion we on *Cote Nord* were anchored next to him about a mile up off Long Beach, New York.
>
> McCarty had a big Newfoundland dog aboard—Sailor was his name—and when it came in the dog's mind, he'd jump overboard and swim over to us. Our fellows would put down lines or a makeshift rope ladder. He'd put his paws in and they'd haul him up aboard. Perhaps he'd stay for two or three hours aboard with us and then you'd see him getting up on the rail and jumping again and go back aboard the *Thorndyke*.

But "Sailor," recalled Noseworthy, was merely a mascot, not a watchdog on the lookout for pirates or hijackers, those who would board a rum-runner to take the liquor illegally. "No doubt if we had been boarded by thieves the dog, had he sensed we were coming to harm, would have tried to defend us, but as for shouting a warning, no."

A FAIR EXCHANGE

THE TERN SCHOONER *Flowerdew* left Grand Turk, West Indies, on October 5, 1927, sailing for Newfoundland with a full cargo of fishery salt. Captain James Bellman had five crew with him: Mate James Watts, Cook Onslow Drake, and three seamen, Wilson White, Arthur Slaney, and Clifford Smith. All were from or lived in Grand Bank, Newfoundland. Captain Bellman had a propensity for Newfoundlands and was more than partial to carrying one on foreign-going voyages—good luck or just good company, no one knows now.

The crew was several days out when they discovered the tern was leaking more freely than usual. Watch was extended on the pumps until, finally, on October 11, all hands were forced to pump continuously.

In the afternoon of that day, despite the manpower at

the pumps, Bellman sensed *Flowerdew* gradually settling lower in the water. Realizing the potential danger, the captain altered course, hoping to make the coast of the United States and save his vessel.

For three days and three nights, without let-up, the labouring crew manned the pumps. As the leaks grew worse and worse, the ability of the men to stop them lessened. Two of the crew fell exhausted to the deck. Finally, the pumps ceased to function. Clogged with the salty brine that sifted into *Flowerdew*'s bilges, there was no way to repair them.

In a last desperate effort, the crew cut the hatches away and dug frantically into the cargo, heaving salt overboard as fast as buckets could be filled. But *Flowerdew* took on water so rapidly that the top of the cargo was covered with the sea that came seeping in. The schooner's rails were dangerously close to the surface of the water as the men continued to jettison salt.

Up to that time, Captain Bellman had sent out no distress signal, but he was prepared to launch the schooner's lifeboat at the first sign of foundering. On the third evening after the pumps gave out, *Flowerdew* was almost submerged. Bellman was certain it was only a matter of hours before the schooner slipped below the cold Atlantic.

When the first smudge of smoke appeared on the horizon, the crew was ready to shout for joy. To see a possible rescue vessel in the distance, at the time they needed it most, seemed incredible. For the first time, Bellman had the distress signal hoisted to the masthead. While the steamer was approaching, the crew, splashing about in water that now submerged the deck, continued to bail water and salt out of the hold. The Newfoundland dog, still playful, could do nothing to help with the bailing, but certainly sensed the crew's anxiety.

The ship proved to be the Italian liner *Benta II,* which steamed up to *Flowerdew.* After he flashed a hasty signal indicating he was abandoning ship, Captain Bellman packed up the vessel's navigational instruments and ship's papers. Each man bagged some extra clothing. Then, at 8:00 a.m. on October 14, the crew lowered a small lifeboat, put the Newfoundland aboard, climbed in themselves, and pushed off from *Flowerdew.*

At latitude 31.56 north and longitude 73.27 west, about 200 miles off Savannah, Georgia, *Flowerdew* gave its final nod and went to the bottom. *Benta II* was bound to distant British Columbia via the Panama Canal. Since this destination was so far from the shipwrecked mariners' homes, the captain of the liner decided to transfer the men to some vessel bound for the United States. Communication was established with SS *Santa Veronica* headed for Portland, Maine.

That night, the men clambered down the side of the Italian steamer and into a boat from *Santa Veronica.* Rescuers and rescued said their goodbyes. Yet, one other sad scene of parting goodbyes occurred.

Captain Nicolo Gaidrossich, master of *Benta II,* had taken a liking to the playful Newfoundland puppy of Captain Bellman. It was the only payment Bellman could offer, so he presented the dog to the Italian before he left for *Santa Veronica*. With no other means of thanking Gaidrossich, that seemed a small token of gratitude for saving the lives of himself and his five crew.

WAR HEROES

"PAL" WAS AS playful and loyal as any Newfoundland dog. He lived in the town of Gander, Newfoundland, with the family of Rod Hayden. One day he accidentally scratched the face of a child of the family and, reacting as most would, the parents became upset with the incident. Not wanting to have the dog "put down" or put to death, they offered the large dog to the Royal Rifles, at that time stationed near Gander International Airport just at the outbreak of World War II.

The Royal Rifles, a regiment of the Canadian Army, accepted the Newfoundland as a mascot for their group, renaming him "Gander" and promoting him to sergeant. In the fall of 1941, when the regiment was assigned to Hong Kong Island, Gander went with them.

The Battle of Hong Kong, the defence of this island against the attacks of the Japanese, began on December 8,

1941, a day after the attack on the US naval base at Pearl Harbor. Gander was a real and courageous soldier, seemingly knowledgeable of his duties to protect the soldiers who had taken him in.

He helped fight Japanese invaders three times. On two occasions Gander's stand or attack slowed or stopped enemy soldiers from advancing, thus protecting groups of injured and fallen soldiers. On a third and fatal incident, Gander picked up a Japanese hand grenade thrown by the enemy and rushed with it in his mouth toward the enemy line. In the ensuing explosion Gander died, but the quick removal of the explosive saved the lives of several wounded Canadian soldiers.

In time the war ended, and surviving soldiers returned home to Canada, but Gander's heroism was not forgotten. Yet it took many years for his story to reach public awareness. It came through the awarding of the Dickin Medal, created in 1943 by Maria Dickin. Maria founded the People's Dispensary for Sick Animals, a veterinary charity established in the United Kingdom.

By 1949, many Dickin Medals, likened to an animal's Victoria Cross, had already been given to dogs, horses, pigeons, and a cat for war bravery. Through the efforts of the Canadian War Museum, Gander was nominated and he was given a posthumous medal on October 27, 2000—the first in nearly 50 years.

The citation reads:

For saving the lives of Canadian infantrymen during the

Battle of Lye Mun on Hong Kong Island in December 1941. On three documented occasions, Gander, the Newfoundland mascot of the Royal Rifles of Canada, engaged the enemy as his regiment joined the Winnipeg Grenadiers, members of Battalion Headquarters "C" Force and other Commonwealth troops in their courageous defense of the island. Twice Gander's attacks halted the enemy's advance and protected groups of wounded soldiers. In a final act of bravery, the war dog was killed in action gathering a grenade. Without Gander's intervention, many more lives would have been lost in the assault.

As a final honour, Gander's name and his medal, at the insistence of survivors of the Battle of Hong Kong, is displayed with the names of those 1975 men and two women on the Hong Kong Veterans Memorial Wall in Ottawa, Canada.

In 2000 a Newfoundland dog, a mascot of a Canadian military unit, was awarded the Dickin Medal (left) for bravery in World War II.

One of the most well-known Newfoundland dog mascots was Sable Chief, who became famous during World War I for his immense size and dignified demeanour. He was often seen marching alongside the troops, keeping in step throughout, and, it was said, the Newfoundland would come to attention during the playing of his country's national anthem (the "Ode to Newfoundland"). He was regarded among the troops as a general morale booster, frequently visiting wounded soldiers. (Photo courtesy of The Rooms, NA 1535.)

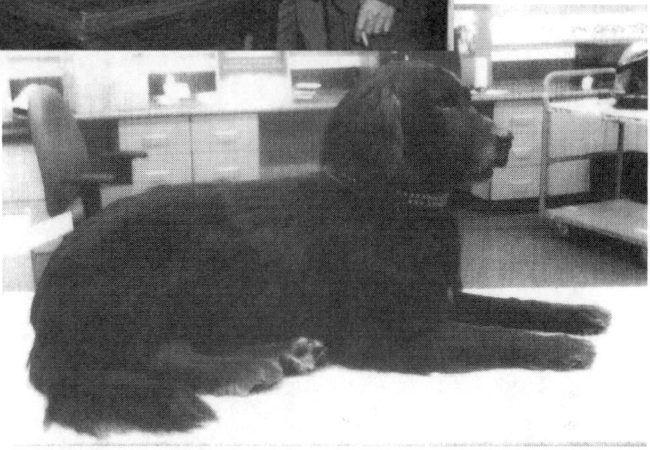

TOP: A group of veterans of World War I admire Sable Chief, Newfoundland dog mascot of the Royal Newfoundland Regiment. L-R: W. Newberry, J. J. Dooley, T. Mahoney, P. J. Miskell, E. S. Hennebury, W. L. Logan (Department of Veteran's Affairs, Ottawa), and E. Kelly.

BOTTOM: Sable Chief was presented to the Second Battalion, 1st Newfoundland Regiment (afterwards called Royal Regiment) on April 20, 1917, by Captain C. W. Firebrace of London, England. Sable Chief was killed in an accident in 1918, but was preserved by a taxidermist and placed in the High Commissioner's Office in London, where he remained until the office closed in 1949. The mascot was then sent to the Great War Veterans' Association of Newfoundland. Sable Chief is currently on display in a sealed clear case at the Newfoundland museum located at The Rooms, St. John's. (Information and photo taken from *Atlantic Guardian*, September, 1950.)

THE UNUSUAL DEMISE OF A NEWFOUNDLAND

NOT ALL TALES of mascots on Newfoundland ships have happy endings, as this next story—one of the longest in this volume—illustrates. It is a tale both heroic and sad, not only for rescuers and rescued, but for the noble Newfoundland dog caught in a situation he could not overcome.

The Newfoundland tern schooner *Harold* under Captain William Yetman was returning home to Harbour Grace just before New Year's Eve, 1904. Before it reached there, however, its story became not just a regional tale of its home port, Harbour Grace, but one shared with the great nation of Germany and a curious interaction of two towns.

Yetman had five seamen with him and a ship's mascot, a large Newfoundland dog. *Harold* had landed salt cod at Malaga, Spain, loaded salt at Cadiz for ballast, and sailed west on December 2. On the third day out, the wind swung south-southeast, very strong, and by December 5, the bad weather changed for the worse. Southeast gales turned to northwest with snow.

Crew of Schooner *Harold* December 1904,
all of Harbour Grace and vicinity
Captain William Yetman
First Mate Mark Stevens
Second Mate Alfred Sheppard
Cook Edward Pike
Seaman John Barrett
Seaman Albert Smith

Harold iced up and had to run for warmer waters to help get the ice off the vessel. Yetman was determined to get home before Christmas, so the next day his crew swung northerly again. They were doing well until December 18, when the winds came up stronger than before.

Although the sails were reefed and the vessel lay to, in order to ride out the storm, waves boarded the deck every minute. Yetman figured the winds were up to 95 mph with heavy rain and sometimes snow squalls. It was impossible to stand on deck without lifelines. A rogue wave, what seamen call an especially large one, broke over *Harold,* while the crew took shelter below.

Yetman took stock. Fortunately, no one was swept overboard, but the sight when the crew went on deck was best described as "devastation": the three masts, as well as the bowsprit, were broken off or severely damaged. Of the two anchors forward, one was gone overboard and the other had broken through the deck. The large lifeboat was missing, four casks of drinking water were smashed, and the stove and furniture in the cabin were broken.

The crew was now without water, the fire in the damaged stove was out, and they worked at getting canvas over the damaged section of the deck. By this time all hands had lifelines on, but when they saw a wave about to break over the ship, they all ran aft to take shelter in a companionway.

The pumps had to be kept going constantly. For 15 days each man rotated for a 15-minute turn pumping. The salt in the hold was melting and its brine was pumped out, but the crew could not keep up against the inflow of water. On the fifteenth day, *Harold* was nearly full of water. All the nourishment the crew had was hardtack or ship's biscuit and the rum or liquor they had brought from Spain.

During this time several steamers—two- or three-stackers—passed in the distance but did not see the labouring schooner. On December 21, the crew, knowing the *Harold* was going down, kept distress flags and signals going day and night.

That night the helmsman saw two masthead lights in the distance. Others looked out into the night but saw nothing. Then, as *Harold* rose on the crest of another tremendous wave, they all saw a large steamer heading westward and in their direction. Captain Yetman had the crew preparing distress flags and getting a small signal fire ready. When the steamer got to within a half-mile, every temporary light and emergency flare on the schooner was lit and its small foghorn blew continuously.

The steamer slowed, came close, and someone asked through the megaphone what they wanted. Yetman replied, "Take us off as the vessel is sinking."

The steamer's spokesman said they would try to help. It came around to the windward and turned on its searchlights. All this time a winter storm raged across the Atlantic, but the steamer's crew was determined and lowered a lifeboat. It immediately broke when seas drove it against the side of the steel vessel. All four smaller lifeboats were smashed in the slings or damaged when they were lowered.

The officers of the ship—which by this time *Harold*'s crew had learned was the German liner *Koeln*—said they would try the largest lifeboat, and if that failed they would wait until daylight or better weather to take the crew off.

The large lifeboat was prepared, the lifesaving crew climbed in, and when *Koeln* rolled on its side, they pushed off. For a moment it looked as if the lifeboat capsized, but its crew righted it and moved toward *Harold*. One of the German sailors aboard the lifeboat was a young seaman, Karl Herget, but that was not really significant to the Newfoundland sailors at that time.

When the lifeboat neared the schooner, Captain Yetman threw a line to the rescuers. One by one each Newfoundland seaman clambered aboard the boat, including the Newfoundland dog. It took an agonizing five hours to effect the rescue—a testament to the ferocity of the elements that night.

When they reached the side of *Koeln*, each person, rescued and rescuers, had to climb an 18-foot rope ladder. Unfortunately, the dog was left till last. No one climbing up could manage to hold the ladder and the dog could not climb up a nearly vertical rope ladder. Thus when the lifeboat filled with water, the dog perished. *Harold* was abandoned at sea and its crew was taken to Baltimore. In time they reached their homes in Newfoundland.

Forty-three years later the story of rescue and near-death at sea took a curious turn. In the following decades, Germany had been embroiled in both World Wars. By August, 1945, World War II was over, but the country was devastated, defeated, many cities lay in ruins, its people hungry.

In September, 1947, Karl Herget, perhaps believing that one good turn deserves another, sent a letter to Newfoundland. It was postmarked Frankfurt main-Sindlingen, Gustavs Allee, Germany, and addressed to the Harbour Master at Harbour Grace. In time, the letter was delivered to Mr. A. Simmons.

Herget told the reader (Simmons) he was one of the lifeboat crew who risked their lives to save the Harbour Grace seamen on the *Harold*, nearly 43 years previously. But Herget's letter was more than a reflection of rescue. It was a cry of distress, just as the Newfoundland tern schooner had appealed for help in 1904.

Things were desperate in Germany since the war had ended in August, 1945, and for Karl Herget and his family. According to the *Evening Telegram* (which printed sections of the letter), Herget says:

> . . . 43 years have passed since the time of that rescue. I suppose you know about the present circumstances in our country by newspaper. Hunger reigns and there are heavy sorrows about how to feed oneself.

Herget, perhaps then in his sixties, reminded the reader of the letter that when Captain Langreuter of the *Koeln* called for volunteers to man the lifeboat, he (Herget) didn't hesitate. Now, in 1947, Herget continued, he, his wife, and family were in great need and asked that if even one of those men from *Harold* still lived to help him and his family:

> Send some lard, bacon or oil, tea, milk powder, sugar, coffee, and soap. These are things which we know only by name since a long time. I don't beg for delicacies, clothing and so on, only for victuals to keep us alive.
>
> Send this letter to any survivor of the *Harold*. If that is not possible, deliver it to some reputable organization in New York and confirm the account of the brave deeds of a German lifeboat crew in 1904.

It is not known what success Karl Herget had with his request, but it is highly likely he was sent a care package by one or several of the crew or by some dependable organization in Harbour Grace. The abandonment of *Harold,* the untimely death of a Newfoundland dog, the bravery of German sailors, and the letter from a despairing rescuer make for a poignant tale of the sea.

8

ODDITIES

Although the origin of the Newfoundland will probably never be known for certain, it was an important symbol of early Newfoundland history, characterized by its loyalty, sagacity and life-saving qualities.

Megan Nutbeem attributes these qualities in the dog to the relationship it shared with the Beothuk: "The Indians regarded their dogs as gifts from the gods and through this mutual relationship of affection and dependence on each other grew two races—the gentle Indian and the dependable Newfoundland."

NEWFOUNDLAND ENCYCLOPEDIA, "DOGS"
MEGAN NUTBEEM, ET AL.

SOLD, FOR 20 SHILLINGS AND A NEWFOUNDLAND DOG

BY OCTOBER, 1918, NEAR THE END OF WWI, many Newfoundland sailing ships and merchant vessels had been intercepted and sunk by German cruisers and submarines. More than a score had been sunk in a period of a year. Stories of sinkings and personal accounts of how and why the enemy put the latest ship to Davy Jones's Locker were common.

In a way the litany of suffering, loss of life and ship, and the setbacks to local industry and the economy was demoralizing. No wonder the local papers took it upon themselves to offset or counterbalance tales of woe with lighthearted fillers and thought-provoking items of a curious nature.

In October, 1918, a Newfoundland paper carried this brief item under the heading "Wife Sold at Auction." With tongue in cheek, the *Bay Roberts Guardian* reminisced about Mary Ann Thompson who, in 1832, was the last wife to be sold at public auction in England. Her spouse, Joseph, after a marriage of three years, decided to avail of the old, yet never legally sanctioned, practice of human auction. He pointed out Mary Ann's good qualities and one of the bidders was successful with an offer of 20 shillings and a Newfoundland dog. Mrs. Thompson went away contented and is said to have lived happily ever after.

Offer Wadham Island.

Latitude 49. 35. 35. N.
Longitude 53. 45. 12. W.

Notice is hereby given that the revolving Light at Wadham Island giving single flashes at intervals of 30 seconds is temporarily discontinued During its stoppage an Occulting Light will be exhibited, giving alternative periods of 5 seconds light and 5 seconds dark.

Due notice will be given when the Revolving Light is re-established.

J. G STONE,
Minister of Marine & Fisheries.
Dept. of Marine and Fisheries,
St. John's, Nfld.,
July 13th, 1918. oct18,3i

Reliable Medical Books

Self and Sex Series
PURITY AND TRUTH.
Size of each volume 4¼ x 6¾ inches.
Rev. T. Albert Moore, D. D., General Secretary of the Dept. of Social Service and Evangelism of the Meth. Church of Canada, who visited Newfoundland

...without giving money's worth. Skilled labor, whether of the hands or brain, is money's worth, and does not fail to obtain it.

Wife Sold at Auction

Mary Ann Thompson was the last wife to be sold at public auction in England, the sale taking place at Carlisle in 1832. She was the spouse of a farmer, Joseph Thompson, and had been married about three years when her husband decided to sell her at auction. This old practice, although it never had legal sanction, had been followed in rural sections of England for centuries. The auction commenced at noon on the appointed day, Thompson placing his wife in a large oaken chair with a rope around her neck. He pointed out her faults and her good qualities to the assembled throng. There were few bidders, but at length she was "knocked down" to Henry Meors, who paid 20 shillings and a Newfoundland dog. Mrs. Thompson went away contentedly with her new owner and is said to have lived happily with him.

Newspaper clipping from the *Bay Roberts Guardian* of October 18, 1918, of "Wife Sold at Auction."

REVENGE IN AN OUTHOUSE

A STRANGE BUT true tale comes from the town of Fortune Harbour, situated in a large, landlocked harbour on the prominent headland of the New Bay peninsula within Notre Dame Bay, Newfoundland. By the 1930s, the town had a population between 200 to 300 people made up of English and Irish descent.

In the summer of 1935, according to an account given to Ray Johnson by Austin Davis of Fortune Harbour, a number of petty robberies occurred in the town. Unable to solve or curb the thefts, the local priest contacted the law authorities in St. John's.

Since there were more policemen serving in St. John's at this time, the Attorney General deemed it possible to send a policeman to Fortune Harbour for a short period. Perhaps he could catch the culprit, solve the crime, and, as a bonus, the whole of Notre Dame Bay would see and feel the presence of the law.

However, the policeman failed to figure out who was responsible. Furthermore, he was a bit of a bully. He liked to walk around displaying the uniform and feeling the weight of the billy, or nightstick. This unnamed man seemed to dislike children and had a strange habit of approaching them from behind and flicking the ears.

He stayed at the home of Austin Davis, whose mother kept boarders. Austin was eight at the time and had a pet and faithful, loyal companion—a large Newfoundland dog named "Champ."

On the way to or from school, the boy, his dog, and perhaps other male companions would meet this representative of the law. The policeman would flick Austin's ears or the ears of his companions. It was not only irritating, but painful. Champ knew this and it upset the dog and made him angry.

Champ would show

his displeasure at the discomfort given his master and growl and bare his teeth at the policeman. To show he was boss, the man would then give the dog a slight tap on the nose with his nightstick. The dog, unused to any harsh treatment, got such a surprise and fright he ran and hid. What could the boy say or do? After all, the policeman stayed at his house and his mother depended on the extra income.

It wasn't long before the aggressive policeman became generally reviled, not only by the children but also by the adults in Fortune Harbour. Needless to say, Champ disliked him and awaited his chance to exact some type of revenge on his tormentor.

Like most Newfoundland outports, many stages and sheds hugging the shoreline had an outhouse. Generally this outbuilding had one or more seats or holes and was built over the water. With the privy built over the water, the rising tide did the flushing. Now some of these outhouses were old, dilapidated, and were not firmly affixed to the stage or wharf on which it was built.

It seems that one day, the policeman visited an outhouse not too far from the Davis home. Champ saw this and waited for his chance. When he figured the lawman was settled away, perhaps with his pants and big braces pulled down, and mounted on the seat reading the Eaton's catalogue, the dog made his move.

Champ knew the teaser was vulnerable and he must have known the outhouse was not firmly nailed down or was shaky. He ran down the hill toward the makeshift toilet, gathering momentum as he ran. Champ hit the outhouse with his shoulder and forepaws with the full force of his 200 pounds.

The force of the blow knocked the shaky structure off its moorings and it fell, with the policeman still inside, into the landwash. The man stood up, sputtering, cursing, and yelling, with the mess of the outhouse around him.

Champ, meanwhile, ran and hid behind some stages. The lawman had no idea who or what had sent him and the remains of the privy into the drink. But some children and a few adults had observed the incident. They burst out laughing and generally could not contain their amusement and smiles whenever they met the man.

The story was passed on quickly, making a laughing-stock of the policeman (who never did find out who was responsible for the petty thefts). Shortly after, he was recalled to St. John's. According to Austin Davis there was never a policeman assigned to Fortune Harbour after that—thanks to a wise and vengeful Newfoundland named Champ.

THE APPARITION

WEBSTER CITY, IN Hamilton County, Iowa, is located at a junction of two or three major railway lines, including the Union Pacific Railroad. In early May, 1887, the engineer of a freight train in the northwestern sector of Webster City accidentally ran down and killed a large, handsome Newfoundland dog.

The engineer declared that since the accident he frequently saw the ghost of the dog as he passed the spot at night. As the train approached a mournful howl was heard, and out of nowhere a white apparition resembling the dog darted out from the roadside. The phantom seemed to disappear beneath the head locomotive.

It happened so often, other crewmen on the train watched for the ghostly appearance at night and saw the strange sight. So real and eerie was the appearance that some of the train's personnel feared the haunted engine was doomed to meet with an accident.

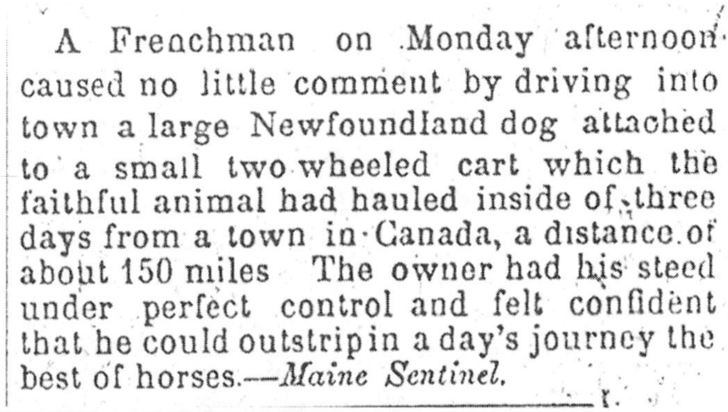

A Frenchman on Monday afternoon caused no little comment by driving into town a large Newfoundland dog attached to a small two wheeled cart which the faithful animal had hauled inside of three days from a town in Canada, a distance of about 150 miles The owner had his steed under perfect control and felt confident that he could outstrip in a day's journey the best of horses.—*Maine Sentinel.*

As Good as a Horse. The newspaper *Maine Sentinel*, based in Waterville, Maine, USA, reported in one June issue, 1887, that a Newfoundland dog arrived in town. There was much comment in the area that the dog was pulling a small, two-wheeled cart on which sat a Frenchman from New Brunswick.

The faithful animal had pulled the cart and owner for three days, covering about 150 miles. According to the paper, the owner had his steed under "perfect" control. The Frenchman said he felt confident he could outstrip in a day's journey the best of any horse.

AN UNPLEASANT POSITION

THE NEWFOUNDLAND DOG makes a much better watchdog than some others of a more aggressive breed—some of which cannot be safely let off the chain. Yet it is possible for the Newfoundland to make a mistake between a friend and an adversary. So said the *Otago Witness* (from a March, 1892, story taken from *Naturalist* magazine) of South Island, New Zealand, which went on to give an example of misplaced guard duty.

A lady paid a visit to the home of a Newfoundland's owner. There was no one home as the woman had gone out with her husband to made a social call to another's house. By some oversight they had left the door of their own house open. The visiting lady, not seeing anyone about, walked in, called out, and, hearing no answer, sat down to wait—supposing the owners would be back shortly.

The dog lying there in the kitchen or living room didn't object and made no moves or action while the visitor walked in and sat down. As soon as she got up to leave (thinking her owner friend wasn't about to make an appearance) the dog showed its teeth as if to keep her in the chair.

Later on the lady became hungry. When she attempted to help herself to some biscuits and tea or tried to look in the cupboard, the movements of the Newfoundland convinced her nothing of the kind would be permitted.

Unfortunately and unknown to her, her friends had been persuaded to remain where they had gone—not only for the afternoon, but also for supper and a game of cards after. They meant to be home at two or three o'clock in the afternoon but didn't arrive until well past midnight.

They walked into their home to find the distressed lady friend sitting upright in a chair, in the dark, half-starved and afraid to move. Meanwhile, the dog stood unforgivingly near the door, dutifully guarding his master's property. And he would have stood there and kept the lady in the chair all night had the owners of the home not returned hours later.

NEWFOUNDLAND YARN.

From the Bangor (Me.) Commercial, Dec. 1.

A man in the central part of the State has four skeins of yarn spun from the fleece of a large Newfoundland dog, every thread of which is jet black. After being carded and spun it weighed 2¼ pounds. It spun as easily and well as wool. Quite a profitable animal to have, not crediting his ability as a watchdog, which is par excellence.

The *Bangor (ME) Commercial*, December 1, 1887, explains another unique aspect of the Newfoundland. The dog's fleece, when sheared, carded, and spun, yielded a jet-black yarn that spun easily and as well as wool. This breed then doubles as a watchdog and a giver of a fabric.

JUMBO'S WRECK

USUALLY WHEN TALES of dog rescue are told, it is the human who is the victim or the injured party and often the strong, wise Newfoundland is the hero. But in the 1901 shipwreck of *Edward M. Young*, the reverse was true.

When the Panama liner *Advance* pulled into New York on December 18, 1901, it had eight extra passengers: seven men and the Newfoundland dog, "Jumbo," from the wrecked schooner *Edward M. Young*. They had been rescued from what remained afloat of the tern schooner off Cape Hatteras a few days previously.

Men and dog had been without water and nearly frozen to death when the *Advance* sighted the wreck. All were perched on top of the deckhouse as the rest of the vessel was below water. All that kept them from freezing to death in the December winds was that they were situated in the warm Gulf Stream. Spray and waves washing them almost constantly were relatively warmer.

Edward M. Young, with a cargo of lumber, sailed from Georgetown, South Carolina, on December 17. Off Lookout Point, Captain John Maddocks, his six seamen, and Jumbo ran into a southeast gale with winds so strong the schooner was driven before the gale. Within hours it was leaking so badly that only the lumber in *Edward M. Young* kept it afloat.

On Sunday morning the gale veered northwesterly and disabled the vessel even more. As sea water rose, the schooner sank lower and lower in the water. Casks of fresh water were spoiled and death from thirst was looming before the haggard crew. The men and dog climbed on top of the deckhouse, the only thing except the masts that was left above water.

The next morning the SS *Daphne* passed close, but either did not see the nearly submerged ship or mistakenly thought the crew needed no assistance. Later that Monday the *Advance* saw the wreck, steamed down, and, using the steamer's lifeboat, rescued the crew and Jumbo.

Only Jumbo had been injured. According to the *New York Times*, "The big Newfoundland dog's back left leg was broken when he was thrown into the rescuing boat from the top of *Edward M. Young*'s deckhouse." Once Jumbo arrived in New York, a city vet tended the Newfoundland's shipwreck injury.

THE OBJECT OF HIS CONCERN

USUALLY THE NOUNS "intelligence, memory, and patience" are used when listing the attributes of the Newfoundland dog. Quite often, too, the Newfoundland uses those characteristics to help others, be they human or other animal. Tales of another breed applying its own wisdom and patience while "pulling a fast one" on the Newfoundland dog are rare, but it occasionally happened.

It seems that in the late 1880s a large Newfoundland dog and a Gordon setter had outdoor living quarters next to each other. They were friends, non-combative with others as well as with themselves. Both were more or less confined to the area around their shelter, but that was fine until one day when a two-year-old collie was temporarily lodged about 50 feet away from the Newfoundland and the Gordon. The bouncy collie had the privilege of wandering about the yard without restraint.

One morning he took the liberty of poking his nose into the feeding pan of the Newfoundland. This liberty was resented and subsequently checked when the great dog gave the collie a sound thrashing.

The collie, it seemed from observation, devised a plan of revenge from that moment on. He went into his kennel and remained there the best part of the afternoon, brooding. Toward dusk he came out and, going to a corner containing a pile of bricks, seized a brick with his teeth. He carried it cautiously and quietly over to the Newfoundland's kennel and dropped the brick in front of the opening. He was undetected.

After dark, when the big dog had curled himself up inside and was deep in sleep, the little collie continued his work. He picked up no less than 60 bricks and deposited each one in front of the doorway of his enemy's house.

At that point the collie was discovered by the man of the house, who had occasion to go into the yard to get a bucket of water. He saw what was happening and stood back watching for 20 minutes.

The collie dropped as many bricks near the doorway as space would permit. He then stationed himself in front and barked with all his might. The Newfoundland responded with a deep growl and made an effort to come out, but the bricks prevented this. Meanwhile, the collie jumped about and gave vent to his happiness with shrill yelps.

THE "HEARING" NEWFOUNDLAND

"BOBO," THE NEWFOUNDLAND puppy, was acquired by the Suffolk School for the Deaf near Lake Ronkonkoma, New York, in 1947. He was trained from the start to "hear" for the 40 children under his charge. He would escort them to the classroom building in the morning and return with them to the dormitory buildings at the end of the day.

Bobo grew to be a huge, but gentle, adult loved by all. He learned to press his paw on the doorbell of the dormitory building to announce the youngsters' arrival. According to the principal, he performed his duty faithfully for eight years.

In the summer of 1955, his age and a heat wave caught up with him. Bobo was taken to a vet for a hair clipping but really didn't want to be there. At the first opportunity, when no one was looking, he scooted out the door and trotted toward his home, several miles away.

Meanwhile, three men were engaged to search for him and found him—exhausted and dehydrated—three miles away, lying in the shade under a tree. Bobo was rushed to a vet and every effort was made to revive him, but without success. The Newfoundland was taken home to Lake Ronkonkoma and buried in the Peter Pan Woods, a part of the Suffolk school tract of land.

CONDOLENCES FROM A PREMIER

"MOOSE," WHO DIED in 2007 at age 13, may have been the first and only Newfoundland dog to receive a letter of condolence from a Newfoundland and Labrador premier. Throughout the years Moose, a Corner Brook native owned by Dave and Betty Lou LeDrew, became a provincial and an international celebrity.

From the time he was a pup, Moose, accompanied by Dave, greeted tourist passengers on cruise ships docking at Corner Brook. He was a tail-wagging, larger-than-life companion who became a perfect host to let guests know they had finally arrived in Newfoundland—the source of all Newfoundland dog legends.

Moose often became the highlight of their visit, leaving a lasting impression. Quite often he would be back on the dock to bid goodbye to his foreign friends. And then there were visitors to Newfoundland's west coast who dropped by his master's store—the Newfoundland Emporium in Corner Brook. Moose was always on hand to provide a special greeting.

His celebrity status rose in the year 2000 when Moose became the official mascot of the Newfoundland Flotilla, a group of about two dozen vessels from North America's eastern seaboard sailing to the island to celebrate the "Vikings 1000 Years!" event.

Moose received copious amounts of fan mail, according to LeDrew. One letter from a couple in Texas in 2003 was addressed simply to "Moose, Newfoundland Emporium, Corner Brook." Other letters came from all over the world, stating their appreciation to Dave and admiration to Moose.

The dog had his own postcard! Dave's self-produced postcard of Moose shows six identical poses, explaining how a Newfoundland dog's face is always the same even when docile, happy, angry, sad, hungry, or full.

When Moose died in 2007, his death made the front page of the Corner Brook *Western Star*. Soon a letter of condolence written on official provincial letterhead came from the premier of Newfoundland and Labrador, Danny Williams. It read in part:

> "I was sorry to learn that your well-known and much-loved Newfoundland dog Moose has passed away . . . Here in his home element he was a true-

blue Newfoundlander with a welcoming attitude and indomitable personality . . . With Flossie to follow in Moose's footsteps, may you enjoy many more years of giving our tourists a warm welcome they will never forget. Yours sincerely, Danny Williams, Premier."

Moose had his own postcards: "Seven Seas Navigator: Welcome to Corner Brook"; "The Newfoundland and the Cruise Ship in Gros Morne"; and this one, "The Newfoundland Dog and His Many Moods." (Courtesy of Dave and Betty Lou LeDrew, Corner Brook.)

RIGEL, OF THE *TITANIC*

THERE ARE MANY who doubt this story of "Rigel," a Newfoundland who survived the sinking of *Titanic*. However, his heroic deed was published in a reputable newspaper, the *New York Herald*, which had a large readership and an existence that lasted from 1835 to 1924. Accounts of various Newfoundland dogs can be found in scores of newspapers all over North America. We have no reason to doubt those stories in other papers. Thus Rigel's tale in the *Herald* may be authentic.

When the luxury liner ship *Titanic* sank on the night of April 14-15, 1912, there were pet dogs on the ship. That would be expected and logical, as there were about 2,200 people aboard, many of whom were passengers—and many well-to-do, at that. Some sources say a dog show had been planned for the morning of Monday, April 15.

Of the ten dogs aboard, only three survived. Two

smaller dogs were saved with their owners, likely smuggled into the lifeboats. The third dog became better known—Rigel, a large Newfoundland owned by one of *Titanic*'s officers. Rigel's story was published in the *New York Herald* on April 21, six days after the great ship went down.

Jonas Briggs, a seaman aboard the rescue ship SS *Carpathia*, claimed ownership of Rigel and told the media of the dog's heroism. Only for Rigel, he said, the fourth lifeboat located, and from which many survivors were taken aboard *Carpathia*, might have been run over by the rescue steamer. For three hours Rigel swam in the cold water where *Titanic* went down, evidently looking for his master.

On that morning of April 15, *Carpathia* moved slowly about as Captain Rostron and his crew looked for boats, rafts, bodies, anything that might be afloat from *Titanic*. It moved closer to a fourth lifeboat, but those in the small craft were exhausted from rowing, weak from exposure and lack of food, and were in a state of shock and disbelief. That lifeboat drifted under *Carpathia*'s starboard bow.

Those survivors were dangerously close to the steamer but were too weak to shout loudly enough for those on *Carpathia*'s bridge to hear them. The lifeboat might not have been seen, but for the sharp barking of Rigel. He was swimming ahead of the craft and barking courageously. His bark attracted the attention of a crewman who informed Captain Rostron, and the captain went to the starboard end of the bridge to see where the noises came from. He saw the lifeboat and immediately ordered the engines stopped.

The lifeboat came alongside the starboard gangway. When all survivors in this boat were helped on *Carpathia,* care was taken to get Rigel aboard. Although tired, the Newfoundland, with the waterproof coat, webbed paws, and tremendous swimming ability, was little affected by his long immersion in the North Atlantic. He stood on the deck barking until Rostron called Briggs and had him take the dog below.

Briggs took charge of the Newfoundland, reporting his story to the New York newspaper. Detractors of this tale and those who do intense, specific research know that *Carpathia* had no crewman named Jonas Briggs. As well, they say, no other paper of the day ran the story of Rigel. In fact, newspapers were so anxious to get riveting human interest stories of *Titanic* that they paid a fee to anybody presenting one. A dog hero tale would give the teller some extra cash and was sure to increase the paper's circulation.

A DOG-MAT-TICK DECISION

MR. JOHN WOODS, a St. John's merchant, won a favourable verdict from a local jury in late 1877. He had issued a complaint against the police, the Newfoundland Constabulary, in May, 1877. His charge: the police had "wantonly" or recklessly shot his Newfoundland dog.

According to court records and testimony, it was a splendid mature dog that had been lying asleep on the doormat of Woods's home. In other words, the dog was minding its own business and was innocent of any crime. For some reason, policeman Sweeney of the Constabulary shot and wounded the dog. It died slowly, bleeding to death.

The news caused such an uproar, "the public sensation of the Woods vs. Sweeney case," as the *Morning*

Chronicle labelled it, that the trial was deferred and finally went before the Supreme Court on November 23, 1877.

When the verdict came down the next day, Woods was to be compensated for the full value of the dog (although the amount was not stated). The jury added a rider to the verdict, that in their opinion, "Dogs, when shot by the police, should be killed outright, and not left to swelter in their blood to the disgust of all humanity."

A junior lawyer representing Woods reminded the police that they had gotten six months' credit—or "tick"—before they were proven guilty. Although displeased with the unnecessary death of a fine Newfoundland, the lawyer, a local wit, said the judge had rendered "A Dog-Mat-Tick" decision.

LION'S TALE

THE NEWFOUNDLAND NEWSPAPER the *Patriot* carried a story in December, 1885, of a Newfoundland dog named "Lion," who gave proof almost daily of his understanding of what was said to him. The following incident illustrated the claim.

One day a certain friend called on Lion's lady owner. After the two women sat in the living room chatting for a few minutes, Lion came in rather shyly, lay down on the rug, and went to sleep. The conversation ran on for ten or 15 minutes and Lion remained asleep. Then the visitor changed the topic to Lion.

"What a handsome Newfoundland you have!"

Lion opened one eye slightly. "Yes," said his owner, "he is a very good dog and takes excellent care of the children."

Lion, without moving his head, opened the other eye and wagged his tail to and fro along the carpet.

"When the youngest goes out he always goes with her, and I feel perfectly sure then that no harm can come to her," his owner went on.

Lion's tail thumped vigorously up and down on the carpet.

"And he is so gentle to them all and such a playmate and companion to them that I would not take a thousand dollars for him."

Lion's tail now went up and down, to and fro, and round and round with great and undisguised happiness.

"However," said his mistress, "Lion has one serious fault."

Lion's tail stopped wagging and at the same time his countenance took on an appearance of great concern.

"He will come in here with his dirty feet and lie down on the carpet. I have told him time and time again that he must not do this!"

At this point Lion, with an air of dejection and humility, slunk out the room totally crestfallen with his once-exuberant tail down.

THE BROKEN HEART

FROM THE *NEW York Times* comes a story of a Newfoundland dog that languished from lovesickness and a broken heart. "Prince's" owner was a Jersey City policeman, Joseph Sweeney. For quite some time the only family pet was Prince, a Newfoundland who had grown up with the children of the family. He became their only playmate, carousing, tumbling, laughing, running, and playing tag and hiding games. He shared meals with them. Often the Sweeney children used Prince as a pillow for noonday naps. Prince walked to school with them in the morning and waited for the children after school to walk back home. Then fun and playful tricks began again with Prince.

But change came to the family. Policeman Sweeney brought a donkey to his little suburban home. His children immediately began to play with and admire their new pet.

Soon joy and laughter rang out in the garden as they showered the donkey with all the attention they once had heaped on Prince.

Prince looked on for a few moments and then turned, with fallen tail, to the house. For a time he could not found. Eventually he was located under a bed in the children's room. There he lay sad-eyed and sighing. The children, now seeing the error of their ways (and with encouragement from their parents), tried to tempt Prince outdoors to play. He would have none of it, refusing to move.

When they attempted to uncover him in his hideaway by moving the bed, the Newfoundland moved with it. No amount of coaxing or entreaties would bring Prince back to his former state of contentment.

Policeman Sweeney, in his final statement about the unique case, said, "Even if we had tried, which we didn't as we loved the dog, we couldn't beat him out with a stick. Even food is refused. He lies there inconsolable and sighing his life away."

Sweeney's final words on the sad situation were, "he has grown very thin and will probably not last many more days."

INDEX A

PLACES AND SHIPS

INDEX B

NAMES

The author and Flossie, the shortened name for Florizel, at the Newfoundland Emporium, Corner Brook. Flossie succeeds Moose (see page 187). Photo by Sadie Parsons.

ROBERT "BOB" PARSONS has been called one of the most popular and prolific writers on the subject of Atlantic Canada's ships and ship disasters. He is the author of 25 non-fiction books, ranging from *Lost at Sea, a Compilation* and *Toll of the Sea* to *Courting Disaster* and *Rock and Tempest, Fire and Foe*. His work has also appeared in a number of newspapers and magazines such as *Downhome*, the *(Evening) Telegram*, *Newfoundland Quarterly*, and *Newfoundland Lifestyles*. A former fish plant worker and educator and a present-day researcher and devotee of all items marine-related, he lives in Grand Bank, Newfoundland.

ABOUT THE ILLUSTRATOR

MEL D'SOUZA IS a self-taught artist who was born in East Africa and went to school in his native Goa—a former Portuguese territory in India. In 1971, he emigrated to Canada with his wife and two daughters and settled in Brampton, Ontario. They spent their summer vacations travelling extensively by road across Canada and the United States, before "discovering" the island of Newfoundland in 1989. Since then, Mel has returned every year to visit as much of Newfoundland and Labrador as possible and now has his "second home" in Francois on the southwest coast.

ALSO BY ROBERT C. PARSONS

Since the phenomenon of the 1997 hit movie *Titanic*, more people than ever have been captivated with *Titanic* trivia and still thirst, seemingly at an ever-increasing rate, for facts about the great ship operated by the renowned White Star Line. *Cape Race: Stories from the Coast that Sank the* Titanic presents 48 stories of tragedy and heroic rescue from the sea surrounding Cape Race, Newfoundland, including the story of the magnificent liner whose sinking off that coast in 1912 was felt around the world.

"Robert Parsons specializes in marine non-fiction, with more than 200 articles and stories published, along with about twenty books. He knows his stuff and this book is testimony to that."
Atlantic Books Today

ALSO BY ROBERT C. PARSONS

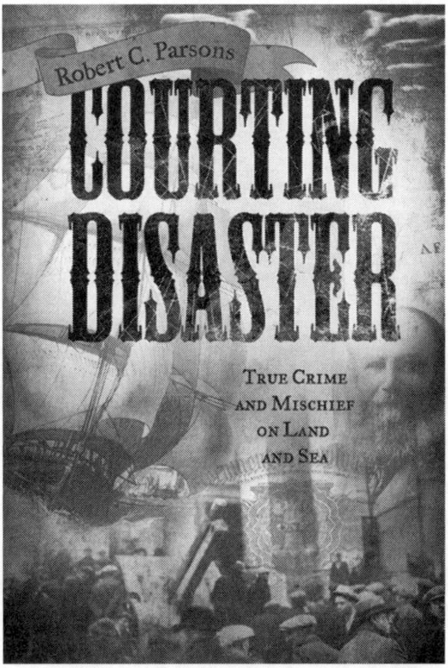

This is a collection of true Newfoundland and Labrador stories about crime and punishment on land and sea. Included here are tales of murder, mutiny, and smuggling on the high seas, as well as riots, assaults, and frauds perpetrated in some of the strangest criminal cases this province has ever seen.

ISBN: 978-1-897317-45-7, $19.95, 317 pages
www.flankerpress.com

ALSO BY ROBERT C. PARSONS

Born Down By the Water is a collection of sea stories inspired by the maritime history of Newfoundland and Labrador. Included are 18 true stories describing the fate of crafts, from massive ocean liners such as the *Titanic* to the small schooners that sailed the Newfoundland-Mediterranean-Caribbean routes transporting passengers, codfish, salt, wine, and rum.

From wrecks and rescues, races across the Atlantic, and war at sea to murder and riot, the tidal wave of 1929, and tragedies of fire, this compilation is an interesting and exciting read. Supporting these stories are dozens of photographs and newspaper clippings.

ISBN: 978-1-894463-52-2, $14.95, 151 pages
www.flankerpress.com

Angel's Wish

Sheila Newberry

W F HOWES LTD

This large print edition published in 2024 by
W F Howes Ltd
Unit 5, St George's House, Rearsby Business Park,
Gaddesby Lane, Rearsby, Leicester LE7 4YH

1 3 5 7 9 10 8 6 4 2

First published in the United Kingdom in 1997 as
The Painted Sky by Piatkus

This edition published in the United Kingdom
in 2023 by Zaffre

A CIP catalogue record for this book is available
from the British Library

ISBN 978 1 00415 669 6

Typeset b[illegible] Limited,

For The Children of The Buck –
Especially Bella

I stood and stared; the sky was lit
The sky was stars all over it,
I stood, I knew not why,
Without a wish, without a will,
I stood upon that silent hill
And stared into the sky until
My eyes were blind with stars and still
I stared into the sky.

Ralph Hodgson

CHAPTER ONE

Angel stood there still, with the dust stirred by the solid tyres of the railway motorbus powdering the shine from her smart shoes. She glanced down indifferently. Seven years ago, after all, she had been wearing boots cracked and caked with foul mud from the ruined fields of France.

The bus was by now out of sight, having rounded the bend, but Angel could hear it rumbling ponderously on towards the next village.

'Well, Angelina Rosselli, d'you intend to take root here?' she mused aloud. Then she smiled faintly at the irony of her words.

She was a slight young woman, of medium height, dressed in a light tussore costume, the skirt badly crumpled by a stout fellow passenger who had sat down heavily beside her, having boarded the train at Ipswich. A round, natural straw hat just afforded a glimpse of short, glossy grape-black hair that curved against the line of her firm, uptilted chin. Her eyes, narrowed against the flurry of dirt thrown up from the country lane, and the relentless afternoon sun, were surprisingly blue, under distinctive brows. Angel's gloved hands, soiled from wrestling with the recalcitrant sash of the train window, gripped the handles of her heavy basket case. She had tucked her fat handbag under one arm.

'Thank goodness,' she thought, 'I had the sense to leave the trunk at the station to await collection by Mr MacDonald.'

Angel had yet to meet her new employer, Robert MacDonald of The Angel, for a mutual friend, his neighbour Edith Fenner had recommended her for this temporary post, duration uncertain, as companion-cum-nurse to his daughter, Alice, convalescing after scarlet fever and a subsequent operation for mastoid.

In the one brief letter she had received, Mr MacDonald said she would be met from the bus. However, bags packed, impatient to leave London, and her sister Louise and brother-in-law Jack, she had come a day early.

What was it the friendly red-faced driver had advised?

'Foller the roses on your right, keep a going till you come to Mrs Newsome's shop, then fork you sharp. Mind the gully in front of the meadow, see the pink house with the pargeting – *then* you'll come to The Angel. Quite a walk uphill on a thirsty night that is, but that Scotsman do draw fine beer.'

So, Angel obediently 'follered' the briar hedge, festooned with tiny roses, for it was June, in shades from deepest to palest creamy pink, each with its golden centre. She couldn't resist plucking a single bloom to tuck in her hatband. Despite the weight of her case, she hurried along, brushing against the tall graceful grasses, averting her gaze from the scarlet poppies, which also flourished everywhere.

There were poppies in France, they said: the seed which had lain dormant for many years had sprung to life where men had fallen, having advanced, retreated then advanced again, over and over the same desolate stretch of land.

She must put those memories away, the nightmare that had almost broken her, begin really living again, looking forward now to the future. That was really what had prompted her to come to rural Suffolk, not just Edith's urging. Could they really resume their friendship after so long?

Her sister and her husband had accompanied Angel, unasked, to Liverpool Street Station.

'Write soon, Angel, oh, promise!' Louise entreated.

Angel nodded, seeing Lou's hands linked so naturally, supporting the heavy swelling of her body. She witnessed that instinctive bonding with the unborn, and pain gnawed at her own insides. Jack's arm lay protectively around Lou's shoulders. He had survived the conflict, he may now have a steel plate in his skull and a nervous hesitancy in his speech yet – *he* was *here,* Angel thought. She must not envy them, for they had waited so long for this precious first baby.

Harry had drawn her close to him, his hand daring to stray beneath the thick knot of her hair, uncut from childhood then – his fingers delicately caressing her neck where it rose above the constraints of her starched collar. Because they were on the ward, where the muttering and sighs betrayed those patients sleepless and in constant pain, she had suppressed the yearning to turn her face towards his, but she knew that her trembling must betray the way she felt . . .

Lou made one final protest when Angel leaned from the train window to say goodbye. '*I* need you, Angel, with the baby coming—'

With tears in her eyes, Angel replied firmly, 'Lou, you and Jack and the baby – you'll be a family, without me. You'll see.' The guard blew his shrill whistle. 'Goodbye – I love you!' she called, as the train steamed away.

Now, she came upon the church, set well back on a rise of ground, with the entrance guarded by a magnificent lych- gate, obviously a recent addition, and beyond that she saw an arch, with a lantern suspended from fanciful wrought-iron brackets, to light the faithful to Evensong on dark winter nights, she supposed.

There were cottages, mere hovels, seemingly built into the bank below the churchyard. The bedroom windows, Angel conjectured, must be on a level with the tombstones on the slope above. THE COTTS, 1790, was carved into the lintel of the middle dwelling of five. The front doors opened directly into the lane. The church spoke of a comfortable living, she thought, the cottages of abject poverty, only partly concealed behind the torn, grimy curtains at the tiny windows.

She sensed that she was being watched as she passed The Cotts by.

It was a relief to arrive next at the school, but this too, was deserted, for the children must have whooped joyfully as they sped homewards some forty minutes ago. The bus had passed several clusters of farm cottages where Angel observed small girls in old-fashioned holland frocks, babies in sun bonnets, playing in the shade of some trees, while their brothers rolled and tumbled on the grass. Rosy-cheeked, country children, she smiled to herself.

The school had been built at a later date than the church, of course, but of matching flintstone – probably in the early days of Victoria's reign.

A large, yellow Labrador barked from the pathway of the adjacent school house, merely a greeting, for the dog's tail wagged furiously. Angel went quickly by, in case the schoolmaster should appear. She hitched her burden higher as if it were no weight at all. She did not wish to meet Edmund, her friend's brother, before Edith.

A pleasant fragrance emanated from the bake-house, but the dimpled windows of the shop revealed shelves wiped clean, and empty. Next door, outside Mrs Newsome's shop, for so the sign proclaimed, a group of women and children were gathered. They turned to gaze curiously at the newcomer.

'Hello – who's this?' she heard, then one called out boldly: 'Nice afternoon!' Angel had the impression of flaxen hair, fair skins, friendly, smiling faces. Descendants of the Anglo-Saxons, all.

Smiling shyly back, she agreed, 'Oh, yes, it is!' It felt like a welcoming, she thought. Then she obediently forked sharp.

The gardener and his boy still toiled in the gardens of what was surely the residence of people of some social standing. The workers were bent double over the flower beds, despite the heat, tossing weeds into their barrow. The house cloaked in green ivy, wore its thatch like an itchy, rakish wig, Angel fancied, just as if scratching hands had pushed it awry.

The lodge, guarding the sweeping drive to the side of the mansion, appeared to have been built around the trunks of four massive oaks, lopped to an even height, but varying in width. The windows here were wide open, and she could eavesdrop on the youngsters chattering at their tea. Hunger pangs struck her, for Lou's sandwiches remained unwrapped in her bag. She marvelled at the vegetables growing densely in the cramped patch, which was all the big house had spared. Not a flower in sight, unless you counted the crimson peeping through the climbing beans. Food obviously took precedence here.

Walking alongside the succeeding water meadows, so peaceful, Angel observed a giant hare, motionless, watching her, as she, in turn, stared back in surprise. A squirrel leaped, almost flying, from tree to tree overhead, leaving the branches swaying. Angel had forgotten the warning about the gully: she stumbled down into a narrow ditch, concealed by hedge clippings. To her relief it was dry, for there had been no rain for days. She bit at her lower lip ruefully as she saw the runs lengthening in her new silk stockings, a parting gift from Lou and Jack. Even as she straightened her hat, and her aching back, she became aware of the grinding of cartwheels, of the smart clopping of hooves. She turned as a pony and trap drew alongside and came to a halt. A man held the reins, a boy beside him.

'Now, you must be the young lady we expected tomorrow – is that so?' the man enquired, in a soft, precise Scottish voice.

Pink cheeked, Angel nodded. She realised instantly who this must be.

'I am Robert MacDonald, of The Angel. This is Tony, my son. We have just been down to the village to collect medicines from the surgery – they told me at the shop I would catch up with a lady walking, a stranger with a case.' Robert MacDonald handed the reins to his son and swung his long legs easily to the ground.

He held out a hand for her case, placed it in the well of the trap and then assisted her up. 'There

– it's but a very short ride now – a pity we did not catch up with you earlier, eh? Your letter advising of the change of plan did not arrive, I'm afraid.'

'I'm so sorry, but I didn't write,' she admitted.

'Ah, I see,' he returned easily, not at all put out.

Angel drew off her gloves, rubbing her chafed hands together, aware that she was already relaxing in his company. Her employer had looked up at her with a kind, quizzical smile, before he had resumed his own seat at the front. She gazed at the back of his neck, reddened from exposure to all weathers, for he wore no hat, at his dark hair, greying a little, cropped short but irrepressibly curly. His shoulders were broad, arms strong.

Tony, the young boy, dark like his father, sat silently and shyly at his side.

'Our friend Edith's house,' Robert MacDonald observed.

There was a sturdy bicycle leaning against the pink house gate, with a delightful riot of cottage garden flowers almost obscuring the flagged path. The place was just as Edith had described in her letters. Albertine roses drooped over the latticed wooden porch; the faded pink of the walls, the pargeting, like a pattern marked on a piecrust, pictures embossed on plaster. If she had come tomorrow as planned, Angel thought, Edith would, no doubt, have been eagerly looking out for her. She had last seen her friend in 1916.

They had arrived at The Angel. The inn stood

facing up the lonely road ahead, where Angel saw trees leaning on either side, forming a leafy tunnel, linked by the buffeting of the east wind. The Angel was situated at the edge, or the beginning, depending on which way you approached it, of the village of Uffasham, in Suffolk.

It was, of course, inevitable that the men in the hospital should call her The Angel. Harry had made her blush, when he told her that. Almost poetry, Harry's next words, ones she could never forget, 'But the word "angel" suggests to me a pale, shadowy being, floating somewhere up above: you, my darling Angel, have substance – so warm and caring . . . you catch your breath when you are forced to cause more agony before you can ease it. "Will it be The Angel, Doctor, with us through the long night watch?" they ask me, "Or will it be Sister Edith?"'

There was the inn sign, with an unlikely angel boldly gilded, hands demurely folded. Despite the oversized halo, it was hardly angelic, Angel thought.

Tony jumped down, to unfasten the gates. Through a courtyard, they trundled, towards a block of stables, past the patrons' privy, with the half-moon cut into the top of the door.

Robert MacDonald said, 'Here we are. Take the path, to the front of the house, for I spotted Aunt Hetty picking away in the asparagus bed. Tony and I will fetch your luggage inside. We must unharness the pony and stow away the trap, but we will be with you shortly.'

A small figure rose unexpectedly from the centre of a lush plot, lifting a rush frail almost full of tender, green shoots.

'Are you calling?' Aunt Hetty enquired: hers was a local accent, excited, light and almost girlish. 'Come you on, inside!'

She led the way through the second door under the porch, for above the first door they came to there was the legend PUBLIC BAR.

Through the open door of that black-beamed, rambling old whitewashed house, Angel stepped.

She was here, an Angel at The Angel, where her past was unknown and where the days ahead looked bright.

CHAPTER TWO

To the right of the spacious flagged hall was a closed door. 'Our front parlour,' Aunt Hetty indicated. To the left, the high backs of two enormous oaken settles partitioned the hall from the bar beyond.

So that was the reason for the first entrance, Angel realised, inhaling the fruity, malty odour that pervaded the hall.

'Out of bounds to the children, you'll understand,' Aunt Hetty remarked cheerfully. 'Kitchen this way, down the short staircase – that's where we spend our days. I'll soon stir the old stove up, rinse out the teapot. You must be tired, Angelina—?' There was a look of kindly concern.

'Oh, Angel, please, Mrs MacDonald,' Angel put in quickly. She glanced around her with unconcealed interest. On one wall there was a handsome brass warming pan, hanging from the handle, on the other side a series of fading prints of horses and dogs. Just before the half-flight of stairs to the kitchen, on the right, a further few steps led up to a door labelled THE SNUG. Opposite, was the main staircase, winding upwards to the bedrooms, with a room on the half-landing directly opposite The Snug, designated PRIVATE.

'My nephew's room. There are five more bedrooms beyond.' Aunt Hetty had noticed her curious glances. 'And you must call me Aunt Hetty – why not, eh? I'm Rob's aunt by marriage, y'know. I was born here, in The Angel – a real coaching inn then, my dear, where they changed the horses before they went on to Lowestoft. Here we are, do you sit down—' She gathered up a sleepy armful of ginger and black kittens from the bentwood rocker, a chair with arms deeply scored from cats' claws, and deposited them on a rag rug by the stove. This aroused a plaintive mewing. Aunt Hetty continued: 'I left here to marry my John and we came back here when my parents passed on. No children of our own, but Rob came to us from Scotland, as a lad, and joined us in the business. 'Course, he was away all the war – milk and sugar in your tea, Angel? – then his wife upped and left me with the children to care for, and my husband died. The Angel was in a poor old way, when her landlord returned – ah, here you are Rob . . .'

Angel found herself blushing deeply again. Rob MacDonald's presence loomed large, for he was very tall, very masculine. She wondered if he minded his aunt hinting at his wife's desertion to a stranger, if this still hurt. Yet, on first acquaintance he looked happy, well adjusted to his position. He was perhaps ten years her senior, not such a generation gap when she, herself, was almost thirty years old. To cover her confusion, she took off her hat, avoiding eye contact with her employer.

Rob said: 'You'll excuse me, Miss Rosselli, but I must prepare now for the opening-up. Shall we discuss your duties over supper? We eat early, whilst we've the chance, but naturally I'll not expect you to start work until Monday next, as arranged – you'll appreciate the weekend to settle in, no doubt—'

Angel found her tongue. 'You're very kind. Oh, I know I'll soon feel at home here – it's such a lovely old house. I do look forward to exploring—' she added impulsively.

That nice, warming smile again. 'A slower way of life, mind, we've not caught up with London ways, as you'll be used to – no water on tap, but a good old pump, oil lamps, can't say I'm sorry. I gather Aunt Hetty has put you in the picture, regarding our circumstances, she has been a grand substitute mother to my children, as she was to *me*, but they will, no doubt, appreciate more youthful company, while we are busy each night.' He turned, went back up the little staircase.

Taking her cup to the sink, Angel glanced out of the window. Somehow, she had not imagined there would be much land surrounding The Angel. She was wrong, for a meadow rolled out beyond the vegetable patch, there was a pond with dipping, leafy willow trees, a coop of scratching red-brown hens, a placid white goat, with two young kids close to her flanks, cropping the long grass – *was that hump an ice house?* she wondered. At the far end of the field she saw an ancient barn, which appeared to be in disuse.

Aunt Hetty, observing her interest, came alongside. 'There is not the necessity for storing so much hay, now that patrons come by bicycle, Angel, by motorcycle or even the motorcar.'

There had been a barn, near the field hospital, adjacent to the abandoned farmhouse which had been requisitioned for the nursing staff. Angel and Harry met there, sinking down on the rotting hay. Once a barn owl had risen from the rafters, startling them, flying straight through the gaping hole in the roof. They heard the indignant flapping of its strong wings before it circled the barn, then flew away. There was a lull in the gunfire, but the acrid, scorching smell was never dispelled. Then Harry gently loosened her hair, buried his face in its dark mass; they were both weary beyond words. War seemed never ending, but at that moment, they were at least together – their loving eased the dreadful pain of it all.

Angel turned away abruptly from the view from the window, looking instead round the square room: at the solid, dark dresser with its Royal Doulton dishes and baskets of fruit and vegetables. Onions dangled from a twisted string and shedding skin, canvas aprons hung from a nail on the back door. The big table had been scrubbed and bleached with the coarse grain – six hard-seated chairs grouped tidily round it. The red coals behind the bars of the stove kept the kettle on top sighing and wheezing. From the side oven wafted a truly delicious aroma of tender meat and pastry. The sink, she saw, the usual deep stone sort, had buckets of water beneath, at the ready.

'I must soon pare the vegetables and set on the hot-me-pot,' Aunt Hetty observed. 'But I'll just steam a bundle of the asparagus first, Alice might just fancy that, drenched in butter, eh? We'll go upstairs then so you can meet her, you'll want to unpack before your own supper I expect. Your room, Angel, is next door to hers.'

Angel smiled back at nice Aunt Hetty. She appeared so small and slight, with her sleeves rolled up to reveal skinny arms with knotted veins, but she must be strong, Angel mused, to have coped here on her own with the children for several years. She really liked Aunt Hetty's weathered face, criss-crossed by constant laughing surely, with eyes almost as bright as they must have been when she was Alice's age. Hetty's hair was fine, fuzzy and white as the ruff round the neck of the plump goose which hung by its feet from the stout hook on the back of the scullery door, jostling for space with oilskins and a heavy plaid scarf.

'Sunday dinner that goose – in your honour, my dear!' Aunt Hetty beamed. 'There's a copper in the scullery, and another sink, that's where we do our washing each Monday morn, rain or shine – oh, and a nice hip bath that Rob bought for his wife, when you fancy an all-over soak. When things get better, when custom picks up, Rob's promised us an indoor bathroom and WC, till then, I'm afraid, it's the chamber pot in the washstand cupboard for the dark hours and trips outside to the old privy in the light. We've got our own, apart from the pub's – just outside – see?'

'I see . . .' Angel watched dreamily, for already the pace of life seemed to be slowing, as Aunt Hetty trimmed the asparagus and deftly tied a bundle with cotton. She placed the stalks upright in a pan of salted, boiling water, then shifted it to the simmering plate and covered it carefully with the lid.

'Edith speaks very highly of you, Angel.' Aunt Hetty began laying up a tray for the sick child. 'See, the larder: would you care to help? Could you cut the crusts from the bread? The poor child hardly eats a morsel . . . You and Edith, nurses together, I hear, in France during the war?'

In her last letter, urging Angel to come: 'It seems so long since we met . . . I promise I will never mention the sad events of that last time . . .' Edith had concluded: 'I always believed in you, regarding the first, and as for the second terrible thing, no one ever knew, except for me. You will find this a healing place, Angel. Well, I have certainly found contentment here, especially since I retired to the pink house . . .'

Angel replied now: 'That's right. Is this the butter to use, Aunt Hetty?'

Aunt Hetty, nodded, pouring cold milk into an almost translucent green glass. 'Nice glasses, bone china – help to tempt the appetite, when you're sick, I find.'

Angel removed the rose, on a sudden impulse, from her hatband. 'May I have a small container? Too pretty to let this wilt, isn't it? Just right for an invalid tray.' The pink egg cup was perfect. The rose would soon perk up.

As they went upstairs to Alice's room, Aunt Hetty remarked: 'There's so much more sky here, y'know, in our part of the world, watch out for the sunsets – they're so beautiful. Lalla, Rob's wife, used to sit by the landing window, come summer evenings, painting the sky. This here is my room, and this little room, squeezed in between, is young Tony's – he needs his old Auntie near at nights, for he has a small problem, you'll understand . . . Linen cupboard – spare room, we put up guests, from time to time. Now, this is Alice's bedroom, the next door is yours, you go in, freshen up, whilst I take in her tray. When you're set, well, just you come through the inner door, eh?'

'Thank you, I will.' Angel turned the brass knob. As Aunt Hetty juggled the tray in opening Alice's door, Angel glimpsed a bed by the window, a table drawn up beside it, and the back view of young Tony bending over a puzzle, or perhaps a game.

Angel grimaced at the bear rug, for it felt wrong

to her to tread on the pelt of a creature which had been sacrificed to provide an ornamental covering for the varnished floorboards.

It was a long room, with a window under the eaves that looked out onto a different view, over the front and the yard, to the pink house opposite.

The walls were freshly whitewashed, the curtains faded by strong sunlight, but newly pressed. The bed was brass railed, plumped up with a feather mattress – Angel fingered the sheets, starched white linen, with eyelet embroidery on the turn-back, matching the frill round the pillowcases. There was a single wardrobe, a simple dressing table with swing mirror, a small chest of drawers and a rather fine washstand, marble-topped, with a bowl and basin set patterned with blue cornflowers. No doubt, she smiled to herself, the receptacle, when revealed, would match. There was a new cake of Pears transparent soap, her favourite, which she lifted to smell, a soft blue flannel, and companion hand towel hanging neatly from the rail.

She poured cool, soft water into the basin and thankfully rinsed her face and hands. She thought ruefully that she was not very suitably dressed for country life: the women she had seen outside the shop like Aunt Hetty still wore long skirts, with long hair severely dressed.

She looked at her face in the mirror. She was still unused to the short bob but, in a way, she supposed it had been a symbolic cutting, for Harry had loved her tumbling tresses. She combed her tousled fringe. No papier poudre, no lip rouge today, for, 'I'm no bright young thing!' she told her reflection.

Her basket case was set on the cane-bottomed bedroom chair. She slipped out of the tussore costume, hunted in the case for the loose-waisted blue dress she had thought suitable for her nursing duties. Then she went through the connecting door.

The pale girl, propped up by pillows, regarded her gravely. Immediately, Angel could tell just how ill Alice had been.

Alice was all eyes, darkly shadowed, her hair shaved and strained away from the dressing over her left ear, pulled back from her high forehead into an unbecoming plait. Aunt Hetty perched on the side of the bed, supporting the tray on her niece's lap, obviously trying to coax the girl to eat. Tony turned, his expression wary, fingering the chess pieces which had been in play, when Alice's supper arrived.

'Hello, I'm Alice, and I didn't really want a nurse, only Dad insisted – but Aunt Hetty says you're really very nice, so I suppose we'll get on, so long as you don't treat me like a baby,' Alice said candidly. She began to nibble reluctantly at the asparagus.

'Fetch Angel a chair, Tony,' Aunt Hetty requested. 'I won't apologise for Alice, Angel, because her mother brought her up to speak her mind, and that's not something as can be cured . . . Thank you, Tony – here will do. Well, if you'll excuse me, I'll carry on with the cooking. Tony – will you bring down the tray later, eh?'

When Aunt Hetty had gone, Alice said firmly, 'Tony's more in need of a nursemaid than I am.'

'I'm not!' Tony was indignant, but he looked more uncertain than hostile.

'That's good,' Angel said equably, 'because I'm not a nursemaid – I'm a qualified nurse – it's my job to ensure that you recover as quickly as possible, even if it does mean I'll be looking for another job sooner, rather than later.' She'd got the measure of Alice, being instantly reminded of herself at that age, rebelling against Lou's strictures.

Alice was frankly surprised. 'You're not going to insist that I stay in bed for weeks and weeks, then? I was six weeks in the fever hospital first, but I was too ill to care. *Then*, when I'd only been home a week, they had to rush me back to Lowestoft for the operation. That meant another month of horrible bedpans and blanket baths, and nurses saying, "Lie still, Alice! Don't you dare move your head!" and tucking me in so tightly I couldn't move if I'd wanted to.'

'Well, *I* shall want to get you downstairs, as soon as your legs are less wobbly, to let you soak up the sun, while the weather's so good, out in the garden. And, I do hope you and Tony will teach me to play chess, for I've always wanted to learn

– I do know all sorts of Patience, with cards from my early nursing days, which I could show you in return—'

'I don't want any more.' Alice pushed the tray away.

'You mustn't hurt Aunt Hetty's feelings, when she went to so much trouble, come on, Alice, try just a little more, please . . .' Angel moved the tray back. To her surprise, Alice picked up the bread and butter strips and began to eat, albeit slowly.

'Are *you* good at art?' she asked between nibbles.

'I used to enjoy painting lessons when I was young, but I've not done anything since,' Angel admitted. 'Your mother was an artist, I gather?' she added casually.

'*Is* an artist.' The correction was swift. 'I'm not very good, myself, but Tony takes after Lalla, our mother – when he gets to know you better, maybe he'll show you some of his pictures – mostly of animals, aren't they, Tony? He did a lovely one of the yellow dog from the schoolhouse, the other day—'

'I can speak for myself!' Tony butted in. 'I'm nearly ten, remember!'

'And I'm already twelve, two years older than you, and always will be. You'll never catch me up!' Alice retorted. However, she grinned at her brother and Angel thought that her tone was not malicious, more that of a bossy, older sister, a state with which Angel was very familiar.

'My sister Lou is *eight* years older than me. My

father, who was from Italy, if you're wondering about my funny name, came to England in the 1880s. He was an Army doctor and was killed in the Boer War when I was a child. My mother eventually married again, and went to live abroad, so I went to live with my sister and her husband. They treated me like their own child, having no family then, which was frustrating for me at times. So you see, *I* know what it is to have a big sister in charge, Tony! But, you know, when you are both adult, the age difference doesn't really matter anymore, in a strange way, you do seem to catch up . . .' The children absorbed this, with interest.

An amused voice from the doorway caused them all to look in that direction. 'Time to catch up with supper, now, Miss Rosselli – Aunt Hetty sent me to fetch you and Tony.'

'Take the tray!' Alice ordered Tony. 'Say, it was delicious and thank you very much. Will you come back and keep me company, Angel, after you've eaten?'

'Now, Alice,' her father said mildly, standing aside to let his son by with the tray. 'Miss Rosselli must be tired after her journey, and that long walk from the crossroads—'

'Of course, I'll see you after supper.' Angel was glad she had obviously met with Alice's approval.

She and Rob MacDonald went downstairs together. He paused by the door marked PRIVATE. 'I shall join you in a moment. Miss Rosselli—'

'Yes?'

What he said next was entirely unexpected. 'Miss Rosselli, I would ask you not to bring up the subject of the children's mother, unless Alice, or Tony, should do so themselves. My wife is best forgotten. This family is happier, more stable without her. You understand, I trust.' His gaze was intense, unnerving even. The disarming smile was not in evidence.

'Naturally,' she found her voice. 'I shall do as you wish, Mr MacDonald. That is what you are paying me for, after all.'

'Good.' He closed his door.

From the landing window, Angel saw a small cloud drifting lazily towards the late afternoon sun. Aunt Hetty was right, she thought, shaking off sudden unease, following her employer's blunt statement, here, there really was so much more sky.

CHAPTER THREE

In the pink house opposite The Angel, Edith Fenner bided her time, absently drumming her fingers on the kitchen table. Really, she fumed, that wretched woman in The Cotts was infuriating. Edith wished to keep her hand in even though she had left the hospital – considering her advice was free to all she deemed deserving – *why* did the villagers continue to turn to one they called 'the wise woman', a self-styled nurse with no regard for hygiene?

Edith had hurried to attend a difficult confinement, having heard from her brother, the schoolmaster, that the young mother was in trouble, only to be turned away from the door with the words: '*I'm* the only nurse wanted here . . .'

Back at the schoolhouse, her brother had remonstrated mildly with her, saying that he always found the folk of Uffasham very friendly. Of course, because of his position, he was afforded a certain deference, which, being a modest man, he was not too sure he deserved.

'Rubbish!' Edith flared. 'You do more, *far* more, than is necessary to educate their children – it's fortunate you are not a married man, no wife would tolerate the hours you spend in that school. I find it hurtful, Edmund, that they will not accept *my* help . . . Thank goodness for my neighbours at The Angel. They were grateful enough for my care of Alice.'

'That reminds me, Edith. The dog was barking at a passer-by, earlier – by the time I came out, the young lady was walking towards Mrs Newsome's shop. The news soon came to me via the village grapevine: your friend is already at The Angel. I thought you said she would be travelling here tomorrow?'

Edith was piqued, she had planned to ask Rob MacDonald casually if she might accompany him in the trap to meet Angel Rosselli. She had wished to be in charge of the introductions to the family, to tactfully hint that she was always available if Angel needed her professional expertise. In fact, she had been loth to relinquish her responsibility for Alice's nursing care – but events over the past year had disturbed her – she *needed* to see Angel again, but how could she persuade her to come, when in the past, Angel had turned down her invitations to visit? Alice's continued need of nursing had proved a godsend . . . She wondered wryly if Angel would have kept up their link if she had not persisted with her friendly letters. She must not suspect Edith's real feelings!

The drumming ceased. Edith rose. Now was the

time to find out if old wounds had healed. She smiled. The fly had landed on the spider's web.

There was an unexpected guest for supper, already ensconced at the table.

'Edith!' Angel exclaimed, surprised.

'I just called in to see what time you were expected tomorrow and Aunt Hetty said: "My dear, she's here!" So I craftily wheedled an invitation to join you for your meal. You're soon to discover that Aunt Hetty is a wonderful cook! Welcome to Uffasham, Angel.'

Angel and Edith did not embrace, for Angel knew of old, that Edith shied away from intimate contact, which was not to say that she did not betray her affection for her closest friends, despite her rather hearty manner. She was not a very feminine person, unlike Angel.

'It's good to see you again.' Angel sat opposite Edith, while Tony dodged between them laying the cutlery, and Aunt Hetty brought forth a glistening brown pie from the oven below the hot-me-pot where the vegetables still steamed gently.

'You look well, Angel.' Edith looked her over approvingly. 'Different, modern, I suppose, well, you were never a fuddy-duddy like me, were you? Tell me, what d'you make of our – sorry! – *your* patient?'

'She's *im*patient to be well – which is a good sign, isn't it?'

Edith looked very little older than the last time

they had been together, Angel thought – though Edith had never looked less than middle-aged, with her homely features, sturdy figure and fine, sandy hair still wound into that uncompromising bun. Solid, dependable, dear Edith. What would she have done without her support seven years ago? She wasn't sure why she had delayed their reunion for so long. She had let Edith down badly, that was still a matter for regret. Lou, however, who only knew half of what had happened, had advised her to cool their friendship somewhat. 'That woman is too possessive, Angel,' she said. Wasn't that true of Lou, too? But in a *different* way . . .

Edith said now, 'I've been holding the fort with Aunt Hetty, of course. At one time, we feared we might lose Alice. All right, Tony, don't look so alarmed, your sister is set to recover, I'm positive of that – and don't you pass on what's said around this table, either! I've been here daily, Angel, as I said in my letters, to change the dressings – but I'm quite sure young Alice will appreciate your youthfulness, and your lighter touch,' she added, a trifle ruefully. 'For didn't the patients in France always ask for Nurse Rosselli to re-bandage their wounds when the doctor had been on his rounds?'

Angel hoped that her involuntary flinching was not visible to Aunt Hetty, now serving the meat pie on to their plates.

Fortunately, Rob MacDonald appeared at that moment, greeting Edith cheerfully: 'Ah, Edith, you couldn't wait to meet up with your friend, I see? Miss Rosselli, will you take some potatoes, runner beans? We must eat up all the jarfuls Aunt Hetty salted last year before the new beans swell! And the carrots come from our patch – ye'll be sampling all sorts of vegetables for our gardener. Also, Aunt Hetty has been busy, as always.'

'Thank you.' Angel obediently helped herself.

'Rob – I do hope you don't intend to remain so formal.' Edith took a heaped tablespoon of chopped carrots, in her turn. 'Miss Rosselli, indeed! Surely you can bring yourself to call her Angel, when she's such an old friend of mine?'

He looked at Angel. 'If there is no objection?'

'None at all.' She wondered if *she* should call him Rob . . .

After the meal, Edith rose reluctantly. 'That was delicious, Aunt Hetty, thank you. I must go, for I promised to go for an evening stroll with Edmund and his dog. He'll be knocking on my door right now, I guess, and wondering where on earth I am. I'll see you again soon, I hope, Angel. You'll be busy for a few days with your patient, I know. Good luck!' She saw herself out.

'*We* must hurry,' Aunt Hetty said, collecting up the plates. 'They'll be trying the bar door, too.' She appeared rather flustered.

'Let me wash the dishes,' Angel offered. There had been two extra tonight, after all.

'That's very good of you, my dear. You'll help Angel, Tony, eh?'

'We'll go up to sit with Alice afterwards, as I promised.' Angel smiled.

'Don't let the children keep you up too late,' Rob said, as he departed for his evening's work. 'Pack Tony off to bed when you're ready.'

'Plenty of milk, if you want a drink last thing,' added Aunt Hetty, tying on her bar apron.

'Aunt Hetty —' Angel called, as she was about to follow Rob.

'Yes, my dear?'

'Mr MacDonald – Rob – we didn't get a chance to talk about my duties as Edith was here.' Angel reminded her anxiously.

'It's obvious you're the best judge of what needs doing, Angel, just carry on, in your own way, and I'm sure Rob'll be well pleased.'

The evening passed pleasantly, but Angel called a halt to the chatting and card games when she saw Alice slipping back against her pillows and looking drained. 'Off to bed now, Tony, for I must see to your sister – I'll put my head round your door to say goodnight, promise!'

She made Alice comfortable, tucked her up loosely, opened the window, for fresh air was important on a warm night, then she turned the nightlight low. 'I'll fetch you some fresh water in your jug, Alice, shall I? Just take this dose of your new medicine first – nasty, is it? Never mind, I'm sure you won't need to take it much longer. It's to help you sleep well at nights, you see, to ease the pain behind your ear. You're a brave girl, Alice,

Aunt Hetty whispered that you never complain about that.'

She fumbled her way downstairs, for the lamps in the wall niches had yet to be lit, although light spilled over from the bar beyond into the hall, illuminating the little staircase. She heard cheerful voices and laughter, although the men thus socialising and relaxing were invisible behind the huge settles.

The big oil lamp burned steadily on the kitchen table. Angel dipped Alice's jug in the half-full pail of drinking water kept cool in the dark space beneath the sink. Then she paused to look out of the window at the sunset. Aunt Hetty was sure to ask if she had seen it tomorrow, she mused. The glorious colours of the sky made her catch her breath in sheer delight – if only she could paint! No wonder the night skies of Suffolk had been such a favourite subject for the children's artist mother. All rose and gold streaks, a hint of mauve, with the dark shapes of the trees and the barn in the distance. The window provided a natural frame for this picture. *Sunset and Shadows* . . . she murmured.

For a moment or two she wondered if her imagination was playing tricks: a shadowy figure emerged from the tumbledown building, slowly and uncertainly at first, then breaking into an awkward run. Her eyes widened, as she realised that this was a man, carrying something in one hand, which glinted in the sinking sun. She watched, mesmerised, as the man climbed atop the mound above the old ice house, stood there, silhouetted against the wide, glowing canvas that was the night sky, and the bright object was raised to his lips.

The sound that issued forth made her gasp, almost drop the glass jug. For what she heard was unmistakable, yet another memory from her troubled past to make her shudder.

The stranger was blowing a bugle: the mournful, searing notes of The Last Post.

As the final, lingering notes died away, another shadowy figure appeared – a woman, Angel conjectured, with flowing hair. She halted a few feet away from the bugler. Then he turned, came down hesitantly from the mound: the two figures seemed to merge together in a clinging embrace. For a few moments they appeared to be motionless, then, the woman supporting the man, they retreated back to the barn, vanishing within the dark cavern.

'Are you all right, Angel?' Rob MacDonald came beside her, as she stared still through the kitchen window. She felt his hand lightly touch her shoulder. This brief contact was strangely disturbing. It was the first time she had been so close to a man, except for Lou's Jack, of course, since Harry. 'I came out to light the stairs, to say goodnight to the children, as I always do,' he added. 'I heard you in here, thought I would just enquire how things are with Alice.'

'She is settled for the night – I just came down

to fill her jug. She has taken her medicine,' Angel managed.

He moved back. 'Thank you. We did not expect all this from you on your first evening.' His gaze was thoughtful.

'I wanted to do it,' Angel said.

'I hope Aunt Hetty and I will not disturb you later. It will be some time before we can get to our beds. I am sure you will prove to be a great asset here. I'll wish ye goodnight then, Angel.'

'Goodnight.' She hoped he could not discern the tremble in her voice.

It was not until she was undressing for bed, herself, suddenly longing to sink down into the soft bed for, after all, it had been quite a day, she yawned to herself, that she realised that Rob MacDonald had not mentioned the mystery bugler, or his companion to her, although, of course he must have seen them, neither had she told him what she had heard. She was only sure of one thing, that her employer had shown no surprise.

At any rate, she thought, just before she succumbed to sound sleep, I don't believe this is anything to be frightened of. I can ask Aunt Hetty, or the children, what they know about the ghostly bugler, in the morning . . .

Others, out and about had listened to the bugler too. In the bar, the banjo had been taken down from its hook on the wall by the fireplace and the schoolmaster good-naturedly played all requests. *I'll Take You Home Again, Kathleen* – the singing was always sentimental, sometimes Irish songs, rendered huskily in broad East Anglian accents. It would soon be time for last orders. Aunt Hetty's feet were throbbing: the Scotsman did indeed draw fine beer with a steady hand.

Some were already sauntering towards home down the lane. 'Last Post! Poor devil . . . Still, he've no old gal to scold him for being late to bed again. Early to rise in the morning eh, Jack? See you then . . . Goodnight, old partner . . .' These were comrades from the trenches.

In the pink house, Edith was still up. She had regarded the bugler too, as she always did, from her bedroom window. In her voluminous white nightdress she resembled a rather overblown angel herself, with long strands of hair bleached of colour in the lamplight. It was strange that the bugler had chosen to play this particular night she thought, for there was no rhyme or reason behind his appearances. Surely, Angel must have heard him, if not seen him: would *she* sleep well tonight? Perhaps she herself would, now the cause of all her bad dreams was just a few steps away across the road.

CHAPTER FOUR

Angel awoke later than she had intended, to sudden bright light that made her screw up her eyes as someone briskly pulled her curtains aside.

'Good morning, Miss.' Another stranger, a girl with tangled conker brown hair tied back from her smooth-skinned young face with a ragged scrap of ribbon. A tall girl, slim-waisted, with a full bosom pushing against the skimpiness of the cheap material of her blouse, frayed at the collar, with sleeves rolled high ready for work.

'I'm Jess, from The Cotts. I saw you yesterday when you went by. Such a beautiful day it is: the Missus sent me up with the tea for she's busy frying – young Tony fetched field mushrooms early on. Guv'nor, well, he's gone to the station to pick up your trunk. I set your cup on your table, mind how you sit up, or you might spill it . . .'

Angel, bemused, duly took care, smiling back at the pretty girl who now perched boldly on the end of her bed.

'Do you work here too, Jess?' she asked.

She nodded. 'I see to the rough work, clean them old spittoons in the bar – coo, they take some scrubbing! Then I fill 'em with nice fresh sawdust. I clear the floor too, wash it over and re-straw it, that soon gets trampled on, I can tell you. Then I go out to the privies and I scrub *them* – use a lot of Lysol here, we do—'

This was rather off-putting for Angel as she sipped her tea. However, the beaming girl obviously took a pride in her duties. She certainly reeked of the disinfectant she had used.

'I live with my nana – she used to be the midwife around here, but old Miss Fenner, when she first come, she say it's time Nana retired, that she would visit them expecting and give 'em advice – tell 'em when they should go to the doctor, like . . .'

That sounded just like Sister Edith, Angel thought wryly.

'Still,' Jess continued, her round cheeks dimpling delightfully, 'My nana still see to warts and pushes and the laying-out, when folks is poor-but-proud, as they say—'

'Pushes?' Angel queried, puzzled.

'Oh, boils, do you call them? My nana, she does all the old remedies, she makes a splendid belladonna plaster, and a hoss liniment the old boys swear by for themselves as well as their hosses!' Although she appeared so friendly, Angel recognised a challenge in those direct green eyes, flecked with golden freckles. 'My nana,' asserted Jess, unaware that she was echoing the words which had made Edith smart so yesterday, 'is the *only* nurse we need round here.'

'I see.' Angel immediately took her meaning. 'Look, Jess, I'm not here as a village nurse, you know, Alice will be my sole patient I assure you.'

'That's all right then.' Jess rose, took the empty cup and saucer. 'Is that real silk, your nighty?' she asked admiringly.

Angel immediately felt conspicuous in her sleeveless, pale-blue slip. 'Yes. A birthday present from my sister. She has a dress shop in London.' Somehow she didn't want down-to-earth Jess to think her frivolous. 'I should get up now, I think,' she added, 'is Alice awake do you know?'

'She is. I propped her up, for her tea.'

As Jess was about to depart, Angel said suddenly, 'Jess, you know everyone round here, of course. Do you—?' How could she put it?

'Do I know the bugler?' The girl turned her head, her expression wary now. 'You heard him, saw him, did you last night? Don't you be troubled, Miss, he's harmless.' Then she was gone.

After breakfast, Angel unwound the bandage, lifting the dressing with infinite care from Alice's ear. She bit her lip as the livid puckered scar was revealed. She could see that it had been a huge abscess.

'I *do* like your hair, I wish I could have mine like that,' Alice said wistfully, as Angel's silky bob brushed her face.

The idea came to Angel instantly. She knew that

Alice could have no concept of the extent of the disfigurement until the dressings were finally discarded. The tight plaits would be far too revealing. 'You could have a similar style, I believe – your hair is fine like mine – I had really spindly plaits as a child! It would be so much easier to care for – you could wash and just brush it through yourself. I used to trim my sister Lou's hair: when you feel better, I'll ask Aunt Hetty if I can bob yours, shall I? A fringe would suit you, too, I think.' A collar-length bob, she thought, would conceal all, very nicely.

'Oh, I *am* glad you came, Angel,' Alice said. 'You're very kind, because you've really got masses more hair than me – I've got hair just like Lalla, Aunt Hetty says . . .'

Angel smiled, but remembering Rob's warning, did not comment further. However, she would ask Alice, too, about the bugler, she thought.

She assisted Alice on to the chair while she re-made the bed. 'Alice, did you hear anything – well, odd, last night?'

'The bugler, you mean?' Alice was direct, like Jess.

'Yes. When I went downstairs for your jug of water, I saw him, from the kitchen window – when I came up again you were almost asleep, so I didn't like to ask you then.'

'Can you keep a secret?' Alice asked gravely, as Angel plumped her pillows.

'Yes, but *is* it a secret?'

‘Sort of. *We* all know, of course, and Jess – and Nana Elderberry – and Edith, because *she* knew him already, you see, from when she was Sister-in-Charge at that convalescent home for ex-servicemen not far from here, by the sea – I expect you knew that?’

‘Oh, yes. She was there several years, wasn’t she, until her aunt died and left her the pink house and a small annuity – she wrote to me all about it.’ Edith’s letters, the early ones, had been full of the broken men she cared for, broken in mind as well as body, some shell-shocked, some still suffering from the terrible effects of mustard gas which had almost destroyed their lungs, or blinded them. Many would live, linger on, but never fully recover. Those letters had been disturbing.

Alice went on: ‘The bugler – his memory is gone – came out here to stay with Edith one weekend. She likes to keep in touch with her old patients in the home. She asked Dad to chat to him, thinking it might help, because he finds it difficult to talk. He took to Dad, it seems, and a few weeks later, he left the nursing home, found his way back here and sheltered in our barn one night, which is where Dad found him. He’s been here ever since—’

‘And will continue to stay – just as long as he wishes,’ a cool voice said from the open doorway which led to Angel’s bedroom. ‘I knocked, guessed you were through here with Alice – I have left your trunk by the window,’ Rob added.

'Thank you,' Angel said. Would he think her a gossip?

'The bugler,' Rob came into the room, bent over his daughter, then lifted her easily back into her clean bed, 'troubles no one. It is a privilege to supply his few needs. The nursing home is happy to let him stay here, especially as Edith can keep an eye on him. He seems to have no family to care for his welfare. Young Jess has taken it upon herself to keep him company, as often as he feels like it. The war may have officially ended years ago, but the bugler is still hiding from the enemy, from his fears. Apparently, he was already an accomplished pianist, but at the home he played the bugle as part of his rehabilitation. Now and again, he obviously feels the need to play it. Quite a legend has grown round this, locally, and we have done nothing to dispel it, ye'll understand. I can rely on your discretion?' His gaze was very direct.

'Of course you can.' Angel collected Alice's breakfast things. 'I'll be up again in a little while, Alice – rest and read now, eh?'

'Angel says she'll cut my hair, just like hers!' Angel heard Alice tell her father, as she went towards the door.

'Well—'

'Oh, Dad! Men are all the same! Or so Aunt Hetty says – Uncle John told her it was unwomanly to have short hair. Angel looks very attractive though, doesn't she, with *her* short bob? You must agree with that!'

'Looks are not everything, Alice. It's the kind of person you are inside that counts. I don't want you to become vain, like your mother. I think there is more to your character than that.'

It was ridiculous, Angel knew, to feel chagrin because her employer had not said he agreed with his daughter about her appearance. It was also obvious to her now that Rob MacDonald did indeed harbour bitter feelings towards his wife. She went slowly downstairs, struggling with her own feelings, the unbidden attraction she was experiencing already – so soon – for another man. It would be just as well if her job turned out to be of brief duration.

'I'm sorry, Alice, I shouldn't have said that about your mother.'

'Was it true? How do I know,' Alice demanded of her father, 'when Lalla left us all those years ago? I can remember she was beautiful, so perhaps she was entitled to be vain!'

'Lively, lovely, loving – she was all of those, Alice . . .'

'But you *hate* her now, don't you? You must do, you won't talk about her – Tony and I have a right, Dad, to know she did care for us once, even if we never get to understand how she could leave her small children – I know *I* never could! *Angel* understands, because *her* mother left her, too, to be brought up by her sister—'

'For someone who protested she didn't need a

nurse – well, you've soon changed your tune, Alice. I'm glad you approve of Angel, she seems already to have altered your attitude to your illness – made you believe you will be well again very soon: cut your hair, if Aunt Hetty agrees, Angel appears to know what's best for you.'

'Oh, Dad – so do *you*! But you didn't answer my question, you know. Do you hate Lalla for deserting us – when she did, when you were away fighting for your country?'

'She wasn't the only one, I'm afraid, Alice. All right, I loved Lalla deeply, I *thought* she felt the same about me. Though, because of her nature, what had happened in her life in the past, I should have known it couldn't last. I don't hate her – but I'm not sure I'll ever be able to forgive her for what she did to you. Now you are growing up, she should have been here for you. Still,' he ended, trying to lighten what had been a heavy conversation between a daughter who was indeed growing up fast and her father, 'I'll do *my* best – promise!'

Rob held her close for a moment, gently stroking her soft hair. If Lalla walked in the room right at this minute, what would he feel? Would they be able to communicate in a civilised manner? He couldn't tell Alice that the love he had felt for his wife was still tangible, although sharply edged with anguish. She had been the only woman in his life. He believed he could never love another, in that way.

'I must go, Alice. Rest and read, eh, as Angel

wisely suggested. You don't need this rug at the end of the bed, do you? I can take it?'

When Angel went to unpack her trunk, just before lunch, she discovered that the bearskin rug, which she had moved and rolled up, had been tactfully replaced by a bright, rag rug. Rob MacDonald, she thought, was a man in tune with other's feelings, after all. Harry, whom she had loved so passionately, and lost, had been just such a man, too.

CHAPTER FIVE

On Monday morning, Angel accompanied Tony to school. Alice had requested more books, for she insisted she was feeling up to her schoolwork now.

'Would you like me to fetch you any shopping?' she asked Aunt Hetty, who was pummelling dough on the kitchen table for the week's supply of bread. The big earthenware crock took four large loaves.

Steam came in gusts from the scullery, for Aunt Hetty and Jess had been busy since dawn, when Rob lit the fire under the copper, soaking and scrubbing the linen ready for the big boil-up. 'You must let me help with the ironing later.' Angel thought Aunt Hetty was a marvel for her age, so energetic.

'We'll see,' Aunt Hetty answered cheerfully, smearing flour on her face instead of powder, pulling on the elastic dough. 'Shopping? I need some more sewing needles, I don't know where they all go to.'

'In the rugs,' Tony reminded her feelingly. 'Didn't I stab my toe on one last week, Aunt Hetty?'

'You should wear slippers 'round the house,

then,' Aunt Hetty retorted. 'Angel, would you ask Mrs Newsome to add some pudding rice to my Friday order, please – what we don't provide for ourselves, you see, we mostly get delivered. Still, its a good old shop to poke 'round in, you always see something you haven't thought of, that's her secret, here's half-a-crown, see if you can find something that might amuse the children – and a few sweeties, eh?'

Jess came out from the scullery, wiping her damp forehead on her apron. 'Miss – if you have the time, like, would you call on my nana, and ask her to come up here afore we have our dinner? She knows all about you,' she added disarmingly. 'Number three, The Cotts.'

Smiling, Angel was quite sure that Nana did indeed know all about her.

The children at the long rows of desks, double-seaters, facing the blackboard in the high-ceilinged school room, scrambled noisily to their feet, obediently chorusing, 'Good morning, Miss!' as the schoolmaster rapped for attention with his pointer.

Tony endeavoured to slip unobtrusively into his seat, but as this was in the middle row, he was, naturally, spotted.

'A little late, Tony – didn't you hear the bell?' The schoolmaster didn't sound very cross. He looked rather young for such a responsible position, the teaching of the junior children, as well as overall responsibility for the whole school, from eight to fourteen years old. The younger children were placed in the front rows, the more privileged older ones in the back seats.

'My fault. I kept him, I'm afraid, while I talked to his aunt,' Angel put in quickly. Behind the flimsy partition she could discern the chanting of the infants, and the tapping of their teacher's pointer as she indicated simple words on her blackboard.

'You are Miss Rosselli, I take it?' The schoolmaster indicated that his class should sit, resume their writing.

'Yes, and you Mr Fenner – Edi – Miss Fenner's brother,' she amended. He was not unlike Edith: much taller, but thickset, with receding hair, fairer than his sister, a contrastingly dark moustache and eyebrows which he had neglected to trim, for, judging by his clothes, he was an untidy man. Angel warmed to him immediately, to the ink and tobacco stains on his fingers, the patches on his jacket elbows, the crumpled handkerchief looping from his breast pocket. Edith's fierce efficiency had obviously not rubbed off on her younger brother.

'You have come to collect Alice's work?' When Angel nodded, Edmund Fenner called to a big girl who was bending over another's desk, obviously helping with a problem: 'Stella, will you take charge for a few minutes, please? I shall be in my study, if you need me. This way, Miss Rosselli.'

When they were inside the cubbyhole, which was almost taken up with a large desk, and laden bookcases lining the walls, Edmund Fenner told

Angel, as he rummaged in a drawer, 'Out of the children's hearing, of course, I presume we may be on Christian name terms?'

'I should like that.' She felt shy, for they were in close proximity in such a restricted space. 'Edmund,' she added.

'Here you are,' he smiled. He handed her a sheaf of paper, a history textbook, in a brown paper cover. 'I have written out the parts to be studied, and the essay to be written – all in good time, for I know Alice has not recovered her full strength as yet. She is a most able pupil, there is not much more I can teach her here, within my restraints. When she is thirteen, I hope she will try for a scholarship to the Grammar School. It is quite a way to travel, unfortunately, but then, a solution might be found – weekly boarders are sometimes considered, for several of the staff live locally. I must return to my class before it is awash with paper darts! I do hope we shall meet more informally soon – Edith tells me she intends to invite us both to dinner, when you are settled in.'

'I look forward to that. Have you lived here long?' she asked as he escorted her to the front entrance. Edmund bent to pat the yellow dog, waiting patiently, stretched out on the step, head on paws, for the first break in lessons.

'Four years. Edith wrote to tell me that this post would shortly become vacant – so I applied. I was tired of working in the city, you see, where I had been since I left the Army, and although it took me some time to adjust, I envisage staying here for as long as the authorities say I may. I felt Edith was glad to have me near. Like you, forgive me for mentioning this, she suffered the loss of someone dear to her in the Great War . . . I do understand, having been so fortunate to come through unscathed myself,' he ended quietly.

Angel hoped that her surprise did not show. Perhaps she had been so bound up in her own love for Harry, so grief-stricken after what had happened, that she had been unaware that Edith, too, had a lover. This was puzzling, but not unbelievable, for at the time, Edith would not have been much older than she, Angel, was now.

The yellow dog nuzzled her hand. 'What's his name?' she asked Edmund.

'Boniface,' Edmund grinned, 'but he's not quite as saintly as his name, or looks, suggest – though he is very tolerant of the children. Well, goodbye, then, Angel.' His handshake was firm and warm.

'Goodbye,' she replied.

They had passed Mrs Newsome's shop on the way to school – being in a hurry, also it seemed practical, Angel thought, to shop on the return journey: just as well, for the history book quite weighed down her basket.

She also intended to visit the bakehouse. Despite the loaves she had seen in the proving at The Angel, she would buy Alice and the others, something extravagant, jammy and creamy, she determined.

Now she retraced her steps of – was it really only three days ago? – to The Cotts. The door of number three was wedged open, just as if she was expected, she fancied. Nevertheless, she knocked politely with her knuckles, awaiting permission to enter.

From the bright sunlight outside she walked into a dim room, cold as charity. The voice that called: 'Come you on inside!' the same greeting she had received from Aunt Hetty, did not sound that of an elderly person. When her eyes had adjusted to the gloom, she saw a tall, straight-backed woman, poker in hand, for she had obviously been riddling the ashes from the stove. The woman must be over sixty, she calculated, but certainly did not look it, with the same red-brown hair as her granddaughter and the same bright, inquisitive flecked eyes. Nana Elderberry's face was not as plump or round, naturally as Jess's – her hands were swollen-jointed and worn – also she had few remaining teeth, whereas Jess's dimpling smile had revealed a splendid set.

'Sit you down, Nurse,' she offered, proffering a chair with rickety legs and a sagging seat. Angel lowered herself very carefully, placing her basket at her feet. So, Nana knew exactly who she was . . .

'I have a message, Mrs Elderberry, from Jess—'

'She wants to stay there longer, to get all the washing done,' Nana stated. 'She wants me to bring the baby up to her, eh? So she can nurse the little scrap? You tell her, Nana'll be with her directly.'

Startled, Angel now perceived that there was a crudely made wooden cradle in the recess by the stove. No one had mentioned that Jess was a mother, she thought.

Nana reached in the cradle and brought forth a tiny baby to show Angel. 'There my dear, isn't she just beautiful? She come into the world, bless her, straight into her Nana's hands and into our hearts. Here, you hold her, whilst I pour you some tea. Pot's still hot.'

Into Angel's arms Nana, smiling, placed the baby.

She felt the sudden rush of tears pricking her eyelids. She blinked them rapidly away. New babies always affected her thus. She could never have been a midwife she thought; for her arms trembled as she shifted the baby to hold her more securely. She looked down into what really was a lovely little face, not just the verdict of a proud great-grandmother she mused. Round eyes, still blue, regarded her solemnly, then the baby's mouth opened emitting a little happy crowing. Angel saw the dimples flash in the soft cheeks. With a gentle finger she explored these tiny indentations, then she brushed her lips against the dark downy head.

'You should have one of your own, my dear.' Nana noisily drained the tea from a handleless cup, removing the tea leaves between finger and thumb, wiping the cup round inside with the corner of her grubby apron before refilling it with strong tea and a mere dash of milk.

'I'm not married, nor likely to be,' Angel said simply. 'I lost my fiancé in the war, you see.' Then she coloured up remembering that Jess had worn no wedding ring.

Nana was not put out. 'I'll have Belinda back again – you drink your tea, before it cools.'

Angel would not have offended Nana for the world, even though she had seen the cleaning of the cup. She took a deep breath, and like Nana gulped her tea down.

'You're not like that Miss Fenner,' Nana told her, Belinda tucked casually under one arm, while she stretched for a lid for the cast iron pot on the stove. 'Told me I was too long in the tooth, she did – that I should give up on nursing – a young gal like her, retired already! Whatever does she find to do, all day, I wonder?'

Angel had to smile at the description of Edith, as a gal. It was obvious that her friend had upset Nana Elderberry, though it was equally obvious that hygiene and Nana did not go together. The baby was clean, mind, but her long gown smelled of dribbled, stale milk. However, Belinda the beautiful was obviously thriving!

'I must get back to Alice,' she said. 'Thank you for the tea, it was most refreshing. I'll see you both when you come along later to The Angel, eh?'

'A touch of olive oil, rubbed gently, that eases the tightest scar,' Nana advised. 'I could've stopped that ear infection, if Aunt Hetty'd called me, as she used to before Miss Fenner come. Retired she may say, but bossy, she be.'

I don't blame her for being indignant, at being ousted, Angel thought, but, of course, I can understand why Edith interfered . . .

She smiled at Nana. 'Jess is lucky to have you mind her baby, while she's working.' She meant it. 'Goodbye for now.'

'Fare ye well,' Nana replied, with old-fashioned courtesy.

Angel left the bakehouse with half-a-dozen jam puffs in a bag, for they looked so delicious; she wanted to treat all the workers at The Angel for elevenses – including herself and Alice too, of course! And not forgetting one pastry for Tony for his tea.

At Mrs Newsome's, Angel made another new friend, her third within the space of a mere hour.

'Just missed the crowd,' Mrs Newsome confided cheerfully. 'They all want to meet you. Now, what can I do for you today?'

Mrs Newsome was motherly, talkative, ample-figured but extremely quick on her feet. Nimble-fingered, too, as Angel saw, watching fascinated, the deft twirling of newspaper 'pokes' to accommodate 2 ounces of aniseed balls, giant gobstoppers for Tony – 'that lad'll crack his jaw!' Mrs Newsome reckoned, and a bundle or two of red and black liquorice skipping ropes. A stout blue bag held a shovelful of shining white rice, dug from one of the sacks in front of the counter: 'Aunt Hetty might be glad of it, before the end of the week – don't need to pay for it today, my dear.' Drawing books and chalks were reached down from a high shelf. The shop was almost bursting at the seams, Angel fancied, as she ducked under streamers of bright ribbons in the haberdashery section, while Mrs Newsome delved for the sewing needles. There was a brass rule along the counter, for measuring the flipped-over bales of cheap and colourful cotton prints; boxes of buttons in every size and hue, from glass to horn; corsets and calico; 'snap' fasteners and hooks-and-eyes; darning wool, waxed thread and good, strong cotton to wear down your teeth when you bit it at the end of a hem – everything for the home dressmaker. The grocery counter boasted round yellow cheese; butter to pat to size; flanks of bacon to slice with a lethally sharp knife. Big silver tins of biscuits with the name embossed: Rich Tea, Osborne, Figgies. And a box labelled: Broken Bis. 3d. per lb.

'You want it – likely we got it – if not, we'll get it.' Mrs Newsome totted up Angel's purchases on the back of a torn paper bag, then tossed the coins into her shoe box till.

'Think you'll like it here, my dear?' she asked next, loading Angel's basket on the long mahogany counter.

'Oh, yes!' Angel was very sure of that. The only little niggle she had, was that the village folk she had met so far obviously did not think too highly of Edith. A fleeting memory struck her, her fellow nurses in France rebelling against Edith's strictures: 'We don't know why *you* always stick up for her, Angel.' But she'd always been nice to Angel, and no one could have been more compassionate when – Angel forced her thoughts back to the present, and to Mrs Newsome saying: 'And here's a little something for young Alice, from me – say Jinny Newsome sent it . . .' The tiny bottle of scent, in its turn, was concealed in a 'poke'. 'She must miss her mother, poor child, even though she was but five, and young Tony only three, when Mrs Fly-by-Night ran off: *he* was heartbroken when he come home from the war and found she'd gone.'

I ought not to let her tell me this, Angel thought, but she listened all the same. It would help to have some inkling of what the children and their father had been through, she reasoned with herself.

'That Lalla,' Mrs Newsome confided, 'come here to paint one summer, lodged at The Angel. Beautiful, she was, give her that, but hoity with it. Aunt Hetty never approved. But Rob was set on marrying her, she stayed on and they tied the knot that Christmas, in our church. Didn't see no relations of hers at the wedding but Aunt Hetty and her husband splashed out – what a beautiful dress she had! From a shop in town, of course. She let Aunt Hetty carry on as before, all she cared for was her pictures – mind, she do some beautiful painting, all them sunsets—'

'I know.' Angel had to put a stop to it, she felt too guilty. 'There's so much more sky . . .'

'That's it,' Mrs Newsome beamed. 'Well, I mustn't keep you, eh? Please call again, soon!'

She was right, Angel thought ruefully, as she forked sharp to walk back to The Angel – she *had* to break in, fascinating as the story of Rob and his wayward wife was – it really was none of her business and she was sure that her employer would not have approved.

She must get back as quickly as she could, or the jam puffs would spoil in the hot sun.

CHAPTER SIX

'Do stay, Nana my dear, and have a bite to eat,' Aunt Hetty offered hospitably, generously slicing at the still-warm, yeasty-smelling bread. 'Pot luck, being washday, but you're more than welcome.'

'I won't say no,' Nana agreed complacently, settling down in the rocker with her plate of bread and cheese with thick brown chutney on the side, and a glass of stout at her elbow, which Rob had poured from a brimming jug brought out from the bar. Belinda slept on her lap untroubled by the crumbs.

It wasn't that long since they'd consumed those delicious jam puffs, Angel realised, she would soon put on weight if this went on! However, she found herself tucking in with relish. She was fascinated by the soft Suffolk sing-song, 'Nana', not clipped but drawled as 'Nanner'. She felt it was rather a shame that the children were encouraged at school to iron-out their use of dialect. To Angel, it seemed that the young ones would forfeit some of the easy almost poetic rhythm of speech evolved over centuries. This was a farming community, though most were tenant farmers or farm labourers, the work-force had been cruelly decimated by the recent war. There would undoubtedly be changes due to this, the emphasis on education would mean that the younger folk would look further afield for employment. They had to 'fit in'.

Jess finished her lunch, '*He* needs his sustenance now,' she said. No one commented when she tied a hunk of bread and a great slice of cheese in a pudding cloth, took the baby from Nana and left the company without another word.

'I must get back to work, plenty to do,' Rob sighed, pushing back his chair. He looked at Angel, 'Later on, I'll bring Alice downstairs as you suggested, so that she can be with you out in the garden. Aunt Hetty will show you where we keep the long chair with wheels. I suggest you put it under the shade of the trees. Goodbye to ye, Nana Elderberry,' he added.

'Fare ye well,' Nana replied, in turn.

Angel was still sitting at the table, facing the window, gazing out idly, as Jess, with beautiful Belinda in her arms, made her way down the meadow towards the barn. Before the treacherous memories could rise to the surface, triggered by the sight of Jess pulling open the barn door then going inside, Angel jumped to her feet.

'I must go up to Alice – shall I take my tea with hers, Aunt Hetty?'

The bugler lay stretched out on his bed, on the crocheted coverlet made by Jess from the odd balls of wool donated by Aunt Hetty and Edith, the opened book face-down on his chest. It was a book he had brought back with him from France, one of the few things he had kept in his locker at the nursing home. He often appeared to be reading, but Jess was not sure that he actually took in the printed words on the dog-eared pages. She wished that she had attended school more regularly, not been in such a hurry to leave, perhaps then she might have learned to read more fluently, perhaps then she might have been allowed to read aloud to him from this old book he obviously treasured.

'Jess . . .' he murmured, slowly sitting up, then swinging his legs to the ground. He closed the book, pushed it under his pillow. Despite the troubled, deep-set dark blue eyes, his pale face was still youthful, clean shaven. The ruffled hair, too long, made Jess want to smooth it back, behind his ears, but she resisted the temptation.

'Brought yer grub,' she said cheerfully, relieving herself of the bundle of food. He unwrapped it slowly, began to eat.

'Thank you, Jess.'

She sat down beside him, laying the drowsy Belinda down between them. Her eyes quickly adapted to the gloom, being used to the poor light in The Cotts. It was she who kept the interior of the barn swept and tidy, but Aunt Hetty, Rob and Edith who had contributed to its furnishings. There was a table; a pair of sturdy but unmatched kitchen chairs; a single bed, which doubled as a couch; coconut matting on the floor; an oil stove; some cooking pots and crocks; a trunk, containing the bugler's personal possessions and change of clothes; and a lamp, hanging from a hook fixed to the beam above. Sacking was nailed neatly across gaps in the barn timbers, and Rob had fixed up shelves: on the top one a long line of books leaned tipsily. On the easy chair, a tortoiseshell cat, ousted by the latest crop of kitlings in The Angel, curled, purring, an obvious deterrent to any lurking mice.

He shook the crumbs from the cloth, folded it neatly and regarded Jess gravely for a moment. Then he lifted the baby, smiling, and held her over his shoulder, gently massaging her back. Belinda obligingly burped.

'You know about babies,' Jess observed. She wasn't going to allow herself to conjecture about this, except *she* couldn't be the first woman in his life . . .

'You're tired, Jess.' His face was concerned.

'I am . . .' she yawned widely, let him take her sore, red hands in his large, warm clasp. Belinda wriggled between the two. 'But I'm never too tired for *you*—' She stretched out, her head on his pillow, closed her eyes with sheer fatigue.

'Ah, Jess – if only—' his hesitant voice was thick with regret.

'You – are *you*. That's all *I* care about.'

When Angel returned from ministering to Alice, she found Nana still resting in the rocker while Aunt Hetty cleared the table.

'Gal all right?' Nana flapped her skirt vigorously at the sly kitling who dared to fancy a snooze on her lap.

'Doing very well indeed.' Angel was happy that Alice should have made such excellent progress since her arrival.

'My old mother,' Nana reflected, 'now she *was* a nurse . . . You recall, Aunt Hetty, I daresay, how when she had a patient failing fast, from that dratted poo-moan-ya, how she walked the street, and all the curtains drawn – carried a pillow, she did.'

'Pneumonia,' Angel murmured, bemused. As for the pillow, *she*, of course, knew the reason, only too well . . . Edith, too. She shuddered.

'Give 'em blessed relief she did,' Nana went on, her shrewd gaze on Angel's expressive face. 'Freed 'em from all pain.'

After a long moment, Angel said slowly, 'No one stopped her?'

'Stop her, my dear? 'Twas the dying, or their near and dear ones, as sent for Mother . . .'

'You're alarming our modern young nurse, Nana,' Aunt Hetty scolded. 'Ah, here comes your Jess – and Belinda ready to go home to her cradle, eh?'

Angel saw that Belinda was drowsy, blissfully replete after her feed. On an impulse she bent to kiss the baby's cheek.

'Beautiful, isn't she?' Jess glowed.

'Oh, she really is,' Angel affirmed.

'Fare ye well, together,' Nana's by now familiar refrain.

Angel followed Rob downstairs, as he carried Alice on his back, her arms tight around his neck. 'And I thought you'd grown out of piggy-backs,' he joked affectionately, for her long legs dangled.

They were still out in the garden, basking in the warmth, Angel feeling just a little guilty at being so lazy, when Tony came running up the path, slinging his school bag, and his lunch tin under the porch, as he spotted them.

'Oh, good, lemonade!' he cried, pouring a glassful and drinking thirstily.

'That was for *us*!' Alice made a half-hearted protest, knowing it was expected of her. 'You can fetch some more now. Aunt Hetty made *pints* of it – it's in the pantry.'

'I'd rather have the fizz from the pub,' Tony said cheerfully, but he took the jug and went to replenish it.

'There's a jam puff for you, if you're hungry.' Angel called after him.

'He's *always* hungry,' Alice said. 'But he's got to do his chores before he has his tea. We used to take it in turn, before I was ill, but *he* has to milk the goat. We don't get much from her, because the kids aren't quite weaned, but what there is, we give to the bugler.'

'Does he ever venture outside, you know, in the day?' Angel was curious, she couldn't help it, the idea of a sad man, badly damaged in mind, by war, living such a reclusive life, intrigued her. He must have suffered greatly, she thought, to have such a memory block.

'I've never seen him close to,' Alice answered.

'Doesn't anyone know his real identity?'

'Oh, Edith must, of course – maybe Dad, too, I don't know. They named him The Bugler at the nursing home, and Edith says it's best left that way. His name would mean nothing to him. Edith says that his mother died in the influenza epidemic just after the war. There's no one else, as far as Edith knows . . .'

Tony returned, a full jug of lemonade in one hand, a clanking, empty pail in the other. 'Aunt Hetty says are you coming in soon, Alice? Dad's setting up the bar. He'll fetch you, after.'

They all watched as the friendly nanny goat came ambling up to Tony, pulling the tethering rope taut. He caught the little kids, one by one and brought them to Angel and Alice. 'Hold them tight – they won't butt in then.'

They stroked and patted the wriggling goatlings, who only had one thought, to return to their mother's flanks. 'One's a boy, one's a girl,' Alice told Angel. 'We don't give boys a name, because we can't keep them. Blossom, I want to call this one, but Tony insists he wants Snowball, just because she's white. The nanny goat is Nancy.'

'I've never been this near a goat before,' Angel smiled. They were bony creatures, she discovered, with tiny protuberances where their horns would grow, and harsh, sparse coats. But their inquisitive noses, their bright eyes, she found most attractive.

Jess, looking really tired, popped out to say she was going, and for them to tell Aunt Hetty, please, for she'd not been in the kitchen just now, but she'd worked her time to the minute. However, she didn't actually leave right then. Without another word, she looked to see if Tony had finished milking, then relieved him of the pail, and went on down to the barn. After a few minutes, she re-emerged, walked back past them, with a cheerful wave.

I wonder how she got to know him, Angel wondered, and if Belinda—? Then she dismissed the thought from her mind.

'Here's your dad, Alice. Back to bed for you, I'm afraid,' she said now briskly, seeing Rob.

'Aw!' Alice protested, but her earlier animation was fading fast, Rob had timed it right.

The kids went bounding back to their mother, no doubt intent on finding out if Tony had milked her dry.

After Alice was settled, Angel and Tony folded the linen piled high in the laundry basket, while Rob carved from Sunday's goose. 'Cold again, I'm afraid, that's Mondays, and running a pub for you . . .'

Aunt Hetty shook the earth from a young lettuce, which she had grown under a frame in her kitchen garden and prepared a hasty salad. Still, there were scrubbed, jacket potatoes wrinkling their skins in the oven, plenty of farm butter and refreshing hot tea, as always. Angel was thoroughly enjoying the good, plain fare served up at The Angel.

She learned the rudiments of chess that evening, with Tony and Alice. When Rob came to say goodnight, he said approvingly: 'It's good to hear you laughing again, Alice. Now you must get a sound night's sleep, for you have your appointment at the hospital tomorrow. Will ye come with us, Angel?'

'Of course,' she said immediately, moving from her perch on the side of Alice's bed, so that Rob could reach his daughter to kiss her. 'That's what I'm here for, Rob. How far away is the hospital?'

'About thirteen miles. We'll be gone most of the day – Aunt Hetty will cope here, and Jess will, no doubt, be willing to work awhile in the bar, until I return. I hope this will be Alice's final visit, just a check to make sure all is well, although the doctor here and Edith – you, too – assure us that it is. We'll need to leave around eight-thirty,' he added. 'Early breakfast – Aunt Hetty will call you.'

They went out of the room together, Tony running downstairs ahead of them, to beg a crunchy Suffolk rusk and a glass of milk from his aunt, before he, too, went to bed.

'I'll see he washes and says his prayers,' Angel offered. 'Aunt Hetty must be worn out after such a busy day.'

He paused, his face concerned. 'You think I should get more help for her, Angel?'

'Oh, I don't think she would accept it.' Angel hoped he didn't think she was interfering with his domestic arrangements. *If his wife was here* . . . she thought involuntarily.

As if he could read her thoughts, Rob said, very seriously, 'My wife did nothing here, nothing at all. Aunt Hetty took it all on her shoulders. She is a wonderful woman. No, we do not miss *her*. Well, I must return to my work, Angel. I bid ye goodnight.'

Even as she returned the wishes, Angel realised that his assertion had been much too vehement. Of course, he must still miss Lalla, whatever her shortcomings, as she still yearned for Harry. The pain of losing diminished, but the gap was always there.

Tony's prayers were a leisurely affair, Angel guessed that he was stringing them out to keep her there – he certainly didn't look in the least sleepy.

'Pity my simple city,' he recited, in the familiar GENTLE JESUS, the children's prayer, which Angel had learned from Lou: 'that should be simplicity, you know,' he put in ingenuously. 'Alice tells me off, says I should say it properly, at my age, but I like it better—'

'*I* always said, "pity mice implicitly",' Angel said softly, 'and that made me give a little shiver, because I was – am! – afraid of mice, and I had to look up "implicitly" in the dictionary – do carry on, Tony, it's getting late.' But she did not sound in the least reproving.

As she left him, nicely tucked in, even though he was quite old, as he so often reminded them – she guessed, not for long, for the nightlight was still burning, and there was *Comic Cuts* tucked under the covers, she heard him singing to himself:

Now the day is over
Night is drawing nigh
Shadows of the evening
Steal across the sky.

Tony missed a verse or two, then he called out, obviously aware that she was lingering outside his door: 'This verse is 'specially for you, Angel . . .'

Through the long night watches
May thy *angels* spread
Their white wings above me,
Watching round my bed.

She didn't know why on earth she should be forced to wipe tears from her eyes. She stopped by the landing window, searching for her handkerchief. Yet another glorious sky spread before her. Had Lalla, the artist, sung that simple hymn with her children each night?

CHAPTER SEVEN

Tony was up early, but his father had beaten him to it and had already pumped up the day's supply of water.

'Will ye fetch the milk this morning, Tony? I must gain time where I can, with being out all day – Aunt Hetty will have enough to do.'

'I don't see why I can't come to the hospital, too.' Tony thought it was worth a try. He fetched the scalded milk cans from the pantry. Maybe, if he showed willing—

'Sorry, but no, old chap. Nurse will be aboard, naturally, Aunt Hetty will be glad of your help when you get in from school. Take your cart, I should, eh?'

The cart was just an orange box on wheels, with a handle to pull. The last thing Tony had carted in it had been a load of manure, from the stable for Aunt Hetty's vegetable plots and he had only given it a perfunctory scraping-out. However, it didn't pong too badly, and he intended to coast downhill in the cart, where he could.

Doing just that, he narrowly missed the girl coming out of the lodge gate, with a china jug dangling from her fingers by the handle. 'Watch out!' she yelled, backing hastily on to the prickly hedge.

'Sorry – Fairy!' The cart ground to a bumping stop, and Tony jumped out, grinned at the girl. 'Put your jug in with mine – I'll walk you down to the farm,' he offered.

It paid to keep on the right side of Fairy Aldred, he thought ruefully, remembering the fat lip she had given him in the schoolyard a month or so ago. Fairy, they called her, and it was obvious why, because she had a great mop of silvery blonde hair which didn't look as if it ever saw a comb. She was two years older than Tony, Alice's age, but she was already reputed to have a regular boyfriend, whom she shared with her best friend, Mina Bird.

'Got a great thorn in me arm, cor blast it,' Fairy moaned. 'Had to get up even earlier this morning, seeing as Dad is taking *your* lot to town . . .'

They went up the long narrow track alongside the great oaks that guarded the Big House, jolting the cart between them to the Home Farm dairy.

Milking was still in progress. ''Lo Mina,' Fairy said to the nimble-fingered girl with her head pressed against the cow's side, squirting streams of milk into her bucket.

'Dad's got a churn already,' she said, squinting up at them. Then, 'Cor blast it!' she exclaimed. 'That's another hairpin gone – pull it out, will you, Tony, and catch me hair back off me face?'

Tony unthreaded the pin from the cow's brown

and white hair. 'Done it, Mina,' he said. He was in awe of these two big girls who ruled the schoolyard when the schoolmaster, or Stella the monitor weren't looking.

'Cor blast it!' he mouthed to himself, delighting in words he wouldn't dare use at home.

Mina's mother ladled the frothy milk into the cans. 'That's yours done, Tony. Skimmed for you, young Fairy? It's still got a bit of cream in it – I can't see why Aunt Hetty don't save her pennies and have that, Tony, eh?'

'We've got to build Alice up – she needs all the cream she can get,' Tony said grandly. But he thought privately that Alice would probably never have lovely firm limbs on her like Fairy and Mina. Tony, like Alice was growing up.

Those years she had spent selling smart frocks to young ladies in Lou's exclusive little dress shop, after Lou had said bluntly that it was high time she began earning her keep again, even if she felt she could not resume her nursing career, had proved worthwhile after all. For Angel possessed a trunkful of garments that she could never have afforded on a nurse's salary.

Clothes bought for a few shillings, marked-down when a collar was marked by lip rouge, a trying-on where a careless heel had caught in a hem, or a seam split when a customer huffily insisted that a frock was the right size . . . None of them, of course, very suitable for her present country existence, for most required careful hand-washing or steam-cleaning. However, they were all she had, except for the couple of sensible dresses she wore every day. She had not kept her uniform, after the war.

It was just the day for an outing, she thought impulsively, and at soon after six in the morning, she was already washed and dressed in a sea-green silk sleeveless frock, mid-calf length and low-waisted. She hoped that the careful darning of her precious best stockings would go unnoticed. She prolonged the life of her cotton pairs by rubbing the heels and toes with beeswax: these were so much more comfortable to wear but very fragile.

Downstairs she went on tip-toe, determined to surprise dear Aunt Hetty with an early cup of tea as a treat. Rob's door was slightly ajar, but then, he was always first up, for there was a day's water to pump up, she thought.

The pails under the sink were indeed brimming with fresh, chill water. She made a big pot of tea, set it to brew, then bent over the pail to fill her dipper, for the kettle must always be replenished. Rob had obviously riddled and stoked the stove fire. She was unaware that he had padded into the kitchen behind her in his stockinged feet, for he had, as all house-trained men must do, left his boots, muddied by the splashing pump water, outside in the porch. She would have coloured-up hotly if she had realised that he could see the dimples at the back of her knees as she stooped to her task, and that he was smiling at the voluminous apron she had donned to cover her dress, hanging almost to her toes at the front, while her skirt rode up at the back.

Angel straightened up, rested the dipper on the draining board for a second and looked out at the morning. That rhythmic sound of water gushing at the pump, was, with his back to her, naked to the waist, the bugler, making his ablutions. Water soused his head, plastered his long hair darkly to his neck and coursed over his shoulders. Pale-skinned he was, due to being shut away all day, she thought, too thin, with jutting shoulder blades. As she stared, mesmerised, she saw Jess coming up the path, then putting down her basket. Jess disappeared into the scullery and emerged seconds later with a towel, which she draped solicitously around the bugler's torso, then, as Angel had seen her do that first night at sunset, she led him away, back to the barn and his self-imposed solitude.

'You are early,' Rob observed, startling her. 'Our friend likes to wash, unseen.'

She recognised the mild reproof. 'I'm so sorry—' she faltered, 'I really didn't intend to pry. It was just – unexpected – that's all.'

He smiled. 'So are you, Angel. A charming sight, at this hour.'

His frank approval of her appearance was unexpected. Now she did blush, covering up her confusion with the pouring out of the tea.

Aunt Hetty was just about to rise and she, too,

remarked approvingly on Angel's appearance. 'You look nice!'

'There's a hat to match, but I think I'd better wear my sensible shoes,' Angel added ruefully, 'if we're to tramp those endless hospital corridors, eh?'

Later, she helped Alice with her dressing, but determined privately to do a little less in that respect each succeeding day.

Alice had been treated as a baby for too long, she thought: Aunt Hetty was so kind, fussing over her chick as she did, but Alice must resume her independence as soon as possible.

She brushed Alice's soft hair back, but did not plait it, merely tied it with one of Lou's wide satin bows. If the dressing came off today, she told herself, she would be able to get busy with Aunt Hetty's sharp, dressmaking scissors.

'I've grown too tall since I've been ill,' Alice lamented, staring at her stick-thin limbs in the long mirror. Her plain dress was not short in the fashionable sense, more outgrown.

'A serious illness, particularly a fever, seems often to have that effect,' Angel reassured her. 'Still, you are at an age, Alice, when you can expect a rapid spurt of growth, after all, you'll soon be a young woman.'

Alice shot her a wary glance. Angel guessed that she was wondering what was coming next. A girl, rising thirteen, needed a mother to talk to, she thought compassionately. Aunt Hetty might not realise this, being older and having had no children of her own. Angel had felt the lack herself, when she was growing up and frightened by the changes in her suddenly burgeoning body. Lou had not thought to enlighten her about one very important thing. 'I must be *dying*, Lou!' she had blurted out, for why else would she be bleeding like that? She couldn't let that happen to Alice.

Now, she said merely, 'If you ever want to talk about things, in that respect, Alice, I am always here. It sometimes isn't nearly so embarrassing to ask questions of someone other than family – *I* know! It may help to remember I am a nurse, then . . .'

'Thank you,' Alice said awkwardly. However, as a country child, she was not as ignorant as the city child that Angel had been.

'Eat your scrambled eggs up, Alice,' Angel coaxed, when Aunt Hetty deposited the breakfast tray. 'If we are to convince your father that you can stand on your own two feet, and walk more each day, well, you have to get your strength back and that means eating properly, you know!'

Tony was dawdling and seemed unwilling to go to school.

'I'll walk you down,' Jess suggested cheerfully. 'I have to go home to feed Belinda.' She'd already done two hours hard work.

How Jess trotted to and fro, always on her feet, scrubbing and cleaning – caring for her friend cloistered in the barn, too.

'I must fetch water from the pond, too, for Nana,' Jess went on. 'She had one of her bad heads first thing: she took two cloves in her tea. She says that'll ease it.'

'You don't have a pump?' Angel was surprised. She realised ruefully that she already thought of the pump as a great convenience, even after having water on tap, in London.

Jess shook her head. 'No,' she stated. 'We like the old pond water. Nana sticks to the old ways, she even makes her own washing soap from lye. Not many do that nowadays.'

'Lye,' Aunt Hetty enlightened, 'is wood ash dissolved in soft water.'

The simple ways of Nana and her only surviving kin, for Angel had learned that Nana had seen six children die in childhood, despite her remedies, only to lose her remaining daughter when she gave birth to Jess, those simple, well-tried mores were practised as they had been over centuries past.

Angel had expected to travel in the trap, she put a soft shawl in her bag to protect Alice's head and shoulders if necessary – the east wind was always a possibility, and Alice's delicate ear must be covered. However, there was a veritable carriage awaiting: a motor car, long and gleaming, with a spare wheel and can of petrol secured to the running board, for garages were few and far between in the country. It was not a new motor, but a splendid one, the Rolls Royce Silver Ghost of 1911, kept under cover throughout the war years at the Big House, now driven by Fairy Aldred's father, Will, who had gained his expertise when driving a lorry full of troops, or vital supplies, in France.

Rob saw them settled into the back seats before taking his own place in the front beside Will. Aunt Hetty, Jess and Tony waved them off as if they were going to be away for a week, instead of just a day.

'Sheer luxury, Alice, eh?' Angel sank down on the soft leather cushion, filled with purest duck down. There was a handy leather strap for clutching when rounding corners, and the hood was up, in deference to the invalid. The Silver Ghost might be an aristocrat among motor cars, but it made light of the uneven roads along which they travelled.

'Did you see the Silver Lady on the radiator?' Alice was excited. 'Aunt Hetty worked for Lady Pamela at the Big House – in service – before she married, you see, and Lady P. always sends the motor for us, on special occasions. I was even whisked off to hospital last time in it! I keep asking Dad to get us an Austin Seven – you know, it's only a *little* motor, but he says we can't even afford that, and petrol is more expensive than hay . . .'

'My brother-in-law Jack, wants to buy one of those. He and Lou could bring the new baby to see me here, then, couldn't they? But I guess it's only a pipe-dream, unless the dress shop does really well this year—'

'Lalla has an Austin,' Alice lowered her voice, although the glass screen between the front and back seats was in position, Will had switched on the speaking tube. 'Gerald, that's the man my mother went off with, bought it for her. She wrote to tell us about it last Christmas. She sent me a pretty dress then, but, you see, she'd forgotten how I must have grown – anyway, I suppose I could never be little and pretty like her, because Dad's so tall – I couldn't even get my head through the neck opening. Tony was luckier, he had a clockwork car, but he'd overwound it by Boxing Day, and Dad thought he should put it away, until it could be mended.'

Angel did not comment on any of this, because she was all too aware of the sudden stiffening of Rob's shoulders, although he did not turn his head – she was sure he had heard every word Alice said.

The town was busy and bustling, but not as crowded as it would be on Friday, market day, Rob told Angel. 'Once a month, I collect up produce from the smallholders in the village and bring it here in the trap. It makes a fine day out, the children love to come along when they are off school, and Aunt Hetty, too, if Jess will mind the bar. We always get back in good time for the evening opening.'

'Aunt Hetty,' Alice put in, 'always says you come back just as loaded as you went.'

'All the bargains, market day, and what better than to exchange your surplus produce, in a roundabout way, for things you don't grow yourself?' he defended himself, grinning at his daughter, obviously putting her remarks in the motor car out of his mind.

'Like fish, fish and *more* fish?' Alice grimaced, as Rob bowled her along the hospital corridor in a borrowed wheelchair.

'Straight from the boat, fresh from the sea,' Rob reminded her.

To Angel, the pervading smell of carbolic, the narrow, high iron beds glimpsed in the long wards, brought back memories of her nursing training: sometimes, she thought, she had had to refuel her determination to succeed as a nurse by sternly reminding herself of her father, the dedicated doctor. He had died in the service of his adopted country: how often, in the depths of her depression, when she thought how she had had no choice in the abandonment of her own wartime duties, had she wished that she might have given her life, like that.

Groups of people waited patiently to see the doctor, sitting on the edge of the hard, wooden chairs. Acutely, Angel felt the throbbing silence, as in church.

After what seemed hours, they were out in the sunshine once more, and Alice was walking, rather unsteadily, but gamely, to the motor where Will, who had been for a look at the sea, and the fishing boats, while they were away, now awaited their instructions.

'You would like to visit your brother and sister-in-law, I expect, Will?' Rob asked. 'Well, if you would be kind enough to take us to our lunching place, you can call back for us when you're ready, eh?'

'I haven't got to go back to the hospital again, Will!' Alice exulted. 'I'm absolutely recovered!'

Angel and Rob exchanged a quick glance. Angel smiled, 'You're discharged into my care for a while, Alice – and I prescribe whatever you fancy for lunch!'

The Rolls moved off smoothly, with Will's gloved hands steady on the wheel, the callouses and marks of his hard work disguised. 'Pansy will have a nice fat herring for me to eat!' Will called in farewell.

A plate of thin, curling pink ham, with just an edge of fat, brownly breaded: small potatoes, waxy white, buttered and sprinkled with fine-chopped parsley; hot, crusty rolls and shredded salad – they'd enjoyed every mouthful, especially Alice, who showed the first clean plate in months. Iced water, with a twist of lemon, to clear the palate before the apple pie and cream was served to Angel and Rob, and the double portion of vanilla ice cream, with a fluted wafer, for Alice.

They didn't talk much, just smiled at each other from time to time. Angel thought how relieved Rob must be that Alice was on the mend, the bulky dressing at last removed and the first hint of colour returning to her cheeks from that breath of sea air which they had all inhaled enthusiastically before entering the hotel.

A little shop in a narrow back street displayed the perfect gift for Tony. A sailing boat, lovingly crafted by the proprietor, a retired seaman, with sails sewn by his wife and working rigging. *THE MERMAID*, was the name of this miniature craft.

'Nana Elderberry believes in mermaids,' Alice whispered to Angel, as their purchase was wrapped. 'She says she lost her husband at sea when a mermaid pulled his boat under in a terrible, rough storm. *All hands drowned*!' she ended dramatically.

'Where will Tony sail it?' Angel wondered.

'Oh, in the stream – we go swimming in the hot weather, in the river, further up – Dad fixed a board for jumping off, and Aunt Hetty reckons the best watercress you've ever tasted grows in the clear, running water.'

'Talking of Aunt Hetty,' Rob reminded them, 'you must choose a surprise for her, too.'

A gardening sun bonnet, the old-fashioned kind, with a wide frill to cover shoulders and neck, prettily patterned, they spied in the very next shop. Angel couldn't resist a tiny replica for Belinda.

They went back to the car, where Will was surrounded by admiring small boys, leaving fingerprints on the polished sides of the Rolls or daring to just touch the Silver Lady.

They were delivered home just before four o'clock, when Aunt Hetty and Tony came rushing out to ask how the day had gone.

'I must change . . .' Angel murmured. 'Alice, sorry, but back to your bed for a rest after all that excitement . . .'

Did she imagine it, or did Rob bestow a special look in her direction as he told Aunt Hetty: 'Despite the reason for going, yes, it really was a special day out.'

CHAPTER EIGHT

Aunt Hetty was thinning out the seedlings in the vegetable patch. Wearing her sun bonnet, she looked much as her mother had, some fifty years ago. Yet, the design of the bonnet was faultless and she was well-shaded from the rays of the sun.

'Do let me help?' Angel offered – so here she was, too, digging obediently with the small fork, wherever Aunt Hetty indicated. The trug was brimming already with small, curly lettuces, cabbages, spinach and spring onions.

'Jess say she has an idea what to do with any spare,' Aunt Hetty straightened her back with an involuntary, 'ooh!'

Alice lay dreaming over her book, on a rug spread under the tree, running her fingers idly through her silky hair, bobbed and loose to her shoulders, which made her feel quite grown-up and infinitely superior to Tony, sprawled beside her. He was sketching Boniface, who had accompanied his master to The Angel half-an-hour ago. The big dog panted, head on paws, tongue lolling, drops of water still quivering on his whiskers, for he had soon drained the bowl of cold water Rob had kindly pumped up to slake his thirst. Edmund, after a few friendly words with the workers and the idlers, had followed Rob into the bar, to quench his own dry throat, he grinned, for despite a dearth of customers, the bar would be open for a while yet.

When Edmund rejoined Angel and Aunt Hetty, Tony ran up to show him his drawing. It was obvious, Angel mused, admiring his effort, too, that Tony had inherited his mother's skill. The pencil marks were bold, often unjoined, but he had captured the dog's expression, for the panting seemed almost palpable.

'I hope you'll let me have this, when it's finished, Tony – it's well worth mounting and framing – you've really captured my old sinner!' Edmund turned to Angel, 'I was wondering, can you take this evening off, Angel?'

'Well, I can – I am! but I was thinking of going to visit Edith—'

'She's so conscientious,' Aunt Hetty put in. She picked up the brimming trug: 'I'll put this in the scullery. You go as soon as you like Angel, my dear.'

Angel felt guilty at not visiting Edith before this, for after all, it was thanks to her old friend she had come here in the first place, to The Angel where already she felt so much at home, and where the day would soon arrive, she acknowledged sadly to herself, when she would no longer be needed.

'Come for a spin first on my motorcycle, Angel – then we'll *both* descend on my sister. She always has a substantial Saturday supper waiting – anticipating her brother's arrival.'

He expects a polite refusal, Angel thought, well, I'll surprise him! Even though I've never been on a motorcycle in my life – how horrified Lou would be!

To Edmund's pleased surprise, she found herself saying, 'That sounds exciting! I'd love to, Edmund.'

'I've got a spare helmet and some goggles. Angel—' he hesitated.

Tony, avidly listening in, and envious at Angel's luck at being asked to ride pillion, interrupted: 'I wouldn't wear silk stockings if I were you!'

'Er – exactly!' Edmund agreed.

'Or a tight skirt!' Tony said it for him.

In fact, Angel possessed the ideal outfit, courtesy of Lou. A divided skirt for bicycling, so much more ladylike than bloomers!

Tony and Alice insisted on cheering them on their way, when Edmund returned with the motorcycle. Angel gingerly mounted her steed, for she hadn't even ridden a bicycle before – there had been no need in London. The neat, close-fitting leather helmet, a thick, woolly jacket with collar turned up, the goggles to protect her eyes from the slipstream – Angel felt well-equipped for the 'spin'.

'Hold tight!' Aunt Hetty sounded anxious.

'I will, don't worry!' Angel promised. Rob was

nowhere to be seen. She couldn't help wondering if he disapproved.

They sped along the narrow lanes, brushed by the hedgerows, through dappled light and shade, past flat water meadows and ancient cottages with reed roofs. She didn't realise that Edmund was throbbingly aware of the warmth and excitement she generated as she tightened her arms round his waist, with her breath tickling the back of his neck.

'Oh, I loved it!' she cried, breathlessly, as they cruised to a halt by a stile. She unbuckled the helmet, pulled it off, shook her hair into a dark cloud, then she sprang lithely over the stile, dropping with a soft thud on the grass on the other side.

'We pick blackberries here in the autumn,' Edmund told her, as they strolled along.

It happened so suddenly that they were both taken by surprise. The blue sky stretched endlessly it seemed, so that Angel had the illusion that when they arrived at the top of the meadow they might just fall off into space. Then the dense blue of butterflies all around them; fluttering in their hair, caressing their upturned faces, silently moving ethereal wings, flimsy creatures, beautiful, elusive, exciting in the extreme.

Angel would never know what came over her. Kicking off her shoes, she whirled around in a dreamy dance of her own, the butterflies whirling round her. The grass was cool to her stockinged feet. Edmund stood stock still, watching her. She hadn't danced like that since she was six.

Papa had a laughing face, such large, dark eyes, with hair as black as his younger daughter's. Tonight, it was not serious, stirring music that he made with the old violin for he loved classical airs, but happy, carefree tunes for little Angelina to dance to. Such a vivacious child, so like her papa: the Latin side very evident this evening, a precious memory for Carlo Rosselli, the Army doctor to take to war with him. His wife, so very English, putting on a brave face for his imminent departure, and Louise, serious and too old for her years, promising Papa solemnly that she would care for her mother and her little sister. Things would never be the same again. The child would not be encouraged to dance like that after her papa was gone . . .

'Papa,' Angel cried silently now, 'I danced again today – in a flurry of butterflies—'

The butterflies were gone, as swiftly as they had appeared. There was a mere smudge of blue on her hand, where she had inadvertently bruised a wing, and that *look* on Edmund's face. A look she instantly recognised, from the early days with Harry. She bent quickly to put on her shoes.

'I couldn't help it. It was so – wonderful . . .'

'You looked so happy – so carefree.' His voice was studiedly light. 'How can they call it the Common Blue, eh? Shall we go back? I warned

Edith we would be coming – she will be expecting us shortly.'

'I haven't felt like that in years,' she told him honestly. 'Please don't tell Edith, though,' she added, 'she will think I have gone quite mad!'

'I won't,' he promised. He took her arm, in a friendly fashion. 'But I must say that it was just as if you were intoxicated – and it was *me* who drank Rob's strong ale!'

'Well, here you are at last then,' Edith said, ushering them into her little sitting room, where the latticed windows were flung wide, and comfortable chairs grouped round the inglenook, though of course, there was no fire. On the trivet, there was a blue bowl full of flowers, mingling with ferny leaves from the tansy plant, which grew weed-like all round here.

'You look very well, Angel.' Edith looked keenly at Angel's face, still flushed. 'I hear that Alice has made extraordinary progress since your arrival – I was right, you still have that healing touch.'

'You *were* right, Edith, to suggest I come to The Angel – I was getting in a rut, and if I had waited until Lou's baby put in an appearance, I would probably have stayed on there, for ever.'

'Like Aunt Hetty?' Edith suggested. 'The invaluable aunt?'

'Perhaps. But Aunt Hetty belongs here, she's so much part of The Angel. It just wouldn't be the same without her. After France, well, I never felt I belonged again in London.'

After supper, pork pie and hot vegetables, rounded off with cheese and biscuits and more than one glass of Edith's cowslip wine, home-made, for as she said, she was determined to be a real countrywoman and make her own brews, Edith despatched Edmund to the piano.

The instrument was elderly and some of the keys squeaked. Edmund played with surprising abandon. Angel stood obediently beside him, told by Edith to sing, while Edith admitted wryly that she'd never yet found a key she was comfortable with and sat in her chair, with her knitting. However, her attention was fixed on them, not her needles.

Angel smiled to herself. 'She's intent on match-making!' When she caught Edmund's sly twinkle meant just for her, she knew at once that he was thinking the same thing. She must have imagined the way he looked at her when she danced, she thought.

It was good to sing all the old favourite tunes, those with a nostalgic theme, like 'Tipperary', 'Nellie Dean' and 'Daisy, Daisy', which last seemed particularly apt, after their ride in tandem.

Over a final drink they played a silly pencil and paper game, vying noisily, like children, to score the highest points.

'Oh, Edith, I *have* enjoyed myself – thank you for making me so welcome!'

Angel and Edith walked arm in arm among the fragrance of the evening scented flowers crowding the path to the gate.

Edmund opened it, stood waiting for them to make their goodnights.

'May I come again soon, Edith?'

'Of course you may! It was just like old times, wasn't it? Remember the singing round the piano before we went to France? All those brave young men, mostly gone like Harry . . .' Why did she have to say that?

It still hurt. Edith had promised silence but how much did Edmund know? Angel exclaimed, 'Another beautiful sunset, oh do look!' Then they heard the first hesitant notes of the bugle. Angel turned impulsively to Edith. 'Poor man, it's so sad, isn't it?'

'I don't believe he's unhappy, Angel, except for puzzling over his past. But I feel that if he *did* have that recall it might be all too painful, too haunting . . .' *As it is for you* – the unsaid words.

'Alice says that you know who he is—?'

Edith's expression became guarded. 'When he is ready, when he can face the world again he will, no doubt, return to a more normal way of living. But who can say when that will be? We – Aunt Hetty, Rob, myself – do what we can, what he will allow us to do—'

'And there's Jess, of course.'

'Yes, there's Jess. She may be good for him right now but later, well, she may have to face rejection.'

Edmund had not entered into their conversation, standing aloof. The music trembled to a stop. 'Look, Angel,' he said, 'here come the regulars from the pub, it must be closing time! You don't wish to be locked out, eh?'

'No! Goodnight, Edith!'

'Goodnight,' Edmund said in turn.

They discovered Aunt Hetty in the garden, pouring dregs of beer into a sunken jam jar. 'I'm trying to drown a few hodmedods – snails! – and a slug or two, 'twill be a good way to go – had a nice time, my dear?'

'Oh I did!' Angel put out her hand to Edmund. 'Thank you for the spin!'

He had wheeled the motorcycle over the road, now he swung his leg over the saddle, ready to cruise back home. She just caught the mischievous whisper, 'And thank you for the entertainment – the dancing!' before the machine spluttered into action.

She encountered Rob as she turned to go upstairs. He was carrying a tray piled with glasses. There was still the washing-up to do. He barely paused, merely said, 'I wish ye goodnight.' Then he went down to the kitchen.

A quick peep at the children and then it was not long before Angel was in her own bed. Yawning, she wondered if Jess had been there to shepherd that poor, bewildered man back to the barn, and, if she had stayed to comfort him . . . Her final thoughts before sleep came were happy ones:

memories of her childhood, triggered this evening, which made her smile.

Edith, casting aside her corset, with relief, smiled too, with satisfaction. She reached for her nightgown. So – Angel obviously had no suspicions regarding the bugler's identity – she was bound to find out eventually, of course, but right now, Edith considered she was in control of the situation. She hadn't considered the possibility that her brother would be attracted to Angel – she had always been able to read Edmund like a book. However, this was something it would do no harm to encourage. This would certainly cause far less complications than a growing intimacy between Angel and Rob, she thought. *That* was not part of her plan for Angel.

She climbed into bed. She felt for the photograph under her pillow. She didn't need to look at it. Her fingers traced the image of the unseen face. Why did love bring such pain? And *hate* . . .

CHAPTER NINE

Sunday morning and Aunt Hetty asked Angel, 'Would you care to come to church with Tony and me?'

She was dabbling her hands in scalding water, waiting for the knob of soda to dissolve to cut the grease from the breakfast plates. Angel turned, looked at Rob. He wore ancient corduroys, his shirt open at the neck; it was obviously going to be just another working day for him, she thought.

He had been rather offhand with her since that day out with Alice, indeed she had begun to wonder if she had offended him in some way. 'Now,' he said briefly, 'no need to ask my permission, Angel. Of course you may go – if ye wish it.'

'Alice can lie abed until we return,' Aunt Hetty decided. 'Nothing as grand as a goose today, but then it's really hot – shall we cut into that great beef and kidney pie, eh? The gravy'll be a nice jelly. Dig a few of them little spuds, Rob, they need just a rub not a scrape.'

'I will do that,' he agreed. Then he went outside and down the meadow.

By the time they were ready, gloved and hatted

despite the heat, with Angel clutching a borrowed prayer book, Rob and two hefty lads from the village were steadily swishing their sharpened scythes in the long grass.

'It's a pity to see the wild flowers fall,' Angel regretted, as the buttercups, poppies and daisies were flattened too.

'Needs to be done, my dear,' Aunt Hetty told her. 'The goat does her best but she can't keep up with it. Anyway, that's her winter fodder. When it's turned regular like, that's the sweetest hay kissed by the sun.'

Beyond the rhythmic scythes, there was a newly turned patch of earth close to the barn. A dark piece, stitched with green.

Aunt Hetty intercepted Angel's gaze. 'Ah, he's been busy that bugler . . . Jess has got him planting up the spare seedlings. She reckons that'll get him out by day, but the poor feller prefers to dig by moonlight, it seems.'

Jess had not turned up for work yet this morning – she worked seven days a week, Angel had soon discovered – she wondered if Jess, too, had been wielding a spade last night and was consequently having an unaccustomed lie-in.

They met up with Edith, tightly corseted beneath her long-sleeved brown silk dress. She wore a prim, matching straw hat, with a self-coloured ribbon, and there were already beads of perspiration showing through the powder she had applied to camouflage her high colour. Angel rather wished she was not wearing that sea-green dress, for she felt conspicuous beside the sober Edith. Aunt Hetty wore a smarter version of her usual attire, with a tiny black velvet bow at her throat. Tony was already wilting in his Norfolk jacket, long woollen socks and highly polished boots.

Angel and Edith walked sedately behind Aunt Hetty and Tony, who was intent on marking their progress with a sharp-ended stick in the dusty road. It was a wavering line he drew.

'I kept thinking last night, after you had gone,' Edith said, 'how good it is that we have been able to pick up the threads of our old friendship after all this time. I really missed you, Angel, when you returned to England – of course, I knew it had to be, but the other nurses seemed to think, so unfairly, that it was *my* fault that you had left the hospital. You could almost say that I was ostracised . . . I know I gave my all to my job, but it was difficult at times. When it was all over, and I was offered the post at the nursing home, well, it was a great relief. It was a nice surprise when Edmund came to live nearby – he has really taken to you, Angel! How d'you feel about that?'

Angel was uncomfortably aware that Aunt Hetty could well have heard all the foregoing. It was almost as if, she thought, Edith was intent on exposing the events which had caused her so much anguish, despite her previous assurances.

'We seem to get on well, Edith,' she replied, somewhat shortly.

It was a relief, after the long walk, to step within the cool interior of the church. Aunt Hetty ushered them into the family pew and closed the little door behind them.

There was a gallery, Angel saw, with youngsters peering over the edge. 'The bell tower is at the back,' Aunt Hetty whispered, as she saw Angel gazing upwards. Just then the bells began to ring, calling the faithful to worship. 'We be early, you see,' she added.

The smell of polish and the gleaming brasses; the niches in the walls, each with its simple vase of garden flowers; the way the worn blue carpet ran straight and true to the altar; the ornately carved pulpit and the choir benches; and the first swelling notes of the organ, filled Angel with contentment. She read the memorial inscriptions, watched as the hymn numbers were changed, kneeled obediently when bidden. It was some time before she realised that it was Edmund playing the organ. The church was packed, despite the fact that many of the children had already attended morning Sunday school, and would be expected to repeat this again in the afternoon. Parents concurred, for it was precious time on their own.

Tony muttered to Angel, as they knelt side by side, while he jingled the coppers in his pocket, to a reproving 'tut' from Edith, 'See that old lady on her own at the front? That's Lady Pamela. She looks about one hundred and two, but Aunt Hetty says she's prob'ly only ninety . . .'

Lady Pamela was all in black. Her straight back and her elegant, broad-brimmed hat, with nodding feathers, made her seem rather formidable, but Angel thought she must be kind, to loan her motor to ensure a comfortable ride for Alice.

The rector had rather a grating voice and a steely gaze. He paused now and then to stare at the less attentive among his flock, which quelled the shuffler or sweet-sucker immediately. Angel was disappointed to find the sermon uninspiring, and later, when the rector shook her hand, as they emerged into the sunlight through the porch, she felt his clasp to be chill and clammy. She hoped he would not ask her if she were a regular communicant – all I know, she thought, is that I have always been able to pray, when I need to . . . She had certainly prayed, in her despair, in France . . .

Edmund caught them up, along the lane. 'Hello, again! I could hear *you* singing, Angel!'

'She sings in tune,' Tony remarked candidly, pulling off the stuffy jacket, and slinging it over his shoulder, 'not like Lady Pamela.'

At that very moment, they were forced to leap hastily to the side, as the Rolls swept by. They glimpsed Lady Pamela, graciously smiling, while giving a little wave of her hand.

'Tony!' reproved Aunt Hetty. 'Show some respect for your elders, my lad. She was a good mistress to me, when I was young – she took me to Scotland with her that summer and there I met my dear old feller. His parents ran the hotel where we stayed – we soon knew we had a lot in common. "So I have to lose you, Hetty," she said with a sigh, but I came on home and waited till my John follered. When he took me back to Scotland as his wife, I liked it there, though it was wholly cold in winter – but I knew I'd come back to The Angel one day, and so I did.'

'Whatever are you mardling about?' came a breathless voice, as Mrs Newsome caught up with them, in her turn. 'Didn't you see me in church, Hetty? I have a right job to hurry in this heat, my dear—'

'Mardle,' Edith interpreted, sotto voce, for Angel: 'Gossip!'

Mrs Newsome had some information of her own to impart. 'Jess – I saw her, when I was nipping along to church – says she missed you and to tell you Nana has been *ablaze* all night—' she paused dramatically.

'Feverish,' Edith whispered. Angel thought the fiery description fitted a febrile patient exactly.

'Anyway, she says she can't come to you, sorry, today, but hopes to, tomorrer.'

'Could we help, I wonder?' Angel murmured to her fellow nurse.

'Leave well alone,' Aunt Hetty had heard. 'Jess knows what to do, eh?'

'Nana don't go to bed at nights,' Mrs Newsome went on, 'she sits in her chair by the old stove. Just like Mr Newsome, when his chest was bad. In the day he shifted into the shop to watch over me, to mardle with folk when he'd got the breath.' She looked at Angel as she continued with an obviously oft-repeated story. 'He said, "Jinny, my dear, should I pass on while you're serving, just drape me quick with a towel or two till the shop be empty . . ."'

Tony couldn't resist it, 'And she did, Angel, she really did!'

Morbid it might be but everyone laughed, even Mrs Newsome. She concluded happily: 'He loved a good joke did Mr Newsome – it was a great way to go and, if anyone noticed – well, they never said . . .'

Time to leave Mrs Newsome, to fork sharp and to walk on home.

'Oh, you're still with us—' Angel remembered, after they had said goodbye to Edith at her gate. Then she felt rather foolish for Edmund laughed aloud.

'I had begun to feel like the Invisible Man,' he said wryly, 'for you were so absorbed in the demise of the late Mr Newsome. I always wet my whistle at The Angel after all that hymn playing and singing, I have to confess.'

Towards them as they crossed over the road came a straggly procession, carefully carrying brimming jugs of beer. Growing lads mainly but also a granny or two, for the bar, as Angel had already discovered, was the domain of men with their dominoes and greasy pack of cards.

As Edmund went through the first door she

noticed that the window was up on the saloon. So this was where the jug-bearers were served, tapping on the glass for beer on tap.

Aunt Hetty was in a hurry with lunch to make ready and Rob busy already in the bar with no Jess to hold the fort while he ate, himself.

'Let me see to Alice, I'll bring her down, then I'll organise the food, Aunt Hetty – look, Rob's set the potatoes to boil already and I do want to help—' Angel offered.

'Thank you, my dear,' Aunt Hetty accepted gratefully.

Angel, Alice and Tony were just wiping their plates clean of the remaining delicious jelly from the pie, when Tony remembered: 'Oh, the bugler!'

Fortunately, there was still a wedge of pie, and Rob had been generous with his spuds, so she was able to assemble a decent plateful, together with bread and butter. Tony went round to the window, to tap for the bugler's beer, and Alice spooned stewed apple into a dish.

Tony took the tray and walked easily down the shorn grass to the barn.

In the evening, after the children were in bed, Angel felt restless. Aunt Hetty and Rob were still in the bar. She went quietly along the hall into the front parlour. This room was rarely used in the summer, as Aunt Hetty had told her, when she first arrived: 'It comes into its own at Christmas when we eat in there, and get a great fire blazing up the chimney.' In the parlour there was a wall completely lined with books. Angel thought romantically she would take a selection back to her room, to read by the light of the moon.

She took down an old favourite or two. The books smelled musty, the room, flooded by the evening light, seemed rather forlorn – cushions too plump, a sharp odour of fallen soot from the grate. There were pictures around the room, all by Lalla, she saw. The children, baby-faced, laughed down at her from over the mantel. Dark-eyed Tony, curly-haired like Rob: Alice, unbelievably bonny with healthy, rosy cheeks. They were dressed alike in simple, blue smocks, and Alice had a ring of daisies round her head. They looked so happy, well-loved, she thought wistfully – Lalla couldn't have captured them like that unless she adored them, surely?

She settled down on a hard couch by the window, swung her feet up, and idly opened the first book.

It was a familiar sensation, yet one last experienced long ago, when her father was alive: the gentle removal of the book, which was wedged under her cheek, the stroking back of her hair. Her eyes were wide now, she gazed up at Rob's smiling face.

'I'm all pins and needles . . .' she apologised, as he helped her rise.

'I wondered who on earth was in here, seeing the door ajar, when I came back to close up the bar. I thought it might be young Tony, it's not unknown for him to prowl about if he can't get to sleep. I apologise, Angel, for disturbing ye, but I thought I should. It would have been a shock to wake up here next morning!'

They walked along the hall together, then upstairs. He paused, before going into his room.

'Goodnight to ye, Angel – I am very grateful for all you do, not only for Alice, and Tony, but for Aunt Hetty – for me. Do not be in a hurry to leave us.'

She felt a little odd, remembering the tender touching of her hair – just as if she was of an age with his children, she thought. She certainly did not want to leave The Angel, especially now.

'I won't,' she replied softly. 'Goodnight, Rob.'

If the bugler played that night, Angel did not hear him.

CHAPTER TEN

'Time to rise up, Angel,' Aunt Hetty said cheerfully, bringing in the early morning tea. 'That's a bit cloudy this morning.'

'Jess not here again?'

'Not yet. But there's time still.' Aunt Hetty took an envelope from her apron pocket and tucked it discreetly under the edge of the pillow.

Angel smiled. She guessed this was her wages: had she really been here a month already? 'Thank you,' she said. *I would work here for nothing – just my keep!* She thought.

As if reading her thoughts, Aunt Hetty remarked, as she turned to go into Alice's room, 'You are worth every penny, my dear . . . Not that times aren't hard. A good many old boys didn't come back from the war and some young 'uns gone farther afield – one or two had to walk to Lowestoft to join the fishing fleet – that bar used to be lively in the old days. Sometimes Rob says he wonders if it's worth all our hard work, keeping it going. Ah well, we'll have to see, eh? If he had a good wife, now—' she sighed expressively.

'Tony says the wild strawberries are right for

picking,' Alice sounded wistful, as Angel saw her downstairs for breakfast. She was really progressing fast, Angel mused.

'How far would we have to walk?' she asked.

'Not far – just along the lane – oh, Angel, d'you think *I* could go?'

'I don't see why not. If you eat all Aunt Hetty serves up today, mind. I've never tasted a wild strawberry, Alice—'

'Then you must!' Alice asserted.

'We'll wait for Tony – go after school – you can have your afternoon rest first,' Angel decided. She gave Alice's arm a gentle squeeze, 'Strawberries and cream for tea?'

'Well,' Alice had to admit, 'they don't usually get as far as the basket!'

Jess arrived all breathless and apologetic. 'I must go straight down to see the boy – do you mind, Aunt Hetty? Nana feels a mite better this morning, but I had to bring Belinda with me. The bugler can mind her for a while.'

Washing day again but Aunt Hetty was too kind to say that they were all behind.

Later, when she helped to peg out the sheets, Jess settled her baby in Tony's box-on-wheels, where she could watch the washing dancing on the line and the goats browsing, but safely tethered for as Jess told Angel: 'There's nothing so curious as a goat except for kitlings, and the goats nibble everything of course.'

The telegram boy caught up with Angel in the

garden. 'Telegram, Miss!' She took the envelope, guessing who it must be from.

Peter Carlo arrived safely, Mother and son doing well. Love Lou and Jack.

Tears came readily into her eyes, tears of thankfulness. She hoped fervently that Lou had not endured a long labour. She must send a telegram by return expressing her joy. It would be so much easier, she thought, if the post office was in Mrs Newsome's shop, for it was a lengthy trek to the village.

'Of course, I'll take you in the trap,' Rob offered instantly.

'Would you get me stamps, dear?' Aunt Hetty asked. 'Don't worry about Alice, she can get on with her school work, eh, if she's to go jaunting this afternoon.'

Alice made a disappointed face, thinking she could have gone with her father and Angel. However, she sat obediently at the kitchen table and ruled a margin or two on her paper.

It was good, sitting up high beside Rob as the pony trotted smartly along, to see the surroundings from a different viewpoint. 'May we stop off, on the way back?' she asked impulsively, 'look in on Nana – I suspect that Jess is still worrying about her.'

'Of course,' he agreed. Then, 'You'd like time off, Angel, I'm sure, to visit your sister?'

Her response obviously surprised him. 'Thank you – not just yet, Rob. In a few weeks' time, perhaps . . .' But he did not comment.

She found herself dabbing at her eyes again, oh, *why* was she always so emotional? It must be a legacy from her father, she thought: her mother was always cool and collected. She wondered if her mother would exert her right to travel home to see the baby first, but she doubted that her stepfather would show more than polite interest.

Rob glanced at her, concerned. Again, he said nothing. They drew up outside the post office, which was among quite a cluster of shops and small businesses – the wheelwright, the forge, the doctor's surgery, the greengrocery, the pork butcher, with his fat sausages festooning the window. There was another pub here, licensed to sell beer only, Angel discovered – more a front room of a cottage, than a real inn, like The Angel. Yet, no doubt a drain on their custom.

Overjoyed news – Welcome to the family, Peter!
Letter & parcel to follow. All love, Angel.

She duly dictated the telegram, then purchased the stamps.

It made her ache inside, to think of her sister, with a baby. If she had only met Harry at another time – if they had married – surely she, too, would have been a mother by now? It would never be, now – how could it? She must try to overcome the attraction she felt for Rob, she thought, for *that* could come to nothing – and who would have her, anyway, if the truth was ever revealed?

'Angel, are you feeling unwell?' Rob handed her up into the trap.

'Just a little sad, when I should be so happy,' she admitted.

'You are thinking of what might have been,' he said intuitively. 'I do that too much, myself. If I had not gone to war – we seemed so happy, my wife and I, before we were parted . . .'

He gave a gentle shake of the reins, to remind the stolid pony to move a little faster. She watched the muscles rippling in the animal's rounded rump, while reflecting on his words. Suddenly, softly, she said:

'I *do* feel at home here, Rob . . .' then immediately, she felt embarrassed, for surely he must wonder what on earth she meant?

He merely replied: 'Good.' He was obviously in a confiding mood as far as his own feelings were concerned, however, for he continued, 'Lalla was much travelled, suffering from a surfeit of it, she said, when she came here, to relax, to paint. She was dazzling, Angel, perhaps not conventionally beautiful – but as Alice may well become, in a few years' time. She probably married me on an impulse, on the rebound from the chap she took up with again, while I was away. She loved us, I do believe that, but we – The Angel – tied her down. Perhaps it was as well, that I was not there to see her leave . . . I believe I am so fortunate to have the children with me still, that she does not interfere in the way I bring them up. That is my great consolation – Alice and Tony are my salvation.'

'When I lost my fiancé,' Angel said simply, 'there was nothing left for me.'

For a brief moment, he placed one warm hand over hers, clasped in her lap. 'There are two children, Angel, *my* children, who are already fond of you – you were just what Alice needed, when she was so low in spirits and health. Edith must have been inspired to think of you! Here we are, at The Cotts, and Nana's door is open, which I think is a good sign. I'll wait outside for ye, eh? No hurry.'

Nana's smile was welcoming, though her eyes showed wariness. 'Miss Fenner come earlier – I sent her packing. I don't want no fussing, I say.'

'Jess says you are better – we've been down to the village – I thought I'd like to call in.' She noted the yellowish tinge to Nana's drawn face, the hand resting on the tender place in the region of her ribs.

'I won't keep it from *you*,' Nana surprised her. '*You* won't interfere. Must be great old stones, eh? The pain's bad, but I didn't tell the gal, nor you won't neither.'

'It could be your gall bladder, Nana,' Angel surmised.

'I don't doubt it. That's a turn-up, me being not

fat nor forty! I took a good dose.' She didn't enlighten Angel as to what. 'That'll send the jarndice through.'

'You must rest; jaundice is unpleasant – watch your diet—'

'Apples, bread and water, that's all I'll touch . . . Tea, but no milk.' Nana looked at the door. 'Well, your guv'nor's waiting. Come another day, and welcome, Nurse. My Jess tells me you have made a big difference with them children – you can tell the *other* one she's not needed—'

'Miss Fenner means well,' Angel told Nana firmly, 'she's a good friend of the family. She's my friend too—'

'Some folk is not as straight as you and I.' Nana would have the last word.

'All right?' Rob asked as they trundled off once more.

'All right,' Angel agreed. She did not mean just Nana Elderberry and nor, she was sure, did he.

The wild strawberries grew on a bank shaded by trees and bushes. They had brought the token basket and Rob had asked diffidently if he might accompany them. Alice exclaimed: ''course you can, Dad! We wanted you to, but—'

'I never seem to have the time,' he finished wryly. He looked at his children. 'I'm sorry I'm always so busy, dear Aunt Hetty too—'

'Oh, we understand,' Alice assured him. 'Anyway, we've got Angel now, haven't we?' Then she looked anxious. 'You won't go, Angel, will you, till I'm *quite* better?'

Rob answered for her, 'You can be quite sure she won't, Alice.'

The tiny scarlet berries were sweet as honey and melted on the tip of the tongue, Angel fancied. She ate so many her lips were stained with juice. 'I'll go a bit further along,' she told Alice, 'the other way to Tony, it would be unfair, wouldn't it, if we didn't take back a generous tasting for Aunt Hetty and Jess?'

She lined the basket with cool, green leaves, so that the minute berries would not be crushed, and, on her knees, crawled along, searching for the little jewels. She glanced up, startled, as after ten minutes or so, of concentrated picking, Rob spoke to her: 'Time to go back, I'm afraid. Sorry, you were in a dream world of your own . . . Aunt Hetty will be laying up for supper and the patrons of The Angel are no doubt washing off the sweat and grime of a long day in the fields, and thinking of coming along shortly for a long glass of beer.' He assisted her to her feet, then added unexpectedly, 'You look as if you have been well and truly kissed – your mouth is the same colour as the strawberries! I don't need to ask you if you like the taste!'

'Nectar, sheer bliss!' she returned. That strange shyness in his company had re-emerged, that stirring of long-dampened sensations; she felt a slight breathlessness. She reminded herself sternly that he was still a married man, that she was his daughter's nurse. This unexpected rapport, she told herself, was merely because they had something in common, they had both been badly hurt during the war. Rob, she was positive, was still very much in love with his wife.

As they walked back to the children, she mentioned: 'Edmund suggested I might go for a walk with him this evening – with the dog – if that is all right, with you? I would see Alice settled first, and would not be out too long.'

She did not say that Edith would be accompanying them, too.

He slipped his arm round Alice's shoulders, helping her along. 'There is no need to ask my permission. Of course.'

CHAPTER ELEVEN

Edith rapped smartly on the barn door. She waited a few moments for she was aware that the girl was inside with the bugler. Not that she expected to witness anything improper, she told herself, but there was fear that she *might*, buried deep inside her. That day in France, when she had stood silently, seething with hurt and anger, watching those two, so much in love – nothing could match that, surely? She had never forgiven Angel for that betrayal.

There was talk, about Jess's baby, but Edith had not been one of those to point the finger, even though she had been spurned, as usual, by Nana Elderberry. Belinda's other parent remained a mystery, but the answer was transparent, Edith thought.

She lifted the latch, cleared her throat, walked in.

The bugler, hunched in his chair, was reading. He looked up with a smile. He, at least, appreciated Edith's concern for his welfare. Jess, with a brief nod, continued with her tidying up.

'How are you?' she asked. Her professional eye

took in his pallor, the slight trembling of his hands, as he closed the book, and rose politely.

'Oh – fair, Edith, fair.'

She pulled a chair beside his, looked meaningfully at Jess, who took the hint.

'Best get home – Belinda will be wailing for her feed, I reckon . . . I will see you tomorrer – unless—'

Unless, Edith thought, as the girl departed, unless he is out on the tiles tonight . . .

'Sit down, we should have a little chat, I think. Any improvement in the memory, old chap?' She kept her finger on his pulse, looking directly at him. She spoke pleasantly, but it was imperative she knew.

He looked uncertain. 'Sometimes – well, I recall things which obviously – were in my childhood. I dream, now and again – of guns – wake up – in a sweat . . .' His voice trailed off.

'That's all?'

'Yes.'

'You know what I have been able to tell you, of course, about your background – do you remember any of that?'

'No. You say I had a wife and child – before I joined up. You say my wife died in childbirth. But, I don't—'

'Your mother looked after your little girl while you were away – sadly, she contracted meningitis, and you lost her, too.'

'Belinda—'

'No, Belinda is *Jess's* baby – that was not your daughter's name. Your mother visited you a few times in the nursing home – do you remember that?'

'I – think – yes. You told me, *she* died—'

'In that dreadful influenza epidemic. Your parents left you well-provided for – I have power of attorney, as your close friend, unfortunately, you have no other family. When you feel you can face the world again, we, Rob and I, will help you find a home, a proper place to live, near us, so we can *always* keep an eye on you.'

'You are very good to me, Edith – thank you.'

'You must get more fresh air, my dear, you show the lack of it. But, at least I know you are well fed: the family at The Angel are very kind to you, which we know you appreciate. There is a new member of the household – did they tell you? Another friend of mine, from the days of war . . .' Edith's gaze was intense now. 'Have you seen her? If so, do *you* know her, too?'

'I have seen her face – at the window.' He looked puzzled. 'Do I – have I met her?'

Edith did not answer directly. She was satisfied with his answer. 'I think it doesn't really matter. I don't know why I mentioned Angel—' No flicker of recognition at the deliberate use of Angel's name. 'Well, is there anything you need – Rob will take your list to town, next time he goes, eh?'

She shook his hand warmly. 'I will come again, soon.'

'I do not lack company – I have Jess,' he said simply.

'Yes, you have Jess.' A man, perhaps especially this one, she thought, had needs, which Jess could fulfil. However, he would eventually have to outgrow his dependence on this young person. *She* was not a suitable match at all, her feelings were of no importance.

School was out – both Edmund and Tony were of a mind to celebrate! A jaunt to the sea was mooted, but Aunt Hetty thought that the wind might be strong, off the water. So, it was decided that it would be safer, with Alice in mind, to picnic by the river.

'Edith and I'll pick a great basket of watercress – full of iron, eh, Angel? Just what Alice needs. Those who swim, can get more'n their feet wet.' Aunt Hetty corked the lemonade.

Angel, buttering a mound of bread slices, passed them to Alice, who inserted the ham, being cut by Rob, while Tony, in his turn, smeared on blobs of mustard. Greaseproof paper to wrap, tomatoes in a bag, apples tucked in the corners of the picnic hamper, old cups and plates: towels and bathing costumes clutched under arms, and the crowd at The Angel were ready.

Edith brought her share, including chocolate cake for the children. Edmund carried a bowl and bag of biscuits for Boniface, plus towels for them both, for as he told Angel wryly, 'The old rogue likes nothing better than getting soaked and shaking himself all over the place.'

Angel found herself walking with Edmund and his dog while Edith and Aunt Hetty ambled along at the rear. Tony bounded ahead, while Alice clung to her father's free arm as he carried the picnic basket with his other hand.

The grass was soft and spongy to the tread as they made their way to the river, where the willows dipped their branches into the clearest, flowing water that Angel had ever seen. Aunt Hetty and Edith vanished behind the bushes to divest themselves of stockings and shoes, re-emerged with their skirts girdled higher, then went off happily with their basket and knives to cut the bunches of cress.

'I can paddle, can't I?' Alice asked anxiously, pulling off her cotton stockings in full view of the company. She was not grown-up at all today. Angel smiled, it was good to see Alice intent on childish pleasures.

'I promised, didn't I?' she replied, 'Just let me change in Aunt Hetty's hidey-hole, and I'll wade with you, before I decide whether I'm brave enough for a total immersion!'

Rob was already in hot pursuit of Tony, who was making for the diving board and deeper water. Edmund, it appeared, was not inclined to swim for a while, so he was left in charge of the picnic and a jumble of discarded clothes. Boniface, barking, raced after Rob and Tony.

Angel's bathing costume was a most respectable affair in navy wool with white trim and a neat skirt designed to conceal curves. However, she still felt over-exposed; avoiding Edmund's eye, she seized Alice by the hand as they stepped into the water together, with little shrieks at its coldness.

Upstream they paddled, to where the river widened, until they were knee-deep. 'Are you shivering, Alice?' Angel was concerned. 'You mustn't get your skirt wet! Hitch it up a little more. We'd better go back, I think.'

Alice didn't say, 'I'm not a baby!' when Angel towelled her thin legs and cold feet vigorously and insisted that she wriggle into her stockings once more. She draped Aunt Hetty's cardigan round Alice's shoulders. 'There, Alice – have something to eat, then keep in the sun and warm up. Tie my scarf round your head – you don't want to burn your neck . . . D'you mind if I join Tony for a swim? I haven't swum since Lou took me to Margate for a holiday, and gave me lessons—'

'You don't forget,' Edmund stated. 'I might join you, when the ladies return from their picking.' He glanced around, whistled to Boniface. He was nowhere in sight. 'Send that wretch back here, if you see him, please, Angel. He knew I was having a crafty snooze while you were all otherwise engaged.' He did not sound overly concerned.

Two heads bobbed side by side – Rob was not taking any chances, Angel thought, with young Tony being more bold than skilful. She tested the springiness of the board tentatively, gathered up her courage, lifted her arms, closed her eyes – and achieved a spectacular belly-flop.

Choking, her legs tangled in green, slimy river weed, and not yet rising from the water, Angel felt a firm grasp on her shoulders. She came, gasping and terrified, to the surface. Rob's arms supported her, his dripping face was full of concern. '*We* know the river, you don't. Let me help you to the bank, Angel. Tony! You are to come out now, too, and run as fast as you can to bring back Angel's towel. No need to alarm Aunt Hetty or Edith, mind!'

She felt stupid, then suddenly sick, having swallowed much water. Rob held her solicitiously while she retched, ineffectually, then apologised. 'Oh – I'm so sorry to be so silly, Rob. I haven't swum for, must be twenty years, and then only in a calm sea in the shallows.'

His arm round her shoulders was very comforting. He seemed perfectly at ease with their close proximity, as if unaware that he clasped her bare skin. She hoped fervently that he would interpret her sudden involuntary trembling as a fit of the shivers, and she was thankful when she saw Tony haring back with her towel. She disengaged herself and wrapped herself in its folds. The three of them walked back together.

She sat between Edith and Edmund while they shared out the sandwiches and nibbled on sprigs of watercress. Bitter, but good, she discovered.

'Boniface still missing?' she asked Edmund.

'He is. Still, we will be returning home shortly, for I understand that Aunt Hetty feels Jess has been left on her own for long enough. Boniface is probably stretched out on the schoolhouse path, sunning himself and snoring, wondering about his dinner.' He sounded anxious, despite his banter.

Unhappily, this proved not to be the case. They heard the dog's excited barking when they were still some distance from The Angel.

'Hold you hard, young Tony!' Aunt Hetty exclaimed, gripping his jacket, as the barking gave way to agonised, high-pitched yelps, and the men set off at a run, abandoning the things they were carrying. 'Here, my lad, you can carry the picnic basket, it's not heavy now.'

Alice, who had been walking with her father, slowed down, wavering a little, her face drained of colour. Angel was immediately at her side, as was Edith, and together they offered instant support.

'Sorry . . .' Alice said faintly, 'I suppose I'm not as strong as I'd like to think I am – is Boniface in trouble, d'you think?'

'Been butted by your mother goat, I expect,' Edith said briskly.

They remained, wide-eyed with shock and disbelief at the open gate. The yellow dog was sprawled on the path, being viciously attacked by a mangy, snarling, brown dog, thin, but more agile, at his throat. Jess, copper stick in hand, was swinging wildly at the aggressor, while Nancy, the goat, trailing her tethering rope was bleating pitifully by the house, her little female kid ducking under her, desperately seeking solace from her pendulous teats. Rob, calling to Edmund, attempting to catch hold of Boniface's collar, threw a sack over the other dog's head, wrestling with it, while Edmund dragged Boniface free. It was a bloodstained struggle – Angel and the others felt powerless.

'Get the children round the back – *inside*!' Jess yelled to Aunt Hetty. Her shout galvanised them into action, Aunt Hetty and Edith propelled Alice and Tony away from the mayhem.

Angel could see that Rob was very likely to get bitten, that he and Edmund, Boniface, too, would need first-aid – even as she moved cautiously towards them, the brown animal tore free, streaked past her, through the gate and bolted down the lane.

'Are either of you – hurt?' she hardly recognised her voice. She watched, as Edmund bent over Boniface's still body. Jess wound the goat's rope round her wrist, and, murmuring soothingly, led mother and kid back down the meadow. Then Angel became aware of a different sound – harsh weeping. Someone – it could only be the bugler – was crouched over something lying in the grass. She guessed at once what that must be, for the other kid was nowhere to be seen.

'We're all right, Angel,' Rob told her, and his voice, too, sounded strange. 'Will ye look at the dog?' he asked.

How could she tell Edmund that Boniface was dead? Probably not from the great gashes in his hide: 'His heart must have given out, Edmund,' she said quietly, as he knelt there, unbelieving, beside her, cradling the dog's head.

'I will fetch the trap, take you and Edith home with him,' Rob said, 'I am so sorry, Edmund – he was a grand old fellow.'

'Brave, too,' Angel added. She straightened up. 'I will see if I can help calm the children and I'll make some tea. I won't tell them what's happened yet—'

'Thank you,' Rob said. 'Edmund, we'll move him first, shall we? Cover him over, in the trap, before Edith comes out.'

Jess came towards her, carrying the other limp little body. Angel took it from her arms, gently wrapped it in her towel, and motioned Jess to go back to the bugler. Poor Nancy kept up her plaintive mourning, re-tethered a safe distance away.

Angel took the pathetic bundle into the scullery for Rob to see to, later. What a sad end to their picnic – her own modest drama paled into insignificance. She carefully sponged the stains on her dress – another thing to keep from the children right now.

There was Alice to put to bed, Tony to reassure

and a quick whisper to Aunt Hetty to put her in the picture. Rob, they agreed, should tell Alice and Tony of the twin tragedies.

Jess sat beside the bugler on the bed. Angel standing in the doorway, could not see his face, for Jess held him close, against her breast. His arms were tight round her waist, and Jess rocked him gently, as if he were Belinda. Angel thought: 'He is crying still, silently now . . .' She suddenly felt like howling, herself. She must steal quietly away, for she felt like an interloper. *As Edith must have felt, coming upon herself and Harry, in the barn, that day.*

'I had to inform the policeman,' Rob said briefly, explaining his prolonged absence. 'They intend to shoot the dog, if they can find it. It does not come from the village, as far as they know.'

'Edmund—?' Angel asked. He must be bereft, she thought.

'He and I have seen to things. Edith will stay with him tonight. Is Tony upstairs with Alice? I'll go to them, now.'

'You will go up when he comes back?' Aunt Hetty asked, 'It is time for the opening up – the bar will be full of the story, no doubt.'

Jess looked in. 'Belinda'll be getting desperate and Nana'll wonder where I am. See you tomorrer, Aunt Hetty, Nurse.' Her face too, was stained with tears.

'Thank you, dear Jess – what would we do without you?'

The children slept at last, after all the upset. Angel went down wearily for a glass of milk. She met Rob, as she so often did, by the stairs.

'Rob—' she said, wishing she did not have to remind him, 'I put – you know – in the scullery—'

'I will see to it, when we are closed.' Then, 'No doubt we shall hear the bugler tonight, Angel.'

And Jess, she knew, would be back.

CHAPTER TWELVE

'We must air this room, Angel,' Aunt Hetty said, opening the door wide to the spare room. 'It's likely to see a visitor soon . . .'

Angel followed her inside. She felt rather like an intruder for Aunt Hetty remarked matter-of-factly that this had been originally Rob and Lalla's room. 'He moved downstairs – he couldn't bear to sleep in here, alone . . .'

It was a large double room with a splendid bed and fine furnishings. Under the window, canopied by the eaves, stood a child's bed. 'We let it as a family room.' Aunt Hetty opened the wardrobe door, rummaged inside. 'Here we are, still in the box.'

Angel found herself sitting on the wicker chair, trying on a pair of leather shoes with strong soles and thick laces.

'I thought they'd be just your size,' Aunt Hetty announced with satisfaction. '*She* turned her nose up at 'em, but you need a good walking shoe round here. Have them, my dear, and welcome. Rob won't mind, I'm sure.'

Angel thought privately that she would not have liked it if the shoes had shown signs of wear, not because she was fussy, she admitted to herself, having worn her sister's cast-offs in the past, but because the shoes had been Lalla's. 'Thank you, Aunt Hetty, I'll be glad to wear them. I've already worn a hole in the sole of mine and patent leather, I've discovered, is not the shoe for country lanes,' she ended ruefully.

Glancing round the room, she unconsciously searched for traces of the headstrong young woman who had shared the large bed with Rob, who had, she surmised, given birth to the children in here too, but the only link appeared to be a photograph in a silver frame on the dressing table. A younger, smiling Rob, unfamiliar in a suit, with his bride on his arm, in shimmering silk, her veil held in place with a garland of flowers. Angel was instantly reminded of Alice.

Aunt Hetty picked up the wedding photograph, dusted it on her sleeve and slipped it in a drawer. 'Best place for *that*,' she stated.

Angel enjoyed applying the bellows to the skirting board, blowing away the dust – Aunt Hetty was well aware of all the 'wrinkles', remarking slyly that a damp cloth would merely smear the paintwork.

Together they made up the bed with starched linen redolent of lavender, smoothing out the creases, giving the pillows a thorough shake by the open window. 'Those shoes,' mused Aunt Hetty, 'remind me of my Dada's new boots. He always had the best, specially made – "a man needs good boots," he said. A young chap came to measure his feet – this is before I went to Lady Pamela's – we got talking, boy and girl like. Well, when he brought the boots, seeing Dada so satisfied, very daring, young Ted – he was Will Aldred's father later, you know – said, "Can I take Hetty to the mission meeting in the village – they've got the magic lantern show – this Saturday evening?" Dada asked Mother what she thought – her being the boss. Mother said: "That's all right I reckon, but Hetty must be back by ten at the latest. We won't worry will we Dada, knowing his father . . ." Well, Ted and I had a lively time, despite the hymns and prayers and all: we ought to have been home in time, but we rather dawdled along the lane – it was quite dark. Suddenly, we heard the rumble of the trap coming our way, and the old horn lantern swinging lit us up, all guilty looking. Dada yelled, very fierce, "Where have you been, my gal?" and poor young Ted, all quaking, whispered in my ear: "Oh, Hetty, I do hope he isn't wearing them new boots – just *think of them hard toecaps*!"' Aunt Hetty smiled dreamily at the memory, not enlightening Angel as to whether her luckless swain had indeed received a boot up the backside, sending him packing.

Angel grinned: 'But for your Dada's boots you might have had that saucy Fairy Aldred in your family, instead of Alice!'

It was Friday and Alice and Tony had gone to the market with Rob. 'Reckon Alice is up to it, Angel?' Aunt Hetty asked. 'She still seems very deaf in her bad ear.'

Regretfully, Angel told Aunt Hetty the truth. 'It won't improve, I'm afraid, Aunt Hetty. Alice doesn't realise it yet, of course. She's adjusting well, and it's a blessing she has excellent hearing in her good ear. It will do her the world of good to get out. Tony, too, they've been so subdued since – the goats and poor Boniface . . . Reminds me, d'you think I could go to see Edmund this afternoon – just for a short while?'

'That's a very good idea – you go,' Aunt Hetty approved. 'Edith says he's still very upset – that dog was his constant companion. The children, at the school, they'll miss the old feller, too, when they return to their lessons in September.'

'Tony finished that picture. I wonder if Edmund would like to have it, now – I'll ask Tony—'

'Oh, I'm wholly sure, he'd be pleased to have it – that'll be a bit of comfort, eh?'

A cooler afternoon, so she laced on the new shoes, which went nicely with the tussore costume. She had helped Tony to mount the picture of the dog on card; she wrapped it carefully in tissue. Aunt Hetty, about to join Jess in the bar, slipped half a pork pie in her bag. 'Expect poor feller will neglect himself, feeling down . . .'

Angel saw Edith in the front garden of the pink

house, weeding vigorously. She paused to tell her friend where she was going.

'Oh, good,' Edith beamed. 'How about you both coming to supper tomorrow night, Angel?'

Angel wasn't sure. 'It depends on the children, really . . .' she demurred. 'I've had most of the day, off, apart from helping Aunt Hetty a bit – but you know how independent she is – with Rob taking them to the market, the children that is, you see.'

'You mustn't let yourself become too involved,' Edith warned her. 'Edmund's a different matter – he really likes you, Angel, I can tell. And, I believe the feeling is reciprocated?' She sounded almost arch, not like Edith at all.

'You know it is, Edith! But don't go too far with your match-making, I'm not sure—'

'You're not sure you'll ever get over what happened – the knowledge *you* and *I* share, is that it?'

'The daydreams and the nightmares, I do feel they're slipping away from me, now – all due to your persuading me to come here! But when you've been as hurt as I was – well, you are afraid that it might always be there to haunt you and that it could spoil any new relationship . . .'

'Edmund is a very compassionate chap. You could tell him anything.'

'I'm sure I could. But I'm more concerned for *him*, at the moment: well, I'll let you get on, Edith! I may see you still hard at work, on my return . . .'

Edith waved her on her way. 'I *insist* you visit *me* soon, anyway!'

Edmund, too, was in his garden – he came towards the gate to greet her. It seemed strange that Boniface was not racing ahead of him.

'Oh, I did hope you'd come,' he told her. 'Cup of tea, Angel?'

'Yes, please!'

It was some time before she gave him Tony's picture. He regarded it gravely, his face very sad. 'I am grateful for this, and please tell Tony I appreciate the title: BONIFACE THE BRAVE. Please thank him, and tell him it will be framed, next time I go into town – I shall hang it in my study at school, I think. In term time I am more there, than here – Boniface was, after all, as much the school's dog, as mine.'

'You'll have another dog eventually, won't you?' she ventured.

'I imagine so. But not yet – I couldn't,' Edmund said.

They were sitting in his kitchen: she saw the dishes piled in the sink, the untidiness overall, and suppressed the wish to do something about it. But she imagined that Edith descended on her brother every now and then, with broom, bucket and plenty of yellow soap – she, Angel should not interfere. Anyway, if she did, it would give Edith cause to think she had protested too much that she did not want to be committed.

'More tea?' he asked. 'Or d'you think it will be too stewed? Edith tells me this place needs a woman's touch, in other words, why don't I take a wife?'

'If you are happy as you are, then you don't need to marry to satisfy Edith.'

'It is probably because she did not wish to remain single, herself,' he said perceptively. 'No sane woman would put up with me, anyway! I have far too many bad habits! I'm not house-trained like my friend Rob. Mind you,' his smile widened, 'I think Edith had an ulterior motive in beguiling *you* to come to The Angel—'

'I'm sure of it!' Angel agreed, smiling back. He really was a most comfortable, honest man to be with: however, she couldn't help remembering the way he had looked at her, off-guard, that day in the strawberry/butterfly field.

As if he knew what she was thinking, he said: 'It's nice to see you on your own, for once – you always seem surrounded by the family up the road! I did enjoy our outing that day, we must do it again.'

'I'd like that,' she approved. 'Especially the motorcycling!'

What he said next, surprised her. 'If ever I did decide to marry, Angel, I would hope it would be to someone like you . . . But, I have never been seriously involved with anyone—'

'Then, at least you won't have the same regrets and heartache for what might have been, Edmund.

As I have. Friendship is so much easier to live with, believe me.'

It was time to go. It seemed quite natural to her to give him a quick hug, to accept the light kiss on her cheek. 'See you soon,' she told him.

'Please.' Then he added quietly, 'I wish I had known you before I went to *my* war, in the Middle East. The only letters I received were from Edith, playing her vital part, as you were, in France. She often mentioned you . . .' He could well have added, 'rather obsessively.'

She felt a moment's disquiet. Had Lou been right, after all? Was Edith's interest in her, a trifle obsessive? Had Edith admitted this to herself?

'*My* sister begged me not to go – but I felt that my father would have expected it of me, d'you understand?'

Edmund nodded. 'I'm sure he would have been very proud of you, if he had lived.' There! He didn't know the whole truth after all.

She flinched. 'In some ways, not in others, I think,' she said quietly. She mustered a bright smile. 'Well, goodbye, again!'

CHAPTER THIRTEEN

Alice and Tony came bursting into the kitchen and hugged both Aunt Hetty and Angel as if they had been away from home at least a month.

'Hold you hard!' Aunt Hetty beamed.

Angel was touched by the breezy affection, *she* was, after all, a paid companion, a nurse, as she often had to remind herself. 'A rest now, Alice,' she told her patient firmly, 'upstairs, not outside, for I'm sure you are full of fresh air, and an hour's nap will do you good, before supper.'

'We made the room ready,' Aunt Hetty said quietly to Rob, who was unloading the great basket on the table.

'Good, thank you, Aunt Hetty,' he said briefly. 'Jess gone?'

'She has. The old boys like her serving, she brings a twinkle to their eye, they say. And Angel here – well *she* has lived up to her name, helping like she does.'

'Fish for tea, Angel – didn't I tell you?' Alice lay down reluctantly on her bed. 'But I wheedled round Dad to get bloaters – you need a lot of bread and butter and plenty of cups of tea to get rid of your thirst, but Lowestoft bloaters are the *best*.'

Downstairs, Tony couldn't wait for the fish to cook, he was already on his third buttered rusk, for sea air had certainly sharpened his appetite. 'Did you take the picture to Edmund?' he enquired through a mouthful.

'I did. He was very pleased indeed, and says he will be along to thank you properly shortly.'

'To see *you* again, I expect – *he's* got a twinkle in his eye—'

'Tony!' Aunt Hetty didn't sound too cross.

'Well, you said it about the old boys in the bar and Jess, Aunt Hetty—'

'That'll do, Tony!' By contrast, Rob's tone was sharp.

After supper, while they still sat around the table, with the cats sniffing round in ecstacy, waiting for the fishy bits, Rob made an announcement. 'Children, I received a letter from your mother this morning. She mentions – that she would like to pay us a short visit – I'm not sure when she is coming—'

'*Why* is she coming?' Alice demanded. For once, Tony seemed at a loss for words.

Aunt Hetty answered, even as Angel realised that this was why they had made the guest bedroom ready, earlier in the day. 'She has been travelling abroad, only just caught up with the post – didn't know you'd been so poorly, Alice, till then – naturally, she says she wants to see you.'

'I don't know if I want to see *her* . . .' but Alice's voice lacked conviction.

'She's your mother. Of course you do.' Rob pushed back his chair and rose. 'I shall expect you to make her welcome, both of you,' he added, as he went off to open up the bar.

'What d'you think, Angel?' Alice demanded.

'Well, I think it's good that she wants to see you – she must want to reassure herself that all is well—'

'She's never worried about us before – or Dad!' Tony put in resentfully.

'You'll need your hair trimmed, Tony. Angel did a good job, didn't she, on Alice – or would you prefer old Aunt Hetty to get the pudding basin out, eh?'

'*You* do it, please, Angel. It was all lop-sided last time Aunt Hetty had a go—'

'Should've kept still, then, my lad.' Aunt Hetty fished out her scissors from the basket beside the rocker. 'No time like the present, if Angel agrees?'

Tony was soon draped round with a towel, and Alice and Aunt Hetty stood too close, offering advice, as Angel pulled out the springy curls and snipped busily. 'It's harder than cutting straight hair, but on the other hand, your mistakes curl up and are hard to detect!'

When Aunt Hetty went to join Rob at the bar, Angel heated soft water from the butt, shredded soap, then washed the children's hair, in turn, at the sink. Alice leaned backwards, for Angel still tried to keep the affected ear as dry as possible. As they dried their hair by the stove, they chatted away, confiding in her.

'I wonder if she'll look like she did – as I remember her?' Alice wondered.

'She isn't an old lady, Alice – I imagine she will!'

'I hope she won't try to be all mother-like,' Tony said, making a face at the very thought. 'We've done quite all right without her, up till now.'

'Give her a chance, Tony. Don't condemn her, before you meet.'

'Off to bed, now – why are you still up?' Rob's voice was sharp again. 'There's a lull in the bar, so Aunt Hetty suggested Angel might wield her scissors on my mop, too – any objections, Angel?'

'None at all,' she answered. 'Go along, Alice, Tony. I'll be up to see you in a little while – I'll bring you some milk, shall I?'

They departed reluctantly.

'So,' she thought wryly, 'he still wants to look his best for *Lalla* . . .'

'Sit down, Rob, here's a dry towel for your shoulders. You like your hair short, don't you?' She could feel herself breathing faster as she leaned over him and took the first tentative snip. She was very glad that she was standing behind the chair and that he could not see her face. The texture of his hair was, indeed, like that of his son's, but he required the curls to be severely cropped, restrained. 'I can't clipper your neck – but it's not too bad . . .'

'*My* feelings are mixed, Angel, regarding my wife's visit,' he said slowly. 'Still, maybe it will be an opportunity to sort things out, finally.'

'A divorce, you mean?' She brushed the hair from his neck, removed the towel, shook it out.

'Perhaps. I was always set against that, it seemed too final – but I can't help wondering what her *real* motive is in coming here.'

'Surely, it's because Alice has been so ill?'

'The children have been ill at other times. She merely wrote then to say she was sorry, and to send money for fruit – an easy way out . . .'

She went over to the sink, 'There's some nice, soapy water still warm, in the bowl – shall I wash your hair for you, too?' Instantly, she wondered why on earth she had suggested such a thing. 'I often washed my brother-in-law's hair,' she added lamely. 'He had to take such care, with that steel plate in his scalp.'

He was actually laughing. 'I'm happy to say – as you will already have seen! – that I have not that excuse, but, well, if you wish it, I accept your offer!'

He stooped, head down and Angel stretched and lathered his hair with firm fingers. He, of course, was completely unaware of the effect his proximity had on her as she reached her arms round his neck.

She was shaking, when she moved back to fetch jugs of cool rinsing water, topped-up with hot from the kettle. He kept his bent stance obediently over the sink as she poured carefully, for naturally, unlike Tony, he had kept on his shirt, although he had unbuttoned it at the throat.

He turned, straightened and caught the warm towel she threw him. 'You can dry it yourself!' She mustn't get too close to him again, she thought.

'Is that an order, Nurse?' he teased.

She said the first thing that came into her head. 'Rob, you remember you said I *ought* to go – I know it's short notice – but I *would* like to visit my sister and her new baby. Alice is so much better—'

'When would you like to go? Tomorrow?' he asked. 'You could make it a long weekend, Angel.' His look was long and searching at her.

'Tomorrow – yes. Thank you, Rob.'

'I will tell Aunt Hetty. And I will drive you to the station, if you go first thing. There, still damp – but I must get back to the bar . . . Goodnight to ye, Angel.'

She busied herself with clearing up, emptying the slops. Was she running away, yet again? she wondered tremulously. Edith would no doubt think so. Though, of course, it *was* time to see Lou and to hold little Peter in her arms.

CHAPTER FOURTEEN

London seemed so noisy, so frantic, reeking of petrol fumes: the Great War had certainly accelerated the use of the internal combustion engine. There were still the humble carts drawn by placid old ponies and even the handcarts, perilously loaded, spilling fruit and veg still weaved along, endangering the public. While the brewers' drays, with their great horses went plodding along as always, and the baker and the milkman remained faithful to their old mode of transport. The bicycle, the delivery tricycle held their own, but the motor bus and electric tram were a cheap and popular mode of travel for the masses.

Angel missed the hansom cabs of her youth, which the square motor cab had long succeeded. However, she hailed the latter, in a moment of recklessness, outside the station, for now she could hardly wait to reach home, that roomy flat above Lou's shop. 'Kensington, please!' she cried.

She paused, for a brief second, to admire the skilful window display, but did not go through the shop: she pressed the bell on the smartly painted white door alongside, having climbed the steps, securely railed on either side. The basement area was used for storage.

Lou looked at her disbelievingly, then thrust her arms out scolding: 'Angel! Why ever didn't you let us know you were coming? Jack is at the Bank, naturally – but he could have taken time off to meet you – oh, come in, do!'

They embraced in the narrow hallway, then, smiling, regarded each other.

'Oh, Lou, you've soon regained your figure – you look – blooming!' Angel approved, thinking, as she always did, how different they looked: Lou, with her fair hair, pale complexion and grey eyes was so like their mother. Lou certainly didn't look her thirty-eight years, motherhood had relaxed her, softened her expression. Perhaps Angel could relinquish her role, at last, as substitute daughter.

'So do you,' Lou told her, 'you look happy, Angel. I was wrong, I know now, to try to keep you here – over-protective, after all you'd been through. The shop wasn't right for you. But, I meant well—'

'I know that, Lou. Yet, what would I have done without you, these past few years? However, it really was time for me to stand on my own two feet again. The family at The Angel – well, they are good friends already, and I am very fond of them all.'

'I am so glad.' Lou meant it. 'I can hear your nephew stirring – come and meet him, then it's time to feed him. Afterwards we'll find ourselves some lunch, though I warn you, I am completely disorganised in that respect. Poor Jack has to take what comes, but he doesn't seem to mind, and the wonderful news is, that Jack hasn't had a single bad turn, not even a little headache, since Peter was born. The Bank are more than happy with his progress.'

'May I?' Angel asked, lifting the baby from a cradle that was very different from Belinda's, this one was hung around with muslin flounces and blue satin ribbons. 'Ah, Peter Carlo,' she discovered to her pleasure, 'you are like our papa – eyes already dark like chocolate! He is wonderful, Lou – you are so lucky!'

Lou, being half-Italian herself, although she seemed so English, would not worry at the tears she was unable to stem, Angel thought.

'Hand him over!' Lou gave a mock sigh. 'Like all men, he is insatiable!' And she unbuttoned her blouse.

They talked of old times while Peter nursed, and Angel, curled up comfortably beside her sister on the bed, slipped off her shoes.

'Angel!' Lou exclaimed, 'wherever did you find those shoes? You really are the sensible nurse again, eh? Not becoming *too* like that fierce friend of yours, Edith, I hope . . .'

'Don't disparage my footwear, Lou – essential country wear!' She refused to allow herself to rise to the gibe about Edith, nor did she relate the history of her practical footwear.

'Peter is such a placid baby, unlike you, when you were small, Angel—'

'You always said I was too quiet as a child.'

'Ah, after Papa was gone, perhaps. But, Angel dear, there was always such passion beneath the surface. That is why you found it so hard to accept what happened in France – when you lost Harry.'

'I was so angry, as well as sad,' Angel said quietly. 'To be accused, as I was, Lou – even though I was exonerated – it was a fearful burden to bear.' She had been able to tell Lou the facts of this – had to, in explaining why she was sent home from France, and Lou had been fiercely protective, ironically, just as Edith had been . . . The other tragedy was a very private affair.

'You must put all that behind you, it's been a long while, Angel; Jack and I keep hoping you will meet the right man, be just as happy as we are, especially now we have our precious Peter Carlo . . . There, my lad, a quick change, and then you can resume your nap, and allow Angel and me to have our meal, eh?'

'I don't have the nightmares any more, Lou . . .' She realised that she hadn't actually thought of Harry in weeks. *I can't tell her*, she thought, as she helped with the baby's changing, *that I believe I have fallen in love again, at long last, but that nothing can come of it . . . Yet, it is still a wonderful feeling to – almost – lay the memory of darling Harry to rest. She must accept Rob's friendship, not look for more.*

Thick soup, crusty bread rolls, cheese – Lou and Angel talked non-stop over their improvised meal.

'The shop is doing well, the manageress is very

enthusiastic, with just the right background.' Lou lit the gas stove to heat the coffee pot. 'Still, you know, Angel, they say this country is heading for a crash – we are fortunate that Jack is in such a safe job, and that we still have a little invested for a rainy day.'

'The country way of living is, I think, the same as it was when the old Queen was alive,' Angel observed. 'Does it amaze you, Lou, to think of me bathing in a tin tub in the scullery? Mind you, there's the pleasure to come of bathing before the kitchen stove in the winter—'

'Not with an audience, I trust?' Lou grinned.

'No! Though Aunt Hetty has offered already to scrub my back! Soft water, out of the rain butt, Lou, you scoop out the creepy crawlies and hot it up. There's lovely Pears soap to wash with, but plain old soap to shred for washing your hair – you must rinse and rinse and *rinse* – but, just look, you end up with twice the shine, don't you? Aunt Hetty bakes our bread, grows our veg, everything tastes so good, so fresh. Mind you, I do sometimes think wistfully of the water closet here, for our "offices" are down the garden path, and even though I was terrified of the geezer over our bath – all that popping and hissing! – I miss instant hot water, too . . . The local people, Lou, they work so hard – there's a wonderful old character called Nana Elderberry, for instance, who treats Edith with great suspicion, says she's far too keen on carbolic – and she has a granddaughter called Jess, who works all the hours God sends, and never complains, to support her old Nana and her baby Belinda. Then there's Mrs Newsome at the shop who knows what everyone is up to, round and about – and Edmund, the schoolmaster – would you believe, I've ridden on the back of his motor cycle?'

'And the family you're so fond of,' Lou laughed. 'But tell me more about this Edmund, though I'm not sure I approve of his method of transport, Angel . . .'

Perhaps it was as well, Angel thought, to talk more of Edmund than, well, of Rob. She didn't want Lou to put two and two together, for she would surely then try to persuade her sister to leave the very place where she longed to stay.

'Edmund is a confirmed bachelor, and as I am now a maiden aunt, we get along very nicely together. No romance – but he's really nice – you would like him, Lou.'

Lou said slyly: 'Sometimes good friends surprise themselves by becoming lovers, Angel! Not all marriages begin with youthful passion, like Jack and I – at twenty and eighteen years of age!'

'Not all brides take on a small sister as *you* did, Lou.'

'It will be better for you, Angel, to stay in London, with your sister,' Mother told her. 'Sidney, after all, is not used to children. He had no family with his first wife, and as he is over fifty, ten years older

than me – it would not be fair to expect him to take you on, you see.' Angel did not discern the distress in her mother's eyes. She could not realise that these words had more-or-less been put into her mother's mouth by her new stepfather. She only knew that she was being rejected. But she did not know that Lou felt the same . . .

Their new intimacy prompted Lou to say now: 'It was hard on me and on Jack, Angel, I have to admit it. But I was determined to keep my promise to Papa, to look after you, while he was away. I felt resentment, for I was so newly married, and here was our mother, abdicating from her responsibility to you, graciously opening an account at the bank, so that *I* could look after you, see you through school, into adulthood. We put off having a baby, then, Angel, because we thought you might feel pushed-aside: you can imagine how we felt, when later, I found it so difficult to conceive. Still, when you decided to go into nursing, we were so happy to see you following Papa, into a caring profession.'

'You tried to stop me going to France . . .' Angel murmured.

'You might have been saved all – *that* – you know, if you had stayed here to nurse the wounded who came "home to Blighty",' Lou reminded her gently.

A key turned in the front door, and Jack, a much more confident Jack, cried, 'Well, I never!' at the sight of his sister-in-law, and Angel was given a warm welcome-home hug and kiss. As if on cue, Peter Carlo woke and gave a hungry yell.

'Feed our lad, first,' Jack told Lou ruefully. But Angel could tell he did not mind at all.

'Let me cook the evening meal, please,' she asked later, picking up Lou's shopping basket. 'I want to treat my favourite sister and brother-in-law to a real Italian meal.'

Pasta, olive oil and garlic; the ingredients for a green salad; strong cheese; and Neapolitan ice-cream, to transfer quickly to the icebox – what better? And a bottle of red wine, of course.

They talked until very late, when Lou again had to scoop up her baby for yet another feed, and, yawning, Jack put the kettle on for a final warm drink.

'Sunday tomorrow, we can have a lie-in, if Peter allows . . .' Lou said sleepily. 'Your bed's made-up, Angel – I kept it aired, hoping you'd be back soon.'

'I promise to come back more often,' Angel said slowly. 'But I want to stay on, as long as they'll have me – as long as they need me – in Suffolk, Lou. Don't forget that Peter Carlo will need a room of his own – he may have mine, with my love. I'm sure he won't mind sharing with me, on occasion!'

Lou looked at her searchingly. 'You see, my intuition was right, there *is* more to it, isn't there, than you'll tell me?'

'Alice and Tony – their mother left them, like

our mother left me. I *understand*, Lou, and, maybe—' she paused.

'Maybe *you* need *them*,' Lou finished. 'Goodnight, dear Angel!'

Surprisingly, she did not fall instantly asleep, despite the late hour. The gentle murmuring of voices heard through the partition wall, then silence, and she knew that Lou and Jack slept with their arms around each other, with their baby close by in his crib.

She cradled the thought of a tall man, with curling dark hair, bending over her, brushing her hair gently from her eyes, and she sighed. He, she thought, would be waiting for Lalla to return, wondering what the outcome would be. They would need her, if they were to be deserted again.

It was good to have said things to Lou that had never been aired before. But she must face the fact that she was envious of her sister, for she had Jack, who loved her dearly, and now, little Peter Carlo.

She would go home, first thing, on Monday morning.

CHAPTER FIFTEEN

They were not expecting her back at The Angel until Tuesday afternoon. So, as she had on the day she arrived, she walked from the crossroads. This time she was sure of the way and she was not so laden.

She was hatless today, and the sun beat down unmercifully on her head. She thought of Edmund out in Mesopotamia in the war, where he'd told her that a soldier who removed his pith helmet to mop the sweat from his head was in instant danger of sunstroke. She suddenly recalled a vivid sentence from one of his letters, read to her by Edith, when they were in France, 'The heat is so intense our rifle steel burns our hands . . .' She stopped by the schoolhouse, but he was not about, and she foraged in her bag for a flimsy scarf, which she tied to protect her head and neck.

A little motorcar rattled to a halt just ahead. The top was rolled back, the white tyres had gathered dust – a cheeky tin-can of a motor, with a lady driver, looking back over her shoulder and calling cheerfully: 'Can I give you a lift?'

Angel realised immediately that this must be Lalla. 'Please!' she called back. 'I am going to The Angel . . .'

'Quite a coincidence,' smiled the lady, as Angel climbed in beside her. 'So am I. You are—?'

'I am Alice MacDonald's nurse.'

'And I am Alice's mother!'

The motor rumbled on its way, swerving round the ruts, causing some mothers and children, who were talking outside the shop, to stare, startled, as it passed.

'Hang on!' Lalla cried blithely, as they forked sharp. 'You don't look like a nurse,' she observed, as they left behind them a wreath of smoke outside the Big House, almost choking Will and his lad with the exhaust fumes.

Angel hoped that Lalla had not noticed her shoes: she was wearing the sea-green silk, but despite its flimsiness, she realised that her face must be red from her exertions and that her upper arms had caught the sun. 'I have been home, to London, for the weekend,' she explained.

'Another coincidence – and such a pity, for had I been aware of your existence, which I was not, I could have brought you all the way, for I have come from there, myself.'

Lalla did, indeed, possess an unconventional beauty, Angel thought, returning Lalla's friendly smile. Her face was sharply featured, but her lustrous dark eyes, long-lashed, and her full, sensuously curved mouth drew the attention. Lips which did not need to be stained with wild strawberries to suggest that they had been much kissed. Fine hair, she had, like Alice, but hers feathered endearingly round her face, much blonder than her daughter's. A skilful hairdresser had no doubt achieved this, but the paleness of her hair complemented the soft, almost white skin.

They swept with panache into the yard at The Angel.

'Here we are! By the way, I'm Lalla and I hope that what you've heard of me, is not all bad . . .'

'I'm Angel,' Angel returned. They stood together by the motor, and she realised that Lalla was really quite short, with a slender, boyish figure quite concealed by a loose, primrose cotton dress, which daringly just skimmed her knees. No darns in silk stockings for Lalla, for her legs were bare; she wore strapped sandals, like the ones in Bible pictures. She looked cool, unflustered, not overheated like Angel.

'How strange, an Angel at The Angel,' Lalla observed. 'Ah, here they come – I knew the motor would announce our arrival.'

Aunt Hetty, shading her eyes against the sun, looked uncertainly from the door. Tony bounded over, then stopped suddenly, a few feet short of his mother.

Lalla held out her arms dramatically. 'Tony – I'd have known you anywhere! Don't be shy!' And Tony went at once into her embrace.

'Alice may still be resting,' Angel said, averting

her eyes. 'Aren't you coming inside?' She moved towards the door herself.

She saw that Aunt Hetty looked tired, as if she had not slept much last night, and that her gaze was wary. She wore her washing-day apron, her hands were reddened and wrinkled from the suds and Angel recalled with compunction that it was Monday after all, not the day for visitors to arrive.

'I decided to come back today,' she explained unnecessarily. 'Lalla gave me a lift – half-way along the lane . . .'

'I'm glad to see you,' Aunt Hetty said fervently, 'Alice is still abed – shall I leave it to you, to fetch her down, tell her who's here, dearie?'

'I will,' Angel said, going swiftly along the hall as she heard Aunt Hetty say, 'It has been a long time, Lalla.'

'Seven years,' Lalla replied. 'Where is Rob, Aunt Hetty – doesn't he want to see me?'

'He's in the bar, we have just opened. There's only two or three old-timers on a Monday – he will see to them, then close up, he says. Go in the front parlour, Lalla. It's upside down still in the kitchen. I'll make some tea!'

'Oh, Angel – good, you're back!' Alice exclaimed, reclining on her coverlet in her petticoat because it was so warm.

'Not only me, Alice – your mother has arrived, too,' Angel told her.

'Oh, Dad said maybe tomorrow – but, how exciting! What does she look like?' She pulled her dress over her head and scrabbled with her feet for her slippers.

'She gave me a lift, up the lane. She must look much as she did when you were little, for she really doesn't look old enough to have a daughter like you—' Angel passed Alice the hairbrush.

'What d'you think – d'you *like* her?'

'Yes, I did – well, I do! She seems a – warm kind of person, I think—'

'Like you, Angel!'

'Oh, Alice, *she's* quite – *beautiful*, go and see for yourself!'

'I will!' Alice cried, but she paused to hug Angel on her way out. 'But she can't be as nice as you, Angel, 'cause if you'd been my mother, you wouldn't have deserted me, would you?'

Angel couldn't trust herself to answer that one, she merely hugged Alice briefly, in return.

In her own room, she quickly changed into her everyday dress. She couldn't – mustn't – compete with Lalla, she told herself wryly. But she wondered how Rob would react to his wife, she couldn't help herself.

Aunt Hetty was just emerging from the kitchen with a tray of sandwiches and cups of tea. 'They are having a little talk, the four of them, on their own,' she said. 'Jess is just pouring out for us.'

But Jess, Angel discovered, was not doing any such thing. She sat, slumped at the table, her head on her folded arms.

'Jess – whatever's wrong?' Angel placed her arm

round the girl's shoulders. The rich, coppery hair was damp with sweat and the steam from the scullery.

'I'm a'weary . . .' Jess's voice was muffled. Then she made a big effort to pull herself together, sat up determinedly, and smiled, waveringly, at Angel. 'It's just – well, Nana has been poorly most of the night – and Belinda, she didn't seem to be satisfied, however often I put her to the breast. Then, the bugler, *he* started and I come along at dawn to find the poor feller still out and about—'

'You're worn out, you try to do far too much, Jess,' Angel said, concerned. 'No wonder your milk is going.'

'I got to mangle them last few bits, hang 'em out, and then there's the copper to empty, the flags to wash—' Jess murmured.

'You won't be doing any of those things, Jess. Look, I'll pour the tea, make my own sandwich, then you go on home when you've had yours and I'll finish up for you here—'

'You've got your own jobs, Nurse . . .' Jess made a move to rise.

'Sit down, Jess! And stay there!'

'You sound just like Miss Fenner!'

'Good! I'm not on nursing duty today, I've got the rest of the day free to help you and Aunt Hetty and plenty of energy after a weekend away. There! Here's your tea, and a sandwich for you – fancy that?'

Jess nodded. 'I had some grub earlier but,' she

looked bemused, 'I *need* to work, you see, Nurse. Nana says with her so poorly it's the workhouse next, we'll be living on the parish like. Mind you, she's handed on her pride to *me*!'

'Wouldn't the church help?' Angel asked, biting into her own sandwich. She had learned that this was a comfortable living for Lady Pamela was generous to the incumbent.

'He – the old parson – pointed me out in church. I used to go most every Sunday, living under the church as we do, but when I was big with Belinda he said: "This gal has committed a sin. Don't anybody have anything to do with her until she repents." Lady Pamela was away that day, maybe he would have held his tongue otherwise . . . Nana said to me, "come on home gal, there's cold charity here. *Every* babe is a blessing from our Holy Father – can't he see that? We won't take a penny from *there*." Aunt Hetty, good old soul that she is, came straight round to ours after the service and told us: "There's always work at The Angel for you, Jess, whenever you feel like it." She judged for herself you see. Anyway, I have my feller to see after, too.'

'Tony and Rob will look after him, I'm sure, and I'll come and see Nana just as soon as I can,' Angel promised, clearing her throat. 'Eat up – then home you go . . .'

Aunt Hetty demurred a little when she discovered Angel hard at work with mop and bucket in the scullery, but she bit her lip in worry, when

Angel enlightened her about Jess. 'Oh, dear, I must have worked her too hard!'

'Not your fault, Aunt Hetty. You need the help, and Jess is desperate to make a living for the three of them. If you say it's too much for her, even though it may be, she'll be destitute. No, *I* can help more – I want to, please. If I'm to justify staying here a while, now Alice is convalescing, well, I must earn my keep. I'm used to this sort of work – from my early nursing days and my time in France.' She longed to ask how Aunt Hetty thought things were going, in the parlour, but it was not her place to do so.

Rob hung a notice on the door:

SORRY – BAR CLOSED UNTIL
FURTHER NOTICE.
OFF-LICENCE SERVICE ONLY.

Aunt Hetty observed to Angel, as they unpegged the dry linen, 'The whole village'll know why. They'll have seen the motor coming – know *who's* back.'

'Is she staying long, Aunt Hetty?' Angel asked diffidently. She watched Lalla walking down the meadow with her children, arms around their waists, Alice already topping her by a good inch, and their laughter drifted back to them, in the garden.

'She don't say. She tells Rob she just wants to see the children – before she goes away again. She and that Gerald are going to Australia, so she says – that's much too far to come on home from there, eh? But *I* reckon she came in hope – just to see if he'll have her back. She may be all smiles, but she don't seem happy to me – lost a lot of weight, too—'

'It is probably too late for a reconciliation,' Rob said, startling them. He, too, gazed after the happy trio, now petting the goat and her remaining kid. Then he turned and walked back into the house, without another word.

'Oh, dear, my fault, Aunt Hetty – I shouldn't have been discussing his private affairs with you . . .' Angel was near to tears. Rob had been hurt enough.

They ate a formal supper together, in the parlour, using the silver cutlery and linen napkins, Lalla and Rob's wedding china, given to them by Aunt Hetty and her husband. More of the cold beef, but with new peas, potatoes and to follow, a freshly made apple pie with cream. Aunt Hetty's quick way with the pastry made it light and flaky. Alice and Tony sat close by their mother, vying for her attention. The others concentrated on their food.

'Your neighbour, from the pink house, came over for a word,' Lalla said. 'A strange woman, I thought – she had the effrontery to tell me that she hoped I had not come home to upset the apple cart!'

'Edith has been a good friend to us, especially recently,' Rob said evenly. 'She is rather John Blunt, I'm afraid.'

'You've still got the picture, the one I painted of the children, I see. I'd like to take you for a day to the sea, children, you could come as well, Angel, of course. Though, forgive me, Alice hardly seems to need a nurse . . .'

'You didn't see her a few weeks ago,' Aunt Hetty stated firmly.

However, they all relaxed, for the children's sake, with no customers to call Rob or Aunt Hetty away. The gramophone was wound up and Lalla produced half-a-dozen new records – lively, fast piano music, American style – the board games came out and they all sat around the table and competed noisily. Angel did not remind Alice when it was her usual time for going to bed, or tell her that she would be over-tired next morning.

Angel and Aunt Hetty went to the kitchen eventually, to tackle the washing-up, while the children packed up their games and at last went upstairs to bed, leaving Rob and Lalla on their own, to talk, if that was what they wanted.

'I'll pop down to Nana's tomorrer, take them a few bits, Jess's money – tell her to take a holiday, poor gal, paid of course,' Aunt Hetty said kindly. 'And just *you* be quiet this night, my lad,' she said, looking out of the window at the distant barn. 'Leave the poor gal in peace.'

Alice called sleepily through their connecting door, when Angel was disrobing: 'Angel, will my mother come in to say goodnight?'

'I'm sure she will,' Angel replied, hoping fervently

that Lalla would not let her children down. *Had they been told*, she wondered, *that this visit was by way of a final goodbye? They had both been so animated, bowled over by her charm. It had been Rob who, despite making a valiant effort for their sake, had betrayed the bewilderment, the undoubted pain he felt, at Lalla's precipitate return. He will lie awake tonight, wondering how he can cope with her being here – how he can allow her to go again . . .* she thought, longing to be the one to comfort him, to be able to tell him that *she* would be here for him, and for Alice and Tony, when Lalla was gone. All she could offer, in reality, was staunch friendship.

Lalla *did* come: she heard the murmur of voices, then Lalla told her daughter: 'See you in the morning, my darling!'

'It's so wonderful to have you home!' Alice replied.

CHAPTER SIXTEEN

Only the children slept well that night. Aunt Hetty lay, worrying over what lay ahead: would Lalla want to take the children away from them? Angel tossed and turned, wondering what Rob was feeling and thinking that when things seemed to be going well, they always disappointed her, after all. Edith was not even undressed: she stood at her bedroom window, waiting for the bugler to begin his lament. She was still seething, from her encounter with Lalla earlier. She determined that Lalla would not spoil her special relationship with the family. Rob lay on top of his bed covers, arms clasped behind his head as if he were waiting for something to happen.

Lalla crossed to the washstand and stubbed out her cigarette in the soap dish. She wore a plain cotton nightgown in pale blue, with a matching wrap. These old houses were never quiet at night, she thought, the creaks and sighs echoed her own disquiet. She sprinkled a little eau de cologne on her palms and ran her fingers through her hair, to disguise the tell-tale smell of smoke.

She inched the door open, padded silently on

bare feet, down the stairs to Rob's room. She gave the door knob a little rattle, an old signal from the days when she was a guest in the house, before they were married. Not that anything untoward had occurred then, she thought, with a sudden smile, Rob was always so proper and Aunt Hetty had always been nearby. Only Lalla had a past . . .

It was a long minute before Rob opened the door, for he had donned his dressing gown and slippers. He did not show surprise. He motioned her inside, pulled forwards the cane armchair, removed his pile of clothes from the seat. She sat down, as he turned the lamp wick up.

'You expected me?' she asked. Without the vivid makeup she looked very pale, young and vulnerable.

'Are you happy?' he returned. He sat on the edge of the bed.

'Do you really care?'

'I care.'

'Am I happy with Gerald, is that what you mean? I only know I can't live without him. He'll never marry me, Rob, I accept that – it's an all-consuming love we share for each other. Please believe that I *did* love you when I married you, that I was sure, then, that Gerald was part of the past . . . If you'd only been here, when he sought me out again—'

'How could I help being away – fighting for my country!'

'I would have taken the children with me, you know, though I guess Aunt Hetty would have fought tooth-and-nail to keep them, on your behalf. But he only wanted *me* – that's why we've never had children of our own.'

'Do you want a divorce, Lalla, is that it?'

'Only if you wish it, if you intend to remarry . . .'

'At present, I intend no such thing.'

'Then, let's not put ourselves through the pain of such a final act: it would hurt the children too, I think—'

'All the while we are still married, Lalla, I imagine Alice and Tony harbour hopes that their mother may return to them, one day. Perhaps it's for the best, I really don't know.'

'I just came, tonight, to reassure you that the children will always be with *you*, Rob. That is the only fair thing I have done for you.' She rose, came over to the bed, sat close beside him, lifted his hand, gently unclenched it. 'Don't let there be anger between us, Rob – I take all the blame, all the responsibility for what happened. I want us still to be friends.'

'Is that possible?' he asked sadly.

She pressed her face against his shoulder. She gave a sly, unexpected nip at his waist. 'You have kept in shape, Rob – no surplus flesh . . .'

'And you are too thin, Lalla, much too thin.' His arm circled her waist. 'I don't think you'd be like this, if you really *were* happy.'

'I've always been a restless spirit. I was born to be on the move, always seeking, I think. Will you kiss me goodnight, for old time's sake, Rob?'

Her lips were as full, warm and yielding, as he had dreamed. It was a brief kiss, then he put her from him. 'You must go back to your room, now, Lalla. Goodnight.'

The bugler played the first, uncertain notes. She was coming swiftly towards him, across the grass.

Edith saw a light in the window upstairs, the room she knew to be Rob's. Was he watching the bugler, too – or was there some other reason? She couldn't stem her suspicions, the stab of jealousy.

'Jess?' the bugler questioned.

'It doesn't seem that she will come tonight. Let *me* take you back to the barn, to your bed, my dear.' The nurse in her was uppermost now.

When Rob brought up the copper cans of hot water, whispering feathery smoke, Angel was in Alice's room, examining Alice's ear, as she scrupulously did each day.

'Aunt Hetty thought it looked rather red inside, yesterday,' Alice told her father, a trifle anxiously.

'No discharge,' Angel reassured her. 'Will you wash and dress now, Alice? You will want to be up earlier this week, with your mother here, eh? The excitement doesn't seem to be doing her any harm, Rob!' she added, for his benefit.

'Good,' he said. 'I'll bring your can through, Angel.'

He placed it on the washstand, after closing the connecting door. Angel was all too conscious that she was clad only in her nightdress. She knew she must present a rumpled, straight-out-of-bed appearance.

As if completing a conversation which they had not even begun, he said, 'She hasn't returned to me, as I always hoped, whatever I avowed, but I'm sure that she *does* still love the children, even though she doesn't love *me*, and she has a right to see them, and they, of course, have a right to be with her . . . It will be hard, Angel, but I would like to think I can be generous enough to make this a happy few days for Alice and Tony – Lalla, too . . . D'you understand? D'you think I am right?' This was a question he had patently agonised over, most of the night, for he looked tired and bleary-eyed.

'Yes, you are right.' She was wryly aware that he had not stopped to think of the impropriety of talking to her in her bedroom and that he had not even noticed that she was still in her night attire. She went on, positively, 'The children will love *you* even more for this, when they are older.' She was very sure of that.

'Thank you, Angel.' His smile was bleak. 'We haven't known you long, but we all have a staunch ally in you, that's obvious.' As he went out through the door, he said, 'Lalla is a night person, she will sleep-in, no doubt. She always had her breakfast in bed, in the old days. Aunt Hetty is already busy at the stove, by the way, and Tony will see to the bugler, while Jess is away.'

'I heard him again, last night,' she said.

'So did I. I looked out and I saw Edith leading him away.'

'He must wonder where Jess is.'

'Edith will put him in the picture. What a good friend *she* is to us, too.'

CHAPTER SEVENTEEN

It was Tony who eagerly took up his mother's breakfast tray and Alice who hastily plundered Aunt Hetty's sweet peas, which climbed alongside the runner beans, and stuffed them haphazardly in a narrow vase, 'For her to smell, when she opens her eyes, to know she's really back in the country at last, even if they *do* mingle with the smell of bacon and eggs!'

After breakfast, Rob suggested that he take Aunt Hetty in the trap to shop at Mrs Newsome's then to visit Jess and Nana, to see how they were. 'It seems very strange,' mused Aunt Hetty, as she actually abandoned the washing-up to the children and a basket of ironing for Angel, 'not to be thinkin' of opening up the bar today – I haven't had a holiday since I got married!'

'Time you did, then, Aunt Hetty – off you go!' Angel said with spirit. She couldn't help suspecting that Rob was intent on keeping out of Lalla's way this morning.

She ironed on the table, over a folded blanket, testing the irons in turn, with a spittle-wet finger, for that satisfying sizzle. The children folded the sheets with a will and Alice volunteered to press the hankies – she really was gaining more energy every day, Angel thought, pleased. The doors and windows were wide open, letting through a pleasant current of air, and Angel dampened the starched linen and enjoyed watching the creases vanish under the pressure of the flat-iron.

'You're all very busy,' Lalla observed brightly, placing her cluttered tray on the draining board. She had hardly done justice to her meal, Angel saw. Lalla wore another loose dress, with billowing sleeves, smocked at wrist and yoke, cinnamon coloured.

'Lalla makes all her own dresses, Angel – to her own designs. She used to make our smocks, when we were small, like in the picture in the parlour – you know?'

'I certainly do, Alice,' Angel replied. She thought it was so easy to like Lalla, while certainly not condoning her abandonment of her family.

Lalla rumpled Alice's hair. 'I understand you were responsible for this nice cut, Angel – thank you. But we really must go out and buy you some new dresses, Alice. I only wish I had time to make them, Aunt Hetty is way behind the times!'

This was tactless, of course, Angel thought ruefully, as she relinquished the cooling iron and hankies to Alice, which she and Tony had pulled hard into squares.

Lalla said quietly, just for Angel to hear, as she followed her into the pantry, where she piled up the clean, muslin cloths which Aunt Hetty used for covering the food, 'That terrible scar – my poor Alice – I feel *shattered* that I had no idea what she was going through, Angel . . . Will she – have that, for life?'

Angel recognised the fear in Lalla's eyes. It was no use prevaricating: 'I'm afraid she will, Lalla. Fortunately, the scar is easily concealed by her hair. It is best, if you will excuse me giving you advice, in my professional capacity, not to comment on it, I think. Yes, a new dress or two is a very good idea, indeed! Alice is growing up, she needs to feel confident about her appearance, especially after such a lowering experience.'

'You are not married – have no children of your own?' Lalla asked. 'Yet you seem so in tune with mine.'

Angel was glad that she could not detect jealousy in Lalla's words. She took them on their face value. 'I love children – no, none of my own – but I seem to have a good understanding of them.' She could not stop herself from adding, 'Anyway, Rob and Aunt Hetty seem to think so . . .'

Lalla's glance was keen. 'Especially Rob, eh?' she said softly. 'Oh, don't worry, Angel, I won't say a thing, but – I can see how things are, with *you*.' Could that be a sigh of regret? She added, 'He is a most attractive man, after all.'

Off to the sea they bowled, in the little motor, as promised, that afternoon. It took only ten minutes to reach the pretty little seaside town with its parade of busy shops; the green where energetic holiday-makers played tennis; the imposing lighthouse, towering snowy-white above all; the carved, painted caricature heads fastened over the doors of a row of seamen's cottages and the great church, with copper spire turned blue-green, with its kissing gates and carefully tended graves. Through the town they drove to the blue-railed promenade with the banks of sea-pinks, thrift and lupins stretching down to the shingle, on which, following a storm, amber might be discovered by those with a keen eye, and beyond, the soft, golden sand and the lapping sea. Fishing boats were beached, against which picnickers leaned, to rest their backs: the old bathing machines were still in use for disrobing and drying-off for more modest swimmers, but the sexes were no longer segregated, nor did the machines trundle into the deeper water for discreet immersing. It was rumoured that a row of splendid beach huts were to be erected, little home-from-homes with balconies – not for sleeping in, it's true, but with facilities for making tea, or cooking simple meals. Since the war, the town was slowly changing, moving with the times, but the salty character would hopefully be retained. It was certainly a popular place, for the beach was crowded.

They did not hire a machine, for only Tony proposed to paddle. Alice spied the ice cream tricycle, and Punch and Judy booth. 'Oh, may we see the show?' she asked, excited. Smiling, Lalla slipped some loose change into her children's pockets.

'Go and enjoy yourselves! Don't let your ices drip, oh, and come back to us here, after the show – Angel and I will just enjoy a lazy chat, I think.' The look at Angel belied this.

Angel thought, '*She* must *realise where my loyalties lie – well, that's obvious, after her earlier remarks* . . .'

'We couldn't come here during the war,' Lalla remarked, 'but this was always a special place for me. We spent our wedding night here, in the big hotel. I really loved Rob then, you know, but there was always Gerald, in the background . . .' They lay, side by side on the sand, but now Lalla propped herself up on her elbow: 'I met *him* at the art school, I was not even eighteen when I fled from home to live with him. My parents were absolutely horrified, they had indulged me in my training, although it was not at all what they had in mind for their only, spoilt child – I was so wilful, Angel, I *always* got my own way. But, Gerald, who was so much older and experienced than me – my *tutor*! – someone so bohemian in their eyes, well, they cut me off without a penny . . . They are both dead now, and I bitterly regret never getting back in touch with them – they never knew Rob, of whom they would have approved, I think, or their grandchildren. I was upset, and surprised, when their money came to me, in the end.' This must be true, for her eyes were suspiciously bright.

'You don't have to tell me all this, Lalla – indeed, perhaps you shouldn't!' Angel put in, 'I am not sitting in judgement on you.' Yet, she longed to hear the rest.

'I *want* to tell you, so that one day, you can tell Alice and Tony if they ask, how it all was—'

'How can you be sure that I will still be around?'

'Angel, I just know that you will . . . I want them to know I did love their father and I do love them, but even though I quarrelled bitterly with Gerald before I fled here, to lick my wounds, I suppose – to find a man as splendid as Rob – I couldn't forget *him*. When he came back into my life so unexpectedly, I couldn't fight my feelings. I would have taken the children, but Aunt Hetty refused to allow it: she was right, I am not a good mother, they needed the stability of their home, the love of their father.' Her voice was husky now.

'So, you really are intending to go away, for ever,' Angel stated. In the clear light she noted the little lines etched on Lalla's face, and knew instinctively that this was a doomed love, just as hers and Harry's had been.

'Yes, I am going away. I shan't see any of them again. I know that.'

'Will – will you divorce him, this time – make a clean break?'

'Divorce is not an issue, we've agreed that and Gerald has never pressed me to marry him . . . But, Rob you know, Angel, is an honourable man.

He will not look for love elsewhere until it is really all over, with me.'

'I am aware of that. Anyway, he does not – see me in that light—' her voice faltered. 'He has asked me to stay on for a while – more the companion than the nurse now, I feel, to both Alice and Tony – but eventually I will have to move on. I had no intention of ever falling in love again – I was so badly hurt when I lost my first love during the war . . . There are things I can't confide, but you can probably guess some of it. In any case, Rob would never want to replace *you*, with *me* . . .'

'Don't be too sure of that, Angel.' Lalla took up her sketch block, a soft pencil and began to draw a tiny girl, in a sagging hand-knitted bathing costume skipping in the foam as the tide receded. She had already done thumbnail sketches of an ancient, nut-brown fisherman mending a torn net and of a little blue boat with white sails moving through the dark green swell of the sea, far out.

The children came running back, Tony with ice cream stains down the front of the shirt which had been still warm from the touch of Angel's iron when he put it on, an hour or two ago.

'The Punch and Judy show was hilarious!' Alice enthused. 'Mr Punch was so bold – so beastly! He really whacked poor Judy with his stick – and there was a *real* Dog Toby—'

'Who opened his mouth and barked and growled at all the right places—' Tony butted in. 'Aren't we going to walk along the beach to the Pier now? You promised, Lalla!'

Angel and Lalla brushed the sand from their skirts and put on their shoes.

They couldn't go back to The Angel without a big bag brimming with the local brown shrimps for tea, of course.

Shoes were shaken in the garden, for as Aunt Hetty remarked: 'That old sand gets everywhere!' She had been busy picking the last of the raspberries, and Rob, who had been catching up on the accounts, had fetched thick cream from the farm.

They were all at ease with one another now, Angel thought, as they topped and tailed the shrimps, ate mounds of bread and butter, except for Lalla, who reminded them that she was allergic to shellfish. She took up her sketch book and with a few swift strokes captured the essence of the happy family seated round the kitchen table – the kitlings mewing in anticipation of a small feast of their own.

'You eat hardly enough to keep a fly on the wing,' Aunt Hetty said, with a shrewd look at Lalla.

Lalla smiled. 'There!' She put her pencil down. 'The drawings may smell shrimpy, but I hope you will keep them, in memory of – a day of sand, sea and shellfish!'

'That's the way to do it!' Tony cried, in a fair imitation of old Mr Punch. 'Here's your share, kitlings!'

I think she meant, Angel thought, to remember *her* by . . .

Even dear Aunt Hetty was relaxing in the company of one she had once been fond of, after all.

'Clouding up – cooler,' Rob observed later, gazing out of the window. He was restless without the usual business of the bar.

'Might be a storm, I reckon,' Aunt Hetty mused, 'Off to bed, children! It's wholly late.'

The first crackles of thunder awoke Angel. She went swiftly to close her window as she heard rain spattering on the panes. It was sultry, sticky: she washed her face and hands with water from the jug. She shuddered, as a longer, much louder burst of thunder reverberated round the room. The scissor of lightning followed almost immediately. The storm must be right overhead. In a panic, she opened her door, saw Aunt Hetty's just closing, and knew that Tony had gone to his aunt for refuge – but Alice appeared to be slumbering unawares. She found herself descending the stairs, past Rob's door, stumbling down to the kitchen, it seemed safer downstairs.

Like a terrible, unrelenting storm the gunfire raged: the casualties came in to the hospital, carried by comrades, often wounded themselves, or stretchered by brave men under the banner of the red cross. There was blood soaking her uniform, blood on her hands, yet compassion overrode shock, fear and anger at the senseless mutilation. She moved fast, looking to Edith to tell her where she was needed most, who might be saved, and who could not. He was brought in late in the day after having gone to see what could be done for those still groaning, alive, pinned underneath an overturned vehicle. He had dragged two men free, when the shell hit him in the back. She was screaming, and Edith's hand struck her cheek . . .

His arms were round her, holding her close, her face against his chest, so that her screams were muffled. She shook violently, as he soothed her, until she subsided limply against the warmth and strength of his body.

'Don't be afraid, Angel,' Rob said softly, still supporting her. 'The storm is passing. But it wasn't only that, was it? A nightmare?'

'A nightmare . . .' she managed.

'Sit down now. I'll make tea,' he told her, and she found herself in the old rocker, with a sleepy kitling curling in her lap.

'I'm sorry,' she said, as he shifted the kettle on to the hot plate. 'Did I wake you?' she asked.

'Well, yes, but I quite thought it was one of the children – so I came to see.' He spooned the tea from the battered old Mazawattee tea caddy. Then he said, 'It was the war, wasn't it? Some nights I, too, wake in a sweat and wonder where I am – Edmund, too. Those of us who went through it, can never extinguish the memories entirely, I believe.'

'Yes, it was the war,' she said. He gave her an encouraging smile, as if inviting further confidences, but she gave a little shake of her head.

'Pour a cup for me, too, please . . .' Lalla walked into the kitchen. She looked at Angel's flushed face, but did not comment. 'Such a storm – such a sky!' she said.

CHAPTER EIGHTEEN

She had to talk to Lalla – she was sure that she had been standing there, in the kitchen doorway, for a few moments before she entered and remarked on the sky. If Lalla thought that there was something going on between Angel and Rob – well, it made a mockery of what she, Angel, had said yesterday on the beach, when they exchanged confidences. There was something else she could not put out of her mind, also. As the three of them had gone upstairs again, Lalla had paused, allowed Angel to go on up by herself, and Angel had heard her say quietly to Rob, as he opened his door, 'May I come in again, Rob? I need to tell you something – I wanted to, last night – but . . .' Rob had barely hesitated before he replied, 'Of course.' Then he called softly after Angel's retreating back, 'Goodnight to ye, Angel. Sleep well the rest of the night.'

Naturally, she had done no such thing. She tapped now on Lalla's door, imagining her to be sitting up in bed finishing off her breakfast. Alice and Tony were making toast in the kitchen. It seemed a good time.

'Come in,' Lalla answered.

She was standing by the washstand, a towel round her shoulders, another, wrapped like a sarong round her narrow waist. Without her makeup, her face was pale, the luscious curved lips almost bloodless.

'Oh, I must apologise, Lalla, I'll come back later—' Angel faltered, taking in the untouched breakfast tray on the chair.

'No, please stay. I know why you've come,' Lalla told her. 'Don't worry, Angel, I saw and heard enough to know that, well, last night – you and Rob – it was all perfectly innocent. Anyway, who am I to judge?' Angel sensed the bitterness behind those words.

Then Lalla let the towel round her top-half drop: she stood there, facing Angel, naked and vulnerable, revealing what the loose clothes had concealed, the swelling and distortion of her left breast. 'You *see*?' she appealed to Angel.

'Yes, I can see,' Angel managed, her eyes wide with pity and shock.

'Come closer,' Lalla asked. 'I would value your opinion: it *is* what I fear, isn't it? I have ignored it for too long and it is too late, isn't it? D'you see, now, Angel, just why I came back to see the children – Rob?'

'I understand, Lalla and I am so very sorry – any doctor would confirm, I believe, your self-diagnosis . . .' Two strides across the room, and she retrieved the towel, covered Lalla, compassionately. Now it was her turn to put her arms round one who was desperately afraid, to hold Lalla close. 'Have you seen a doctor?' She knew instinctively that Lalla had not. She felt the shuddering, almost the pain suffered by this woman.

'What is the point? The only answer would be surgery, I *couldn't* come to terms with that. Didn't you notice how I felt about Alice's terrible disfigurement? It is not only that I am not brave enough to face the knife – I am too vain, Angel. I have always exulted in my looks, my body . . . Gerald had to know, of course – *now*, he seems loving, supportive, but—' she assayed a wry smile. 'I expect him to abandon me, when the time comes. He has no patience with the imperfect.'

'Stay here,' Angel pleaded. '*I* could care for you – you would be with those who love you. Rob still cares, anyone can see that—'

'I don't intend to allow my children to see me, as I will become, Angel. That is why I thought of Australia – so far away – impossible to visit . . . I'm not being noble, I'm being selfish – I want them to remember me as I was, as I *seem* to be, right now.'

'Did you tell – Rob – last night?'

'Only that I was going to a drier climate for my health – that I might not make old bones, which he refused to believe. I told him I would always keep in touch, but that he should find someone else to share his life. Don't worry, I did not mention your name!'

'I am grateful for that, Lalla.'

'I want you to forget what you have seen, Angel. Promise me you will say nothing – I am going away tomorrow, sooner than I intended. The children will be disappointed, I will have let them down yet again, but – I can't keep up the pretence.'

'If I promise, in return you must write to the children as often as you can . . .'

'You must amend that to, for as long as I can. I am not thinking in terms of weeks, or even months. I am fatalistic, Angel. I need a further promise from you, I want you to be here, when the time comes.'

'I promise. Whatever you may think – you *are* brave.' Angel told her simply.

'Thank you!' Lalla turned back to the basin of cooling water. 'Will you take the tray – explain that I feel a little sick, due to yesterday's overdose of sun, eh, – say I am off my food, please? I will be down shortly, then we'll take the children shopping – and leave Rob and Aunt Hetty in peace . . .'

'We'll open up at lunchtime, shall we, Rob?' Aunt Hetty asked, as the others made ready for the outing to town.

'We might as well,' he answered slowly.

Perhaps he would have liked to have been included in the shopping party, Angel thought, but it would be easier without him – the sooner life resumed as normal, the better.

It was obvious that Alice and Tony were still unaware of their mother's imminent departure, though Aunt Hetty had whispered to Angel that Rob had told *her*. They laughed and sang as the motor sped along, and Alice said, 'Not as luxurious as Lady Pamela's Rolls, but isn't the motor the most wonderful invention, Lalla?'

Angel mused to herself that she liked the rides in the trap, with Rob beside her, holding the reins, just as much.

They waved to those they swept past in the lane: to Edith, first of all, as she pedalled on her bicycle to Mrs Newsome's shop; to Edmund, turning in at the school gate; and to Will, busy in the Big House garden. And there was Jess, waiting by The Cotts, as if she knew they'd be passing, with Belinda held up in her arms to see, smiling and waving back. 'See you tomorrer!' she called cheerfully. The holiday was drawing to a close for all of them, it seemed.

Boxes piled between the children: Tony had been kitted out, too. Lalla was certainly not short of money. 'You don't need those thick stockings in the summer, let the air get to your legs – wear cotton socks!' she told Alice. She stuffed the stockings in her bag, 'I'll answer to Aunt Hetty for you!'

Tony was overwhelmed with his giant box of paints: the sable brushes pointed fine and thick; sketch blocks in several sizes; charcoal and chalks; Indian ink and mapping pens; and pencils and squidgy pink rubbers. 'You *shall* be an artist, Tony – if I have my way!' Lalla cried, her eyes sparkling.

To the bookshop next, and Alice, given carte blanche, was soon in a transport of dreamy delight. 'Choose as many books as you like – why not?' Lalla called after her daughter, already engrossed in the crowded shelves. 'Will you wait with her, in here, Angel? Tony and I have another shop to visit. We'll be back within the hour – anyway, you'll have plenty to occupy you, won't you?'

They actually returned empty-handed, and Tony, looking smug, was obviously hugging a secret to himself.

'Fifteen – look, Lalla!' Alice indicated the pile of books on the counter, 'I hope it's not too many—'

'Wrap them, please!' Lalla instructed the bemused bookseller.

Lunch was merely a sticky bun and a glass of milk apiece, for they were all too excited from their shopping spree to want more.

Back at The Angel, Aunt Hetty had prepared a large meal, so perhaps it was just as well they had eaten sparingly, earlier. She had roasted a rabbit – the children were given the delicacy reserved for the young – the 'lantern' or ribs, to pick off the tender pinkish meat clinging to the bones. There was a light sponge pudding to follow: 'How do you get them so airy?' Angel marvelled, as like Alice and Tony she dribbled threads of golden syrup over her portion.

'I beat the eggs with a splash of cold water – that's all.' beamed Aunt Hetty.

After supper, Aunt Hetty hurried off to open up the bar, Angel and Tony washed up, and Alice went into the parlour with her mother to wrap some presents, which Angel guessed were for Rob and Aunt Hetty.

Rob said quietly to Angel, as he, too, prepared to go to work, 'Lalla has told you – about tomorrow?'

She paused in the scraping of the plates: 'Yes, Rob.'

'Life is full of disappointments,' he said. Then was gone.

It was an evening filled with music from the gramophone, when Tony and Angel joined the others in the parlour. The muted sounds from the public bar drifted over. Alice and Tony cuddled close to Lalla on the sofa while she made them giggle over stories of all the eccentric folk she encountered on her travels in the artistic communities of Europe. Angel sat a little apart, writing a long letter to Lou, telling her of all that had happened since she returned to Suffolk, apart from sharing Lalla's confidences to her. She did not wish to intrude.

In the morning, Rob silently carried Lalla's luggage down to the motor – Alice and Tony, both tearful, clung to her, begging her to stay longer. She disengaged herself gently; over their heads, her eyes met Angel's troubled gaze. 'Time to go . . .' Lalla said.

The children clung now to Aunt Hetty, so constant in their lives, while Angel returned the warm pressure of Lalla's handshake, and said her goodbye to someone she, too, would not forget.

As Rob held out his own hand, Lalla flung her arms round him, raised her face and kissed him soundly. Angel had to turn away, as she saw his arms convulsively enfold her.

'Wave, children. Make sure you have a smile on your face—' Aunt Hetty cleared her throat. Lalla's farewell gift nestled in her apron pocket.

The motor moved off slowly, Lalla squeezed the horn as she manoeuvred it round, gathered momentum, down the lane.

A hand touched Angel's shoulder, 'Will you rock Belinda for me, a bit, Nurse? I must get on,' Jess said, just as if she knew that Angel needed an excuse to leave the family on their own for a while.

CHAPTER NINETEEN

The bicycles arrived by carrier the next day. '*You* knew, didn't you, Tony?' Alice accused, seeing his wide grin.

''Course I did! I showed Lalla what to buy while you and Angel were in the bookshop. She wanted it to be a surprise for *one* of us—'

'She wanted to make-up for going away again so quickly,' Alice said, and they all knew this was undoubtedly the case.

Edith came upon them, as they clustered round their new steeds, trying out the bells, squeezing the handlebars, examining the unsullied tyres and stroking the shining metal of the frames. Tony cocked a leg over his saddle, keeping one foot on the ground, while Rob held the bicycle steady.

'I came to ask why you are all neglecting me – but, oh, I say!' Edith was full of admiration. 'Still, it looks as if you are in need of some lessons, and as *I've* been pedalling for years—'

'Thank you,' Rob told her. 'I'm sure Alice and Tony would appreciate that. And, I must apologise, Edith for not asking you over to meet Lalla properly – though I understand you chatted, outside, when she first arrived? You realised, I'm sure, that her visit was a fleeting one—'

'I did indeed. Perhaps it's just as well, less unsettling for the children . . . Can you ride, Angel? I've got an old bicycle you can borrow – no time like the present, eh?'

'I can't – but I'd like to learn,' Angel confessed. She wondered if Alice's balance had been affected by the operation on her ear, but decided to say nothing: Alice had looked pale and mopey before the carrier came, mid-morning. Tony was more resilient, but it was obvious from his remarks that he expected to see his mother again in a year or so: 'It's a long way, but she's got *plenty* of money – she'll probably send for us to go out to Australia for a holiday. Don't worry, we'd come back, Dad,' he added quickly.

'Excuse me,' Rob turned away, time to open up. 'Be careful, you two. And don't be late for lunch. Do as Edith and Angel tell you.'

The children wheeled their bicycles carefully over the road to the pink house.

Angel dashed indoors quickly to change into her divided skirt.

Aunt Hetty observed, as she tied on her serving apron: 'One way of buying affection, Angel—'

Angel paused briefly: 'It's hard for us to understand, Aunt Hetty, but I do feel Lalla loves them, even though she puts her own desires first—' If only she could put Aunt Hetty truly in the picture . . .

'I set myself against her,' Aunt Hetty said, 'but when I saw her again, well, she twisted us all round her little finger you see. My poor old Rob will have to get over it all over again,' she sighed. 'You enjoy your ride, my dear,' she added. The subject was now closed.

'Wobble – more like!' Angel smiled ruefully.

Tony took to his bicycle like a duck to water, and Alice, after a few shrieks and wheel-spins, soon got the hang of it, too. Angel was not a natural at the art of cycling, but with Edith's hearty encouragement, she ignored her grazed shins and elbows and finally took off with a yell to, 'Keep clear!' She managed around twenty yards before she landed in a heap, fortunately on the grassy verge, narrowly missing a huge clump of nettles.

'Get back in the saddle!' Edith shouted, holding the bicycle steady, just as if she was remounting after a fall from a horse and must recover her nerve.

'You can't hurt the bike,' Edith continued. 'It's much sturdier than these modern contraptions, splendid though they may look. It really lives up to its name, The Safety Bicycle. You'll see! Now, shall we all ride on to Edmund's and surprise him?'

Angel surprised herself as she pedalled cautiously, but steadily, following the children, with Edith bringing up the rear, in case she should disgrace herself again.

'Hello!' Edmund was very pleased to see them.

'I see I shall have to abandon my motorcycle and rescue my old bike from the potting shed, cobwebs and all. How about a ride this afternoon – all of us – to see if the blackberries are ripe? The holidays will soon be at an end, eh, we always go and fill our baskets around this time, Angel.'

'I expect Aunt Hetty'll say it's too far for me, that I can't ride well enough and that there's blackberries nearer home, growing round the meadow—' Alice heaved a big, dramatic sigh.

'Ah, but not like the ones that grow you-know-where, as big and sweet as the cultivated sort. Aunt Hetty was the one who told us their secret location, Edith and I—' Edmund said, adding, 'And you look very competent to me, Alice, a true bicyclist.'

'I'm afraid that I'm the one who is probably not up to a longer ride,' Angel put in ruefully.

'Nonsense,' Edith said briskly, 'I'll pack the bandages and iodine just in case! As for Alice, this will be a good test of her stamina, with school coming up – I'll tell Aunt Hetty so.' She was letting Angel know that she was still her superior.

And she did tell Aunt Hetty. Angel walked back with her to the gate, while the children went to wash before lunch.

'I knew you'd be good for Alice, the lad, too, Angel. It worries me a little that they hardly mix with the village children, they rely on each other too much. No doubt, Tony will now be out and about on his new bike, but Alice – I think it will be just what she needs, if she can get that scholarship, and go away to that nice girls' school. Though, of course, then *you'll* be out of a job—' Was there a hint of spite in that?

'Oh, I agree, Edith. But you can't blame Aunt Hetty for not encouraging them to have their friends come here to play, you see, she is always so busy, like Rob, and the two of them are enough responsibility.'

'They are lacking a mother,' Edith said, in her forthright manner. '*She* shot through, like a dose of salts – what did you make of her, Angel? I found her rather insolent, I must say.'

'I actually liked her, Edith. I don't think her visit affected Tony so much, because he was very young when she left – but it must be difficult for Alice, at such an impressionable age.'

'I think Mrs MacDonald, if that's how she still styles herself, should now keep her distance and leave the upbringing of the children to those of us who really care about their welfare. I imagine she resented the fact that *I* am the one who Aunt Hetty, and Rob, turn to, when there is a problem.'

Is she warning me, Angel wondered uneasily, that I should not consider myself indispensable? It's obvious *she* would resent it, if it were true.

She turned, 'Time to eat! See you around two, then, Edith . . .'

Angel managed the trip without mishap, but had a sneaking suspicion that not only would she be suffering from aching calf muscles by the evening, but also a very tender rear. Edith's old bicycle did not have the sprung saddle of the newer models.

Edith, bossy as always, was directing the children where to find the largest berries – 'I'll hook the branches down with my stick!' They had one large basket between them, but stout paper bags in their pockets, for only Edmund had a carrier on his bike.

He waited for Angel, to help her dismount. 'No butterflies today, but plenty of other buzzing, whirring insects – watch out!' he smiled.

'I do wish Boniface was with us,' she said, remembering the soft yellow coat, the lolling tongue, the geniality of the dog. Edmund must still be missing him sorely.

'I guess he is with us in spirit. I've been invited to look-over a young dog which has recently lost his owner – not of Boniface's ilk, but, maybe that's all to the good. A water spaniel, two years old, called "Whistle", of all names – well-used to children, that's the main thing. I was going to ask you, how would you like to come with me – to see what you think? Rob would lend us the trap, no doubt – tomorrow evening, perhaps?'

'Don't you think, Edith—' she began.

'I'm asking *you*!' he said.

'Come on, you lazy pair,' Edith called. 'Stop mardling and start picking!'

'I'll come,' she agreed, as they moved obediently

towards the others. 'If Rob and Aunt Hetty don't mind, of course.'

Alice, still pale, which worried Angel a little, displayed her hands, which were already purple, 'But you should see Tony's!'

Again they progressed slowly to the edge of the world, the crest of the field, and the berries plummeted juicily into the basket until it was brimming.

They rested awhile from their efforts, sprawled out beneath the shade of a great horse chestnut and Edith produced apples from her pockets, and Edmund a bottle of water, most welcome. They wiped the neck of the bottle in turn and drank thirstily. Tony concentrated on making fish bones from a large leaf, carefully removing the green with finger and thumb nail, leaving the thin veins.

Alice stretched out beside Angel. 'Not feeling too tired, Alice?' she asked, trying to sound casual.

Alice smiled dreamily. 'Not at all. I've learned to ride a bike today – I never thought I'd ever own one, 'cause Aunt Hetty's nervous about bicycles. I expect she's worrying right now that we'll return in several pieces! To think that, at the start of the day I thought this was going to be an awful day and really it's been a happy one, after all. That makes me feel rather guilty, Angel, you see, I ought to be feeling sad and missing my mother, but I hardly knew her before and now she's been back home with us for such a short time, it'll soon seem as if she was never here at all . . .'

'Oh, I think one day you'll be able to look back

on her brief visit and have good, warm feelings about it, Alice,' Angel said quietly.

'I'll never understand, though, why – you know—'

'I know, Alice. After all, my mother left me, too.'

She was right, it was difficult to settle that night, with all those aches and bruises. She heard Alice padding about in her room, around midnight. Suppressing a groan, she went to see if all was well.

'I'm glad you came.' Alice lit her candle. They sat together on her bed. After a moment or two, Alice said uncertainly, 'You know you said – if I needed to talk about things, well, I think – it's *happening* . . .'

'Nothing to worry about, Alice dear, we'll sort it out together,' Angel told her. She slipped her arm comfortingly round Alice's shoulders. Lalla should be here, now: she hoped fervently that she would be able to say all the right things, to help Alice step confidently into womanhood.

CHAPTER TWENTY

Angel chose her moment next morning to discreetly put Aunt Hetty in the picture. 'You won't fuss over her, will you?' she asked, hoping that Aunt Hetty would not bridle at the advice. After all, she had taken care of Alice all her life until now, she thought. 'I've explained everything—'

'She didn't ought to ride that bicycle today,' Aunt Hetty worried.

Angel knew she must be firm. 'She's not ill again, Aunt Hetty – perhaps we should let her be the judge of what she feels like doing, eh?'

'Well, you're the nurse!' Aunt Hetty smiled. 'But she's not to wash her hair for a few days, my old mother had very strict rules on that.'

She also spoke to Rob later on, about her proposed outing with Edmund.

He said immediately, 'Of course, you go. Borrow the pony and trap, you say? Then you might deliver a cask of ale on your way to Tillott's farm for their wedding on Saturday. I know where the dog is, I hope he suits for I told Edmund about him.' He added rather too casually, 'I'm glad you and

Edmund hit it off so well, he needs a little female company, we always feel Edith puts a damper on that! However, she can hardly disapprove of you, as you are one of her oldest friends, Angel.'

Was he trying to give her a little push in Edmund's direction, she wondered?

Edith had enjoyed the cycle ride too. She had the satisfaction of knowing that she had reasserted her authority over the children. Surely Rob would be grateful for her expertise in teaching his children to ride the bicycles their mother had bought them. Currying favour, buying their affection, she thought contemptuously.

She was not quite so sure about the old feelings which had been stirred when she had steadied Angel on her old bicycle, helped her to her feet, dusted her down after her early tumbles.

As she hurried through her household tasks before going over to The Angel to suggest a repeat performance that afternoon, she unwillingly recalled the first time she had met Angel.

She was already a Sister at the hospital, in charge of the new intake of nurses. The girl's late father was still remembered with affection there, for he too had ministered there after completing his training, before he joined the Army. Angel had been pointed out to her by the Matron as a nurse who would surely go far in the profession.

She had felt attracted to other women before, but firmly put such wayward thoughts from her.

In fact, later on, it had come as a relief to realise that she could also have strong feelings for the opposite sex. But Angel, she immediately realised, would become her special protégée. The girl was shy then, did not mix well with the others of her own age: Edith soon learned that Angel had been brought up by an older sister on whom she had been very reliant. It was easy then to fill this role herself, to become the one whom Angel would turn to, confide in, a wise always helpful friend.

Her special coaching brought rich rewards. She saw the girl gain confidence, become an excellent nurse. She had needed no persuading to go with Edith, to be part of her dedicated team in France.

It remained a chaste relationship, with one always obedient and deferring to the other. She had not reckoned on Angel becoming so reckless, defiant in love. Harry was older, much more experienced, but it was soon obvious that he was not out to take advantage of a pretty young nurse but deeply in love himself. What happened was inevitable. She threw herself into her demanding work but bitterness and disappointment grew within and perhaps, she could admit to herself now, she had become a little mad . . .

Yet, she could not let Angel go. The girl, she was sure, was unaware of her true feelings. She would keep her dangling, on the end of the line of friendship through her letters but when the time was ripe . . . In June, when she began to worry about the possibility of the bugler regaining his memory, it was time to 'reel her in'. Already there were complications. But at least she had the relief of being sure that the bewildered man in the barn remembered nothing of either of them in France, after all.

Now, Tony was knocking on her door. 'Are you coming out for a ride after lunch, Edith? Angel's going out with Edmund, to see a dog,' he added casually.

She concealed her annoyance. Edmund had said nothing to *her*. What was it about Angel that attracted men so? She mustered up a smile. 'I'd love to!' she agreed.

'I missed you, Jess,' the bugler said. 'I didn't like to think you were unwell. It worried me . . .'

She paused in her sweeping to give him a swift hug. 'I wasn't really ill, just tired out. I take on too much Nurse says—'

'Edith?'

'Oh *no* – Alice's nurse, who came to take care of the gal when she was really poorly. Miss Fenner sent for her. Chalk and cheese but firm friends they say, from the war. Bundle up your washing, old boy, will you? Nana's been sick too, poor soul. In a deal of pain. I should've been a nurse myself!'

'Sorry to hear about your nana. What's the trouble?'

'Stones, she says – they grip her something terrible, she bites her lip with the pain . . .'

'She should see a doctor—'

'You tell her that! I've known the old doctor down in the village ask *her* advice – didn't I trust her, not Nurse Fenner to deliver my baby?' She looked at him. '*Our* baby . . .' she said softly.

He sighed. 'Oh, Jess . . .'

She straightened his bed covers. 'There, you'll do!'

'I haven't seen Rob for a while either—'

'Talking more, aren't you? That's a good sign! No, he had his wife home, but she didn't stay. He must be disappointed, I reckon. But, she's not the one for him, Aunt Hetty says. In her opinion, the young nurse would be just right, but, of course, he'd have to get unmarried first. Anyway, it seems Mr Fenner has his eye on her and his sister actually seems to approve.'

'She – Edith – has been trying to jog my memory, Jess. I know now I had a wife – a child – before, but I lost them both . . . I *can't* picture them, Jess – that makes me sad—'

'You've got *me* now, me and Belinda,' she asserted, but her mouth trembled. 'Well I must get on. You can't live in the past, the Guv'nor must think that – and so must you.'

'Jess, come here . . .' his hands were on her shoulders.

'You love me, don't you?' she whispered a while later.

'I love you, darling Jess – no one can take *that* away from me.'

'Nor from me!' Why should she think of Edith, at this precious moment?

Whistle was a black sturdy dog with a stumpy tail and shorter flap-ears than the spaniels Angel had seen before. He eyed them rather warily from the home-made kennel in the yard of the farm cottage.

'Got a dog of my own,' the woman told them. 'I've been looking after him since Dad died. He misses him, been moping ever since. He needs a man's hand through his collar – a firm touch. Obedient? Yes he is, Dad saw to that. Whistle, come you on out, you rascal and greet the schoolmaster – if you show him your grin, he'll take you home, no doubt.'

'Not all spaniel, I believe . . .' Edmund surmised. He did not approach too near the kennel, respecting the dog's space and allowing him to become accustomed to the scent of strangers. Angel stood quietly beside him, a trifle apprehensive herself, for she was unused to dogs, Lou always said the city was no place to have a pet.

Whistle rested his head on his paws, regarding them from anxious brown eyes fringed by extravagant lashes. His tail gave a hesitant thump.

'More spaniel than not,' the woman said. 'His ma was one of Lady Pamela's. His pa might have been her cheeky Jack Russell – but maybe, *your* old dog—' she added hopefully, hoping that this would clinch matters. 'He costs very little to feed – but, still too much for me, I have to think of my family . . .'

Harry said, 'My father wants to retire when I come home. He has been in practice in our village for almost forty years. My brothers are much older than me – were, for both were in the Reserve and were killed within a few days of each other, right at the beginning of the war . . . Neither of them went in for medicine – but I have promised, I will take over. I just needed a few year's grace, I always intended to be an Army doctor, you see.'

'Tell me about your father, your mother and your home?' Angel asked. He was standing by the desk, as she wrote her evening reports. They hoped to share a precious hour together while Edith was not about.

'My father? I take after him, or so they say. He is tall and quiet. His patients love and trust him – rightly so – it will be very hard for me to follow him! He still does his rounds in the gig, with my old spaniel sitting up beside him – not your pretty cocker spaniel sort, more a working dog with a touch of Labrador maybe – you'll love my father, and my dog, Angel! My mother is a little lady, immensely energetic, she's always busy running this and that, in the village – she thrives on being a grandmother! I know she will thoroughly approve of you! We live in a small village, but my father covers two more – our house is big and shabby – cold as charity in winter, but it's home, and I love it – you will, too . . .'

So many loves, unfulfilled.

The dog ventured out, sniffed at Edmund's outstretched hand, allowed him to caress his silky ears. 'Coming, are you?' Edmund asked, 'That's good.' He slipped the rope through Whistle's collar.

Angel saw a little money discreetly change hands. 'For his food,' Edmund said tactfully. 'I will let you know how we get on together, but I'm sure he will soon settle in at the schoolhouse.'

Whistle crouched at her feet, when they were in the trap, and Angel felt the spasmodic shivering of his body, against her legs. Suddenly, the dog raised his head, rested his chin on her lap, and gazed at her soulfully. As she had seen Edmund do, she gently stroked his head, spoke soothingly to him: 'There, Whistle – you'll soon be home, old fellow . . .' She was gaining confidence herself.

'He's certainly taken to you,' Edmund approved.

Angel wondered if Harry's old Whistler, named after the famous American painter – how strange, the coincidence of the names! she thought – was still alive, but it was unlikely, she realised. She had written to Harry's parents for a while but Harry's father had a stroke right at the end of the war from which he did not recover and eventually, his mother had ceased her correspondence. But Harry's father had sent her his son's signet ring, 'I think he would have wanted it to come to you.' It fitted her middle finger, she would wear it all her life. Harry had wanted her to take it, in lieu of an engagement ring in France, but she had felt it was neither the time or the place, for they had endeavoured to keep their relationship secret, fearing that Angel might be sent elsewhere, but they had stayed together until that fatal day.

'Good boy – good old Whis . . .' she said softly now, as the dog began to shiver again as they trundled into the yard at The Angel, no doubt anticipating more new experiences.

'Whis? Now, that's just right – Whistle's a bit of a mouthful, isn't it?' Edmund said.

Rob was holding his excited children in check: 'He'll be nervous enough, without you crowding him,' he said.

'Whis—' Angel recalled. It was what Harry called *his* dog for short.

Edmund did not stay long – just long enough to introduce Whis to his friends, and to his sister, who had come rushing over from her house.

'Well,' Edmund smiled, 'now you have all approved of him, we're walking home, and I'll soon find out, won't I, if Whis really walks to heel, or not.'

'I'll walk with you,' Edith put in quickly.

'Thank you for your company, Angel, and the way you handled Whis,' Edmund told her, as they parted at the gate. 'Will you – and the children of course – join us for a long walk tomorrow afternoon?'

'I'd love to!' Angel said sincerely.

'So would we!' Tony spoke for himself and Alice.

'I presume I am included in this invitation?' Edith asked.

‘Of course, that goes without saying, Edith!’

When the children were in bed, Angel fetching her milk as usual, met up with Rob, as she often did.

He looked at her reflectively: ‘I’m very glad that you and Edmund liked the dog . . . fate seems to have played a hand in that . . .’

Was fate’s name, ‘Rob?’ She wondered – if only he knew!

‘I like Edmund very much,’ she admitted, ‘but don’t you all go reading much more into it, please . . .’

‘Goodnight to ye, Angel,’ he returned. Then, he added quietly, ‘It would be good, however, if one of us – you, in particular – could find happiness for a second time.’

She could not trust herself to reply.

CHAPTER TWENTY-ONE

They cycled to school, nice and early, the first day of term. Others had the same thought, the playground was already crowded. Angel wheeled Edith's bicycle in after the children, for she could not go past, she thought, without saying 'hello' to Edmund. Alice and Tony positioned their precious steeds with care, in the shed at the back of the school next to the latrines. Fairy Aldred and her mother had cleaned these with a will and today, at least, there was the familiar smell of carbolic and scrubbed boxes.

'You have all beaten me to it, it seems – I'm glad to see you so eager to begin lessons!' She heard Edmund say, as he came in at the gate, arms full of books, smiling at his pupils, nodding encouragingly at the little ones with solemn faces, clinging to the hands of older siblings, wondering what school was all about.

'Good morning – nice to see you,' he said to Angel, and Whis, who had been at his heels, came lolloping forward for a pat and a word or two.

'Good morning,' Angel returned demurely, just as if she hadn't seen him only yesterday, at Edith's house. 'Whis seems to think I am Whistler's Mother!' she added, referring to the artist's famous portrait. On several occasions, when she was out in the garden at The Angel, the dog had sidled in at the gate then bounded up to her, before she reminded him that he was *Edmund's* dog and despatched Tony to escort him back to the schoolhouse.

'Whistler's Mother?' he repeated. 'Ah, I see the connection – Whistle to Whistler, eh? I shall keep him in the study until he learns not to roam during school hours! Well, Alice, fit and ready for the day?'

'I certainly am!' Alice said happily.

'The holidays went much too quickly!' Tony did not sound really regretful.

'I'll probably come down to meet you this afternoon but if not take care as you ride home, no dilly-dallying,' Angel told her charges. She did not give them a kiss for they were too old for that in front of their classmates and, anyway, she was not their mother, she reminded herself. Still, she knew she would miss them. She wondered once more how she was to justify her continued employment now that Alice too was at school all day.

She decided to cycle on to Nana Elderberry's to see if she, like Alice, was fighting fit again.

'Hello!' Nana was standing in her doorway, obviously expecting her to call. 'Kettle's a singing, Aunt Hetty sent me some of her old tea leaves, as she only uses them once I can brew you a good strong cup – are you ready for one, and a mardle?'

Angel recognised the scones as some of last week's batch from home, which Jess had been given. Aunt Hetty always cut her scones square, not round and even stale they were palatable, thickly spread with butter. But this morning she had one dry, and wished she could bring herself to soak it in her tea like Nana. At least she had her own cup on this occasion.

'Yes, I'm improving, gal,' Nana observed before Angel could ask. 'Got to be, haven't I, with Belinda to look after?'

Belinda, sitting up now, was propped on a cushion on a chair, hopefully secured round the waist with an old leather belt. She kicked her legs and babbled as she chewed on a scone with her hard little gums and four front teeth.

'They haven't let you go, then,' Nana said next. 'The Guv'nor needs a good gal like you, not *her*, who comes and goes at her fancy.'

Nana always made her blush with her observations, Angel thought ruefully, but it was nice to feel accepted, with the familiar use of 'gal' instead of 'nurse.' 'The children's mother, she *does* love them—' she began.

'Not enough,' Nana stated. 'Still, she won't come again.'

How does she know that? Angel wondered. It was a trifle spooky, to say the least. She washed the last of the scone down with a full mouthful of tea, to her relief.

'Look at my Jess,' Nana continued, 'She loves

her baby, she loves her feller. Nothing perfect, o'course – she has to stay with her old nana, after all, but *she* won't ever run away, from them she loves. Count on that. No more'n *you* would – if you had a family of your own.'

Angel did not know what made her say it, but she did. 'I knew many soldiers like the bugler in France, in the war, Nana. I might even have known *him* – Edith certainly did. I haven't actually spoken to him yet. I was sent – came back – with all the shell-shocked, others badly wounded in the dreadful Battle of the Somme, in 1916 . . .'

'Ah,' Nana sighed softly, her keen gaze wavering, waiting to see if there was more.

The cloud of suspicion had not lifted from her, though Edith's staunch defence had swayed the verdict of those hastily summoned to consider her guilt or innocence. It was obvious to them that she was ill, exhausted herself. She was put on the boat to Blighty, ostensibly to care for, ease the distress of, those who had some chance of survival. She knew she would never return to France – that she would have to, with some semblance of dignity, ask to be released from her nursing duties, that she would go home to Lou.

He did not seem to know her: physically he should recover, she thought but who could tell how long he would have to endure the terrors which clouded his mind? Was the reality of what happened that night, suppressed within his troubled head, for ever? If he could only have spoken then . . . Yet, he obviously trusted her still, for, when he had been dreadfully sick, and she had tenderly wiped his face, he had leaned against her, groaning, seeking solace. When he slept, she held him close, and the slow tears dripped down her wan, tired face. When he was taken from her, she did not say goodbye, although she never expected to see him again – she turned to help with the stretchering of the others . . .

'Edith says the bugler has no ties, no family living; he is free to love your Jess,' she said simply now. But of course Edith had not added *that*.

'More tea?' Nana asked, then, 'We have a new person, didn't Aunt Hetty say, eh? Reverend Goodchild – young he is, with a bonny wife and five little gals, she hardly had time to breathe between 'em it seems . . . He came to see us, didn't he, Belinda? Breath o' fresh air after the old parson. *He* said, if Jess wanted to marry her feller well, he'd have pleasure in saying the words. But that's up to her, he said. Come to church and welcome anyway.'

'Yes, Aunt Hetty did mention it, I'm afraid I've only been to one service since I came here, but I believe I'd like to meet the new parson!'

She stopped off at Mrs Newsome's on her way home.

'Hello!' Mrs Newsome exclaimed in her turn,

pleased to have a customer for there was always a lull after the early morning rush. 'Time for a cup of tea, I daresay?'

'Just had one – sorry! – at Nana's,' Angel told her. Still, she took the proffered chair, while Mrs Newsome flipped over the bale of soft white cambric on the counter, alarming the snoozing cat, who leaped down all ruffled.

'Blouse you say, m'dear?'

'Mm. A surprise for Jess. Aunt Hetty said, "She'll want more than I usually have, me being so skinny and Jess—"'

'Jess being full-bosomed, like?' Mrs Newsome's hands sketched an expressive curve. 'Leave it to *me*, eh?'

'Aunt Hetty mentioned small pearl buttons – eight she thinks – and some fine lace for edging—'

'For the Meet the Parson party?'

Angel nodded, smiling. She watched dreamily as the sharp scissors nicked the edge of the material, then Mrs Newsome took it in her strong hands and tore it across. 'There, nice and straight! Yes, the new preacher says, "All welcome!" He wants to meet us all then – can you believe it? He says we'll have a grand old kick-your-heels-up – a dance! – to follow the supper . . . I penned a poster, it's up in my front winder – have a look when you go, eh?'

And Angel did, while Mrs Newsome beamed proudly.

Meet the new Parson and his family!
PARMINTER'S BARN – by kind
permission of Lady Pamela
SATURDAY NEXT. SUPPER PROMPT
5 p.m.
(Cakes and sandwiches appreciated)
Dancing to 9.30 p.m.
MUSIC by THE GOOD OLD
ALDRED BOYS.
ALL WELCOME!

'Tell Aunt Hetty she'll have to get busy – you'll come o'course? With your feller?'

'My feller?' Angel was hot under the collar once more as she fastened her parcel by the long loop of string over one shoulder, and made ready to pedal off.

'The schoolmaster,' Mrs Newsome remarked complacently. 'I've seen the two o' you together, with his new dog. Miss Fenner actually approves it seems . . .'

'Now, Mrs Newsome—' Angel began, wondering how to put it.

'No smoke without fire!' Mrs Newsome twinkled back. Then she returned smartly to her post behind the counter for a customer was approaching.

Aunt Hetty was pleased with the material. 'I'll make the gal short sleeves, eh? Then Belinda can have a bonny new frock too.'

'I could sew that,' Angel offered. 'While you're busy on the machine, I like sewing by hand.'

'That's it,' Aunt Hetty was pleased at this notion. 'You'll come to the parson's party – with Edmund?' she added slyly.

'With Edith – and all of you – and Jess and company, I hope,' she answered airily.

'The pub'll close up – just for the evening, for the whole village'll be at Parminter's barn. Mind you, it'd be perfect, my dear, if you were to be on *Rob's* arm that night—' She shook her head regretfully at Angel. 'Still, Lalla didn't do the right thing by him, and like my John, his uncle, he's a little strait-laced, as they say . . . I ought to be pleased you've picked Edmund for your feller—'

'Oh, Aunt Hetty – *please*!'

'Quick, put this lot away – here comes Jess, for more water. Reckon we might offer the gal a bath here – tactful like – before she dresses up next Saturday, Angel?'

'I reckon that's a good idea . . .' Angel was relieved at the change of subject.

'Hello, talking about me?' Jess beamed.

'As if we would, dearie,' Aunt Hetty returned demurely.

Peeling the potatoes at the sink, Angel dreamed of smocking, french-knots and pink embroidered rosebuds. Belinda the beautiful must live up to her name, after all.

CHAPTER TWENTY-TWO

Edith, as an intimate friend, always used the back door of The Angel. She had one of her stabbing headaches today and wore that pained expression which had made the nurses steer clear of her in France.

Jess was at the water butt, dipping her pail for soft water, for washing. She looked up, as Edith approached.

'I want a word with you,' Edith began, without preamble. She glanced in at the kitchen window: Aunt Hetty and Angel must, fortunately, be elsewhere, she thought.

Jess stood the bucket on the ground. She said nothing, waited for Edith to continue.

'You're missing a button on that blouse,' Edith stated, staring disapprovingly at the soft swell of bosom thus revealed.

'Is that it?' Jess asked, in disbelief.

'Don't be impertinent! I don't know how Aunt Hetty puts up with you. No, I want to know why you are spreading these rumours about the poor man in the barn—'

'Spreading rumours? That's ridiculous, Miss Fenner!'

'Is it? I heard, you are hoping he will *marry* you – do you deny that?'

'*I* never said so! Anyway, that's my business, not yours.'

'He is still my patient: discharged by the nursing home into my care—'

'Why isn't he in your house, then?'

'You know very well, why not. Because he is not fit to face the world, cannot communicate—'

'He talks to me, all right.'

'More than *that*, I think,' Edith literally spat at her.

'I said, that's my business. He needs me, more'n you, Miss Fenner – or have you got your eye on him, too?'

'How dare you! I shall speak to Aunt Hetty – to Rob, about your rudeness to me—'

'Edith, I think you have said more than enough, leave Jess be, come inside, I think we need to talk . . .' Rob had come up behind them without them being aware of it.

He opened the door, shepherded her firmly inside. Jess, tears welling in her eyes, fled down the meadow to the barn.

She wedged a chair against the door, sobbing in great gasps. The bugler stood there helplessly: 'What is it, Jess – tell me!'

Then she was in his arms, and for the first time since they had met, it was he who comforted her.

'Miss Fenner – she says I'm out to catch you—'

'I—don't understand . . .'

''Cause of what the new parson say, I reckon, that he'd tie the knot 'tween us – marry us! – *if* we wanted that—'

'Jess—' He led her gently to the bed, where they sat, side by side. He looked down at her: 'You've lost a button,' he said.

Jess began to cry again. He put his hand across the gap. His touch soothed her. 'Nothing that can't be mended,' he whispered.

'You *say* you love me—'

'I do. But, who would marry a wreck like me – with a muddled memory and too many fears—?'

'I would! I would!'

'You're so young, Jess, so sweet – so giving. I owe – a lot – to you.'

She gave herself up to the caressing, content in his arms. Aunt Hetty would wonder where on earth she had got to. She was glad she had barricaded the door against intruders.

'I never intended—' he murmured, his lips against her face.

'What?'

'To take advantage of you . . .'

'Whatever were you thinking of, Edith, railing at that girl like that? We *all* know that she is responsible for the bugler's continuing, slow recovery—'

'What about *me*? I give him the skilful nursing care he needs – oh, not of the body, now, he is superficially healed in that respect, but he needs the expertise of one with experience of damaged minds. I am prepared to carry on, however long it takes, you must be aware of that?'

'Of course. But why this patient in particular? You must excuse the intrusion, but – are you very attached to him, is that it? I can't see why else you would resent Jess's involvement.'

'You don't understand, Rob. I have a special responsibility to this man. That's all I am prepared to tell you. Did I condemn the girl, when she had that baby? No, I accepted that she is a victim of her desires—'

'It takes two, Edith. Maybe that was what the bugler was lacking – warmth, affection – it can be a lonely path, without a woman in your life.'

Edith looked hard at him. 'I should never have brought Angel here . . .' she muttered.

'Angel? What on earth has *she* got to do with it? You took my meaning: I still regret losing my wife. We should let the two of them work out their own destiny, I believe. Meanwhile, I think an apology from you, to Jess, is in order – then we can forget this conversation, eh?'

'You don't understand, Rob,' she repeated dully. 'But, I will say I'm sorry. I have such a wretched headache, this morning – I didn't intend to fly off the handle. Will *you* forgive me, too?'

'I said, we'll forget it happened. I will just add, we couldn't cope here, without her help – you will go now? And I will make the tea, and call the others, for a break, too.'

Edith lifted the latch but the door seemed to be struck. She gave a push – it did not yield.

Jess clapped her hand across the bugler's mouth. 'Ssh!' she breathed. They lay very still.

'Jess – are you in there?' Edith called. 'I – wish to apologise for my words earlier. It was quite unnecessary – I am sorry . . . Let me in, will you?'

Let her stew! Jess thought. She suppressed a nervous giggle.

The latch moved again. 'Jess!'

The clock on the bugler's bedside table ticked the minutes away. Then they heard the sound of retreating footsteps. Edith had given up!

'Guv'nor, dear man – *he* put her right,' Jess said, with satisfaction. She sat up and retied her hair. 'Got to go. Have to finish up the chores then run home to feed Belinda. I'll bring her up for you this afternoon, shall I?'

'Please, Jess,' the bugler said.

Edith was very quiet, Angel thought, as they sat round the table and sipped the hot tea.

Jess fetched her cup and did not look at Edith as she asked Aunt Hetty: 'Got a spare button,

Aunt Hetty? Mustn't go back down the lane all a'gape, or folks might talk, eh?'

'Look in the sewing basket, dearie – no, wait a minute, there's something you shouldn't see – a surprise, like – I'll find you a button, in a minute. Sit down and drink your tea, first.'

'Running late, Aunt Hetty – but, all right.'

'You look pale, Edith, are *you* all right?' Angel asked, concerned.

'Just a bad head, Angel. I really just came up to confirm that Edmund and I may join your party, on Saturday.'

'Of course, no need to ask!' Aunt Hetty put in, adding, 'The Good Old Aldred Boys, eh? Long time since they got together to play: Will's the oldest, Angel – there are four brothers, we used to wonder how them big fellers slept in that little old house at nights – just the two bedrooms, you see. No room for beds, we guessed – the fellers lined up, side by side, on the floor. No wonder, the younger 'uns run off to sea . . .'

'Did well, the sailors,' Rob observed. He had remained standing up, by the door. Now, he said, 'Like Jess, I've got to get on. See you Saturday, then, Edith, if not before. Excuse me.'

When he had departed, Jess took off her blouse, turned her back on Edith, and deftly sewed the button back in place. When she was dressed, she addressed Edith: 'Satisfied, Miss Fenner?'

'Why should it concern me?' Edith asked innocently. 'Well, I'm off.'

'Don't forget to take a powder . . .' Aunt Hetty called after her.

Angel wondered if she had heard aright. Had Jess *really* muttered: 'How about *arsenic*!'

CHAPTER TWENTY-THREE

The bathing of Jess was a jolly affair. Alice hung a notice on the scullery door: LADIES ONLY! Nana Elderberry, on the rocker by the stove, where the big towels warmed on the airer above, was prepared to shoo away not only kitlings and cats when it was time for the drying, but any male – well, Rob and young Tony, anyway – who dared to poke his head in there.

Jess sat in the tub with steam gently rising from a generous amount of soft water, heated in the copper, with Belinda, solemn faced, sitting on her lap, for this was a first total immersion for both of them. Angel rubbed at Jess's damp hair, washed with the usual gooey melted soap, then rinsed with the juice of a precious lemon added to the jug of cool, clean water. The coppery glints were pronounced now, Angel thought admiringly, and the curls were crinkling back already. She averted her eyes tactfully from Jess's full, fine young breasts, thinking wryly of her own slight figure, but Alice stared in frank amazement, no doubt wondering if she would ever achieve such a splendid shape herself.

Aunt Hetty had scrubbed Jess's feet, 'We all need

help in that direction, eh?' Now, she plied her little silver scissors: 'Nails are easy to pare when soft from bathing . . .'

Alice was trying to make Belinda laugh, while Jess soaped the flannel and washed her baby all over. Belinda's downy first hair had rubbed away over the months since Angel had first seen her, and instantly fallen under her spell, and now she, too, had a cap of bronze curls, but hers were damp from a dunking in the bath.

'That's beautiful in here . . .' Jess breathed. 'I could lie here all night . . .'

Angel scooped up Belinda and Alice rushed to fetch a towel from the kitchen. She couldn't resist kissing the soft, pink face peeping from the folds of luxurious terry towelling. 'I'll take her through to Nana to dry,' she said.

Nana did not altogether approve of all this washing. But she blotted her great-granddaughter thoroughly, and accepted the clean, small garments passed to her by Angel without comment. The new vest knitted gamely by Alice, never mind the occasional lapse from single-rib to moss-stitch, was a most creditable effort, Angel thought approvingly; the pilch to conceal her cloth napkin, folded triangular-wise and pinned firmly in the middle; the pristine long white socks and the simple petticoat; and finally, the flouncy, pretty dress, duly rosebudded and french-knotted which had seen Angel sewing far into last night, sitting up in bed, by candlelight.

'Sewed with love,' Nana remarked shrewdly. She never missed a thing, Angel thought, *she* could sense the longing in her heart, the feeling for what might have been, that time she could never, ever forget.

Jess made do with her own shabby underthings, for they must not undermine her pride, Aunt Hetty had been adamant regarding that, but she donned the new blouse with evident pleasure and surprise, tucking it in her skimpy skirt. Never mind her wrungover boots, Jess had been reckless for once and purchased new stockings from Mrs Newsome's. 'A bargain,' kind Mrs Newsome assured her, 'pinned together – that leaves a spot of rust, you see – but you'd need one of them magnifying glasses to see it . . .'

'Oh, do leave your hair hanging loose, Jess – it looks so nice,' Angel said impulsively. Tony, allowed in at last, gallantly presented a white marguerite from the garden, to pin at one side.

Jess took the baby from Nana. 'See you all later,' was all she said, but everyone knew she was going down to the bugler, to show off her finery.

Nana heaved a little sigh. She, of course, had not dressed up for the occasion, but she had removed her apron and squeezed her feet into a pair of Aunt Hetty's shoes. 'I'll make tea,' she offered, 'while you get ready, yourselves.'

Rob joined them in the kitchen, not changed yet, either, for there was the bath water to empty first. 'Give me a hand, Tony, there's a good chap,' he said.

Angel mopped her damp brow with her apron. She tended to make these little gestures, she thought ruefully, whenever she came face to face with Rob nowadays, possibly to conceal what she was afraid must be obvious to someone as perceptive as he – the way she felt about him. The last thing she wished to do, was to embarrass him. It was probably best to foster the illusion that she and Edmund had the makings of a pair – *although was that very unfair to Edmund?* She wondered.

Unexpectedly he said, 'Will ye wear your green dress this evening? The one you wore when we took Alice to the hospital? It suits ye well.'

'More the dress for high summer . . .' she answered regretfully. Yet she decided immediately she would wear that, not the dress laid out ready on her bed, just because he liked it. There was a cashmere shawl, which she had never worn, tucked somewhere in her trunk, which would go with the dress very well, and the promised dancing would no doubt banish any shivers. 'I will see you later,' she added, following Alice up the short steps.

Alice was very excited at the chance to wear one of the new frocks Lalla had chosen for her – plaid seemed very appropriate for a girl called MacDonald! She discovered a little note tucked in the soft, woollen folds:

BEE HAPPY & ALWAYS BEE FULL OF BUZZ DEAR ALICE!

was written in Lalla's extravagant hand under a picture of a large-as-life bumblebee. As she smoothed the paper out, Angel saw that Alice's eyes were suspiciously bright.

'Yes, you must certainly *buzz* tonight!' She gave Alice a swift hug.

'So must you,' Alice returned, stroking the cobwebby shawl, crocheted with a fine needle in pale grey. 'Edmund – Mr Fenner – is very keen on country dancing. I know that, from school.'

'Then I had better wear some comfortable shoes, eh? If you think he will ask me to dance!'

'Oh, he'll want *you* as his partner, all right. Mrs Newsome said you've made quite a catch, Angel!'

'Did she . . . Why is everyone trying to marry us off, d'you think?' Angel joked.

'Because he's so nice, and so are you and because Edith actually approves of you – well, she must do, as she got you to come here.'

Angel wasn't so sure about Edith's motives for persuading her to come to Suffolk, now. She thought uneasily that Lou might have been right about Edith, after all.

She looked forward to dancing with Edmund, after all, folks couldn't read more into it than they already had – but, she really hoped that Rob would ask her to dance, too.

It was Alice, a devotee of the schoolgirl annuals so much in vogue, who labelled the meet-the-new-parson party a 'bun-fight'. Buns were indeed piled high on plates, together with potted meat sandwiches, slices of pork pie, quivering with rich jelly, cold apple tarts alongside jugs of cream, and sausage rolls, fat and flaky or undersized and overbrowned.

Lady Pamela sat serenely, graciously nodding at all the guests as they arrived, positioned at the centre of the top trestle table, which was covered by a proper damask tablecloth instead of the starched sheets thrown over the other tables. Next to her, naturally, was the parson, who was short and plump, with a boyish face with plain steel spectacles that slipped down his small nose but could not disguise his friendly, blue eyes. He had sparse, gingery hair, and his colouring had been passed on to the five little daughters, giggling in their matching pretty frocks. His wife, Lilian, in contrast, was tall, gawky almost, with thick black hair piled high and, although she appeared more reserved, Angel couldn't help noticing that she was obviously holding her husband's hand under cover of the tablecloth, for, to her surprise, she had been ushered to the empty chair on Mrs Goodchild's left. Edmund sat alongside Angel, but on the corner of the table – along the side row were placed Aunt Hetty, Edith, Alice, Tony, Nana Elderberry, and at the end, Rob. The five girls opposite grinned and pulled faces at Alice and Tony.

Jess had told them to go on without her, that she would join them shortly.

The Good Old Aldred Boys were older than boys. The sailors sported whiskers, only Will was clean-shaven. They wore coloured waistcoats, baggy trousers and spotted neckerchiefs – a fiddler, a piano-thumper, one with a squeezebox and Will with the tin whistle. They were energetic and exceedingly tuneful, with a wide repertoire – they made music while the food vanished from the plates, managed a bite or two themselves and quaffed tea from big enamel mugs.

'So, you are the young lady who is the subject of so much speculation . . .' Lady Pamela observed, graciously accepting a third slice of pork pie, which after all had been made in her kitchens, from quiet Mrs Goodchild, who was obviously content for her ebullient husband to do the talking for them both.

Angel shot her a startled glance, for as they were two seats apart, these were the first words Lady P. had bestowed upon her. She was aware of the parson's twinkling side-look, for how could he and his wife do anything but listen in? 'I'm not sure—' Angel began, uncertainly.

'You are not sure of my meaning? Remember, I regard Hetty as one of my oldest friends. The *village* may have you marked as a schoolmaster's wife, but Hetty sighs that if only it were possible, you would be the ideal companion for her adopted son, the mother figure his children need so sorely, the future mistress of The Angel.' The wrinkles beneath the pink powder on the angular face betrayed the speaker's advanced age, but her eyes, although pouched were shrewd and very direct.

Angel was grateful that Edmund was deep in conversation with Edith and Aunt Hetty. She heard Aunt Hetty wondering: 'Where on earth has young Jess got to?'

She was saved from replying to Lady Pamela when the door to the barn swung suddenly open. There was an instant hush, a pause in the music as Jess proudly propelled the bugler, holding Belinda, to the table where Nana had reserved their places.

Angel caught her breath sharply, almost choked. She knew him at once of course.

CHAPTER TWENTY-FOUR

There was a general intake of breath, then a concerted expelling of same, for the bugler, looking rather dazed, wore a crumpled uniform, which had obviously been packed away for some long time – a dress uniform, now rather hanging on his spare frame. Jess, beaming proudly, had obviously spent some time coaxing him into his attire, which explained their late arrival.

Nana had already piled plates in readiness: now she took little Belinda on to her lap, to feed her tidbits from her own plate, urging Jess and her escort to duly tuck in themselves.

The chattering resumed, those who were replete, rose to dance, perhaps unwisely, in an area cleared and designated for this purpose.

'Would you care to dance, Angel?' Edmund murmured unexpectedly, his breath tickling her cheek.

'You really ought to ask Mrs Goodchild, first . . .' she whispered back. She was still in a state of shock, knowing now, who the bugler was.

'You think so?' he smiled. He repeated his request to Lilian.

Edith, Angel saw, was lining-up with the ladies, opposite Rob, Tony was hurrying Aunt Hetty to join in and the parson, making his excuses to Lady Pamela, came along to Alice to say: 'Music's about to begin! Would you do me the honour – Alice, isn't it?'

Will, with a firm push in the back from his wife, was despatched to ask Lady Pamela to dance. Fairy and Mina, bowing exaggeratedly, took the floor as partners, gazing slyly and hopefully along the line of men.

Angel was without a partner, some distance apart from Nana, the bugler and Jess. She did not try to catch their attention, along the now empty seats between. She stared instead at the energetic dancers, at the men circling their partners, the top couples galloping in turn with sheer abandonment between the lines of exuberantly clapping onlookers. She gazed at the sight of Mrs Goodchild's tumbling-down hair, which softened her face and the ever-enlarging split under one of Edith's arms. For Edith, she thought ruefully, always wore clothes a fraction too tight. Angel's thoughts were in turmoil: Edith must have known that eventually she and the bugler would come face to face – would he, in turn, recognise her, too? What would be the outcome, if he did? Would she be forced to retreat, yet again, when she was so happy here despite the fact that it seemed her new love could never be acknowledged . . .

She saw Alice, animated, chattering away

nineteen-to-the-dozen to one who was, after all, very used to the company of a large number of young girls. These daughters were actually enjoying a bun-fight with the remaining rock cakes!

'Will you take Belinda, please, Nurse?' Jess asked diffidently, startling her, for she had been so studiously avoiding catching their eyes, she had not noticed Jess and the bugler leaving their chairs. '*He* has asked me to dance, you see, and Nana has just dodged out to the privy . . .'

Angel looked directly at him then and he smiled shyly over Jess's shoulder. There was a big difference in his appearance, of course, but it really was he. Relief washed over her as she realised that he was not aware that they had met before.

'Of course, enjoy yourselves . . .' she said softly and cuddled Belinda up in her cashmere shawl, for the baby was becoming drowsy. Jess looked so young tonight, she mused, as the tempo of the music changed to a dreamy waltz, the dancers caught up with their original partners, and the bugler tentatively took Jess in his arms. But it was Jess, Angel observed, now unafraid of looking at them, who was unsure where to place her feet, and the bugler who gathered confidence with every step. When the music faded to a close, he and Jess were by the piano, just as that Good Old Aldred Boy announced his intention of sliding off for a short break – and a mug of something stronger'n tea, eh? 'Come on, you boys!'

Disappointed, the dancers began to drift back

to their tables. In the general movement, the fact that the bugler had taken the vacant seat at the piano passed unnoticed.

'Such a dear little soul,' Lilian Goodchild said softly, gently stroking Belinda's hair. Angel smiled back. She had a strong feeling that she and Lilian were destined to become real friends.

The music began again, tentatively at first, but the keys of the ancient piano were fingered by the sure touch of one who obviously loved to play. The talking died down to a muted muttering as all heads slowly turned to gaze on the pianist.

'Chopin,' observed Lady Pamela. 'That gel – Mrs Elderberry's granddaughter, Jess – she must be seventeen or eighteen now. His child, is it? Mrs Newsome intimates it is.'

Angel was shocked into silence. Jess, sensible Jess; somehow Angel had assumed a maturity which she could now see that Jess did not possess. The bugler must be some twelve years her senior perhaps more, but it was Jess who was the stronger of the two, who mothered him just as she did her Belinda. *Were memories being stirred for him as he played on?* wondered Angel. They certainly were for her.

Edith decreed that tonight all who were embarking for France on the morrow should let their hair down, allow the excitement of the party to override their natural apprehension. Angel wore a blue costume, her glossy hair restrained with a satin bow. He already sat at the piano. The carpet was rolled back and the furniture shifted to make room for the dancing. The party was taking place in the splendid drawing room of the house belonging to one of the senior surgeons of the hospital where all the nurses had trained. The pianist had a sad face, Angel thought. Edith had whispered that the young doctor had recently suffered a bereavement. Angel couldn't contain a shiver at the notion that this would be the last time any of those present would be so carefree. Yet this was the first time she saw Harry, too.

The man at the piano shifted effortlessly from the lighter classics to snatches of opera to popular songs, fervent in their message to those about to go to the war zone. Sentimental singing triggered tears, for some the abandonment of caution, the prelude to loving. But for Angel, that meeting with Harry meant her first real kiss and the unspoken promise of being together.

'You must meet my friend,' Harry said, 'like me, medicine is in his blood.'

So it was for Angel. Following in her father's footsteps.

Edith's voice stridently invaded the hushed atmosphere. 'Edmund, you must take me home, yes, *now*; I have one of my migraines, please ask Mr and Mrs Goodchild, Lady Pamela, to excuse us . . .' her face was utterly drained of colour.

Angel was instantly on her feet in her concern for her friend. 'Shall I come with you?'

Edmund smiled reassuringly as the music flowed effortlessly on. 'No, no, I can manage, thank you, Angel. I will wait until Edith is safely in bed and feeling easier. This will take a day or two for her to get over, but I imagine you remember that?'

Actually she did not. Edith had been tireless, never ill in France. But she acquiesced, because she could interpret the desperate appeal to her in Edith's eyes, to go along with this. Of course Edith too must have been swamped with memories when the bugler began to play.

As they left the bugler rose from his seat at the piano as abruptly as he had positioned himself there, and he and Jess came shyly back to their table to a spontaneous burst of applause from the rest of the company.

Nana came to collect Belinda from Angel. 'The baby must go home now with her old nana, Jess and her feller can stay awhile. You should have a chance to dance yourself, not play nursemaid all evening.'

Tuning up accomplished, the Good Old Aldred Boys, thoroughly refreshed began a lively if not entirely accurate repetition, due to muzzy heads, of their earlier music. It was then that Rob asked Angel to dance.

No slow romantic waltzing, she was relieved to find, but a flying polka, which entailed much cannoning into other excited couples. There she was, all breathless and laughing, ending up near Alice, Tony and Aunt Hetty when she discovered that Jess and the bugler had slipped away, after all.

The parson made an informal warm speech, the crowd gradually diminished, the Goodchild girls yawned widely and Lady Pamela, peremptory as always, declared an end to the party.

'May I call at The Angel one afternoon?' Lilian asked Angel. 'When our children are at school?'

'Yes do!' Angel smiled, knowing that Aunt Hetty would be pleased.

Outside the barn it was dark and there was a definite nip in the air. Aunt Hetty grabbed Tony's arm, 'Full steam ahead, lad!' she ordered briskly. 'Shine the torch for us all, mind!'

Angel, recalling Lady Pamela's words, made sure that Alice was the one in the middle, between her and Rob. She couldn't help thinking that there was inevitable sadness ahead for this family, it would be cruel for her to complicate matters.

Alice's voice seemed to come from far away. 'Oh, it was such a lovely party! Angel, did I *buzz*?'

'Alice dear, you did . . .' Angel agreed quietly, squeezing Alice's hand for a secret shared.

In the barn, Jess folded the bugler's uniform and replaced it in the trunk. 'You made me very proud tonight,' she said.

'How good you are to me, Jess,' he replied.

'Now, you won't go outside again, will you?' she asked.

'I shall sleep tonight. Will you stay?'

'Just a little while. Belinda needs me, you know that.'

'She's the only one I can bear to share you with. Jess—'

'Yes?' she breathed, eyes shining.

'When – everything's clear – in my head again, I *will* marry you, I promise . . . I've nothing to offer you now, you see . . .'

She was close to him, he could smell the sweetness of her freshly-washed hair. Her strong young arms encircled him. He could feel the throbbing warmth of her through the soft stuff of her blouse. 'You're the love of my life,' she whispered fancifully. 'That's something that will never change, just you be sure of that.'

She's there in the barn with him, Edith thought. But he didn't recognise Angel, that was certain. However Angel had certainly realised who he was. Wasn't this what she had expected, hoped for indeed when she asked Angel to come here? In any case, if the worst happened and the truth of that traumatic time came out, surely all she would have to do would be to deal with the situation as before. Had she really become so revengeful over the ensuing years that she had desired to expose Angel, pay her back cruelly, once and for all, for loving someone else too well?

She sniffed the eau de cologne on her hanky. She had told Edmund to go home. She shifted restlessly in her bed. She had been blind to what was happening under her nose. She had seen the way Angel looked at her employer. She had seen that longing in her eyes before. She felt she still knew her well enough to believe that Angel would continue to hide her feelings. What about Edmund? She had been ready enough to sacrifice him. He was obviously smitten with her erstwhile friend. Why was her relationship with Angel such a tangled one? Why on earth had she invited her here, to cause such complications?

Footsteps were passing the pink house, voices raised in happy talking. She was out of bed in a flash, crossing to the window, gazing out. The lamp shone outside The Angel. Rob held the gate open, Aunt Hetty and the children walked through. Then he and Angel walked together along the path.

Edith experienced the gnawing pain of suspicion. Was she always destined to be the loser?

The two figures paused for a brief moment, while the others went inside the house. Shadowy they might be, but she was sure that the taller figure bent over the shorter one.

She flung herself on the bed face down and drummed her fists on her pillow.

'You go straight up to bed, I'll tidy up downstairs,' Rob said. He kissed her cheek. 'I enjoyed our dance, I wish we had had more. Goodnight, dear Angel.'

'Goodnight . . .' she repeated.

CHAPTER TWENTY-FIVE

Lalla sent letters to the children from every port en route for Australia. Rob pinned a map of the world on the kitchen wall and Alice and Tony plotted their mother's progress with mapping pins.

Aunt Hetty found an empty chocolate box with a pretty picture on the lid for them to keep the letters, which Lalla had illustrated with evocative little sketches.

Angel was privileged to read these, after Rob and Aunt Hetty naturally and was touched to find that she was invariably mentioned with the words, *Remember me to Angel.*

'Your geography will improve by leaps and bounds,' approved Edmund when he called in to see the record of the long journey and to hear extracts from the letters:

Gibraltar – oh the mighty ships of the King's Navy! On the crest of the great rock the warning guns gleam. There are narrow lanes running away from the shore of the bay in a series of crumbling steps . . . Here's a picture of a Barbary ape for you!

Shouldn't show this one to Edith! The stokers, stripped to the waist caused an excited fluttering among the ladies in our party invited to watch them at work . . . They seemed oblivious to their audience as they bent to their endless sweating labour, as they shovelled tons of best coal into the hungry furnace. Their rippling muscles, their lean, wringing wet backs, their expressionless faces stubbled and dark red, like sunburn, made me want to capture for you, if I could, the raging heat and exhaustion, the sheer doggedness of these men . . .

There are many families travelling steerage – how lucky we are! They are cheerful and uncomplaining despite the overcrowding. And are so eager to begin their new life in the new country . . . Here are some children playing with marbles while their fathers released from the necessity to work for a while, gossip over games of cards or beer and their mothers nurse their babies, worrying because a case of chickenpox has just been confirmed . . .

I was terribly seasick before we reached Naples! Oh, those beastly sick pans sliding across the floor every time the ship lurches and rolls! This is me, lying prostrate on my bunk, with my face turned to the wall, incommunicado . . .

The Bay of Naples made me catch my breath, it is so beautiful. The curve of the bay continually modifies as the gulf fills up. Some forty years ago, I'm told there was a devastating cholera epidemic here. Naples has apparently changed beyond all recognition since that tragic time due to the Risanamento, the scheme designed to purify by the destruction of the old decaying disease ridden hovels.

In 1906 the great volcano Vesuvius erupted, just twelve days before the San Francisco earthquake. Liquid, molten fire spread rapidly and cinders cascaded on the roofs of Naples causing them to collapse like a house of cards . . . Here is how I imagine this . . .

The Suez Canal is crowded with ships both large and small. We all waved like mad! The heat is blistering! All we crave is iced water . . .

And here we are in Melbourne – quite built in the English style – well, London style, with which none of you (except for Angel, of course) will be familiar . . . We are here for a few days before we re-board the ship for Sydney . . .

I felt as if I would explode with excitement as we steamed into Sydney harbour. There was so much to absorb, all those miles of coastline, 'the doll's houses on stilts' peeping above the brush-wood and the shivery feeling that we were now steaming steadily through shark infested waters which were first traversed by Captain Cook . . .

I must dip my paintbrush deep in the blue paint, for here above and below, are blue skies, blue water, blue mountains . . . I shall be at peace here . . . It may be a little while before you receive my next letter for soon we must face a long, tiring train journey . . .

The letters all ended with the same sentiments:

Give my love to Rob and Aunt Hetty, be sure that I love you both very much, Your mother, Lalla.

There would be no more letters and no address for Alice and Tony to write back.

One weekend, at Aunt Hetty's urging, Rob took Angel and the children on an excursion from the little seaside town that they had visited with Lalla. It all seemed strangely long ago.

They walked along the dyke wall of the estuary to the steam ferry, paid their pennies to cross the water and made their way through bracken and purple heather towards the ruins of an ancient church. Occasionally they looked back at the sea, at billowing sails and circling gulls. The ruins, the crumbling stones, the gaps were smothered in ivy, hiding the sad decaying of centuries since the church was ransacked during the Reformation.

They stood silently and respectfully within the stark walls lost in their own private thoughts. This was not a blue place like Sydney as Lalla had described it Angel thought, but purple like the heather.

'We could cycle here one day by the lanes,' Rob said.

Later, back sitting on the dyke wall, they dangled their legs and ate fish and chips steaming in a newspaper parcel.

As the sun sank and stained the sky, they gazed for a while over the water.

Rob had another surprise in store. They were going to the evening performance at the Picture House! Angel and Alice tried to comb the sticky sea-blown tangles in their hair so they would not appear too excursion-untidy while Tony told them excitedly to, 'Oh do hurry up!'

There was already a patient line of people waiting in the main street. The Picture House was a newish building, smartly painted, with an impressive foyer and photographs of the stars of this evening's film smiling down at them from the walls as they filed slowly but surely towards the box office.

Their tickets were clipped, and the young lady with the beaming torch led them to plush seats in the centre row. Soon the seats were all taken and the magic began.

Angel would always remember that night, sitting

between Rob and Alice while Tony passed along a bag of aniseed balls and the four of them sucked these until their tongues were sore.

'I should have bought you two ladies some chocolates . . .' Rob whispered, but they didn't hear because the piano was reaching a trembling crescendo as a long-haired girl with wide eyes floated perilously down a raging river clinging to a log, with her mouth open as she shrieked in silent terror.

Alice was clutching Angel's hand and she, lost in the drama held on to Rob, who glanced at her absorbed face and smiled.

When the lights went up and the weary pianist flexed her fingers and yawned before striking up with *God Save The King*!, Angel began to wonder if they would have a long walk home. They had been fresh, of course, when they started out this morning. She needn't have worried. Rob had arranged it all. Will waited outside the Picture House to ferry them back to The Angel.

Edith was talking to Aunt Hetty in the kitchen. When she heard what they had been up to she looked disgruntled. 'You might have asked *me* to come! It's ages since I went to the Picture House. Anyway, Angel, I thought you had promised to go with Edmund one evening?'

'And I shall,' Angel returned, for she was not going to let Edith spoil what had been a wonderful day out.

'They had no idea they were going to see a film

today,' Rob put in. 'You are very welcome to come along next time we have such an excursion, Edith, of course; I must apologise for not thinking of you on this occasion . . .'

'Hungry?' asked Aunt Hetty.

Despite the fish and chips and the overdose of aniseed balls, surprisingly they were.

The idea of the cycle ride to the ruined church sounded like a challenge. Angel rather fancied going on her own. It was unlikely that Rob would take more time out for some while, she thought ruefully. She couldn't help thinking how he had gently freed his hand from hers when *The End* flashed on the screen. And this time she had been oblivious to their closeness!

The children were going to tea at The Vicarage after school. A free afternoon!

'You go, I should!' Aunt Hetty told her. 'But remember it gets darker earlier now . . .' She sketched the route on an old envelope.

'I will,' Angel promised. She felt very guilty as she sneaked past the pink house. She couldn't explain to herself why she did not want to be with Edith on her own. Edith so often snapped her head off these days. She had even asked Angel if it wasn't high time she thought of going back to London, the family really didn't need her now. *She* knew that they did, and there was her promise to be there, to *Lalla* . . .

She was a proficient cyclist now, spinning along

the winding lanes feeling carefree and happy. She met no one else on her way. She propped Edith's bicycle against a tree and began the trek across the heather.

She had not realised that on a weekday this would appear rather a desolate place, particularly when there were lowering clouds in the sky. She had been foolish not to bring a mackintosh but the sun had been shining when she left The Angel. She began to feel rather apprehensive, glancing behind her but the heathland was indeed deserted.

With some relief she reached the ruins and stepped within the walls. Aunt Hetty had told her that this was a favourite sketching point for artists from all over the country. When she asked if Lalla had set up her easel here Aunt Hetty had replied: 'No, the place gave her the shivers . . . When the Iconoclasts smashed and ruined the churches, they trampled down the heather and set about destroying this one. The beautiful stained glass windows, the statues – *all* hammered beyond recognition . . . Yet, it's still a holy place, I reckon.'

Perhaps she had really ventured here to think of what the future might hold. The happiness she had found with the folk she couldn't help thinking of as her new family still seemed fragile as if, like this, it could all be knocked down around her. Edith still had a hold on her life – had done even all those years they had been at a distance one from the other.

The sky was really black now, the rain did not

begin as a drizzle, gaining momentum; the downpour was instant, torrential. There was nowhere to shelter for she was halfway between the ruins and the roadway. She stumbled along, it was difficult to run because the roots of the vegetation snared her feet: she was off-balance, for she had flung up her arms to protect her head, but she was already saturated.

When at last she reached the tree where she had left the bicycle she discovered with dismay that it was no longer there. She looked round wildly – could she be sure that this was the tree? But it must be; the tallest among a few stunted specimens in this exposed area.

She had left home at three – it was already nearly half-past five.

She hoped fervently that she could remember the way back. Aunt Hetty's directions were pulp in her pocket. How far was it? About three miles she supposed. She had wasted valuable time searching in vain for Edith's bicycle, which seemed to have vanished in thin air. It must have been taken while she was within the ruins she supposed. She wouldn't get back home before seven and it was already darkening due to the cloud and rain. She began to squelch along, chilled and apprehensive.

About a mile from The Angel she took a nasty tumble. The ground seemed to come up and hit her as she fell heavily on her knees on the stony surface of the road. Shaken, she stayed where she was for a long moment, then rose slowly and looked down at the damage. She had holed both her stockings and blood was spurting from her right knee. She pushed up the sleeves of her cardigan, the elbows of which were ragged, and found both arms sore and grazed. The rain still coursed down relentlessly.

She was crying, she couldn't help it when she heard and saw the trap coming towards her, with the welcome glow from the carbide lamp that had replaced Aunt Hetty's old horn lantern.

'*Rob!*' she shouted in her relief. But it was Edmund who leaped down and lifted her up while Whis comforted her with his licking and wagging tail.

'Where's the bike?' Edmund asked.

'It's been stolen,' she gulped. 'Edith will be cross!'

'Of course she won't,' Rob told her, patting her arm consolingly, 'Like us, she'll only be concerned and relieved that you are all right. We wondered where on earth you had got to, you see. We'll soon be home!'

She was glad of Edmund's arm around her and the horse blanket tucked round her lap. As she had done that first time, she gazed at the back of Rob's neck as he drove her home.

CHAPTER TWENTY-SIX

She sat in the rocker while Rob dragged in the tin bath from the scullery and replenished the sticks under the copper.

'You're about to enjoy your first bath in front of the stove, dearie,' Aunt Hetty said cheerfully, shooing Tony upstairs and ordering Rob to keep his back turned, while she deftly helped Angel out of her wet clothes under cover of the blanket and draped her round with a huge towel which Alice had rushed to fetch.

'I feel better already,' Angel said, managing a smile.

'Oh, your poor old knees – and your elbows too . . .'

'The knees hurt but my arms are just sore, Aunt Hetty.'

A knock on the kitchen door and Edith entered. 'Edmund put me in the picture, he thought it best to tactfully disappear home as it was obvious, he said, that a tub would be the first priority. Injured, I gather – I brought some salve and I guess Aunt Hetty will soon rustle up some bandaging, eh? Alice, can you fill the basin with warm water my dear?'

She was in her element and Angel was grateful for there was grit to be coaxed from the wound and the more damaged knee was already stiffening.

'Edith – I'm so sorry about your bicycle – I must pay for it of course—'

'Oh, don't be so ridiculous, Angel! It wasn't worth anything much and I have another, newer one after all – I may not have said so, but I intended you to keep it when I could see how much you were enjoying its use—'

Rob, eyes still averted, as he poured the first pails of hot water in the bath, put in: 'I think it's not really stolen, just borrowed by someone caught in the rain on their way home, who couldn't see any owner in sight . . . My guess is that it will either be mysteriously returned to the tree where it was taken, or abandoned in the village. All we have to do, is to ask around.'

'Shouldn't you and Rob be in the bar, Aunt Hetty?' Angel asked belatedly.

'Keeping an ear open my dear for customers – not likely in such weather, I'm afraid. Haven't pulled a single pint tonight . . .'

'Well, I'll hold the fort now,' Rob told them, 'I'm only getting in the way here. See you later, Angel!'

'Rob—'

He turned slightly at the door. 'Yes?'

'Thank you, for coming to find me . . .'

'Well, we can't afford to lose *you*,' he said lightly.

'*Ouch*!' Angel gasped as Edith applied her tweezers to an embedded piece of grit.

'You'll do,' Edith said. 'In the water with you! Need any help?'

Long ago she had had no choice and been glad of Edith's practicality, she thought. Now she said, 'I can manage, thank you!' and Aunt Hetty made things more private with judicious use of the clothes horse, and took over the rocker while Edith sat up at the table looking over the precious letters from the chocolate box (with one exception, Angel hoped!) with Alice.

'Your supper's keeping hot in the oven for you,' Aunt Hetty said. 'You might just as well get straight into your night things, eh, then—'

'An early night I suppose?' Angel asked wryly. 'I'm all right you know, just thankful to be in one piece. I could understand it if I'd fallen from the bike but – well, I must have tripped over my own feet!'

When Edith had anointed and wound the torn sheeting into place, she excused herself. 'I'll pop over tomorrow to make sure all's well.'

'You don't really need to fetch us from school, you know – not that we don't like being met – she can have the day off, can't she, Aunt Hetty?'

'Of course she can, we will enjoy cosseting *you* for a change Angel!'

She did settle down in bed some time after ten, wincing as she moved her legs into a comfortable position. Reading for a while she drowsily turned a page or two without really taking anything in.

As she shut the book and went to nip out the candle, there was a tapping on the door.

'Come in!' she called, thinking it was Aunt Hetty.

Rob stood diffidently just inside the door. 'I thought you'd be pleased to know the bike has turned up! One of the old boys discovered it at the end of the lane, thought it must be Edith's and took the opportunity to ride up here for a drink! He gave it back to Edith before he came over the road.'

'That's good . . .'

'Angel—'

'Yes?'

'Why did you go off on your own like that?'

'I—'

'I wondered if we, all of us, are, well a bit overwhelming at times – you help us over and above the call of duty, you know—'

'Rob!' She sat up, brushing her hair back from her eyes. 'I love it here . . . I wish I could – stay here for ever!'

'The children will grow up – much as we enjoy your company, you ought to be somewhere more lively perhaps, where you are likely to meet that special person, Angel. You really should be married and raising a family of your own. But, I guess you are unselfish like dear Aunt Hetty . . . Don't leave it too late though, will you?'

'I won't . . .' she promised. She hoped he couldn't see the longing in her eyes.

'Goodnight,' he said softly, then he was gone.

The minute the outer door closed, the inner one opened. Alice, bearing her candle, came over to sit on the side of Angel's bed and to whisper with a grin: 'Did he kiss you goodnight?'

'Alice – really!' Angel protested.

'Well, you ought to have seen how worried he was when you weren't back for supper, knowing you were on your own, too. Anyway, Lalla has someone and I don't see why Dad shouldn't be the same . . .'

'Alice, remember he and your mother are still married—'

'That doesn't seem to matter to Lalla,' Alice said candidly. 'But I don't feel so bad about it since we saw her again.'

'Good. School tomorrow, remember. You'd better get back to bed double-quick!'

Alice bent over the bed, gave her a brief hug. 'I hope your knee won't be too painful tonight, Angel. It didn't take *Tony and me* long to love you lots . . .'

'I love you both lots too! Now, goodnight!'

Nana was rocking to and fro in her chair by the stove, her hands pressing where the pain stabbed her. Her breath came in little wheezing sighs. Where's that gal got to? she said to herself. Belinda had been fretting all evening and had only just gone off to sleep.

The door opened cautiously and Jess came in. She, too had been caught in the rain, but had borrowed Aunt Hetty's big black umbrella. She shook it outside, put it down, for everyone knew you mustn't have an open umbrella indoors, that could bring you nothing but bad luck.

'Late, gal, you are,' Nana stated equably. 'You take care now, Belinda's no age at all.'

'I *know*, Nana! But that's not to say I don't want a big family when the time is ripe, mind!'

'Wait till you get a ring on your finger, I say . . .'

'He'll wed me when he's well, he said so . . . Oh, I *do* love my feller, Nana – I just wish I could help him more'n I do.'

Nana said wisely, 'You got the healing touch I reckon, like me. You've put your heart and soul into getting that poor feller back to where he should be. But, like I said, Belinda's enough for now. Can you make me some hot peppermint to shift this old pain, Jess?'

'Oh, Nana – I wouldn't have stayed out so long if I'd known you was suffering—'

'You need to get out, I know that, after working so hard all day.'

Jess knelt at her grandmother's side, put her head in her lap. 'Nana, don't ever leave me, will you?'

'Dear girl, you know the answer to that . . .'

The rain had ceased its rattling on the roof. Edith was contented tonight. She combed her hair and replaited it, turned back the bedclothes and sank into bed. She felt that she had been able to convince Angel tonight that the old concern for her welfare was still there. She knew she could live with it if Angel and Edmund became closer. As for Rob he would need a new partner eventually and he wouldn't need to look very far . . . The secrets she and Angel shared with the bugler, not the whole of what had happened of course, appeared to be locked away in his fragmented memory. Anyway, she reassured herself yet once again, why should anyone believe either of these if the truth did come out? Angel would certainly not want Edmund to know, for one.

She would need to pop in frequently for a bit to see how Angel's knee was faring. Those gritty places often went septic. She would certainly be limping for a while. Sister Edith was back on duty.

CHAPTER TWENTY-SEVEN

September and October, Angel mused, were the months for meetings both small and large. The Snug door firmly closed each Friday evening on the Christmas Club Committee at The Angel, who had taken the place of the Boot Club members who had already enjoyed the ceremonial paying out of savings. They now had the satisfaction of seeing their families decently shod for the worst winter could bring.

The scything and sharpening of blades on whetstone; the stooking of the sheaves of wheat and barley; the unbroken straw bundled for the thatcher's art; the gleaning women seeking for family and fowl, all were gone. Now the fields were dark, turned by the plough. The harvest from farms and cottage gardens was safely gathered in. There was the Harvest Thanksgiving in the church, when the parish gifts were distributed later to the workhouse, followed by the traditional Harvest Supper. During this time Angel came to know Lilian well. Of course, Edith was usually there too when they met, making clear in not too subtle ways that she was a long-trusted friend of the family and, in particular, of Angel.

In Aunt Hetty's kitchen one Wednesday afternoon there was a gathering of chutney makers. Angel, with Lilian, wept over the endless chopping of onions; Edith sliced the pounds of green tomatoes and apples; Nana Elderberry gave advice from the rocker and Aunt Hetty stirred the bubbling brown mass in the giant pot crying cheerfully as she batted at the drunken wasps, 'Stir 'em in, add a bit o' meat to it!' Jess weighed out the sultanas, the brown sugar, measured the vinegar and washed the cobwebs from the old glass jars, brought in from the shed.

'Pickling walnuts was easier,' said Angel ruefully. 'I enjoyed testing the green nut with a thrust of my hat pin, you have to pick them before the shell forms—'

'I hope you left a few on the tree, I adore walnuts,' Lilian said. 'Like you, Angel, I'm a city girl, but I am thoroughly enjoying learning all the country ways! How thrifty folk are round here, eh, just look at Aunt Hetty's army of preserves marching along the pantry shelves.'

'I am writing down all the local recipes,' Edith put in, 'and all the ways of doing things, like picking currants with a fork, pulling them through the tines and letting them plummet straight into the pie dish. Just add the sugar and water and roll out a quick short-crust, oh, the time that saves!'

'Here's another thing for your notebook, Edith.

Did you save the cherry stones, when they were in season, like I said?' Aunt Hetty asked.

'I did, washed and dried them as you said, I got a jarful. What next?'

'Well, when tha's wholly chilly at nights, gal, just you put them stones in a hot oven for a while, them pour 'em into a good strong flannel bag. Tie the top, then warm your bed before you venture in.'

This was obviously not one of Nana's economies. She advised Edith with more than a hint of malice, Angel noted, knowing why, 'Get a man, Sister Edith, more comfort than old spit-out cherry stones.'

'Now, now, Nana,' Aunt Hetty reproved her cheerfully. 'Come on, you can brew the tea for us, while young Belinda's snoozing.'

Angel and Lilian cycled down the lane later together to meet the children. They waited at the gate for the school door to open and the youngsters to spill forth. Whis preceded them, bounding over to greet them both with warm, wet licks and wildly waving tail.

'You'd think he was *your* dog!' Lilian observed as Angel caressed his head.

'Oh, Edmund very kindly allows me to share his affection and his walks, but he acknowledges Edmund as his master, Lilian.'

'Perhaps he is trying to bring you two together? The dog, that is. My hands still reek of onions. Do yours, Angel?'

'They certainly do.'

Here came the untidy Goodchild girls, stockings wrinkled and ribbons untied, hugging their mother boisterously. Coming up behind them, wheeling their bicycles were Alice and Tony, and Angel thought with a sudden sharp pang just how much she would have loved such a public welcome, too.

'Such an abundance some are blessed with,' Lilian said suddenly, 'while others have little or none at all.'

For a brief moment Angel thought that Lilian must be referring to the fact that she was blessed with five daughters and that she, Angel was not so fortunate. But as Lilian continued, she realised that she was wrong in this assumption.

'All those vegetables, Angel, stored away. The clamps of potatoes, roots under straw, marrows, great strings of onions, oh, I know the villagers did the Harvest Festival proud, but—'

'Aunt Hetty is always most generous with her surplus,' Angel put in quickly.

They moved aside from the gate, to let the other children past. Pinched in the face and hungry, some of these youngsters were hurrying home not to a meal already steaming on the stove as the MacDonalds and the Goodchilds were, but to bread and scrape and fatty bacon if they were lucky. Times were indeed hard since the war and work was becoming more and more scarce.

'Oh, I'm sure she is and there are others like her. But I've been mulling over an idea: couldn't some of this produce be used to make soup, to nourish and sustain the children at school at lunchtime? Those close to home can run home for refreshments, some are provided with an adequate packed lunch—'

'Some pounce on apple cores or discarded crusts,' Alice said thoughtfully. Alice joined in adult conversation very often now.

'Would you mention this to Edmund please, Angel? You know him so much better than I do, as yet.' There was no guile in this.

'Oh, I certainly will, and I know Edith will want to be involved, too!' Angel decided to tell Edmund right now. No time like the present.

Each morning now, after The Angel chores were done, when the children were in school and before Aunt Hetty went into the bar, the chopping and stirring of the donated vegetables was achieved with much light-hearted chatter. Baskets arrived almost daily from the local farms and more prosperous households. The delicious smell of the great pot of soup was heartwarming in itself. Parcels of meaty bones came from the butcher to add to the goodness; occasionally, when Aunt Hetty had suet to spare she would make dumplings. The bakery donated the previous day's unsold bread when there was any, to be sliced and crisped in the oven as rusks.

'Good for the teeth, all that crunching,' as Aunt Hetty wisely remarked.

One morning Angel looked up with a start to see the bugler standing diffidently just inside the kitchen door. Her hand actually trembled as she put down her chopping knife on the board. Edith, working alongside her, broke the silence: 'Did you want to see me?' she asked.

'I brought—' he began, then held out a curly cabbage.

Jess came to his rescue. 'He wants to help, you see. I told him what you're up to. He grows some fine green stuff round the barn,' she added proudly.

Edith took the cabbage. 'Thank you. All grist to the mill! We are just going to have a cup of tea when the pot's brewed, eh, Jess? Will you join us?'

He looked at Jess. She nodded, indicated that he should sit in the rocker.

Jess pulled up her chair alongside him. Edith, Aunt Hetty and Angel were grouped round the table hoping not to intimidate him.

Lilian came through the door, quite breathless. 'Sorry I'm so late! We had a caller at The Vicarage, I had to hold the fort until my husband came . . .' She glanced over at Jess and the bugler.

'My feller,' Jess said simply. 'You *know*, Mrs Parson.'

'Of course I do,' Lilian replied warmly. 'Shall I pour myself a cup?'

Angel was breathing a little easier. It was the first time she had seen the bugler close to since the party in Lady Pamela's barn.

Edith's large warm hand closed over hers for a

brief moment. Was this a warning not to say anything? Or did she intend to reassure her that her secret was safe? Angel realised that she had been deliberately avoiding being with Edith on her own. On the surface they were friendly and relaxed in each other's company. However, she knew that she could no longer trust Edith as she had in the past.

She began to slice the stale bread. The oven was nice and hot, the rusks would soon brown. She arranged the bread on a baking tray. As she straightened after shutting the oven door, she felt a touch on her arm. She looked into the eyes of the bugler. He smiled. 'I believe I know you,' he remarked.

'I was a nurse, like Edith, in France . . .' she managed.

'D'*you* know him, Nurse?' Jess demanded, excited.

'I believe I do,' she repeated the bugler's words.

'There were so many wounded soldiers,' Edith's voice was loud. 'Impossible to remember them all. Don't you agree, Angel?'

She turned her attention to the soup pot, stirring steadily. She couldn't let Edith have it all her own way. 'There were some it is impossible to forget,' she returned quietly. Like Harry, she thought. It was a shock to realise that *he* was no longer constantly in her thoughts.

Just before opening time, Rob hitched the pony to the trap and the servers climbed aboard with the soup. They took this duty in turn, two at a time. Today it was Lilian and Angel who would wield the ladles. Edith crossed to her home, waved them on their way at her gate.

Lilian looked at her thoughtfully. 'Anything you want to talk about, Angel?'

'Not now, Lilian, thank you. One day perhaps . . .'

The soup was kept at the simmer on top of the tortoise stove in the classroom. The children's noses twitched in anticipation while they wrestled with their long division, longing for the bell to ring.

Lady Pamela had come up trumps with a great stack of discarded china, so soup was occasionally scraped to reveal a faded crest, or rusks piled on a Crown Derby plate.

Angel and Lilian set out an array of bowls on the table, which Edmund had provided.

Edmund glanced at his watch, lifted the bell and shook it. Desk lids slammed. The children formed a queue to first wash their hands in the bowl of hot water provided and set on a chair, then turned to line-up for their lunch.

'My tummy's rumbling!' Angel confessed, as she filled Alice's dish. Edmund had decreed there was to be no discrimination, the soup was free to all. That way, the poorer children would not feel that they were receiving charity, he thought.

The bigger children took it in turns to wash up while the younger ones rushed outside to rustle and tumble in the autumn leaves, to bowl hoops or to play ball on the blank side wall of the school.

Edmund had a brief word with Angel before she returned to The Angel for her own lunch. Rob would collect the empty soup cauldron later.

'This has made a big difference to the children, Angel, they are no longer so tired in the afternoons—'

'It was Lilian's idea,' she reminded him. She did not want him to give her all the credit.

'Angel's angels, I call you!'

She was touched. 'You *are* nice, Edmund!'

'Nice enough for you to want to come out with me, on your own for once, one Saturday? I thought we could go to the picture show and have a splendid tea at a restaurant I know: what do you say?'

'I say, that sounds *very* tempting! But may I let you know? Rob and Aunt Hetty are always busy on Saturdays, the children are glad of my company then.'

'Of course the children must come first.' There was no sarcasm in that. 'When you can take time off, no hurry . . .'

Poor Edmund, she thought, as she walked home. It really would be for the best if she did not encourage false hopes that their warm friendship could grow into something much more. Yet she was throwing away a chance of happiness perhaps . . . She did like him so much, felt so comfortable in his company after all.

The bugler was gaining steadily in confidence since he had first ventured indoors at The Angel. It could only be a matter of time surely before he became aware of just how well they had known each other during the war, before he remembered the triangle of Edith, Angel and Harry. She clung to the memory of their journey home together from France. He had not repulsed her then – did he know the *real* truth of the matter? Could she, or Edith, cope with any such revelations?

She might still find herself impelled to leave The Angel.

CHAPTER TWENTY-EIGHT

It was Angel's turn to clear up the debris in the kitchen today. Edith and Lilian were the servers of the soup.

She scrubbed the table, humming happily to herself, before she set to as promised preparing lunch for Rob, Aunt Hetty and Jess, who was staying on today.

'You made me start!' she rebuked Rob mildly as she mashed the potato to serve with the cold meat and pickles. Aunt Hetty was holding the fort in the bar while Rob transported the soup and the ladies to the school. Jess had popped home to feed Belinda but would be back shortly.

'I wanted to catch you alone, you always seem surrounded by others nowadays,' he said. His voice was husky, as if he had a cold.

She watched the golden nut of butter as it melted and spread over the floury potatoes. 'I'm sorry, we've been so busy with the soup making, I do hope you don't feel I am neglecting my other duties?' She experienced a sudden rush of fear. Would he say after all that she was not needed any more? Alice was so well, both the children were becoming quite independent, but The Angel was barely paying its way, she was well aware of that.

He was in need of another haircut, but she was not going to offer to play the part of barber again if she could help it, remembering the last time. Now he ran his fingers through his curly crop and looked down at her from his considerable height. 'No, I should never feel that,' he said flatly. Slowly, he brought out a letter from his jacket pocket. There was a long pause. 'I have heard from Lalla's friend . . .' he told her finally. 'Will ye read this, Angel?' Then he sat down heavily in the rocker resting his head in his hands.

She felt her heart pounding as she stood there, reading the single sheet of paper.

My dear Robert,

I am afraid I have bad news for you. Lalla is suffering from inoperable cancer. She is now in hospital. She does not know I am writing to you. I felt you should know, although I realise that you will not be able to come here. In any case there would not be time. You may wish to prepare your family (and yourself) for the worst. I shall, of course, keep you advised. You are within your rights to feel angry, bitter, because of our lack of regard for your feelings in the past. You will, no doubt, regard me as the kind of person who would desert Lalla at such a time. This blow has brought home to me how very much I do care for her and I am devastated . . . I assure you I shall be with her to see this through. What more can I say?

Gerald
P.S. She talks of you all, often.

Angel wanted to tell Rob that Lalla had confided in her during her visit but she knew instinctively that this was not the moment. 'I am so very sorry, Rob,' she told him instead. 'Is there anything I can do?'

He lifted his head, gazed at her and his eyes were dark with pain and disbelief. 'Just be here, for the children – us – Angel. You see, *we* need you,' he almost whispered.

As she went impulsively to him, he rose, held out his arms to her. They embraced each other slightly, silently for a few minutes. The clock ticked on and there was the sudden, unmistakable smell of burning, for Angel had set the saucepan of drained potatoes back on the hot stove. As she moved to disengage herself he cupped her face convulsively with his hands and kissed her parted lips. It was a hungry kissing, born of despair, she knew that. Rob was seeking solace for his pain. Then his hands slipped to her shoulders and he muttered, 'I am sorry, Angel. Will ye forgive me?'

'It's all right,' she managed, snatching the pan up and quickly transferring the contents to the waiting tureen. 'I understand, Rob. I won't des—, leave you, I promise . . . You should tell Aunt Hetty now while Alice and Tony are not around, I think.' Cold water hissed in the scorched pan.

'I will. Such a shock. I see now why Lalla came.'

'Yes, I'm sure that's the reason.' Mechanically, Angel set the table. Her feelings were in turmoil. Had she responded to the unexpected kiss? Would he now suspect the true nature of her feelings for him and his family? She must not take advantage of his present vulnerability, that was the only thing she could be sure of.

'Your birthday, Rob, this weekend. The children are looking forward to it, they have their surprises, that's a sure thing,' Aunt Hetty said, after they had managed to eat some of their lunch. Jess had finished hers, looked keenly from face to face, then excused herself, going down the meadow to the bugler with his food.

Angel had tactfully made herself scarce for ten minutes while Rob had told his aunt the sad news. 'Wait until that's over, eh, dearie?' Aunt Hetty advised, now. 'They'll know, soon enough.'

'It should be a landmark, being forty,' he observed.

'And I shall be thirty on the Monday,' Angel said out of the blue. She had kept quiet about it, for when the children mentioned their father's forthcoming birthday she had not wished to steal his thunder. However, Edith would probably let the cat out of the bag, she realised and, of course, there would be cards and parcels from Lou and Jack and hopefully her mother.

'Then you are still young, Angel, while I am already middle-aged.'

She was convinced that he was deliberately pointing out the gap between them, and not only in years.

'Age doesn't matter to me,' she returned, aware that Aunt Hetty was looking from one to the other of them and no doubt wondering . . .

When Alice and Tony discovered her secret they determined to have an extra-special party for them both. 'Fancy you not telling us, Angel!' Alice reproached her. 'Aunt Hetty, we can ask all their friends, can't we? Like Edith and he who can be called Edmund just for the day! Nana, Jess and Belinda, oh, and Whis of course! Mrs Goodchild? And the parson, if he can come—'

'Your father and I will have to work as usual in the evening,' Aunt Hetty pointed out. 'But I don't see why the fun and games can't go on regardless for a while, eh?'

'I s'pose those Goodchild girls will have to be invited too?' Tony heaved a huge mock sigh.

'Well, they can hardly leave them at home on their own, can they?' Alice reminded him.

'And the bugler, Alice, if Jess can persuade him to come,' Aunt Hetty reminded her.

'And the bugler,' Alice concurred. 'We'll make the cake, won't we, Tony and we can play all Lalla's records, we'll have something to write to her about then, what fun it will all be! I wish *she* could be here, too!'

'Not too much fuss, please, children,' Rob said briefly.

'Why not?' Angel surprised herself. 'It seems the season for parties after all.'

'I'll design and paint all the invitations,' Tony said importantly.

'Angel and Rob – "thirty and forty"; all entwined,' Alice teased. 'Aunt Hetty, can we go in the parlour to plan it all?'

'Go on, then,' Aunt Hetty agreed. 'Angel and I will wash up, have you seen to your goats, Tony? Do that first. Almost time to open-up . . .'

The skies were streaked earlier now, of course. Some time during the evening, when Angel was in the kitchen by herself, thinking of turning up the lamp wicks, loth to draw the curtains to shut out the painted sky, Rob came into the kitchen to wash some glasses.

'For once, a busy night,' he observed, setting the tray on the draining board.

She constantly changed her mind, she thought in confusion. One day she decided to keep her distance, the next, as now, she was standing close by him, with his arm resting lightly across her shoulders as they watched from the window.

Jess was back again, running lightly towards the barn, hair gleaming red in the last rays of sunlight.

'The bugler hasn't been out playing for weeks now . . .' He turned towards her. 'Thank ye, Angel, my dear: it is a great comfort to us to have you here. Especially now.'

She wanted to say, 'But you see, I love you.' Instead, 'I'm so glad,' she said.

CHAPTER TWENTY-NINE

'Parlours in't for parties, they're for laying out,' Nana stated, seating herself firmly in the kitchen rocker. She had given the kitlings what she called 'an oyster', hoisting 'em up and out. 'I'll watch the kettle,' she continued, 'and top up the pot. You'll need a lot of tea to wash down all them fancy cakes.'

Alice and Tony had really gone to town. There was icing sugar everywhere, or so Aunt Hetty mildly scolded. One basic bun mixture and a dozen imaginative toppings. Tony had dipped his paintbrush into cochineal and other food colourings and a rather garish likeness of Angel and Rob, with the thirty and forty indeed intertwined adorned the large, rather lopsided birthday cake.

Angel, somewhat overcome, hugged them both for making her birthday so special. She wore Lou and Jack's gift, a cream wool costume trimmed with navy-blue braid. Rob, not one for dressing up, pleased his aunt by slipping on the bottle-green pullover she had knitted lovingly for him. Never mind that she had got rather carried away and not counted the rows, for it stretched almost to his knees. To Angel, this had the rather touching effect of a boy wearing a garment his mother hoped 'he would grow into'. Mrs Newsome's shop had only two sizes of men's slippers, large and medium, and only one style, cheap and cheerful, but Rob expressed pleasure over his children's gift just as if they were made of the softest leather. Angel and Rob had exchanged token gifts. She received a pair of woolly gloves, also a Newsome staple, and it was no surprise when he unwrapped a similar, bigger pair from her.

'The weather for gloves,' they chorused, then exchanged sheepish grins.

Another of the guests chose to stay in the kitchen. Lately, almost making them hold their breath in case they should alarm him, and cause him to flee abruptly, the bugler had come in diffidently to sit by the stove. Without comment, Rob had brought downstairs another battered old chair to complement the rocker and Aunt Hetty had furnished it with one of her patchwork cushions, filled with goose feathers from various pluckings.

Jess went in and out and, in passing, would give him a swift touch, a pat on the arm maybe and once, a brief laying of her cheek against his hair. When Belinda was sleepy, she was tucked in the crook of his arm. No words seemed necessary between them in company, merely a shy smile. The nocturnal Last Post now seemed a thing of the past.

Angel thought that deep down he might well know who she was. He had always been a quiet man, sensitive to atmosphere. One day though surely all the anguish must surface. If the bugler told all he knew about that dreadful occasion, would the ones she had come to love so dearly feel compassion or revulsion? She was aware of Edith's gaze whenever she saw them in the same room.

In the parlour she sat by Edmund on the sofa, Whis snoozing at their feet. Edith's look was approving, encouraging now.

The Ginger Biscuits, Tony had nicknamed the Goodchild girls, who ranged in age from five to eleven years old. They were extroverts like the parson. Their names all began with a 'C': Carrie, Clare, Cissie, Connie and Charly, who was named for her father, Charles. They were bossy too, for they had come with their own list of games and were determined to play them whatever others Alice and Tony had picked.

Lilian sighed, made an expressive face at Angel. 'I'm sorry. It's hard to dampen their excitement, once they're roused!'

'Oh, they are really livening things up, Lilian! Don't worry, it's good for Alice and Tony to have some competition—'

'They've never mixed much with other children, what with us with a business to run,' finished Aunt Hetty.

'Shall I try and persuade the others in the kitchen

to join us?' Edith asked. She was flushed from the roaring fire, maybe needed to cool off.

'Leave it, gal,' Aunt Hetty advised. 'You see he reminds me of my first old cat, Tiddlieweeze I called him, that's a fair time ago . . . All these kitlings round the place come down from that wild black cat that came from nowhere, in the middle of a cold raw night . . .'

They all looked expectantly at Aunt Hetty, sensing there was more to come.

'He never came indoors whether it was blowing a gale or a snowstorm. He took shelter in the old barn, nestling in the hay, rather like the bugler. I used to wait there, coaxing, with tasty bits and top of the milk in a saucer. Then, one day he stepped daintily into the scullery and watched me doing the washing. I said: "Good little old cat, good – now what shall I name you? Mother always called the cats here Tiddlieweeze so that'll do. I believe you're a she, not a he." Sometimes she came in, sometimes she skittered with a wave of her tail. I had to accept she'd come in when *she* wanted to, not when I'd like her to. It's the same with the bugler. If we say too much, expect too much, he won't come in here again.'

'Dear Aunt Hetty,' Angel murmured softly, 'you're a bit of a philosopher, you know!'

Lilian whispered to her, 'No wonder you all love her so much, every family could do with an Aunt Hetty.'

Carrie cried impatiently, 'Get the paper ready,

Tony, and plenty of pencils. This game's a bit like *Consequences*, only more *literary* Dad says, don't you, Charlie?'

'You're very irreverent to the Reverend,' Tony got his own back.

'I can't write properly yet,' the younger Charly reminded them.

'Charlies together, Charlies united,' the parson said cheerily. 'We'll share our paper and pencil.'

'"Book Titles:" write your choice, turn down the paper, pass it on. Then a sub-title, turn and pass; author's name, then the opening words of the first chapter. Finally, what the critics said about the book.'

As each followed their own story-line, the unfurled papers, read aloud in turn, saw much merriment.

After a rather hazardous game involving a new penny in the centre of the table and the bouncing of rubber balls by a team on either side trying to dislodge the coin and thus win it, Aunt Hetty wisely decreed it was time for tea, so the table must be cleared.

The birthday celebrants were seated at either end of the table, facing each other over the splendid cake. Alice lit the candles: 'Three, 'cause we couldn't possibly squeeze *seventy* on it!' Jess loaded plates for the bugler, Nana, Belinda and herself and said she would bring back the tray with the teapot and the rest of the tea things.

There were groans when Aunt Hetty and Rob

reluctantly excused themselves for there was the bar to open. 'You play more sedate games, mind,' Aunt Hetty warned them. 'I don't want to hear my ornaments crashing in the hearth . . .'

As the fire flames licked up the chimney, they turned their chairs to the warmth and told stories and recited half-forgotten poems in the firelight. Angel looked up at Lalla's portrait of the children and swallowed hard. Yes, she thought, Lalla would want them to enjoy today for she was that kind of person. Jess had been sharing her time with the two parties and now she sat discreetly in a corner nursing Belinda and Angel was sharply aware of the contented little gulps of the baby and Jess humming softly to her daughter. A picture of contentment, the two of them.

At some time during the evening, Nana came to the parlour to take the baby home. The bugler followed her and, as he had done that day in Parminter's barn, he sat down at the old piano and began slowly to explore the yellowing keys. He played fragments of music and even the ebullient Ginger Biscuits fell silent and listened.

But the spell had to be broken some time and at eight o'clock the Goodchilds made their farewells for they had a full day ahead of them, with church and Sunday school.

'Don't get up, Angel,' Lilian said, for Whis was on her lap by now, twitching and snoring as spaniels do. 'Happy birthday for Monday! I'll see you then, of course, at the soup making.'

'Many happy 'turns!' The Ginger Biscuits cheerfully kissed Angel in turn.

Aunt Hetty and Rob popped out from the bar across the way for a moment to say goodbye and thank you for coming.

The party was breaking up, for Jess and the bugler went hand in hand down the short stairs, then outside to the barn.

After another half-hour Edmund sighed, 'Time for us to make a move too, I'm afraid. Whis! I know you want to stay, but we must see Edith home, then go for our constitutional, old lad. Also, your supper awaits!'

Carefully, he tucked a small parcel in Angel's hand. 'Open it on Monday!'

She gave him an impulsive hug and a brief kiss. She turned to see Edith smiling at them. Oh, I do hope she doesn't get the wrong idea, she thought.

'I'll bring my present then,' Edith said, 'Aren't you lucky to celebrate *twice* this year?'

'Very lucky . . .' Angel agreed.

Angel, Tony and Alice tidied the parlour, placed the guard round the dying-down fire.

'We'll wash up, Tony and me,' Alice said firmly. 'Down to the kitchen, brother!'

They stayed up by mutual consent, until The Angel shut and Aunt Hetty shooed them up to bed. 'You two'll have your eyes closed till midday, I daresay!'

'Happy birthday, Rob,' Angel filled her glass with milk. The curtains were already pulled in the kitchen. She thought he looked tired, drawn, now the excitement was over.

'I imagined I was over it all, you know,' he said, and she knew what he was referring to. 'I had learned to live without her very well, I thought. I don't think we could have ever taken off where we left off, that sort of love was long gone. She didn't love me, in that way anymore, I accepted that. But I can't believe this terrible thing, Angel. Lalla is such a vital person – whatever she did to us, her family, we can only mourn her when she is gone . . .'

'I know,' she told him. She tried to put the thought out of her mind that he would soon be free.

In the barn the lovers embraced. 'Can you stay, Jess?'

'Nana's tired, Belinda might wake up, better not. You enjoy the party?'

'I think – yes, of course. Jess, I know who *she* is now.'

'Who, my dear?'

'The nurse. Edith's friend. When they called her Angel today it suddenly came to me. She *was* an *angel* to us – in France . . .'

'She's a special young lady, we all know that. But why doesn't she say she knows you, too?'

There was puzzlement in his eyes. 'Perhaps I have changed, Jess. I can't be the man I was, can I?'

She drew him close again. 'You're getting there, old feller and I'll help all I can . . .'

'She must have her reasons.'

''Course she does. Stop mardling and give me a kiss to warm me all through the night . . .'

Angel and Rob went upstairs together, paused outside his door. For one wild moment she longed to follow him inside to offer him comfort, loving, just as Jess did with the bugler. But she said merely: 'Goodnight and God Bless, Rob. The children won't forget this party, eh? Didn't they do us proud?'

He bent and kissed her. A chaste, brotherly brushing on her burning cheek, so aflame because of those errant thoughts. 'Goodnight, dear Angel. See you in the morning.'

CHAPTER THIRTY

'Could you use these?' The bugler diffidently unloaded his offerings on to the kitchen table. A bunch of carrots and three fine swedes. The early morning mist had dampened his hair, sparkled in droplets from his brows and lashes.

It was certainly the weather for good, warming soup. Angel smiled and said, 'Thank you.' She and Jess were already busy chopping the vegetables.

It was market day and Aunt Hetty and Edith had gone with Rob in the trap, intending to do some early Christmas shopping. 'We'll stir the old Christmas puds tomorrer,' Aunt Hetty reminded them. Lilian had promised to come along later and the parson had promised to collect and deliver the soup to the school in good time. The Angel would not open at lunchtime today.

Jess, Belinda slung on one hip, for now she was crawling she was getting a bit of a handful for Nana to look after all day, paused in scraping a giant carrot. 'Take Belinda for a bit?' she asked the bugler. He nodded. She passed the baby to him and he settled in his chair by the stove.

Belinda did not seem to be her usual cheerful little self. 'Cutting more teeth I reckon, eh, Nurse?' Jess asked.

Angel looked thoughtfully at the baby. 'She certainly has red cheeks today, Jess. Is that her chest grumbling?'

'Yes. I have to keep wiping her nose and she don't like that . . .' Jess sounded anxious.

Angel was aware of the bugler's shy regard. She smiled back. Just a small improvement in his confidence, she thought, but added to daily. He was comfortable with the baby that was obvious. It was right that Belinda had two parents to love her.

When the diced vegetables were simmering nicely, Jess said suddenly to Angel: 'We should call the bugler *Francis*, Nurse, for that's his name. You *do* remember him, from France, don't you?'

She was glad that Edith was not there. 'Yes, I do,' she agreed.

'Did they call him Frank then?'

'No, it was always Francis, Jess.' Although he seemed absorbed now in gently rocking the fretful baby she had the feeling he was listening intently.

Perhaps it was time to talk. She would be giving nothing away, just passing on information already divulged by Edith to Rob and no doubt Aunt Hetty.

'Did he tell you his name himself, Jess?'

Jess nodded.

'He is Captain Francis Taylor. He was a doctor in France, Jess, a great friend of my fiancé, Harry. They were at school together. They – were wounded together . . .' What had Edith told him of his past? How would he react to what she was saying?

'Harry died.' A sorrowful, soft-spoken statement from the bugler.

'Don't upset Nurse,' Jess cried impulsively, 'she still grieves for him, I know it.'

'It's all right, Jess. It was a long time ago. D'you remember *me* now, Francis?'

'He knows your name – 'cause he does, Nurse – he tells me they called you Angel in the hospital – and I knew he was a cap'n, from the uniform . . .'

The bugler's speech was still slow, but recently had become much less hesitant. It was as if the warmth, the welcome of the big kitchen relaxed him. Like Aunt Hetty's old cat *he* was gradually regaining his confidence, his trust confirmed in those who had befriended him. 'We called you Angel, *then*,' he repeated.

As Lilian gave her usual knock and entered, the bugler suddenly betrayed alarm. 'Belinda is burning up – she's twitching!'

With a cry of fear Jess snatched Belinda from him. 'Nurse – Belinda's having a *fit*!'

'Lay her on the table, Jess – quick, we must strip her off!'

But Jess was shaking herself with terror, unable to do as Angel asked. Lilian grasped her arm, turned her round and led her to the sink. 'Fill the basin with water, Jess. I've been through this with one of mine. Angel knows exactly what to do. Remember she's a nurse.'

Belinda's eyes had rolled up, showing the whites. Angel turned her rigid head to the side, gently eased her tongue forwards to prevent her swallowing it. The relentless jerking of her limbs continued. Then the bugler was helping Angel, expertly sponging the baby down, calling for fresh water and flannels from time to time, while Angel held Belinda steady.

Jess and Lilian tipped away water, rinsed the flannels: Jess rushed outside to pump up more in the buckets.

The juddering very gradually lessened to spasms of trembling and Belinda let out a thin, reedy cry.

At Angel's behest, Jess fetched a thin cotton sheet from the pile ironed first thing and awaiting transfer to the airing cupboard. The bugler took it, wrapped the baby loosely. 'She should rest now, Jess. She's over it, thank God, but you must watch her closely for some time, for the rise in temperature is unpredictable.'

Jess clutched at his arm. 'Stay with me!' she appealed.

Angel could see that Jess was suffering from shock. 'Take Belinda to my room, Jess, you can lay her on my bed. It's cooler up there. Just keep her covered with this sheet for the time being. You lie beside her, while she sleeps, but don't cuddle her, will you, or she could easily become overheated again, as – Francis – says. You'll go with her, won't you?' she asked him.

He lifted the baby from the table. Her eyes were already closed. 'Lead the way, Jess, I'll carry her,' he said quietly.

Lilian was making tea. 'One of us will bring you a cup in a short while.'

Angel realised that this would be the first time the bugler had ventured so far into the house.

Angel and Lilian sat at the table, drinking strong tea with plenty of sugar. 'You are shaking yourself, Angel, you know,' Lilian observed. 'Well, I suppose I am too. I lost *my* baby son, Angel . . . We must pray that little Belinda will recover quickly.'

'She will.' Angel willed herself to be positive.

'A small miracle don't you think, Angel, that sad, lost man jolted into the reality of the present? Can the transformation last, I wonder?'

'I can't answer that. My training was more concerned with mending the body than the mind. Edith would be the person to ask. Yet, after the war, it did become apparent to me that the two are inextricably linked, that often the body heals long before the wounded spirit. But I *do* know, Lilian, that something extraordinary has happened here in Aunt Hetty's kitchen . . .' She put out her hand and pressed Lilian's. 'I'm so sorry, Lilian, about your baby son. You never spoke about it before—'

Again, that wistful expression. 'It was a while ago. He was our first baby, Angel; Charlie and I were so very thrilled with him. Charlie was an impoverished curate then. Arthur was about

Belinda's age, just starting to crawl and to babble a bit. People said he looked like me, the only one to do so . . . In his case the convulsion was caused by the onset of meningitis. Oh, Angel, you don't think?'

'*No*! Belinda doesn't have the other signs . . .'

'Afterwards, Angel, all those lovely girls – a bad time with young Charly and my doctor advised, no more. I still *ache* for my little lost son. I always will, I think.'

The soup suddenly spilled over on to the stove. Angel leaped up, rushed over and stirred the pot gingerly. 'It's all right, Lilian, not yet burning on the bottom! A dash more water should do it.'

'Thank goodness,' Lilian sighed, 'Aunt Hetty and Edith are blissfully unaware of all this.'

Even as Angel was about to add, 'What about Nana?' Nana herself came in, all breathless, followed by the parson.

'Got a lift with the young parson didn't I, had the bad feeling something's up here!'

'Now, Nana – we could have done with *you* here half-an-hour ago,' Angel knew she must be tactful, 'but don't worry, all's well now. Follow me, Jess is with Belinda in my room.'

Lilian swiftly put her husband in the picture, 'We can take you all home, Nana; Charles and I must deliver the soup shortly to the school, we are the servers today.'

Belinda was relaxed now, sleeping and making

little sighing noises now and then, still naked within the folds of the sheet.

'Do you think she can be dressed now, Nana?' Angel deferred quite naturally to Belinda's great-grandmother.

Nana nodded, giving a long look at the bugler as he and Jess sat side by side on the edge of Angel's bed. 'The gal needed you today. I thank you for your help, feller.'

She gently unwrapped the baby, eased on some of her garments and then carried her downstairs in her arms.

Angel saw the bugler giving Jess a quick comforting embrace to let her know the crisis was over.

He did not go with Jess, Nana and the baby in the trap, but walked slowly back to the barn without another word.

It was quiet in the house. Lilian had called, as the pony moved off, 'I will be back later, Angel, then I can let you know how things are. We can go together to collect the children from school. Mind you have that soup I put out for you—'

'I will,' Angel promised.

She sat at the table, eating in a desultory fashion. One of the kitlings leaped up onto her lap and she stroked the soft fur taking comfort from the dreamy purring. A friendly animal was not the same as a child to cuddle but it helped. She pondered on the sad story of Lilian and Charlie's infant son. It was inevitable that the events of that second trauma, which had followed so close to Harry's death, should come at last to the fore.

Edith quietly suggested that she stay in her quarters although she knew how urgent the need was for every single member of the hospital staff to be on duty. The emergency operations continued, the wounded arrived hourly. 'You will be going home,' Edith told her, 'nurses are needed to care for the patients on board ship. Relief staff will be arriving here at any time. It's best you rest, you are still in severe shock . . .

She cried at last, now she was alone, because she had not been able to say farewell to Harry, to tell him the news. She had no way of knowing whether he would have been shocked, or glad, despite what this would mean for them both, especially her . . .

How could anyone believe she would have contemplated such an action, just two days ago?

The agonising pain began low in her back. She felt fearfully, for it was dark, still in the early hours in that deserted dormitory, knowing what the dampness, the stickiness of her nightgown must mean.

When the agony was at its height, she dragged herself somehow to the wash basin, clutched at towels, collapsed, writhing on the floor by her bed. She thought she heard a scream, emanating from deep within herself, but the name conjured up was, 'Lou! oh, Lou, help me!' Not 'Harry!' or even, 'Edith!' She had called just so for her sister when she was a child, whose mother had left her.

She was past all calling when she realised it was over, finished.

Edith came then, mercifully alone. She did not question, merely got on, stoicly, with what needed to be done, concealed. It was not the first time she had had to deal with such a situation, after all. Others had suffered like Angel. She felt the needle prick her arm then oblivion until dawn.

The realisation came then, the terrible blow. She was not even to have the solace of carrying and bearing Harry's baby. That part of him too had gone.

Edith warned, 'No one else must ever know. Angel, can you hear me?'

A gentle touch on her shoulder, as she sobbed bitterly, head in hands, still slumped over the table. The soup congealed in the bowl, the bread not eaten.

'Angel, can you hear me?' The echo of Edith's words. 'Tell me all about it,' Lilian whispered.

Angel turned to her new friend, to pour out all that her old friend had forbidden her to ever tell.

CHAPTER THIRTY-ONE

Angel crossed over to the pink house; Edith was languishing on the sofa in the darkened parlour with one of her sick headaches. She carried a jug of Aunt Hetty's lemon barley water 'to clean the system' and the suggestion: 'Two cloves in a fresh cup of tea, so Nana says, clears a bad head fast . . .'

Aspirin, Angel mused, would be Edith's own prescription. It was a wonder that Nana had not reminded them of the ancient habit of chewing a bit of willow bark. Well, wasn't that exactly what aspirin was derived from?

Young Belinda was now happily recovered to everyone's relief but Angel was instantly reminded of that awful day a week ago when she saw that Edith had a damp flannel spread across her forehead. She did not appear particularly pleased to see Angel, muttering, 'Thought you'd be too busy with your new friend to worry about *me* . . .'

Angel poured out a glass of the barley water. 'Try this. Aunt Hetty made it specially for you, Edith.' She refused to rise to the sarcasm. You had to make allowances when someone was obviously unwell.

A few reluctant sips then Edith waved it away, 'I don't care for it today.'

'Have you been actually sick?'

'Don't remind me. In the night – more times than I wished to count. Flashing before the eyes, too. I rose first thing but really couldn't face breakfast. When Lilian knocked to see if I was ready to go over to The Angel for the soup preparing, she persuaded me to lie down in here. I gather she told you?'

'Well, of course she did. Is the headache—?'

'*Excruciating*!' Edith moaned.

'I'll stay until you feel better then, Edith. I told the others I probably would. They can manage without me. Francis will help with the chopping-up I expect.'

'Francis! Francis! Is all revealed now then?' Edith's voice was shrill.

'I told you the other day Edith, he remembers *me* now from the old days. I don't think that he recalls – *that* time but I'm just thankful that he is so much improved. I didn't realise myself who he was until that evening of the parson's party. I will have to take the chance that he does not turn against me eventually when his memory is fully restored—'

'That may never be the case.'

Angel had spent sleepless nights recently agonising over all this. She removed the flannel to cool it.

'We must think of Jess and Belinda, too. Perhaps there will be a happy ending for them at least . . . There, is that better, Edith?'

Edith reluctantly conceded that the fresh compress was soothing.

'Happy ending, do you *really* think so, Angel?'

'Yes, I do.' Angel escaped to the kitchen. She felt sad that Edith obviously resented her easy-going relationship with Lilian. What would be her reaction though if she knew just how much Angel had confided in one so recently met? Why was Edith so bitter about Jess? Where was the compassion that she had shown when she had cared for Angel, covered up for her when she had lost Harry's baby? She had seemed a loyal, loving friend then. Had Edith been acting a lie?

She entered the barn. He was already there. 'Five precious minutes, Angel, we shouldn't have come at all . . .'

Then Edith's voice, sharp and shocked: 'Whoever? Angel, is that you? Harry? They are calling for you, Doctor, you are needed immediately, please go! Nurse Rosselli, wait, I want a word with you!'

'I'm sorry,' Angel whispered.

'How could you?' was all Edith said.

Later, as the gunfire rose to a crescendo she added, as she and Angel endeavoured to comfort a mortally wounded man, as if carrying on with that brief exchange in the barn: 'Why Harry, why him?'

There was no reply Angel could give. She had betrayed Edith's faith in her.

She took the tray in to Edith. 'Perhaps I will go home. Maybe you'd rather be alone, Edith. I will call back later and make you a light lunch.'

'Yes, you go *home* as you call it. Lilian will be pleased to see you back . . .' Edith turned her face away.

She went in to Alice that night. The smothered sobbing was barely audible but she had expected it for this evening Rob and Aunt Hetty had sat down with the children and told them the grave news of their mother. She guessed that Aunt Hetty was already saying her own words of comfort to Tony.

Alice sat up in bed, clutched at Angel and wept. The tears ran down Angel's bare throat. 'We hardly knew her, Angel, it wouldn't be so bad though if she hadn't come back this summer and made us *love* her—'

'She came back because she wanted to see you, so much, all of you, Alice, one last time. She wanted to reassure herself that you were well-adjusted and happy, for don't you think she always felt guilt for leaving you as she did?'

'*When*, d'you think, Angel?'

'It could be soon. If only she had sought treatment earlier, Alice, the outcome might have been better. It's a cruel disease, no known cure, not yet.'

'I don't want her to die! Even if she never came back to see us, ever again.'

'I know. I know. It will do you good to cry, Alice. You aren't crying alone, I'm sure.'

'Tony, you mean? Dad, too?'

'Yes. And Aunt Hetty.'

'Aunt Hetty never approved of Lalla. She says Dad should have married someone like *you*. She's right—'

'Lalla was the one he chose. He really loved her, Alice.' She hugged Alice to her. 'Try to get some sleep now. You have to go to school in the morning, remember. And it won't hurt to pray for your mother—'

'It's no use praying for her to get better!'

'You can pray that she will not be in too much pain, pray because you love her and you always will. She would be pleased at that.'

The door opened slowly. Angel turned and in the light of the dying candle, burning down into the soft wax spilled in the saucer, she saw Rob.

'Is Alice really all right?' he asked, outside the door, when Alice was settled.

'Alice is being very brave, bless her.'

'So is young Tony, he's in with Aunt Hetty, of course.'

As Angel made to open her own door he added: 'Thank you, Angel. For all your caring for this family.'

The letter came from Gerald at the beginning of December, when the tall trees shivered, bare of leaves and a cruel wind whooshed down the chimneys and caught at insecurely latched doors. The goats sheltered in the barn with the bugler and in the school, the children huddled round the teacher and the stove and were thankful for the hot soup, even when their fingers felt too numb to grasp a spoon. Fires roared at The Angel and the good old boys came to the comfort of the inglenook in the evenings, more for the warmth than the beer, for wages were lower than ever. They were thankful to have a job, whatever it paid.

They learned that Lalla had passed peacefully away. The service had been simple as she requested. She had not wished to be brought back even if this had been possible. 'We can't even put flowers on her grave,' Tony said solemnly. In fact, as Gerald said, she had expressed that she was actually glad that Rob and her children would, due to the distance and time factor, be unable to come to her funeral for: '*She wanted you to remember her as she was.*'

There were farewell notes enclosed for the children and Aunt Hetty, firmly written, cheerfully urging them not to be too sad, hoping that they would grow up, Alice and Tony, as she fondly imagined they would: clever, kind, imaginative people who would lead happy and fulfilled lives. Rob did not reveal the contents of the longer letter he received except to say that he was to contact Lalla's solicitor in London.

In a short while he learned that as Lalla's husband he would be in receipt of a considerable sum of money. The children were also generously provided for.

'Money won't bring her back but it'll be a godsend right now,' observed Aunt Hetty. 'I don't think we could've carried on here much longer otherwise, Angel dear.'

'Do you still want *me* to stay on?' Angel had to know.

'Once it was me, but *you're* our linchpin now. You know what I hope for, in time—'

'*Don't* say it, Aunt Hetty. Please!'

'I won't. But another might ask you first. That worries me.'

'I can't make any plans. I can't predict the future. I'll just say, well, *you* are *family* to me now, Aunt Hetty . . .'

'Knew you'd fit in, moment we met, among the asparagus.' Aunt Hetty said.

CHAPTER THIRTY-TWO

Aunt Hetty saw something coming, which Angel did not. One Sunday afternoon she and Edmund walked Whis along by the river. It did not seem a magical place now as it had that day, before she had almost drowned, before the tragic end of Boniface.

Mud oozed, clung to their walking shoes, the water had risen, the willows waved wildly in the wind. 'Better turn back.' Edmund called the dog to heel. He added quite casually: 'I have been meaning to ask you for a while now to marry me, Angel . . .'

Overhead the clouds hung low. There was too much sky today. Grey, wintry sky. Their breath hung in smoky drifts.

'Why? Why now?' She asked simply, wiping her damp face with the back of her glove. She wore Rob's birthday gift to her, the coarse woollen gloves. The soft kid leather pair she had brought with her from London remained unpacked in her trunk.

'D'you want me to say I have fallen deeply in love with you, Angel? I *do* care for you very much but, to be honest, I don't know if I have yet experienced the kind of love you obviously felt for your lost fiancé . . . What I have for you is a good, solid affection, perhaps the most one can ask of a stolid person like me, eh?' His smile disarmed her. 'We get on so well together, don't we? We already share old Whis, you would be an ideal schoolmaster's wife. And – we both would like a family, I know that too.'

'I have a family to care for already,' she said simply.

'A *borrowed* family, Angel. A family you will have to leave eventually, I think.'

She looked at him, face to face. 'Did Edith put the idea into your head?'

He looked surprised. 'Edith? No, though when you first came here I suspected, well, a touch of matchmaking, as I'm sure you did too. It was *Rob*, Angel. He came down to see me at the schoolhouse the other evening, after The Angel had closed. He knows I am always late to bed. I think it helped him to talk to someone not directly involved with his recent loss. He reminded me that the kind of love he and Lalla experienced in the early days of their marriage sometimes burned itself out. That the warm affection and companionship between you and I might be a better and more lasting foundation for a good marriage. He felt that we are, well, *right* for each other.'

'It is not for *him* to say!' She walked away, ahead of him so that he could not see the tears blinding her eyes, the disappointment she felt, for she was really fond of Edmund and the last thing she wished to do was to hurt him.

'You don't have to answer immediately, of course,' he caught her up, took her arm and hugged her close to his side as they walked along. 'Forget it for the moment. I have obviously not picked a good time. I'm sorry.'

'Don't be. I don't want to lose your friendship!'

'You'll never do that. Whatever you decide.'

'Edith has been very constrained with me recently—'

'Yes, I have been wondering about that. Perhaps there is more behind these headaches than she is admitting? I'm sure she doesn't *mean* to be so cool.'

Privately she felt she knew the reason for Edith's recent behaviour.

They parted at Edith's gate. 'Why don't you join us for tea, I'm sure she won't mind.' He looked into her troubled eyes.

'The children need me, Edmund. It's difficult for them, seeing Rob so sad. They feel guilty because it is not so bad for them; they are used to not having a mother around.'

He closed the gate between them. 'Perhaps *Rob* needs you more. Don't say anything, think about it. I will see you soon, my dear . . .'

'Why didn't you invite Angel in?' Edith asked, fussing over his dirty shoes, poking at the fire to warm and dry his damp clothes.

'I did ask her,' he said. He put up with the solicitude because Edith had always been the same. He would always be her little brother, he thought wryly. 'She wanted to get back to Alice and Tony.'

'They are coping well, children are very resilient,' she gave him a sideways look. 'I had the feeling, you know, when you said you were going for a walk despite the weather that you were going to issue – *another* invitation . . .'

'I did,' he said equably.

'And?'

'She didn't exactly turn me down, but I believe the answer is still "no".'

'She's a fool then!' Edith flashed.

'She is not! I thought you two were great friends—'

'*Once*!'

'I can't pretend to understand what all this is about, Edith. Please don't turn against Angel, that's all I ask. I only wish she would have me. However, she can't be blamed for not being in love with me. Maybe there is someone else.'

Tea overflowed his cup, spilled into the saucer. Her hand was shaking. 'Why? Why *now*?' she cried, just as Angel had done earlier.

As Angel was passing Rob's door on her way upstairs later he came out of the room. His look was rather quizzical and she guessed that he was wondering if Edmund had taken up his suggestion to speak to her.

Something seemed to snap inside her and she blurted out furiously: 'I do wish you would mind your own business, Rob! Edmund told me you had spoken to him, about me. *If* I ever marry, I would prefer to choose my own husband, thank you!'

Hurt and surprise clouded his face. 'I only thought, we can't expect you to stay here for ever, that it would be good to have you not far away, you have become such a friend of the family . . .'

She pushed past him, went swiftly to her room and firmly closed the door. After a few moments she heard the stairs creaking as he continued downstairs.

Weeping, face down on her bed, she did not hear the door open or Aunt Hetty coming in.

'Now, what's this all about, Angel? Care to tell old Aunt Hetty, dearie?'

'I quarrelled with Rob, the last thing I should've done, after all he's had to endure recently—'

'He feels it more poor chap y'know, 'cause he isn't devastated like he would've been, for it's been such a long time, the war as well, the two of them apart, eh? He's so sad, I am too, Lalla being so young. Such a cruel way to go. But, till she came back like that, I guess he had days, maybe even weeks, when he scarcely gave her a thought. He was getting on with his life you see, we all have to . . . Now, what on earth did you two find to have words about?'

Angel told her.

'It'll make him think,' Aunt Hetty commented wisely. 'You wash your pretty face now and come down for supper.'

'I don't know if I can face him—'

'You *can*. The children heard something you know. It's the last thing *they* want, another upset.'

'I'm so sorry.' She was crying again.

'Don't be sorry for having feelings . . . Can't say I'm not glad you don't intend to be the schoolmaster's wife, though I'm wholly sorry for Edmund. Dry your eyes! Five minutes, then I'll dish up!'

She splashed her face with cold water, changed quickly into the cream wool costume. She rummaged in her bag, brought out the neglected rouge and rubbed a little on her pale cheeks.

There was a tapping on her door. She heard Rob's deep voice, the gentle Scottish burr pronounced, as it always was when he betrayed emotion. 'Angel I am so sorry if I upset you, *please* forgive me.'

She did not open the door. 'I must apologise too, Rob. I reacted stupidly. I know you meant well. Please say no more about it. I'll be down shortly.'

'Are we still friends?' he asked urgently.

'Yes, of course. Friends, Rob.'

CHAPTER THIRTY-THREE

'Here you are then, gal,' Nana stated as Jess opened the door of Number 3 and stepped straight into the living room. It was past midnight and the fire was low. In winter Nana kept on her top garments and wound herself in an old horse blanket while sitting out the night. She cat-napped now and then but prowled around the room when her limbs stiffened or wrapped her chilled hands round yet another cup of stewed tea.

Jess shook a powdering of snow from her hair, then from her shawl. She peeped into the cot Lilian had lent her for Belinda when the baby outgrew the cradle. The baby slumbered peacefully in her stove-warmed recess.

'Anything left in the pot, Nana?' She slept on a mattress on the landing above where she could keep an eye on her daughter through the rails.

'You can't carry on like this, Jess.' Nana jiggled some fresh water round the tea leaves. '*He* can't move in here with us, Nurse Fenner'd never allow it, and I'm not having that baby brought up in a barn—'

Jess suppressed a grin. Far more space in the

barn and it was no more draughty than the cottage! 'He says we'll get married – *soon*,' she volunteered.

'Reckon he's fit enough, do you, gal?'

'I love him Nana, he loves me – *us*. And I've got my job—'

'*Now*, you have. But what if you fall again, eh?'

'I worked carrying Belinda, and you'll help out as you always do, if it comes to *that*!'

'I won't always be here as I tell you . . . I still get that old pain—'

Fear flashed across Jess's expressive face. 'Then I'll have to care for you too, Nana. You *know* I will!'

'I'll have a word with Aunt Hetty – you get some sleep now . . .'

'Yes, Aunt Hetty'll have the answer, you can count on that.'

Ever nearer Christmas and Angel was wondering whether she ought to tell them that she was expected to spend the holiday with Lou, Jack and Peter Carlo. However, a letter from Lou caused her to change her mind. Lou wrote that their mother and stepfather would be in London during the Christmas period and were anxious to see as much as possible of their first grandchild:

Isn't it amazing? Mother seems to want to make amends for her lack of maternal attention in the past! Probably because Sidney seems to have mellowed considerably and is willing to indulge mother in her new role! Of course, Angel, you are still welcome to come, because they will be staying in a hotel, Sidney is not yet the complete family man! If you can manage sharing with Peter as you suggested, though disturbed nights are more than a possibility . . . Or do you feel you should stay with Alice and Tony after recent events? We will understand if this is the case. Can you let us know soon?

All love from us three,
Lou

Angel was learning how to make and apply the marzipan for the Christmas cake under Aunt Hetty's expert guidance. 'Bit late in the day, Angel, ought to have done it a while ago, but till the children broke up from school and we could forget the soup pot, well, we've got behind on the Christmas jobs . . . You'll be here with us, I hope? We must make an effort for Alice and Tony and we always have Edith and Edmund, and Jess and Nana, Belinda too of course this year, come for their dinner.'

'Yes, I'll be here, Aunt Hetty. But I must write to Lou today and tell her that's what I've decided.'

'The bugler too,' Aunt Hetty mused, measuring out the ground almonds. 'We have had an idea about *him*, Rob and me.'

'It's good he is helping Rob with the cellar work and the outside chores now. He really seems so well in himself. Sawing logs is definitely therapeutic!'

'Edith's very cagey about his past, before the war, you know. All we know really is that he has been married before, but lost his wife and child. She did say that any money left by his family was used up long ago when he first came back from the war. Rob knows she has the handling of his service pension. But we provide, and gladly for his simple needs while he stays here . . .'

'He was a good doctor once but I don't think he'll ever be able to take up that profession again, Aunt Hetty. He was so resolute and brave in France. My – Harry thought a great deal of him. They were such good friends.'

'His old life may be lost to him but he has young Jess and that beautiful baby, bless her, and his music to soothe his soul.'

In came Alice and Tony, red-cheeked from the cold, excited at the first drifts of snow. It had not laid so far this winter.

'Dad says it won't come to anything but Tony hoicked the old sledge out of the woodshed and the bugler's looking it over for us.'

Rob followed them in. 'Well, I've asked him, Aunty Hetty! I stressed it might be a long hard winter and to my surprise he agreed – he didn't need to be persuaded! Maybe Jess had already put the idea to him, for you asked her opinion, didn't you?'

'I did that,' Aunt Hetty said with a saucy twinkle.

‘This is all very mysterious . . .’ Angel rolled the pliable almond paste into a ball in a sprinkling of icing sugar.

‘Francis, for we try and remember to call him that now, eh? Is to move soon into Rob’s room. He can keep his privacy there—’

‘It says PRIVATE!’ Tony pointed out, sneaking a crumb or two of almond paste from the table.

‘—and I shall move back into my old room,’ Rob ended evenly.

Angel wondered immediately, what about Jess? Thinking of the clandestine meetings in the barn.

Aunt Hetty might have read her mind. She mouthed at Angel: ‘None of *that*, not with our young ’uns around . . .’

Alice was too observant. ‘Not until they get married, Aunt Hetty. Jess is asking the parson about *that*!’

‘You know more’n we do, then. Wagging ears I suppose?’

The children looked suitably bashful. ‘Come on, Alice, let’s see if the sledge is ready yet!’

Rob looked at Angel: ‘It will be up to Aunt Hetty of course, but we *can* afford live-in help now. Jess *and* Francis . . . That means you, too, Angel. How d’you feel about being a companion to all the family, rather than a nurse to Alice?’

‘I can’t do without you!’ Aunt Hetty prompted.

‘I can’t do without you all, either,’ Angel, feeling warm and happy inside, unfurled the marzipan from the rolling pin and laid it carefully over the

Christmas cake which she had previously made tacky with marmalade, to keep it in place.

Edmund, she thought, with compunction, must have intimated to Rob that she had indeed as good as turned him down. She would be staying at The Angel!

Being so busy was good for all of them. Rob and the bugler humped furniture between the two rooms. Angel noted that the big bed that Rob and Lalla had shared was exchanged for the smaller double bed, with simple wooden headboard, which Rob had grown accustomed to. Jess and Angel were most industrious with bucket and mop and Aunt Hetty washed mats and covers which steamed round the stove for it was not the weather for extra washing or indeed, any washing at all. Sheets hung limply and dolefully on the garden line but fortunately did not freeze as they well might in a week or two; underwear festooned the airer. There was an aura of yellow soap, condensation on the windows.

'All set for the new year!' Jess informed them jubilantly.

Angel put down her mop and hugged the girl to her. 'Oh be happy, dear Jess, well, I *know* you will! You and Belinda are his salvation, you see . . . But won't dear old Nana miss you both terribly?'

'Nana says, "Just you be happy, gal!" I won't ever desert her, she knows that. And now Belinda's crawling, she'll be with Nana every day as always. It's easier now she's weaned at last.' She twisted Angel's mop to expel the water. 'Some say I'm a bad gal, but Parson says he'll make an honest woman of me and Mrs Parson says I'm a good mother when there's others as aren't so—'

'My sister will be having her usual sale in the new year, I'll ask her to look out for something special for your wedding day. Would you accept that as a gift from me?'

'From *you*, I would. Nothing too fancy, mind. I'd thought about that nice blouse Aunt Hetty made me, I only wore it the once—'

'Then perhaps a warm skirt and jacket? We'll see what Lou can come up with!'

Aunt Hetty had departed for the bar. Rob was already installed.

'Guvnor's bearing up well, Nurse, isn't he? *He* ought to wed again in time. Men have needs you see—'

'Women too,' Angel reminded her quietly. Then she hugged Jess again. No need to say more.

The Snug was the venue for what was for some the annual hair-cutting. A tidying up for the festive season. The barber travelled from village to village with his sharp scissors and clippers that nicked the neck if you were mardling and didn't keep still. There was the constant call: 'Any more hot towels ready, Missus?' This was a men-only occasion of course and Edmund and Francis took turns with Rob and Tony in the barber's chair. Sixpence for a short-back-and-sides, a penny tip expected if the head was over-shaggy. Angel sneaked a look at what was going on when she was despatched with the towels for Aunt Hetty and Jess were pulling the pints tonight.

'Haven't had a skull job like that since they shaved us for the lice in the Army,' Will moaned. 'That's wholly cold without my thatch.'

Tony felt the nape of his neck gingerly. 'Barber pulls teeth as well, Angel, with a pair of pliers! Alice nearly fainted when he showed us a tooth with a hooked root he'd yanked from Will's jaw last Christmas!'

'See?' Will proudly displayed the gap. 'Healed a treat that did. My missus she say it's barbaric, she pays that posh chap in town. He put her out with a good old whiff of gas. But it made her sick 'cause it went down on her stomach.'

Angel beat a hasty retreat. She might be a nurse, but enough was enough!

'I don't know about good old boys, *tough* old boys!' she said to Jess later.

'Francis has got time for his hair to grow afore the wedding, what a bit o' luck!' Jess replied with feeling.

Rob looked younger with his short crop. 'Clear sky, look at all the stars they'll dazzle you, Angel,' he told her, much later still.

I've been dazzled ever since I came here . . . she thought, and smiled at him before they reluctantly shut out the night and went their separate ways to bed. They were nearer now, of course, now he had returned to his old room. She couldn't help wondering if the memories of Lalla were constantly with him as he lay awaiting sleep.

CHAPTER THIRTY-FOUR

Talking to the parson had been no problem at all. But now it was time for Jess to face Edith. She must have had an inkling of course, particularly when Francis moved into The Angel and began to work there, at present on a part-time basis.

Jess took Angel along for moral support. Edith was expecting them and the pink house door stood ajar.

'Come into the kitchen,' Edith called. She was not entertaining Jess in her parlour.

They sat around the table, drinking tea from delicate cups and made polite conversation for a bit.

Jess made the first move: 'Francis and me are getting married in the new year. I come to ask for your blessing, you being concerned on his behalf.'

'Very little money left for him to be married on, Jess,' Edith stated.

'That's no problem. I'll carry on working and he'll do what he can.'

'There's his pension, I'll see to that for you. You've thought about this very carefully, I take it?

Bear in mind that this will be a huge responsibility. Particularly with regard to his health. He could have a relapse—'

'I will be around, should Jess have problems in that respect,' Angel put in. She was actually surprised that Edith was taking it all so well.

'Ah, *you* are staying on I take it?'

'I am. Alice and Tony still seem to need me.'

'It doesn't matter *now*,' Edith said, puzzling them both. 'I will relinquish my interest in Francis from now on. But I don't expect you to come running to *me* if things go badly wrong. Well, I'm afraid I have work to do, so if you'll excuse me—'

However, they had not reached the gate before Edith called Angel back. 'Oh, Angel, a quick word with you!'

She said what had to be said on the doorstep. 'I gather you have turned Edmund down. He hasn't given up hope, you know! He is a good man, Angel.'

'I know that. We are good friends, Edith.' As you and I once were, she thought.

'You were always too impulsive. Don't let your feelings run away with you this time. I needn't spell it out. *Edmund* would never hurt you, let you down.'

'Edith – oh, I don't think you understand. I thought you did, in France, but you've changed—'

'So have you. But I think I still know what goes on in your mind. And there is always that shared secret, of course.'

Was there a veiled threat? Yet Edith was smiling now. 'Goodbye, Angel. See you soon!'

'It isn't wrong, is it, to be excited and enjoying all this?' Alice and Tony were sprawled on the end of Angel's bed, having woken her at some unearthly hour with their 'Happy Christmas!' She reassured them that Lalla would want them to be so.

By candlelight she watched as the children delved into Rob's boot stockings, until only the bulge in the toe awaited the winkling out of the small, sweet oranges, no doubt they would spill juice on her nice coverlet! There was a special, poignant reminder of their mother. Gerald had parcelled up her drawings and sent them to Rob. He had framed a self-portrait of Lalla, colour-washed, laughing at a private joke as she drew her reflection in the mirror. She was in the pretty brown smock she had worn during her visit, her hair glinted with highlights. In one corner there was the extravagant flourish, LALLA. On a plain card, Rob had penned: *For Alice and Tony. Always remembering their lovely mother, Lalla MacDonald.*

'It can hang in your room if you like, Alice, as you're the oldest,' Tony said solemnly. 'But we'll always share it, won't we?'

''Course we will,' Alice agreed, blinking fiercely.

'Will you two give me a chance of getting up now, please? You've plenty to keep you busy! I want to surprise Aunt Hetty this morning with a cup of tea, we were really late home from the Christmas Mass . . .' Angel yawned widely.

'I suppose Lilian said you had to go—'

'Not at all, Alice. I wanted to be there. There's something very special about welcoming in Christmas Day like that . . .' It had begun as they walked under the bright light of the archway lantern.

'Dad didn't go—' They bundled the presents back into their stockings.

No, but we said a special prayer for him, for you all, she thought. 'Shoo!' she said fondly. 'Tea for you, too?'

'Please; we'll be in with Aunt Hetty. We're just going to jump on *her*, aren't we, Alice?'

Angel was rinsing the teapot when she felt her hair fingered out from under the collar of her wrapper. 'I see *you* decided to escape the demon barber, Angel. Like most men, I like longer hair . . . Happy Christmas to ye.' Her neck tingled deliciously from his light touch.

'Happy Christmas, Rob!' She turned, holding the teapot between them. He ignored the barrier and bent to kiss her. She had been intending to renew her sleek bob when next she went into town, now, she thought, she would grow her hair, for him.

It was a chaste kiss. 'I intended to be the tea maker this morning,' he said, setting out the cups for her. 'But I'll provide breakfast instead, eh?'

In the pantry lay covered trays of mince pies and

sausage rolls. The goose had cooked gently in its juices overnight, now was the time to riddle the stove and get the heat rising, for the pudding must be steamed and ahead of the womenfolk was the massive task of preparing all the vegetables. They would not have to sacrifice Rob and Aunt Hetty to the bar today for Christmas Day was sacrosanct.

There were soft-boiled eggs and home-cured ham; toast browned by Tony at the glowing bars of the stove, slice after slice; milk fetched, frothing in the jug from the farm, together with a bowl of thick cream, white under a golden crust. 'How we'll find room for the Christmas *dinner* . . .' Angel expelled her breath ruefully, after cleaning her breakfast plate.

'Oh you will, dearie, you will. Ah, here come the others already, all of 'em, I wonder if Edith has remembered the bottles of her special wine?'

'I certainly have,' Edith said breezily, unloading her basket. She was very cheerful today, quite her old self, as she wished them all cheer of the season and suggested a sample glass before laying up the table again, for Jess and her family to breakfast.

The bugler had walked down to The Cotts first thing, to escort Jess and Nana and to carry Belinda.

'Parcels in the parlour!' Alice cried. 'Follow me!'

Angel wore Edmund's necklace of sparkling blue stones set in silver. 'Look nice on my pinafore, don't they? Thank you, Edmund, I do love to have new jewels at Christmas!'

'Not real, I'm afraid, they'd be much smaller if they were! Happy Christmas, dear Angel!'

She received another brotherly kiss, on her cheek, so flushed from attending to the stove.

The sprouts seemed endless. Angel pulled them from the stalk and cut the traditional cross on the base of each one, before she added them counting under her breath, to the deep pot.

'Half-a-dozen each, I always reckon,' Aunt Hetty advised, peeling potatoes skilfully as always, so that the long curls of brown peel fell straight into the chicken's cauldron, as she called it, to boil up and mix with bran, for 'the fowls treat' as she fancied it to be.

Nana dug the eyes out from the finished spuds, tutting a little, for she considered that an unnecessary chore. Jess washed up their breakfast dishes, while Alice amused Belinda, and Edmund and Francis joined Rob in the chopping of logs, for as Rob said cheerfully: 'We need to get a steam-up, sharpen the appetite again after that huge breakfast and to get me feeling fit and ready to carve for all of you.'

Later, Alice and Tony took charge of the laying of the table, with help from Edith, who had been polishing up the best glasses.

When all was ready, and the kitchen toilers had ladled the vegetables into the big blue, gold and white tureens, stirred the gravy and heaved the goose on to the biggest serving dish they had, it was time to whip off the aprons and to call the entire company to eat. It was exactly one o'clock.

Alice was in excellent form. 'Plenitude in the Parlour!' she sang out, for the table, with the extra leaf wound out, groaned under the giant serving dishes, splendid Crown Derby, shining cutlery and glasses. Starched napkins and centre, the rather tipsy decoration fashioned by the children, prickly with holly, inclining candles and tinsel balls.

The men tackled the piles of washing-up and the ladies took off their shoes, Edith was forced to loosen her corset and Nana lifted Belinda from the high chair which Aunt Hetty had kept for the children who had not come to bless her marriage but which had also served Alice and Tony well in turn.

'Here you are, Nurse, you take her,' Nana said. She looked slyly at Angel. 'Don't fret, dearie, your arms won't always be empty, I *know* it . . .'

By unspoken agreement they did not play the usual riotous games but settled down with Christmas books, or in Nana's case a crochet hook which dipped in and out of the loops of wool of a shawl she was making for, 'When it gets wholly cold.'

Whis curled up on Angel's stockinged feet, the baby slept comfortably in her arms and some time during the evening Francis sat down diffidently at the piano and played a selection of carols, which set them all singing. A piece of cake, a last glass of wine and the party ended before ten o'clock.

Outside it was indeed a *Silent Night*; would the bugler play out there tonight? The bugle hung on the wall of his room, untouched for many weeks.

Angel lay in bed and sleep seemed far away. Tony's door opened and closed; a glimmer under her door revealed the fact that Alice was still reading. She touched her wrist: a watch with a slender leather strap, a joint present from all the family, 'because *you* never watch the clock, so Aunt Hetty says,' Tony grinned. It had been a jewel of a Christmas she thought, what with Edmund's pretty necklace, a silver brooch from Edith, a spider in the centre of a filigree web, a hat-pin from Jess, Nana and Belinda. Even Francis had shyly presented her with a small diary with a brass clasp to lock away her secret thoughts. Jess would soon proudly wear a gold band on her finger. If she had accepted Edmund, she would have worn that symbol too.

CHAPTER THIRTY-FIVE

It was a double celebration that first week of the new year. Belinda was baptised and Aunt Hetty, Angel and Rob stood as her godparents. Then, while the congregation remained seated, Jess retreated to the back of the church then stepped forwards proudly again as a bride, on Edmund's arm. He had been privileged, he said, to be asked to give her away. Nana slipped the baby a bit of paddywack, the chewy piece from the weekend joint, which Aunt Hetty had saved specially for this occasion. The Ginger Biscuits surreptitiously passed boiled sweets along the pew to Alice and Tony.

'Best to come well prepared!' Lilian whispered to Angel with a rueful smile.

Edith seemed preoccupied, gazing at the bride and groom, keeping her distance from Angel. It was difficult to get through to Edith still, which made Angel feel extra sad today. She could not understand why Edith should show such jealousy of her easy camaraderie with Lilian.

However, today was Jess and Francis's day and, of course, Belinda's too. The day when Belinda

Elderberry became Belinda Taylor like her young mother, Jess. She looked neat and bonny in soft, navy wool, with a pleated skirt and braided jacket, which complemented Aunt Hetty's blouse. Her hair was restrained by a matching petersham bow. Nana's gift, little golden hoops, gleamed on her earlobes. 'All the brides in our family show 'em off.' The bugler, tactfully advised by Rob had bought Jess new, shiny boots, for she scorned the idea of wearing shoes. Belinda was nicely in line for inheriting clothes from Charly, Lilian's youngest, and she wore a coat and leggings, good as new, in raspberry red with a poke bonnet.

No choir, no bells, but the organ played by Edmund when he had fulfilled his role in the ceremony. Rob changed roles too, from Godfather to Best Man.

Jess and Francis walked back up the aisle not to the strains of the 'Wedding March' but to her favourite hymn 'All Things Bright and Beautiful'.

It was a typical January afternoon where the mist still clung to the trees on one side of the road so that they appeared floating, ethereal. The Ginger Biscuits were coughing, Nana wound Belinda round more securely in her blanket, the Bride and Groom, with daughter and grandmother were driven off in style in Lady Pamela's motor while the rest of the company caught up with them in their own time for the Reception, or tea party was being held at The Angel. Where else?

Aunt Hetty and the children climbed into the

trap: Angel and Edith elected to start walking before Rob returned to pick them up. The parson, Lilian and the five little girls waved them all a cheery goodbye before returning to The Vicarage for the parson had a meeting to attend to in an hour or two. Edmund took Whis back to the schoolhouse, for the dog had been in his usual place in church, by the organ stool, to feed him and to leave him there for once. 'I'll catch you up I expect,' he called.

Angel slipped her arm into Edith's, ignoring the stiffening and the move to shrug her off. Edith had been surprisingly good about the wedding after all, and had even bought the newly-weds a warm blanket edged with satin ribbon for their bed.

'So, they've tied the knot. *Your* turn next, I imagine, Angel? You seem to have put all thoughts, regrets about Harry behind you at last . . .' These were bitter words.

Ah, was this it? 'I loved Harry dearly, you of all people know that, Edith.'

'Oh yes, I know *that*. Have you ever wondered just why I invited you to come here, Angel? Certainly not to enchant my brother, only to reject him when you set your cap elsewhere . . . Don't I know *everything* about you? Wasn't I the only one to stand by you through all that sorry mess?'

'I'll always be grateful—'

'I didn't do what I did to earn your undying gratitude. I was your best friend—'

'Harry was fond of you too, I know.'

‘You really *don’t* understand! What’s the use of talking about it? I was wrong to write to you. It – it re-opened old wounds.’

‘You baffle me, Edith.’

‘The bugler can’t face up to what *he* knows. Now he has married young Jess, made an honest woman of her, perhaps you should go away and leave them in peace!’

‘What *are* you talking about? They asked me to stay, Rob, Aunt Hetty, the children, why should I leave now? Surely you wouldn’t be so cruel as to tell them—’

‘It depends.’

‘On what?’ Angel’s desperation showed. She could hear the clop of hooves, the grating of wheels: Rob was returning for them, although the pony and trap were not yet visible in the limited vision ahead.

‘What’s the use of going on about it? You’ll never fathom my true feelings, I should have realised that long ago.’

Rob’s cheerful voice: ‘Here you are then, ladies! Not too damp and dispirited, I hope?’

Somehow, back at The Angel, Angel managed to present a cheery face to Jess who was smiling so happily, even if old habits were hard to break and she would insist on waiting on them all although they barred her from the sink.

There was a combined Wedding and Christening cake and Angel had achieved the decorating of same without instruction this time.

'Wishing you both, and Belinda of course, every happiness . . .' Rob brought forth a bottle of champagne from its hiding place in the pantry. Alice produced a tray of wine glasses.

Nana said, 'Too gazzy, I reckon. I'll stick to tea. Aunt Hetty makes such a good, strong cup.'

When the small celebration was at an end, Jess and Francis climbed the stairs to their room and firmly closed the door. Rob made ready to take Nana and Belinda home to The Cotts, for Belinda would not move into The Angel until tomorrow, and Edmund escorted Edith over the road to the pink house.

'You'll miss your gal . . .' Aunt Hetty whispered to Nana.

'Ah, I have my precious, one more night, Aunt Hetty, and she promised, I'm still to have her when they're busy . . .'

During the evening, while they cleared up, Rob told them: 'No reason we shouldn't see about that bathroom now.' It was unsaid, *with Lalla's money*.

'Alice is growing up, that's for sure, she won't like bathing in the scullery soon. And you know *I* like the idea.'

'You won't believe this, but *I* have actually enjoyed all the palaver of the old tin tub.' Angel confessed wryly.

'That's 'cause you haven't had to put up with it for ever and ever, dearie! We must move with the times!'

'I'm for an early night, if you don't mind?'

'You look pale. Hope you're not coming down with something.' Rob's face showed his concern.

She shook her head.

'I'll bring you a nice hot drink later, Angel.'

'Thank you, Aunt Hetty. Goodnight, everyone.'

The newly weds had not re-emerged. She was treading quietly past their door when it opened a little and Jess whispered, 'Just wanted to say thank you and goodnight from Francis and me . . . You all right?'

'Yes! Just tired, I don't really know why. It was such a lovely wedding, christening too, Jess. See you in the morning!'

Love each other, always, you two, she thought.

Francis appeared behind Jess, his arms sliding round her waist. 'I thank you, too, for the nice costume for Jess. I will get stronger, well at last I know, with Jess and all of you behind me . . .'

'He says they called you "The Angel" in France, just like they call *him* "the bugler" here. You *have* been an angel to me and mine!'

She smiled her appreciation, went on up to her own room. There was a great deal for her to mull over but whether she would arrive at any conclusion was doubtful.

Jess nestled down in the soft bed. 'Ooh! I won't *ever* want to rise from *this*!' Despite the fact that they had anticipated this night in the old barn over the past year or two and had Belinda to show for it, she felt shy in the unfamiliar surroundings and self-conscious in the flowing nightgown with the embroidered yoke which Aunt Hetty had tucked discreetly under her pillow. 'Put the candle out!' she added.

His arms went round her. 'Darling Jess, I love you.'

'Don't you *dare* steal out with that bugle tonight,' she told him tenderly.

'Morning!' Jess put down the teacup.

'Well, I didn't expect *you* to bring my tea this morning, Mrs Taylor!'

'Well, I have to admit that feather tickling was hard to resist! Francis says the same, he says it's the lap of luxury for us two!'

'Can – can he recall the old days at home, Jess?'

'Afore the war? Seems so, lately. Just *that* time, the time he was wounded, in hospital, he can't pump up.'

'Guess Nana is missing you this morning—'

Jess's dimples flashed. 'She's already arrived, Nurse, with Belinda. Aunt Hetty says, "Stay to breakfast, eh, Nana?" and Nana says, "Might just do that. Bacon smells good, Aunt Hetty . . ."'

Angel felt weak and rather sick. 'Bacon, oh, I don't think I could face a fried breakfast this morning—'

'You stay just where you are. Poorly I see. I'll tell Aunt Hetty. House scoured top to bottom for the wedding, have a day off, why not?'

'You're the one who ought to be taking time off, not me! No honeymoon, Jess?'

'What, with Belinda around? No, we're happy just to be together official like, one room, The Cotts or the barn – what matter? I'll stick to my feller whatever life throws up.'

'I'm sure you will! He is so lucky to have you.'

'I s'pose you can put it all down to old Miss Fenner,' Jess said thoughtfully, 'if she hadn't brought him here that time, well, we'd never have met. Must go. Drink up, then snuggle down again. Got to call Alice up now.'

It was Alice who brought a dainty breakfast tray with lightly boiled egg and toast fingers, 'Remember how you used to spoil me when I was ill, Angel?'

'Yes, but *you* deserved it. I feel as if I'm malingering!'

'Dad says we expect too much of you—'

'Oh, Alice who could work as hard as Aunt Hetty and Jess – or your father?'

'Well, he's got the bugler now to get the water in and things like that till Tony gets more muscles, and when the bugler's ready, Dad says, he and Jess can look after the bar sometimes so he and Aunt Hetty can spend more time with us.'

'That sounds promising! Sorry but I don't think I can finish all this toast—'

'I'll have it then. You keep telling me I'm a growing girl and need to fill out!' Alice made short work of the surplus toast and marmalade. 'Angel—' she said tentatively.

'Mmm?'

'I know it's not the right time yet – but Tony and me, well, we keep hoping that Dad might—'

'No, Alice, it's *not* the right time. I can guess what you're trying to say, but your father probably has no thoughts of marrying again, ever. Your mother was such an unusual, attractive lady, *I'm* very ordinary. Not at all like Lalla.' She passed the tray. 'I think I'll take a nap now then I'm sure I'll feel well enough to get up later on.'

Alice said awkwardly, 'Sorry, Angel, I didn't mean to upset you, really.'

Her voice was muffled by the pillow. 'I'm sorry too, you must know how much I think of you all . . . Let's please carry on just as we are.'

When she went downstairs at last, Edith was there, taking tea with Aunt Hetty. The children were out on their bikes and the others were not around.

'I'll make myself scarce, shall I?' Aunt Hetty did just that.

Edith actually smiled at Angel. 'I came to apologise. I hinted to Aunt Hetty that I had inadvertently upset you.'

Angel waited. She had come to the conclusion while lying in bed that things would never be the same between them. Not only was she hurt that the one she had once trusted so could have spoken like that, she was sure she could no longer trust Edith to keep her secret.

'You can blame it on my age if you like! I could have bitten my tongue out afterwards. It's probably because I've been worrying about this marriage. Francis is still badly affected by the traumas of war.'

'It wouldn't have been right to prevent it. It's obvious that they adore each other and surely little Belinda deserves to have her father around? You can't run others' lives for them!'

'I mustn't make decisions for you either, is that it?'

'Yes. In my own good time, when *I* want to, I will tell what really happened in France. I know I was innocent – *you* believed that too, didn't you?'

'I said, I came to apologise. Am I forgiven?'

Evading the issue as Edith had done, she replied, 'Let's not mention this again.'

'Tea?' Edith poured her out a cup. 'I feel much better now I've got that off my chest!'

Angel managed a smile in return. Then the children burst in, hungry after expending much energy riding far afield. She opened the tin of Suffolk rusks. 'Dig in!' she invited.

CHAPTER THIRTY-SIX

Alice had her study books spread all over the kitchen table. Aunt Hetty, balling dumplings in floured hands to drop in the bubbling stew, silently signalled to Angel.

'Don't want to stop you, Alice, but it's almost supper time,' she apologised. She took up a handful of knives and forks.

Alice sighed, closed the books and piled them up.

'It won't make any difference what you do tonight,' Aunt Hetty said wisely, 'you'll just addle your brains. You've worked hard for that old exam, all you can do is your best tomorrow. We're not going to scold you if you don't pass – anyway, you *will*! Edmund believes so anyway.'

'I'm glad you're coming along for the ride, Angel, even if you won't be able to come anywhere near the examination room.'

'Well, *I'm* thinking positively. I'm going to take the opportunity to go shopping – I want to get some wool to knit you a High School jersey!'

'Tell you what,' Aunt Hetty was suddenly inspired, 'we'll do something far removed from putting pen to paper, eh – we'll make some toffee!'

Rob, crossing to the sink to wash his hands before supper, turned and grinned at his aunt. 'Last time you had a toffee-making evening there were sticky trails everywhere, even in my hair—'

'*You* ate enough of it as I remember, Rob. Crackjaw you called it—'

'Toffee is *just* what I need to cheer me up!' Alice decided.

'And me,' added Tony, joining his father at the sink, having come in from his chores. '*You'll* have the afternoon off, that's not fair! While I'm still slaving away at school here.'

Angel enjoyed the toffee-making as much as the children. Rob was busy in the bar of course, but Aunt Hetty was in charge in her kitchen. She and Alice weighed out the ingredients as they were called out.

'One pound brown sugar; two ounces of butter; one overflowing tablespoonful of treacle, flour the spoon first, then it'll just roll off into the pan – watch out, Alice, you're getting it everywhere! Tony, take the gill jug and dip it in the pail, that's the right amount of water – oh, and you can measure out a teaspoon of best vinegar . . . What else do we need? Nearly forgot the pinch of cream of tartar!' All went into the heavy-based pan on the stove to be stirred with Aunt Hetty's wooden spoon, stained almost black from much chutney making. The final ingredient was a few drops of powerful peppermint oil.

The mixture boiled steadily for fifteen minutes, bubbling and smelling delicious. 'Don't stand too near,' Aunt Hetty advised. 'It'll stick like glue and burn if you get splashed . . .'

Then came the part they all enjoyed the most. The testing of teaspoonfuls of molten toffee in a cup in a little cold water. Rather like the jam setting test which Angel had helped with in the autumn, when the jam showed a satisfactory wrinkling when cooled and pushed with the thumb; when ready, toffee, Angel discovered, formed brittle threads, which the children fought good-naturedly over to taste.

'Now, we *could* pour this into well-greased tins, mark into squares when almost set, to break into pieces when hard, but – shall we do the door-knob pull?' asked Aunt Hetty.

'Yes please!' cried the children in unison.

When the toffee was still warm and pliable, Aunt Hetty began to pull it out into a long, glistening rope. Then she looped it over the only door-knob in the room, for the doors were mostly latched, and they took turns on pulling the toffee while sitting on a chair, moving constantly so that the rope was held firm. Paler and paler the stretched toffee became, until, as it hardened it was in danger of breaking. They were all busy then, twisting, plaiting and chopping.

As they dropped the little spiral cushions into a deep dish Tony cried in triumph: '*Humbugs*!'

Rob put his head round the door, 'Oh, I was hoping for plain toffee, but never mind – pass the dish to me!'

As Angel obliged, he whispered in her ear, 'Watch out for the brassy flavour, Jess rubbed-up all the brass a day or so ago after all!'

However the peppermint satisfactorily masked the taste of door-knob.

Toffee did indeed get absolutely everywhere Angel discovered. She was still busy with her damp cloth after the children had gone to bed. 'Don't you dare open those books again,' she called after Alice.

Sometimes she worried a little that she had slipped into the mother-role all too easily. Suppose Rob eventually married again; it was a possibility that had to be faced for although she was sure of his easy friendship she would be deluding herself if she imagined that things had changed in that respect now that Lalla had gone.

She looked in on Alice. 'Not asleep yet?' She asked softly.

'No! Just hoping I won't get toothache after a surfeit of humbugs, Angel . . . I want to ask you something—'

'Yes?'

'Well, I hope I pass the test of course, because I really have worked hard towards it and if I go to the High School I'll have the chance of a real career when I leave there. Or I *might*, as Dad hopes, go on to university – *he* never had the chance, you know . . . But—'

‘What’s worrying you, Alice?’

‘I don’t know if I’d be happy away from home, all of you, all week, you see. I’ve never been away apart from hospital, and you can’t count that! And, Angel – I know you’re our friend now not my nurse, but you might want to go and work for another family, because nursing’s *your* job not helping in the house, isn’t it? You must get bored with *that* at times—’

‘Look, Alice, you may be taking the examination now but you wouldn’t be going away until September. That’s months ahead! And while you all want me here – just you try getting me to leave!’

‘That’s all I wanted to know – goodnight . . .’ Alice said.

Another ride in Lady Pamela’s Rolls, and a new companion, Fairy Aldred, whose head still smarted from the comb dragged through her mass of hair by her determined mother. Like Alice, she was subdued, anxiously checking her bag from time to time to make sure she had the required pencils, pens, rubber, ruler and mathematical compass and protractor.

‘I aren’t keen to go to that old High School,’ she grumbled. ‘*Mina’s* leaving school in the summer.’

Will, driving as always, mildly rebuked his daughter. ‘You’ve got the wits, gal, so just you use ’em and make something of yourself.’

Alice squeezed Angel's hand. She was a little afraid of fierce Fairy and couldn't imagine being forced to have *her* as a constant companion, as they came from the same village.

There were six of them this morning, sitting at single desks in the big school hall, while outside the hubbub of school life went on, and passing girls peeped curiously through the glass in the double doors. It was all so different to the little school at Uffasham.

The invigilator passed out the examination papers, face down; ruled foolscap, blotting paper, checked that the inkwells were full and free-flowing. She glanced at the clock. 'Right. You may begin. Turn your papers over, please. You have an hour for this paper. There will be a short break at eleven o'clock after the next paper.'

Alice rubbed her damp palms on her skirt, took a deep breath. Among the titles to be chosen for the composition was *The Journey*. Instantly she knew what she would write about. 'We left Tilbury on a dazzling spring morning, having embarked the previous afternoon . . .' The journey to Australia, inspired by her mother's delightful letters but written from her own imagination unfolded in a rush of words. She really *was* the young convict girl being transported to a wild new world . . .

She came down to earth later when she had to tackle the tricky arithmetical problems. Edmund's patient coaching paid off for both girls here. They scratched away confidently with their new pens and Alice only made one blot.

There was a rainbow selection of wools in the fashionable draper's. Angel liked to have some knitting always on the go, but she usually patronised Mrs Newsome's shop for trips to town were infrequent and anyway it was right, as Aunt Hetty insisted, to use the village shops nowadays when life was such a struggle for most financially.

It might be tempting fate she decided after all, to buy the grey-blue High School wool: there was plenty of time after all for that. Alice was filling out at last, most of her last year's woollies appeared skimpy: Angel made up her mind to find an attractive vibrant colour in a soft fine wool to knit up into a special jersey.

So instead of serviceable blue she bought what she immediately thought of as butterfly blue, together with an odd ball of white to trim the collar and cuffs. Even the pattern the assistant suggested seemed apt for it was designed in blackberry stitch. She hoped it would not prove as difficult to knit as it looked!

When they met up again outside the school, Alice was delighted.

'You always know what I like, Angel – thank you!'

'You're sure to get a boyfriend in that!' said forthright Miss Aldred. She thought Alice was backward in that respect.

'How did it go, girls?' Angel asked them.

'All right, I suppose . . .' Fairy admitted unwillingly.

'All right,' echoed Alice casually, but she gave Angel's hand that special squeeze to show how pleased she was with the wool and that all was *more* than all right . . .

'Not back yet?' Edith enquired. She had felt piqued at not being invited to go along. A few months ago, she thought, her presence would have been taken for granted.

Aunt Hetty was simmering beef broth for Nana. She had been worried about her old friend since she popped in to see her a few days ago, and today Jess had reported Nana was still 'under the weather' and not eating much at all. 'No, not until teatime I reckon. The tests went on until one, then Angel was going to take the girls for a bite to eat before coming home. Will had some shopping to do for Lady Pamela, too. Did you want to see Angel?'

'Not in particular.' Edith looked meaningfully at the kettle.

'Cup of tea, Edith?'

'Yes, please. Actually, I'm glad to see you on your own for once, Aunt Hetty. Rob's busy, is he?'

'Clearing up in the cellar.'

'Good. How are things these days?'

'With Rob, you mean?'

'Yes.'

'He's doing well, bearing up. It helped, him and

her having been parted long ago, of course. He'd got used to her not being around. Sad business though . . . Angel's a wonderful help with the young 'uns, I don't know what I'd do without her now.'

What was it about Angel that she worked her way so easily into people's affections? Edith wondered jealously.

'You might not have much choice,' she said, with assumed lightness. 'My brother is quite smitten with her, I believe.'

'I'm aware of that . . . But, she might have other ideas—'

You have, you mean, Edith thought. 'If you're referring to Rob, well, *that* wouldn't last, it rarely does, on the rebound, eh?'

Aunt Hetty looked worried. 'You think I shouldn't encourage them in that direction, then?'

'She's rather young for him, I feel. He needs a more mature woman – when the time is right . . . Well, thank you for the tea, I must get back to my gardening.'

She passed Jess on her way out. 'I hope you haven't been getting my patient *too* excited, Jess—'

'I can guess what you mean by that!' Jess answered rudely. 'I've been tidying the bedroom if you really want to know.'

In the kitchen, she saw Aunt Hetty's expression. 'What's she been saying to you, Aunt Hetty? Nana's right, she's an old busybody!'

'Oh Edith means well . . . Look, the broth's

ready, when it cools a bit I'll pour some in a bottle. You tell Nana, Aunt Hetty said she's to drink every drop!'

Jess helped herself to a humbug. 'Need something to take the taste of *her* out of my mouth . . .'

CHAPTER THIRTY-SEVEN

'One of the family now, I see,' smiled Mrs Newsome. She separated the great hank of wool and doubled-up the four ounces of white angora that Angel had requested. 'Cap and mitts for your nephew you say?'

Angel nodded, smiled back. 'I'm longing to see him again. He's sitting up now, I hear.'

'Going up to London soon, then?'

'Yes, in a couple of days' time actually. I shall see my mother, too, she lives abroad with my stepfather, they've been back home for a few weeks and their holiday is almost finished.' It made sense to tell Mrs Newsome what she would only winkle out of you anyway!

'Understand Rob MacDonald is going up there, too?' A wicked twinkle from Mrs N.

'Going *down* as a matter of fact Mrs Newsome!' Angel couldn't resist that. Still, she might as well enlighten her further, she thought ruefully. 'We're travelling on the train together but I will be staying with my sister of course and he will be elsewhere in London on business.'

'Coming back together?'

'We *might* . . . He has to collect his wife's car, decide whether to dispose of it or keep it.'

'Poor chap deserves everything he can get from that direction. Business is still slow, don't I know it, now *he* can carry on with no worries, eh?'

This was going a bit too far. Angel placed her parcel in her basket and bade Mrs Newsome a cheerful farewell.

She couldn't get used to Rob in a suit. He looked ill at ease in it. He sat beside her instead of opposite as she would have preferred. She opened her magazine and began to turn the pages. He moved slightly so that there was a gap between them, unfurled his newspaper. She expelled her breath involuntarily. She did not take in a word she was reading.

They had made an early start and she had scarcely slept the night before. Ridiculous, she chided herself, worrying about being alone with him all day when it should have been an event to look forward to! She was also fretting about the reunion with her mother. She had still been deep in depression the last time her mother visited London and she had been sharply told to pull herself together, 'the war has been over for years and unlike others you suffered no physical disability. Of course, I appreciate that you lost your fiancé but didn't I go through the same experience when your father was killed? You are bound to meet someone else as I did, Angel. But you must stop feeling sorry for yourself first . . .' Cruel words, lacking understanding, but, in a way, her mother had been proved right.

She closed her eyes. She did not expect to fall asleep but she did.

They were within ten minutes of Liverpool Street Station when he shook her arm gently. She opened her eyes and looked up into his face. Her head was on his shoulder and his arm gently supported her weight. As she had the first time they met, she thought what a nice strong face he had; such a kind, quizzical smile directed at her. 'D'you feel refreshed?' he asked. 'I'm sorry I had to wake you but we're almost at journey's end . . .'

It was a relief to discover that she did indeed feel rested and comfortable in his company. She did not immediately pull away but smiled back. 'Thank you. Yes, I do feel better,' she replied simply.

Before he put her in a taxi bound for Lou's, she scribbled down her sister's address and telephone number.

'Thank you. I will telephone you before I leave the hotel on Wednesday morning. Let you know whether we will be travelling home by train or motor!'

'You *can* drive, I suppose?'

'I learned in the war: you don't imagine I would contemplate sitting behind the wheel if I hadn't, eh? The children will be joyful if I do decide to keep Lalla's little car, of course.'

'You won't get rid of the pony and trap though, will you?' she exclaimed. It was a form of transport which she very much enjoyed; leisurely looking round at the countryside, the smell of horse rather than the fumes of petrol.

'I promise you, I won't! Goodbye for now, Angel. Enjoy being with your family, won't you?'

Peter pulled the fluffy cap off his head. 'So that's what you think of my knitting!' He didn't sit still for a moment, Angel thought fondly. She put him back down on his rug on the floor and he immediately rolled over and renewed his efforts to crawl.

'You look very well, Angel,' her mother observed. She had arrived before her daughter. Angel was relieved to see that her stepfather was not in evidence today. 'He had some business to attend to and will call for me later. We will be dining at our hotel. I imagine that you and Louise have quite a lot of confidences to catch up on.'

For the first time it occurred to Angel that perhaps her mother was hurt by the closer tie between herself and Lou.

'You don't look any older, Mother.' She took in her mother's slim elegance, the knot of still fair hair, the pink and whiteness of her face. Lou had left them with the baby while she popped out for a loaf. Maybe it was a ruse to force them to talk to each other.

'Why don't you call me Sylvia? Lou has done

so for years. I don't feel much like a mother . . .' she added wryly.

It was time for a truce. Angel had been taught a valuable lesson through Lalla's reconciliation with her family. 'I want to say that you were right – Sylvia. I was wrapped around with misery when we saw each other last. I'm over it now—'

'You've found someone else then?'

'Yes. It may come to nothing because he doesn't, maybe he won't *ever*, feel the same way about me . . . But I know he's fond of me and I value his friendship very much.'

'I'm going to be very honest with you: I didn't love Sidney in the same way as I did your father, but I set my cap at him because I was, well, hungry for affection—'

'You had *us*—'

'You must know that I am not a maternal person. Anyway, Lou was grown up and you were at an awkward stage; I'm ashamed to say that I shelved my responsibility. You were always your father's special one. I have to admit I was jealous of your closeness at times. When he was home from the Army I wanted him all to myself. You – you have his warmth, his caring nature, perhaps you reminded me too much of Carlo, what I had lost.'

There was a long silence between them then, broken by a disgruntled cry from Peter demanding their attention.

'Lou is a wonderful mother—' Angel coloured

up when she realised what she had said. She bent and scooped up Peter in her arms.

Sylvia smiled. 'It's all right. Yes, she is. She had plenty of practice with *you* after all.'

'Sylvia—'

'Yes?' There was hope in the way she asked that.

'Is it possible for *us* to begin a new relationship? It's no good crying about what might have been. We have a great deal in common, you know. We both loved someone and lost him. You're happy with Sidney, aren't you?'

'Rather to my surprise, I am. He's not like Carlo at all, cooler, not passionate, but I'm sure of his love and protection.'

Lou came in and Peter beat an excited tattoo with his bare feet when he saw her. She looked keenly at Angel and Sylvia. 'Did he behave?'

'Of course!' Angel grinned. 'And so did *we*!'

It seemed unfamiliar to eat so late in the evening, after Peter was tucked up and Lou and Jack could relax. Angel was used to having supper with the children at what Lou called teatime. There was red wine, too, replacing Aunt Hetty's bottomless teapot. Angel felt quite dreamy and giggly after a glass or two. They were still sitting at the table when the telephone shrilled.

'It's for you, Angel,' Lou called from the hall.

'I just wanted to be sure you had arrived safely,' said Rob's deep, unmistakable voice.

'Well, as you can see, I have!' laughter bubbled

up within her, spilling over. 'S— sorry!' she added, 'I'm not laughing at *you*, Rob—'

'Why not? I guess I'm treating you as if you were Alice's age— I'm sorry, too!'

She was aware of Lou hovering in the doorway. 'Ask him over –' she hissed.

'Would you like to come here, meet my sister,' she managed.

'Tonight? Rather late, isn't it? How about tomorrow, when I've seen the solicitor, settled things and decided about the car?'

'He says tomorrow?' she mouthed back at Lou.

Lou nodded vigorously. 'Dinner at seven, say, Angel . . .'

Despite sharing a room with the baby, she slept like a top that night.

It was fun selecting clothes from Lou's shop, from the marked-down section naturally. Silk patterned scarves, with miniscule drawn threads for the womenfolk back home, she chose; a crêpe de Chine blouse for herself, a long, thick woollen purple jacket with matching tam-o'-shanter, sheer stockings for the next big occasion.

'Wear this tonight!' Lou ordered, producing an evening dress. 'Sylvia and Sidney will expect us to be dressed-up! Oh, we have to say goodbye to *all* of you tomorrow! What's he like, your Rob?'

'He's my *employer* remember, Lou! He's about your age: I imagine you'll think he's nice-looking in a rugged sort of way, he looks a real Highlander!

I can just imagine him in a kilt, but I do hope he doesn't wear one tonight, or I might get another attack of the giggles . . .'

Hot food and a fierce fire; Angel certainly did not shiver in the shimmering black dress with its yoke embroidered with sparkling silver sequins. She slipped Lou's bangles up her bare arms, tucked her hair behind her ears to display the drop-earrings her mother had presented her with earlier.

Rob wore his suit, a clean shirt that she had pressed for him herself the night before they left Suffolk. He was at ease in the company she was glad to see and it was obvious that her family approved of him.

She sat beside him on the sofa, vibrantly aware of their closeness. 'Ye look very handsome tonight,' he told her approvingly.

'Lou's smart frock, not mine!'

'We shall travel tomorrow in the motor, if you agree,' he said.

'Of course I do!'

He was the first to leave. 'I'll see you out,' she said.

In the hall, he put his hands on her shoulders, stooped to kiss her. She resisted the temptation to fling her arms round him. 'Goodnight, dear Angel. I will telephone you as we previously arranged. I have very much enjoyed our evening. You will have to come down to earth again in Suffolk, I fear.'

He had nothing to fear, she thought. 'Goodnight, Rob. Yes, see you tomorrow.'

It was not such a comfortable journey as the train. But despite cramped seats, for the little car certainly had none of the luxuriousness of Lady Pamela's Rolls, Angel enjoyed every minute. They did not talk a great deal until they reached the country roads for Rob had to concentrate on his driving.

Lou had packed them a picnic lunch and they stopped in a quiet spot by some trees. They sat in the car and Angel shared the rug then with Rob for they were both chilled and hungry.

'They will be opening up about now,' he observed, shaking the crumbs out of the window. 'How do you think Jess and Francis will cope?'

'Oh, don't worry about them, Rob. Enjoy your time off!'

'I have, I am,' he said. He laid his hand lightly on her cheek. 'You've got your colour back already, you looked pale in London!'

'Well-powdered!' she joked.

'I wonder how long we'll be able to keep you; I know you've refused Edmund, poor chap, but you are far too pretty to be tucked away with *us*, you know . . .'

'There's no place I'd rather be. Honestly!' she said softly.

CHAPTER THIRTY-EIGHT

When the winds howled round The Angel on wintry nights, Angel comforted herself by the thought that the inn had been standing for centuries and had not been blown down yet. When she went walking with Edmund and Whis they were buffeted and blown about. One Sunday afternoon he asked her again to marry him and this time she told him honestly, 'I can't. I'm so sorry, Edmund . . .'

Dark mornings still and the cock crowing before there was any glimmer of light. The first three months of the year were not the months for star-gazing or looking for colours in the sky. Rain, and muddy boots lined up in the scullery. Jess and the bugler made a big difference to the working day, even though there was now a real crowd round the kitchen table sharing even bigger pots of stew.

Yet there were bright patches, like the day at half-term when Rob took Angel and the children to the sea in the motor. The water was grey but as still as a millpond. The beach was totally deserted.

Alice and Tony whooped along searching for

treasures. No amber, but green glass from ship's bottles smooth like pebbles but bright like emerald. Driftwood, bleached and fragile in ghostly fragments, cork and torn fishing-netting. The water lapped their boots, cleaning the mud and giving a deceptive shine. Cuttlefish from which, Tony informed them, sepia was obtained and on which the gulls swooped.

They ate sandwiches and drank fizzy pop from the bottle. Angel sat with her back against the sea wall, feeling sleepy and very content. The sea birds quarrelled over the crusts Alice threw them. Angel rubbed at a spot of tar on her skirt.

'Butter will shift that,' Rob told her.

'It's only an old skirt, I don't really care – it's just lovely to be here on a winter's day, Rob!' She yawned. 'The sea air always has that effect on me . . .' She thought of herself and Lalla, last summer, lying out in the warmth of the sun, and talking.

Rob's arm went easily round her shoulders. 'Have a little nap then! I might even succumb myself – though I suppose I must keep one eye open to see what Alice and Tony are up to . . .'

It wasn't long before their heads inclined together and they both slept.

The children surveyed them, grinning. 'Old people always need a nap after lunch.' Tony observed. 'Let's have a paddle shall we, Alice? They can't say it's too cold if they don't *know*, can they?'

'You can if you like! I've got more sense,' Alice retorted. 'I'm going to watch *them* – wonder what'll happen when they wake up and look at each other . . .?'

'Girls! All you think about is romance!'

'Wouldn't you like Dad and Angel to get together then?'

''Course I would! But *I'm* not going to be a – Peeping Tom!'

In April the local builder arrived to dig the foundations of the new bathroom, off the scullery and the weather had improved so much that Aunt Hetty decreed: 'A spot of whitewashing won't come amiss!' So Angel, in ancient paint-spattered overalls was shown the way to mix the distemper. Most folk had their own recipe for perfect whitewash, she discovered. Aunt Hetty's way was to mix five pounds of whitewash in a pail with a tablespoon of powdered alum and enough cold water to leave a puddle on top. Then size, first dissolved in hot water was added and then more hot water until the mixture reached the consistency of thick cream. Water! Angel thought dreamily. How wonderful, soon it would be *piped*!

'Slap it on, dearie, that's it! The big brush'll soon cover the walls. Pantry first, then you can do the kitchen if you feel like it?'

'You're doing an excellent job,' Rob approved in passing. She glowed at his praise.

She really took to the whitewashing like a duck to water, thoroughly enjoyed herself, even though as Tony said, she got it on other places too . . .

While this was all going on at The Angel, the school soup making was taken over by Lilian at The Vicarage. She had a helper in the house now, young Mina Bird, who had been determined to leave school as early as she could. Jess went down there too for it meant she saw more of Belinda, whom Nana brought along. Edith naturally was involved so that meant they saw much less of *her* at The Angel. Angel couldn't help feeling a little guilty relief.

One bright, breezy morning in April she went with Rob to market. She wore the purple woollen set and wondered idly if he had noticed that her hair swung and dipped to her shoulders now, a longer bob like Alice's. Alice had made a good job of her fringe with the aid of Aunt Hetty's sharp scissors. It was so nice, she thought, that Alice seemed like a younger sister; they had chuckled over the snipping of the fringe, drinking bedtime cocoa in Angel's room.

Rob glanced at her appreciatively. 'You really do look like a country girl now, such rosy cheeks!' She felt so happy. He had lost that haunted look, the children and he were able to talk of Lalla quite naturally these days. It was nice to be in the trap, not the motor.

They were bowling along, not talking a great deal, busy observing all the welcome signs of spring in hedgerow, garden and field when Rob said, 'I've grown so fond of you, Angel, you know, as have we all at The Angel. I realise I am older than you, a widower with children about to arrive at the awkward age, not at all a romantic catch for a lovely young woman like you, but we *do* seem to get along together well, don't we, and if, like me, you would be willing to settle for companionship and family life, well, what d'ye say?'

It wasn't the proposal she'd dreamed of, no mention of love, but affection surely, an honest asking without frills. She knew it was sincere.

He added when she did not immediately respond: 'I did think a while ago, you might change your mind about Edmund—'

'He's not for me. We are very good friends of course,' Angel said shyly. She pushed aside the thought that Edmund had also proposed in a matter-of-fact way. She looked directly at Rob. 'I accept, Rob. I would like – would be honoured – to be your wife. On the terms you suggested.'

The pony slowed to a walk, they were approaching the town.

'Bless you, Angel. Thank you. I shall endeavour to ensure that you will never regret your decision. I know that the family will be absolutely delighted. Aunt Hetty has been hinting blatantly!'

'Rob, there are things I feel I should tell you, before—' she faltered. They were encountering other traffic, and Rob must keep his eye on the road and a firm hand on the reins. Market day meant that the world and his wife were about.

'Nothing you could say, I'm positive, could shock *me*, Angel . . . I will guess that this concerns Harry?

What happened between you is your affair, there is no need for you to tell me *anything*. I appreciate the pain you suffered in losing him. I am hoping you will consent to a very brief engagement. There seems absolutely no reason to wait, does there?'

'I feel exactly the same! Just a month, time for the bans, but let's not make any plans until we can talk it over with the family!' She felt as if she would burst with joy and excitement.

Like the day they had travelled together when she learned of the arrival of her nephew, he took one hand from the reins and covered her own clasped hands, transmitting his warmth and strength. As if sealing a bargain, she smiled tremulously to herself.

They did not immediately make for the market place but went to a smart jewellers in the Parade. 'You must have a ring, or Alice won't consider that we're properly engaged! And why not look at the wedding rings at the same time? We have a very busy time ahead if Aunt Hetty has anything to do with it!'

'And I thought I was just coming to market!' She kept her hand in his after he helped her down and escorted her into the shop.

She chose a simple ring, set with a blue sapphire, because it reminded her of the butterflies even though she had been with Edmund, not Rob that day. Again she picked out a plain wedding ring, a wide, gleaming band. 'Ye do not have expensive tastes, Angel!' Rob mildly chided her.

Later she could not remember consulting Aunt Hetty's lengthy shopping list but she must have bought the most important items because Aunt Hetty did not say: 'Oh, didn't you get so-and-so, dearie? I'm right out of that . . .'

They waited until the children returned from school but made their announcement before Jess finished for the afternoon and went to collect Belinda from Nana's.

'Haven't you noticed anything?' Angel asked, holding out her hand and displaying the ring. Then came the flurry of exclamations, hugs and kisses from Aunt Hetty, Jess, Alice and Tony and a grave handshake from Francis who hoped they would be just as happy as were he and Jess.

Alice cried: 'You are mean, Angel, not letting on—'

'Believe it or not I had no idea myself until today!'

'Rob, just you come here and give old Aunt Hetty a kiss! I've been waiting for this I can tell you now . . .'

As Rob obliged, smiling broadly, Angel thought, he didn't kiss *me*!

'Nana'll say, "I told you so!"' Jess clung to her husband's arm.

They didn't get another moment alone until after the bar closed. Angel lingered in the kitchen, hoping he would come, but she was actually longing for her bed, she needed a good sleep after all that excitement! She wondered if Edmund would take the news well and as for Edith, well, there was no doubt she would be confiding in Lilian before she spoke to *her*. At the thought of Edith a chill little feeling flickered within her, her heart began to thump. She was sure, from the way he had spoken earlier, that Rob really did understand how things had been between her and Harry and would never condemn her for it.

She was crying, how ridiculous when she had her heart's desire. He was there. He held her close, as he had the night of the storm. She leaned against him, sighing and it was as if a load was lifted from her.

'Don't say anything,' he murmured. 'Just be still . . .'

'Will you wear that pretty dress for me?' he asked.

Aunt Hetty ladled brandy generously into the cake mix. 'Oh, her sister'll be sending the latest fashion, no doubt—'

'I wish you would wear a long white dress and that you'd let me be your bridesmaid,' lamented Alice.

'Oh and me, a page-boy – no fear!' Tony was drawing a wedding card at the other end of the kitchen table, shielding it with an arm but obviously hoping to be asked, 'What are you making Tony?'

Angel got a word in at last. 'Jess had a *lovely* wedding, no fuss, and that's the way I'd like it too.'

'Suits me,' put in Rob. He was in and out from

the bar, where Jess and Francis were in charge: 'You are going to ask Lou and Jack though, aren't you?'

'Of course. But my mother and stepfather won't be able to come. Still, I must send an invitation.' Angel's needle was flashing in and out of the endless hem on a soft, lawn petticoat. Every woman she thought, should sew some of her trousseau, even if this was a marriage of convenience, not the romantic affair Alice fondly imagined it to be. She added, not looking up but sensing he was still waiting for an answer: 'It's a favourite of mine too, that silk dress – yes, I'd like to wear it.'

The blue stone in her ring flashed as she plied her fine needle. She was seated in the rocker and the kitlings batted soft, sheathed paws as the material spilled from her lap. She smiled to herself.

Edmund had been generous in his congratulations to them both: Edith had gruffly said that she supposed it was to be expected and could she lend a hand with the food, on the day?

'Would you like to go away for a day or two?' Rob had asked, a day or so back.

She was about to refuse, for what was the point, when he went on: 'We could leave the family to their own devices for one night surely? We never seem to be alone for long, to, well, *talk*, do we?'

She prayed he wouldn't take her where he had stayed with Lalla on their wedding night.

'I thought, we might go to the hotel where we went with Alice to lunch that day we took her to the hospital, when we had the good news of her recovery, what d'ye think, Angel?'

'Yes, I'd like that . . .'

Another ten days she thought dreamily and she would be Angel MacDonald of The Angel.

CHAPTER THIRTY-NINE

Lou sprayed her generously with French perfume, despite her protests and lent her a ruched garter for her stockings. 'Your ring will provide the something blue, eh? Angel, do keep still while I outline your lips – *no*, Peter Carlo! You are not going to climb on Auntie Angel's lap and dribble all over her! Alice dear, will you take this little monster to his father please?'

They were in Angel's bedroom, to which she would not be returning after their night away. Lou and Jack were going to use the room tonight and Mrs Newsome had been pleased to lend the old cot that had been halted in its rounds among the new grandchildren. Already Angel's things had been moved into the big bedroom. She had been able to empty the trunk and tuck it away under the bed for there was plenty of room in the wardrobe. The wedding photograph of Lalla and Rob had been spirited away tactfully by Aunt Hetty.

'Oh you look *lovely*!' Aunt Hetty wiped away a sentimental tear. 'Tony's gone to the church with Edith and Edmund; Rob is about to set off in the trap, he'll take Jack and the baby. Jess laid a cloth over the table, she's worked so hard, dear gal, and she and her feller have already gone to The Cotts to stir old Nana up and to make Belinda pretty.'

'You're coming with me, Alice and Lou, aren't you, Aunt Hetty?' Alice had got her wish to be a bridesmaid!

'Traditionally, it should be just you and your – father—'

'I'm glad *you* agreed to give me away Aunt Hetty!'

The Rolls glided smoothly. It was almost a year since Angel had arrived at Uffasham.

Lilian was at the back of the church dispensing the prayer books. Angel breathed in the heady scent of the lovely sprays of flowers lovingly arranged by her friend and the polished wood of the pews, buffed by Aunt Hetty and Edith. Lady Pamela was there, inclining her head with a smile; there was Nana wearing an unfamiliar bonnet, and Belinda, trying to escape into the pew behind to join the Goodchild girls with their strict young guardian, Mina. Lou hastened to join her Jack and Peter, Aunt Hetty led Angel forwards, with Alice a few steps behind. Tony sat with Edith. Francis was at the organ with Jess close by to give him courage to play, for the remaining pews were packed with familiar and unfamiliar faces: the regulars from The Angel, most of the village had turned out it seemed. Mrs Newsome had certainly spread the word!

Rob, standing beside Edmund, his best man, turned slightly as the music swelled and Angel arrived at his side. She carried pink roses and Aunt Hetty's prayer book.

The parson made it a special service despite respecting the request for brevity, simplicity.

Am I dreaming? Angel wondered. *Am I really being married to Rob? I never believed I could be so happy, ever again . . .*

Aunt Hetty gave her a discreet push when the parson said: 'Now you may kiss the bride!' Rob smiled down at her, then their lips met briefly to unexpected applause, gingered-up by the children, who else?

Outside in the sunshine there was the photographer and Tony darted about too with his birthday box camera.

Belinda held out her arms and Angel took her from Nana. There were smiles in a week or so when the wedding photographs were sent for their approval, for there was the bride, babe in arms. 'Whatever will Sylvia and Sidney make of *that*?!'

Angel could not recall eating much of the wonderful spread and she did not seem to see much of Rob as they talked to guests in the parlour. Suddenly it was time for them to depart, for the Rolls had been sent for this purpose again to deliver them to the hotel in style.

Ten minutes followed of embraces, laughing and thank yous. The presents were piled on the parlour table, Aunt Hetty was crying: 'Only 'cause I'm so happy, bless you both!' Alice whispering: 'I can still call you *Angel*, can't I?' and Tony produced a large envelope from its hiding place. 'I made it specially!' he said gruffly. 'A wedding card!'

'I shouldn't worry about all the food being left, my girls intend to stay at the party until it's all gone!' Lilian teased.

Edmund said: 'I'm glad I remembered to bring the ring!' as he hugged her tight and whispered for her ears alone: 'You married the right man, Angel dear!'

Edith came forward last of all. 'Good luck,' was all she said, but she gripped their hands warmly, in turn.

She had undressed swiftly while he was in the bathroom. Perhaps it was foolish to wear such a frivolous slip of a nightgown, but Lou had made it specially and she had promised, blushing, to wear it tonight. She lay in the vast bed, with the sheet primly tucked under her chin, relieved that the lamp was on his side, and turned down low.

Rob's hair was rumpled, his expression serious, his face freshly shaven, as he slipped in beside her, leaving a space between them.

She studied the William Morris wallpaper, rose pink shades and then looked down at the matching quilt. Would he notice that she was wearing something made from that same favourite sea-green silk? Lou had said: 'When I heard you were wearing that dress I hunted out the last piece of the material and made it from that!'

'It was a lovely day, wasn't it?' he said, after a minute or two. 'Thank you, Angel, for doing me the honour of becoming my wife . . .' He leaned towards her, kissed her lightly, first on her mouth, then on her forehead, brushing her fringe to one side. 'I should have said, I do not expect anything of you until *you* feel the time is right . . . Goodnight. You must be tired. I know I am. We should go for a walk perhaps, along the front tomorrow before breakfast for that is not served until nine. We can do that talking we promised ourselves then, eh?'

He turned aside, switched off the lamp. She lay still, trying to calm her breathing. He had not noticed the colour of the nightgown, the narrow straps, her bare shoulders, she thought. How could he, she realised, when she had covered herself up? Had he taken note of this and said what he had, thinking that was what she wanted to hear? Then again she recalled his words when he proposed, offering her companionship and family life, no more . . .

She *was* tired. Young brides might lie abed on their wedding morn, however, despite Aunt Hetty's protests she had gone downstairs at the usual time, for weren't Lou, Jack and Peter Carlo on the road already in their newly acquired second-hand car? They would be arriving mid-morning. Lou was driving. She enjoyed it more than Jack.

But sleep was elusive. Her mind was in such

turmoil. Was Rob awake too? She wondered. Fancy shedding silent tears on your wedding night she chided herself!

She could bear it no longer. She moved deliberately closer, slipped an arm round his waist, pressed her damp face against the warmth of his broad back, so decently clad in warm flannel, contrasting with her own attire. For a long moment there was no response and she was about to withdraw, rebuffed, when he turned abruptly himself and drew her unresisting, almost roughly into his embrace. One of her thin shoulder straps tautened, snapped, Lou's sewing had of necessity been in haste. She felt his lips urgently seeking the racing pulse in her throat then, just as unexpectedly, he let her go and rolled over on to his back. She sensed that he was clasping his hands under his head on his pillow.

'Angel, forgive me . . .' he murmured, 'I've been too long – on my own.'

She was shaking. Dare she say it? The words spilled out. 'It's the same for *me*, Rob. It's all right, really it is!'

She awoke, still in the circle of his arms and saw that he was solemnly regarding her in the rosy light diffused through the still drawn curtains. Confused, she was aware that the other strap had come unstitched some time during what had been, after all, a long night of sweet passion. She was no longer undercover, she thought ruefully, returning his quizzical smile.

'I did not dream—' he began.

'*I* did!' Her candid answer suddenly had them both shaking with laughter.

'That walk I proposed – would you rather have breakfast up here? We'll be returning to The Angel after all, this afternoon—'

'I know *exactly* what you mean!' She hadn't told him yet that she had married him because she loved him, nor had he confided that he felt the same way. It didn't really matter because all she longed for now was to be with him, like this.

CHAPTER FORTY

'You look just like the kitlings when they've stolen in the pantry and been at the cream!' Jess whispered as they washed and dried the dishes.

'I seem to be spending most of my time blushing nowadays!' Angel returned.

'Guv'nor looks quite young again—' Jess said in her normal voice so that Aunt Hetty could hear.

'That he does,' she agreed, scraping the porridge pot for the said kitlings. A new batch of them were now struggling to oust their older kin from the rocker.

'Good news about young Alice, getting her scholyship eh?'

'Certainly is, Jess. But we'll miss her, won't we, Aunt Hetty, when she's away at school all week?'

'Growing up them two. Be nice to have a new young family at The Angel . . .'

'Belinda will have to do! Rob says he's not keen to start *that* all over again.' There, she was all aflame again. She'd thought she would be disappointed when he had intimated his feelings but she was so content with her life, and loving, right now, she felt that was all that mattered.

So, it came as a surprise, though really it shouldn't have, when she recalled their wedding night, when she realised a few days later that she might well be pregnant. She knew, although they had not discussed it, that Rob had been careful this should not happen since their return home.

She regarded herself apprehensively in the long mirror. She had been very nauseous first thing which had been difficult to conceal from sharp-eyed Aunt Hetty and Jess when the bacon and eggs were served up for breakfast. No hot cheeks today, she was completely drained of colour. Her breasts felt full, she winced at her own touch.

Yet her reflection showed a slender figure, no hint of what was to come. She trembled suddenly as with cold, fearful as she recalled the agony of what she had suffered when she lost Harry's baby . . . Maybe she should see a doctor before she told Rob? Was it possible for her to ask Edith's opinion now that they were more-or-less back on a friendly footing?

They walked down the meadow together later, for Edith had come over to see the new goat kids just born in the barn. Tony had entrusted them to Francis's care while he was at school. The episode of the ravaging dog still lingered in his memory.

'You're quite a stranger,' Edith remarked, 'now we've stopped making soup and are supplying the school with the first fruits off the garden instead . . . How's married life?' Her glance was keen.

'Married life is – all I hoped.' It was silly to feel so shy.

'I suppose I can take the credit, eh, for getting you two together in the first place? No regrets, Angel, about the past?'

She winced. 'I can't say that. But, the past *is* the past, Edith. What I have here is – *everything* to me!'

'Excuse me, but isn't this a marriage of, well, convenience? I always believed that *Harry*, rest his soul, was the great love of your life – and Rob, of course, was besotted with Lalla, devastated by her desertion.'

She knew that Edith would not begin to understand if she tried to explain her joy in her marriage. She put out her hand, indicating that they should pause before entering the barn.

'May I ask your advice? I, well, it's come as a surprise but, I might – I believe! – I am having a baby—' Happiness bubbled within her.

'You want me to tell you that all will be well this time, is that it? I can't give you any such assurance at such an early stage, Angel, you know that . . . Remembering all you went through last time, however, it was perhaps inevitable, wasn't it? Life for you *here* should be conducive to a happier outcome. What does Rob think?' Edith's voice became sharp and shrill.

'I haven't told him yet. You are the first—'

'Then I suppose I should be honoured!' No mistaking the venom now.

Angel was immediately aware that she had upset Edith with her confidences.

Then she could hardly believe what she was hearing.

'You have it *all* Angel, you always did. What would Rob say if I was to tell him exactly what I know? For if you said anything to him, *anything* at all, you wouldn't have dared to tell him *that* . . .'

They spoke of amputation. Harry was conscious but so far they were managing to contain the awful pain for him. She could not even be spared to stay by his side to comfort him with her closeness. In the bed opposite lay his old friend, Francis, tossing restlessly, he had lost a lung from a single bullet wound, was still grey with shock. His breathing was hoarse and laboured. He mumbled incoherently, he was shell-shocked too, that was obvious.

Was either of them aware that the other was injured too, that they were together on Edith's ward?

The sounds of war were diminishing: the walking wounded slumped in an uncompromising daze. Some still lay on stretchers awaiting attention; some were dying, others would do so shortly. Overhead was the eerie sound of a single aeroplane, but which side it belonged to seemed of little importance to those in the hospital.

Near dawn she stumbled wearily towards Harry's bed. There was a screen around; hastily pulled leaving a gap. From the bed opposite, Francis, eyes staring, mumbled something.

She snatched the pillow from his face. Deeply indented it was for it had taken resolution and force to keep it firmly in place while he struggled for life. It was over, nothing she could do now would be of any avail. Harry was dead. Still warm but not breathing. Released from what would surely have been, to a man like Harry, unbearable . . .

She did not recognise the awful screaming as emanating from her own mouth . . . They led her away, not kindly, to all the questioning and all the while she clutched the pillow to her. The only thing she could say was, 'Ask Edith . . .' Then Edith came at last. 'I am sure she is innocent,' she told those who accused Angel. 'She could never bring herself to do such a thing, even though it must have been done in mercy . . .'

'*I didn't do it!*' she cried out now, in renewed agony. 'You believed me then, Edith, you know I—'

'I know I was wrong to support your claim: I know *you killed – smothered* Harry that night! Oh no doubt he pleaded with you to end his suffering, to help him die but as a dedicated nurse you knew only too well that was wicked, wrong—'

'I *didn't* do it! I *didn't*! How *could* I? I loved him too much!'

They were unaware that Rob, who had been painting the outside wall of the new bathroom, was running towards them, thoroughly alarmed by the screaming. Or that the bugler had emerged hesitantly from the gloom of the barn.

He acted first. 'Stop it!' he cried, pushing between them for Edith had actually raised her hand as if to strike Angel. 'I know what happened! I was there – helpless – unable to communicate but, *I saw it all*!' They had never heard him shout before.

'*What* did you see, Francis?' Rob pulled Angel into his arms, held her tightly against him, still facing Edith, whose face was white and contorted with fury.

'I saw *her*! Sister Edith, holding Harry down! He struggled to get free, you see he wanted to live, however handicapped, for The Angel . . . When he was still at last, she bent over me and told me: "*You saw nothing . . . You must never tell . . .*" I could feel her breath on my face, see her eyes staring, but I could say nothing – *nothing*! She went away and then The Angel came and found him with the pillow over his face . . . They thought *she* had smothered him and I – I still couldn't speak . . . Later, it all seemed like a nightmare. Like everything else, I blotted it out from my mind, I couldn't cope with it.' Now, he was almost inaudible.

'You let me suffer—' Angel whispered unbelievingly to Edith.

'I told them you were innocent!'

'I *was*! Why didn't you confess, Edith – why, *why*?'

'You really don't know why, do you?' Edith raged cruelly. '*So* innocent, Angel, in *some* ways! First, I loved *you*, in my eyes we were more than friends – then you betrayed me with Harry! It was a bitter twist when I found myself in love with *him*, too . . . The two of you cared not a jot for my feelings – Harry was attracted to you because you were younger, prettier, not inhibited like me. I began to hate you then – yes, I was jealous – and I hate you now! They made love, Rob MacDonald – does that shock you? She doesn't live up to her name, *she* is no Angel! She miscarried Harry's baby – did she tell you that?'

Angel turned in his arms, clinging to him like a drowning person, weeping bitterly. He tightened his grip, spoke over her head to Edith. 'She didn't need to tell me. Such things happened in those terrible times. The world seemed upside down. I can only feel compassion for what Angel had to endure. I'm not sure that I can forgive *you* for what you made her suffer then—'

Angel's muffled voice: 'She helped me Rob, to conceal . . . I thought she was my friend – I didn't realise—'

'Are you going to take this further?' Edith challenged him.

'What would be the point? It would only mean more anguish for both Angel and Francis . . .'

'He would have died anyway, poor Harry. Yes, you had it all,' Edith said stonily to Angel. 'You were too blind to see that for a second time you were depriving me of the chance to marry. You can't deny it, Rob, *we* got on so well before *she* came – I would have been here for you and your family when at last you were free from your first marriage . . .'

'Please go away, go home, Edith. Leave us alone!' Rob led his weeping wife up the meadow. 'Come too, Francis, old chap, your Jess is there for you.'

He took her past Aunt Hetty, giving a slight shake of the head at her questioning expression. 'Look after Francis, I'll see to Angel . . . Get Jess, *quickly*, Aunt Hetty . . .'

He helped Angel undress, tenderly tucked her up in their bed. She felt herself fearfully, but there was no pain, as there had been before, that dreadful day. 'Rest now. You don't need to say anything until you want to—'

Aunt Hetty's head peeped round the door. 'I don't know what all this is about, nor does dear Jess, but she's rallying round, bless her – poor Francis is in a daze. Shall I bring you some tea up, my dears?'

'Please, Aunt Hetty. They've both had a shock—'

'Something to do with Edith, I gather?'

'I'm afraid so.'

'I won't be long . . .' and tactful Aunt Hetty was gone.

'Rob—' Angel said quietly.

'Yes?' he waited. He sat on the edge of the bed, took her hands in his in that warm, comforting way.

'Rob, I *love* you, I have, you know, right from the beginning.' Tears were coursing down her cheeks once more. He mopped her face tenderly with his handkerchief. Then he kissed her, a long, reassuring kiss.

'You make me feel humble,' he said simply. 'It took me rather longer, Angel, to realise that I felt the same, that I loved you too . . . I felt so happy until today – how dare Edith attack you, and Francis in that way—'

'There's something else, please don't be cross . . .'

'Why on earth should you think I would be?'

'I think – well, I'm sure we're going to have a baby, you see, but after what you said about having enough family already, I—'

He stopped the flow of words with another hug, another kiss. 'Doesn't that show you just what I feel about *that*? Dear Angel, a baby of our own sounds just wonderful!'

'Can we keep it between us, until I've seen the doctor, Rob? I want to be sure that all will be well, this time . . . I only wish I hadn't said anything to Edith, triggered all that off—'

'At least the truth is out now. Jealousy is a terrible burden to bear, Angel. I know. Lalla was right, brave, to come back as she did last summer, to try to explain how it all was. I still don't understand how she could leave Alice and Tony but I know now it's possible to love again. You taught me that! I was astounded when Edith said she thought that I would eventually turn to her. Yet she was a great help to us when Alice was stricken. I can't help feeling sorry for her, and for Edmund, for I feel I must put him in the picture. She seemed unbalanced to me—'

'And to me.'

A tap on the door. Dear Aunt Hetty, bearing a tray with steaming cups of tea and the sugar bowl. 'Put in plenty – you need it, dearie . . .'

Jess followed her in. 'Francis told me – a bit – of what happened out there – I'll never forgive old Nurse Fenner for upsetting you both!'

Angel sat up, sipped her tea, winced at the sweetness, for Rob had ladled the sugar in. 'We must, all of us, Jess. She's suffered, too, being tormented in her mind, just as much in her way really as Francis was . . . War did that to *her*, as it did to Francis, and me.'

Jess dabbed her eyes with her apron. Aunt Hetty turned to her, instantly concerned. 'Come on, Jess, let's get back to your feller.'

'I'll be down before the children get back from school,' Angel called after them. '*They* mustn't know what happened today.'

But first, she and Rob needed to be alone, hugging their secret and each other.

CHAPTER FORTY-ONE

Edmund let himself into Edith's house with the spare key. Rob had gone to see him after school, to explain the situation. It was difficult to comprehend for Edith had never confided in him, apart from the brief statement years ago that she nursed and lost her lover; just one among the thousands who had died or been mortally wounded in the senseless battle of the Somme. It was almost exactly eight years ago, he had realised that, as Rob spoke with compassion, despite what she had done, of his sister.

She was upstairs, lying on her bed, fully dressed, dry-eyed but drained of colour. She stared up at the ceiling, did not acknowledge his presence.

He sat down on the wicker chair, wondering what he should say, how he could help her.

Eventually she spoke first. 'I suppose they've told you what a monster I am – how I tricked the hospital staff into believing that Angel had held Harry down until he died, then defended her and persuaded them to let her go without charging her – getting her neatly out of the way!'

'Yes, I know all that. But, like me, they now see that you must have had a mental aberration—'

'I knew what I was doing! It was a *mercy* killing, the man I loved was dying, in excruciating agony before my eyes. It was no more than has been done, quietly, in such situations – here, in this village no doubt, by – *that* woman and her ilk over the years . . . If *she* loved him, as she has always claimed, why didn't she do it? She *could* have done it—'

'But she didn't, Edith. How could you treat her as you have? How could you try to spoil her chances of happiness with Rob? Or did you both care for *him*, too – was that it? Yet *you* encouraged Angel to come here in the first place!'

'I was frightened: Francis was regaining his memory, I thought he might denounce me. It was a – sort of test – a reassurance to me, if they met without knowing one another.'

'It caused *me* pain, indirectly,' he said wryly. 'Did you reckon on your brother falling in love – the dry bachelor schoolmaster?'

'I'm sorry for that.'

'I told her on her wedding day that she had married the right one. It is hard for me sometimes, but I am glad to count them both as my close friends. As Angel was once, in your eyes.'

It was time for a painful revelation. He had obviously not been told *that*. 'Once, she was more than that to *me* too, Edmund . . . Oh, unworldly as she was she had no idea of my true feelings towards her. I thought I hated her – after Harry – now, I don't know. But we can never be close ever again. I accept that.'

'I'll make tea,' he said heavily. He already knew what must be done. It would be better for Edith to leave this place, to start afresh well away from temptation and inevitable traumas in the future. If Edith went, so must he. He would very much regret leaving this little school where he knew and cared for each and every one of his pupils: where he was appreciated and accepted by the families round about. He would miss village life, he would miss all the friends he had made, particularly those at The Angel. It would be difficult to start all over again. But Edith's breakdown left him no alternative. He would need to start writing letters, putting out feelers immediately, if they were to be somewhere else at the beginning of the new school year in September. Edith mustn't be allowed to live on her own again . . . There would be no hoping to find a replacement for Angel: his sister was now his responsibility.

He didn't feel he could tell her what he had decided, today.

Angel guessed that her changing shape was the subject of speculation both at home, and in the village but it was Nana, naturally, who brought things out into the open. 'Got your heart's desire I see, Nurse . . . My Jess whispered she thought as much! Belinda'll like a playmate, eh? Aunt Hetty's wondering when you're going to say the word, you know. She don't like to ask.'

'Oh dear!' Angel, calling in to see Nana and to enquire after her health, had not expected this. Aunt Hetty had merely asked today, 'Not going on your bike, dearie?'

Angel smiled sheepishly at Nana. 'You're right, Nana. Does *everyone* know?'

'Most, I reckon.'

'Then I must tell Aunt Hetty when I get back, the children too!'

'Were you feared of something? You can tell old Nana.'

'I know I can. I suppose – well, I didn't want to disappoint the family if things didn't—'

'Didn't go well? You'll be all right, take it from me. Carrying nicely, past the time you might lose it . . . Believe me, you've got no worries. Not to say things might not be more difficult later on though. You're not a spring chicken like my Jess. You got to rest up more!'

'The doctor says the same . . .' Angel confessed.

'Doctor? Well, I suppose,' grudgingly, 'he's better'n some. Like old Nurse Fenner . . . Still, *she's* going, I hear – she won't be around to deliver your little 'un, and for that be thankful! Ask Aunt Hetty to make you raspberry leaf tea – that makes for an easy labour.'

'And how are you, Nana?'

'Still a trifle yeller as you can see. Groan quite

a bit I do. But Belinda makes me forget my troubles,' she gestured at the little girl, fallen in action, covered with a blanket as she lay on the old rag rug. 'Might have a shut-eye myself now . . .'

Angel made her excuses. Walked home.

The children came home from school now on their bikes. Tony had intimated that he was a bit old to be met now. Fairy Aldred had said so!

'How was Nana?' Aunt Hetty asked, waking instantly from an unaccustomed nap herself. Rob must still be in the bar with Francis, and Jess was washing a tray full of glasses at the sink. She could turn on a tap now!

'All right, I believe.' She caught Jess's sidelong glance. 'I give in! Nana tells me you've already guessed that I'm expecting a baby round about next February . . .'

'About time you divulged,' Aunt Hetty smiled happily.

'Divulged – *bulged*! You can't keep secrets round here!'

'Sit down, dearie. Take the weight off your feet. I couldn't be more delighted. Rob's the same, I can tell.'

'He is!' And Angel sat down in the rocker obediently.

'More news, Angel. Edith came over to say she and Edmund will be moving on in a month or two. Hadn't seen her since, you know, when – I tried not to make her feel awkward. Jess was going to make herself scarce when Edith said she'd something to say to *her* too.'

'Reckon she saw *you* going past earlier, and dodged over so she wouldn't have to face you. She said, Nurse, that she'd never sell the pink house, it being in the family so long like, but she would like me and Francis to be sort-of caretakers of the place. I did say Nana'd never come, but she said she wouldn't dream of asking *her*, them not getting on, see; but young people should have a home of their own and a bit of privacy – not that you all aren't good to us on that – so, what did I say? Francis came in just then, so I said, "ask him yourself then!" and she did, and we both said yes we would, and gladly.'

'Oh, Jess, I'm so pleased for you both! Edith's trying to make amends I believe. Of course, Edmund had already mentioned that he was applying for posts up north and that he would be taking Edith with him – he must have heard something definite, I suppose.'

She thought that they would miss Edmund, but when Edith went it would be a relief.

'I'll have to get sewing.' Aunt Hetty observed, 'before you split that skirt, Angel!'

Alice and Tony came breezing in, hungry as always. Jess, with a wink, gave Francis a shove and said it was time to go down to Nana's and collect young Belinda.

Angel had already told Rob that an announcement was imminent! 'You'd better sit down,' she said to the children. 'Ready for a surprise?' Aunt Hetty chuckled as she poured out five cups of tea and buttered some rusks.

'Let me guess . . .' said Alice. 'I know, I'm going to be a very old sister indeed and Tony's going to be a big brother – am I right? If I am – *whoopee*!'

'Whoopee indeed!' their father agreed. 'Isn't Angel wonderful?'

'We're all agreed on that,' Aunt Hetty said.

End of term, and Edmund had to say goodbye to the school. The parson came along to make a presentation, for the children had pooled their pennies. Edmund was very touched with the splendid fountain pen. He would be vacating the post of organist at the church too, of course, and Francis had not needed too much persuading to fill the gap there.

In a few days' time Rob would drive them to the station and he and Edith would say goodbye, he privately thought, for good, to the place both of them considered to be home. It was not in his nature to feel bitter that it was because of Edith he too was being forced to leave. He had already bequeathed his dog to Angel. 'He already thinks he belongs to you and I could not condemn him to life in town, Angel.'

'The children will help walk him, I know,' she said. She gave him a quick kiss. 'I'm so sorry things are – as they are. We'll miss you!'

'All I ask is – please keep in touch,' he said quietly.

'Dear Edmund, you know I will . . .'

It was not so easy for her to say goodbye to Edith. She waited with Aunt Hetty while Rob brought out the pony and trap having given them the choice of that or the little motor. They saw Edith closing the door of the pink house for the last time, watched her coming slowly along the path, nipping off a dead flower head or two, catching a thread of her cardigan on a rose bush in passing. Silently, she handed over the house keys to Jess and Francis, standing just outside the gate.

'We'll take good care of the house, and the garden,' Jess said.

'Thank you for all you did for me in the past,' Francis said. 'Goodbye, Edith.'

They were to pick Edmund up at the schoolhouse. He had already made his goodbyes the previous evening to his friends. He did not want Whis to see him depart. The children waited under the porch, holding on to the dog's lead. They waved to Edith. 'Goodbye! Hope you like your new home!' they called cheerfully, being unaware, of course, of the real reason for this moving away.

Angel moved forward at last. She faced Edith. 'Goodbye,' she said quietly.

'Goodbye, Angel.' Edith motioned slightly towards her waistline. 'Take care of yourself . . .'

Then Rob helped her aboard. She did not wave back to them, or turn her head. She did not want them to see that she was crying.

CHAPTER FORTY-TWO

'Another visitor!' Rob told her as she sat up in bed holding court, for Lilian and the girls had arrived a little earlier. Whis insinuated his body round the door and wagged his tail vigorously in his delight at seeing his mistress again, even though he bestowed a guilty sidewise look at Rob because up here was usually strictly out of bounds.

'Come on, old boy,' she coaxed him. 'Don't you want to see the newest member of our family?'

The last weeks since Christmas had been difficult ones. Angel's blood pressure had soared and she suffered from swollen ankles and what Tony described candidly as 'sausage fingers.' She dutifully drank Nana's prescribed raspberry leaf tea and stayed in bed as the doctor ordered. Rob seemed to wear a continually anxious expression on his face. Lou wrote often, worrying about her sister but she was unable to visit at present for she too was very pregnant.

It took all that time to produce one baby eh, and then, a second one follows fast on young Peter's heels! Jack blames it on the Suffolk air – when we came up to your wedding! But isn't it wonderful, the two of us having babies eh? Wonder who'll have the first one?

Now Angel knew the answer! Of course, she had to choose the coldest night of the year, when Rob couldn't get the car started despite frantic cranking and Aunt Hetty yelled through the window, 'Come back up here, Rob – we need you!' Jess, over the road heard all the commotion, and came haring over to help.

Angel and Rob's tiny daughter came into the world all in a rush, delivered by her proud father, with quite an audience, including a wide-eyed Alice, home from school for the weekend and determined to be in on the excitement. Angel was past caring who was there, except for Rob, and it was next morning before Alice admitted bashfully, 'I was there – until Aunt Hetty spotted me and booted me out! It was the most exciting thing I've ever seen! Tony was fed-up he missed it . . .'

Angel was glad that Alice had found it exciting rather than frightening. 'You should have seen Dad's face, Angel, when he held the baby up to show us all – I thought he was going to cry!' Alice added.

She looked down at the baby in the crook of her arm and a great surge of love shook her. Right now she and Rob felt that Lalla, as they had called her, would be their only one, completing their family of three. But she suspected they might change their minds later on . . . A telegram from Lou and Jack today – Patricia had arrived!

Tony was being very nice about the baby brother he had hoped for being a sister instead and Aunt Hetty, naturally cuddled and crooned to the baby at every opportunity.

Rob was as bad, Angel smiled to herself now, catching Lilian's wink. He lifted tiny Lalla from her cradle and placed her against his shoulder, making a show of getting up her wind. The puny legs kicked and the oversized pink knitted boots, a present from Mrs Newsome, slipped off one by one. 'Think she wants her mother . . .' He reluctantly handed her over.

The Ginger Biscuits watched wide-eyed as Angel unfastened the front of a nightgown as far removed from sea-green silk as it was possible to be. Flannel was best for nursing mothers and after all it was not yet spring.

'You go downstairs with Rob and see what Alice and Tony are up to,' Lilian told her lot. 'I'm sure Angel doesn't want such a large audience!'

'I had no choice a couple of nights ago!' she said ruefully.

When they were alone Lilian settled herself on the bedside chair and took some knitting from her capacious holdall.

'Sorry, I haven't nearly finished that little jacket I promised you—'

'I know how busy you are, Lilian! I am already

wondering how *I* am going to cope when I am up and about—'

'What? With all those eager nursemaids?'

Angel smiled. 'But can it last?'

'Her name came as rather a surprise . . .' Lilian picked up a dropped stitch. 'Oh well, it's a holey pattern fortunately!'

'Lalla? It was my suggestion and the family all agreed. I liked her you know, I couldn't help it . . . But I think our Lalla is going to favour my father and be quite Latino. Isn't she beautiful, Lilian – or am I a besotted mother?'

'Well, you are, but she is!'

'D'you think I should write to Edith? Edmund says in his last letter that she is very much better. Perhaps, dreadful though it was, when the truth finally surfaced that awful day it began the real healing process for us all. I wonder though if she has really forgiven me for finding such happiness here with Rob, for having his baby—'

'Why not write? She can only rebuff you, she can't hurt you any more, Angel.'

Angel had confided in Lilian, she was the friend that Angel had once believed Edith to be.

The baby had taken well to the breast. She felt so contented with her lot. She gently stroked the dark little head and whispered: 'Love you, Lalla! I'm going to write to your Auntie Lou and Uncle Jack first and tell them all about you and, then – then I'll write to poor Edith . . .'

Aunt Hetty came in with more tea. She was

disappointed when she saw the baby was busy. 'Jess made the rusks today, fancy one?'

'You know me, my appetite is *enormous* since Lalla arrived!'

It was a joy to Jess to have her own home. Edith would have approved of the way she kept it spotless. She had left them some of the furniture, but the men had moved over the grand bed from The Angel.

Belinda had her own room next door to them. Jess checked that she was sleeping peacefully, left the door ajar and then went thankfully to her bed. She still worked a long day at The Angel but then Francis did too. They were so lucky that the rent was so low, she thought. They managed very well.

Maybe, now and again she missed those clandestine moments snatched in the barn, but it was nice to be accepted in the village as Jess Taylor and living in the pink house was quite a social step up.

The best thing of all was that Francis was so well. They had Edith's piano here, which was good because he often played for them. She never worried now that he would slip out with the bugle and play to the stars.

Nana was a bit of a worry: Jess wondered if there was more up with her beloved grandmother than she would admit to. One day, she suspected, Nana would just go quietly whether or not she reached three score years and ten. But Jess as a child had believed Nana to be immortal.

She was glad to see the Guv'nor settled down with such a sweet new wife. They hadn't wasted any time having that baby she smiled to herself.

She let her skirt drop to the ground, raised her arms and took off her blouse, then her chemise. 'You still awake, Francis?' she asked, as she swung her legs up into bed.

He answered by turning to her and embracing her. 'Best moment of my day . . .' She sighed, as she always did. Then, 'Francis, I got something to say—'

He caressed very gently the roundness of her stomach. 'Think I didn't know, Jess?' he joked. 'Remember I was a doctor – once . . .'

'You mind?' She sounded rather anxious. 'Belinda still being so young and all—'

'Mind? Darling girl, I'm delighted, my only fear is you won't ease up on your work when the time comes.'

'I won't ever change. But I'd like a little lad this time, wouldn't you?'

'Another like Belinda would be fine! I'm just happy I'll be *with* you this time.'

'So am I.'

Edith opened the letter slowly, read it through twice. Edmund watched her over the breakfast table. He had recognised Angel's writing of course. Perhaps it was as well that he had been forced to put a distance between them, he thought ruefully. He still missed the school and the children, his friends in Uffasham. To be truthful it had hurt to see Angel and Rob together, loving and loved. He hoped they had believed his assurances that he was happy for them for that really was true. The business about Edith had come as an awful shock. He had found it hard to forgive her although he had never let her realise that fact. Probably he would never marry now. He and Edith would grow old together. They must make the most of their new life. Now that she was so much improved, she was proving quite an asset to the school. A schoolmaster needed a woman at his side.

'Angel has had her baby,' she stated. 'It is a girl. They have named her *Lalla*, of all things!'

'All's well with them all?'

'Seems so.' She looked directly at him. 'It's not fair, Edmund!'

'Life is not always fair,' he stated. 'But forgiveness goes a long way to redressing the balance . . .'

'D'you think she has forgiven *me*?'

'I imagine so. Why else would she have written to you, after all this time? Certainly not to gloat over you, that is never Angel's way.'

'Have *you* forgiven me, Edmund?'

'I hope so. I do hope so . . .'

'At least I didn't lose *you*! She spared me that. Here, would you like to read the letter?'

Give my love to Edmund, he read.

Angel came down the stairs, yawning widely. The baby had only just settled down, after two feeds in less than two hours. Rob had not yet come up to bed.

He was looking out at the night sky. He turned at her approach. 'Tired, Angel? Everyone else is abed!'

She leaned her weight against him. 'I can't settle without you, Rob. I need you to squeeze me tight . . . Sometimes I feel quite inadequate as a mum, your daughter seems to drain me dry!'

'Milk,' he said solicitously. 'You must drink lots more milk. I'd forgotten how you always sneaked down here for a glass each night, or was it only in the hopes of meeting up with *me*?'

'Goodness no! Like you, I love the Suffolk skies . . . No bugler tonight, Rob . . .' And the lights were out in the pink house, she thought.

'Nor any night, for months now,' he mused. 'I'd like to do something with the barn – all that money of Lalla's – we *must* give something back. I was wondering, what about a studio for young artists to use, to come and stay for very little; Aunt Hetty's good food – it might be something for Tony to run, later on, when he becomes a fully fledged artist himself. Lalla would be proud of her children, I think – Alice will go on to university I hope.'

'It's a *wonderful* idea!' She yawned again.

The baby was awake once more making snuffly noises, working up to a louder cry for attention. Alice, reading in bed, laid down her book, listened. She had been aware a little earlier of Angel treading quietly past her door on her way downstairs. She missed the opening of the inner door, Angel coming in for a chat. She hoped that the room next door would be little Lalla's in time. Of course, as she was almost fourteen years older she did not expect that the two of them could become close as she and Tony still were, but she was proud to have this unexpected sister anyway.

She threw back her bedclothes. Angel obviously had not heard the baby's wails. It was time for some sisterly ministrations!

Aunt Hetty and Tony came out of their doors simultaneously. The three of them exchanged sheepish grins. Rob was apparently still up and about for the lamps in the niches were still flickering.

They bent over the cradle and the baby, instantly aware of their attention, stopped crying. Alice looked at Aunt Hetty. She nodded. Very carefully Alice lifted the baby, wrapped in her shawl. They sat side by side on Angel and Rob's bed and while Alice held her in her arms the other two made what they imagined to be soothing noises and waited their turn to nurse her.

After some time, Aunt Hetty went to the top of the stairs and called down: 'Lalla's awake, but don't worry *we're* looking after her till you come up, you two!'

'What *would* we do without dear Aunt Hetty?' She asked as she so often did.

His fingers threaded through her silky hair. She lifted her face for his kiss. How fortunate she was to be here at The Angel with Rob and his family. Would Harry have been happy for her? She knew he would.

Two lonely people had come together and delighted in their closeness. Perhaps the shades of Lalla would never quite leave The Angel. But they were both happy to live with that thought.

'I love you, Angel MacDonald,' he murmured.